CW00743041

LIBRARY OF NEW TEST∠
461

Formerly the Journal for the Study of the New Testament Supplement Series

Editor
Mark Goodacre

Editorial Board

For

W. Hall Harris and Francis J. Moloney, S.D.B.

CONTENTS

Contents

PREFACE

I started thinking seriously about Johannine characters when I began work on my doctoral dissertation in 2005. Since that time there has been a tremendous growth of interest in the subject. As I was in the process of putting together the proposal for this volume, I discovered that another volume devoted to Johannine characterization was simultaneously in the early stages of preparation. That volume – soon to be published under the title *Character Studies in John* – is devoted to providing a study of every character or character group in the Fourth Gospel.[1] After a series of conversations with the editors, it became clear that we were producing very different works with complementary aims. There was even a brief discussion of combining our efforts and creating a two-volume work, though that did not materialize for a number of reasons. This volume is concerned with methodological approaches to character as well as exegetical studies of important Johannine figures. It is my hope that this book will be used with benefit by students of the Fourth Gospel and that it will also serve as a useful complement to the forthcoming volume that is being produced by Professors Hunt, Zimmerman and Tolmie.

I want to express my appreciation to the editorial staff at Bloomsbury T&T Clark, particularly Dominic Mattos and Prof. Mark Goodacre, series editor of the Library of New Testament Studies. I am grateful that both regarded this project as a worthy pursuit. At Mount Olive College, where I serve as professor, I am privileged to work in a department in which all of the members genuinely enjoy working with one another. Though our areas of expertise are quite different, I am particularly grateful for my colleague, Dr Hollis Phelps. His intellectual prowess and exceptional insights inspire me to strive for clarity and substance in my own scholarship. I am thankful for his day-to-day reminder of the importance of the life of the mind. I would also like to thank Susan Ryberg, the references and extended services librarian at our campus library. She helped me to locate a number of hard-to-find and obscure resources while I was researching for this book.

---

1   See Steven A. Hunt, Ruben Zimmerman and D. François Tolmie (eds), *Character Studies in the Fourth Gospel* (WUNT; Tübingen: Mohr Siebeck, forthcoming 2013). Several of the contributors to this volume have also contributed studies to that volume; see Cornelis Bennema (the crowd, Judas, and the chief priests), Sherri Brown (the Greeks), Mary Coloe (the mother of Jesus, the servants at Cana), R. Alan Culpepper (Nicodemus), Susan Hylen (Jesus' disciples), James Resseguie (Beloved Disciple), and Christopher W. Skinner ('the world', Malchus).

For those who know me well, there is little doubt that my wife, Tara, and our children, Christopher, Abby and Drew, are the collective glue that holds my life together. Things like dinner-time 'best and worst' reports, three-on-one wrestling matches, bedtime sing-alongs, and family reading nights continue to ground me and remind me of what is truly important in my life. I am especially thankful for a family that understands my passion for what I do and encourages me to pursue projects like this one.

Finally, I want to acknowledge the two professors who have most shaped my experience with the Gospel of John, Dr W. Hall Harris and Dr Francis J. Moloney, S.D.B. While studying under Dr Harris, I was introduced to both the Greek text of John and the important works of scholars such as C. H. Dodd, Rudolf Bultmann, C. K. Barrett, John A. T. Robinson, Rudolf Schnackenburg, Raymond E. Brown, D. Moody Smith, Robert Kysar and R. Alan Culpepper. With guidance from Dr Harris, I wrote a master's thesis on the 'Lamb of God' title in John 1.29, 36 and became enthralled with all-things-Johannine. Once I decided to pursue doctoral studies, I chose to attend the Catholic University of America with the goal of studying under Frank Moloney. Many personal conversations with Frank, as well as numerous hours spent reading his books and articles, have enriched my knowledge of this most important and enigmatic Gospel. As much as I admire his scholarship, I am even more grateful for Frank's friendship. Over the years he has treated me with unwavering kindness, once even offering to pay for my semester when it looked as though my funding was going to fall through! Even six years after his formal retirement from life in full-time academia, Frank is still among the pre-eminent Johannine scholars in the English-speaking world, and more importantly he still takes time out for his students. I consider it a tremendous privilege to have studied with both of these men. Their pastoral guidance, keen insights and careful readings have profoundly shaped my understanding of the Fourth Gospel. I dedicate this book to them with appreciation.

LIST OF ABBREVIATIONS

AB	Anchor Bible
ABD	*Anchor Bible Dictionary*. Edited by David Noel Freedman. 6 vols. New York, 1992.
ABRL	Anchor Bible Reference Library
AcBib	Academia Biblica
AnBib	Analecta Biblica
ANTC	Abingdon New Testament Commentary
AusBR	*Australian Biblical Review*
BDAG	*A Greek-English Lexicon of the New Testament and Other Early Christian Literature*. Edited by W. Bauer, F. W. Danker, W. F. Arndt and F. W. Gingrich. 3rd edn. Chicago, 1999.
BDF	*A Greek Grammar of the New Testament and Other Early Christian Literature.* Edited by F. Blass, A. Debrunner and R. W. Funk. Chicago, 1961.
BETL	Bibliotheca ephemeridum theologicarum lovaniensium
Bib	*Biblica*
BibInt	*Biblical Interpretation*
BIS	Biblical Interpretation Series
BJRL	*Bulletin of the John Rylands Library*
BNTC	Black's New Testament Commentary
BSac	*Bibliotheca Sacra*
BTB	*Biblical Theology Bulletin*
BZ	*Biblische Zeitschrift*
CBQ	*The Catholic Biblical Quarterly*
CBQMS	Catholic Biblical Quarterly Monograph Series
ConBNT	Coniectanea biblica: New Testament Series
DJG	*Dictionary of Jesus and the Gospels*. Edited by J. B. Green, S. McKnight and I. H. Marshall. Downers Grove, 1992.
DRev	*Downside Review*
EBib	Études bibliques
ECC	Eerdmans Critical Commentary
EDNT	*Exegetical Dictionary of the New Testament.* Edited by H. Balz and G. Schneider. 3 vols. Grand Rapids, 1993.
ESEC	Emory Studies in Early Christianity
EstBib	*Estudios Biblicos*
EThL	*Ephemerides Theologicae Lovanienses*
ExpTim	*Expository Times*

GBS — Guides to Biblical Scholarship
HKNT — Handkommentar zum Neuen Testament
HTCNT — Herders Theological Commentary on the New Testament
HTR — *Harvard Theological Review*
Int — *Interpretation*
JBL — *Journal of Biblical Literature*
JETS — *Journal of the Evangelical Theological Society*
JNES — *Journal of Near Eastern Studies*
JR — *Journal of Religion*
JSHJ — *Journal for the Study of the Historical Jesus*
JSNT — *Journal for the Study of the New Testament*
JSNTSup — Journal for the Study of the New Testament Supplement Series
JSOTSup — Journal for the Study of the Old Testament Supplement Series
JTS — *Journal of Theological Studies*
LeDiv — Lectio Divina
LNTS — Library of New Testament Studies
LSJ — *A Greek-English Lexicon.* Edited by H. G. Liddell, R. Scott and H. S. Jones. 9th edn with revised supplement. Oxford, 1996.
LTPM — Louvain Theological and Pastoral Monographs
LXX — Septuagint
MT — Masoretic Text
NCB — New Century Bible
NCBC — New Cambridge Bible Commentary
Neot — *Neotestamentica*
NIB — New Interpreter's Bible
NICNT — New International Commentary on the New Testament
NIDB — *New Interpreter's Dictionary of the Bible*
NIGTC — New International Greek Testament Commentary
NIV — New International Version
NovT — *Novum Testamentum*
NovTSup — Novum Testamentum Supplements
NRSV — New Revised Standard Version
NRT — *Nouvelle Revue Théologique*
NTAbh — Neutestamentliche Abhandlungen
NTG — New Testament Guides
NTM — New Testament Monographs
NTOA — Novum Testamentum et Orbis Antiquus
NTS — *New Testament Studies*
NTTS — New Testament Tools and Studies
Pac — *Pacifica*
PNTC — Pillar New Testament Commentaries
PRSt — *Perspectives in Religious Studies*
PTMS — Princeton Theological Monograph Series
RB — *Revue Biblique*
ResQ — *Restoration Quarterly*

RevExp	*Review and Expositor*
RevThom	*Revue thomiste*
RTR	*The Reformed Theological Review*
Sal	*Salesianum*
SBFA	Studii Biblici Franciscani Analecta
SBLDS	Society of Biblical Literature Dissertation Series
SBLRBS	Society of Biblical Literature Resources for Biblical Study
SBLSymS	Society of Biblical Literature Symposium Series
SNTSMS	Society of New Testament Studies Monograph Series
SP	Sacra Pagina
StudEv	*Studia Evangelica*
TDNT	*Theological Dictionary of the New Testament.* Edited by G. Kittel and G. Friedrich. Translated by G. W. Bromiley. 10 vols. Grand Rapids, 1964–76.
TrinJ	*Trinity Journal*
TS	*Theological Studies*
TynBul	*Tyndale Bulletin*
VT	*Vetus Testamentum*
WBC	Word Biblical Commentary
WTJ	*Westminster Theological Journal*
WUNT	Wissenschaftliche Untersuchungen zum Neuen Testament
WW	*Word and World*
ZNW	*Zeitschrift für die neutestamentliche Wissenschaft und die Kunde der älteren Kirche*
ZTK	*Zeitschrift für Theologie und Kirche*

LIST OF CONTRIBUTORS

David R. Beck is Associate Dean of Biblical Studies and Professor of New Testament and Greek at Southeastern Baptist Theological Seminary in North Carolina, USA. He holds the PhD from Duke University in Durham, North Carolina.

Cornelis Bennema is Associate Professor and Head of the Department of New Testament at South Asia Institute of Advanced Christian Studies (SAIACS) in Bangalore, India. He is also Academic Associate of the Research Institute for Theology and Religion, University of South Africa. He holds the PhD from the London School of Theology, Brunel University, UK.

Sherri Brown is Assistant Professor of Religious Studies at Niagara University outside of Niagara Falls in New York, USA. She holds the PhD from the Catholic University of America in Washington, DC.

Raymond F. Collins is a visiting scholar in the Department of Religious Studies at Brown University in Rhode Island, USA. He holds the STD from Katholieke Universiteit Leuven, Belgium.

Mary L. Coloe is Associate Professor at Australian Catholic University in Melbourne. She also holds the ThD from Australian Catholic University.

R. Alan Culpepper is Dean of the McAfee School of Theology, Mercer University in Atlanta, Georgia, USA. He holds the PhD from Duke University, in North Carolina.

Stan Harstine is Chair of Religion and Humanities and Associate Professor of Religion at Friends University in Wichita, Kansas, USA. He holds the PhD from Baylor University in Texas.

Susan E. Hylen is Associate Research Professor of New Testament at Candler School of Theology, Emory University in Atlanta, Georgia, USA. She also holds the PhD from Emory University.

Craig R. Koester is Professor of New Testament at Luther Seminary in St. Paul, Minnesota, USA. He holds the PhD from Union Theological Seminary, New York.

Dorothy A. Lee is Frank Woods Professor of New Testament and Dean of Trinity College Theological School, MCD University of Divinity in Melbourne, Australia. She holds the PhD from Sydney University.

Judith Christine Single Redman is a minister in the Uniting Church of Australia. She is a PhD candidate in Religion at the University of New England in Armidale, NSW, Australia.

James L. Resseguie is Distinguished Professor of New Testament Emeritus at Winebrenner Theological Seminary in Findlay, Ohio, USA. He holds the PhD from Fuller Theological Seminary in California.

Christopher W. Skinner is Assistant Professor of Religion at Mount Olive College in North Carolina, USA. He holds the PhD from the Catholic University of America, Washington, DC.

Introduction

Characters and Characterization in the Gospel of John: Reflections on the Status Quaestionis

Christopher W. Skinner

I. Introduction

Over the past three decades biblical scholarship has shown an increasing openness to the application of literary theory to the narratives of the Hebrew Bible[1] and the NT. Since the late 1970s, literary methods have been applied to the biblical narratives from seemingly every conceivable angle and the results have been nothing short of dramatic. In the new millennium narrative criticism and its related hermeneutical trajectories have become organic elements within the exegetical process even when practitioners are unaware of their methodological choice.[2]

Within Gospel studies narrative criticism traces its formative stages back to the early 1980s. In 1983, R. Alan Culpepper published his seminal work,

---

1   Some early narrative-critical contributions to the study of the Hebrew Bible include (in chronological order): Sean E. McEvenue, *The Narrative Style of the Priestly Writer* (AnBib, 50; Rome: Pontificio Istituto Biblico, 1971); Jacob Licht, *Storytelling in the Bible* (Jerusalem: Magnes, 1978); Shemaryahu Talmon, 'The Presentation of Synchroneity and Simultaneity in Biblical Narrative', in Joseph Heinemann and Shnuel Werses (eds), *Scripta Hierosolymitana* (Jerusalem: Magnes, 1978), pp. 9–26; Michael Fishbane, *Text and Texture: Close Readings of Selected Biblical Texts* (New York: Schocken, 1979); Shimon Bar-Efrat, 'Some Observations on the Analysis of Structure in Biblical Narrative', *VT* 30 (1980), pp. 154–73; Robert Alter, *The Art of Biblical Narrative* (New York: Basic Books, 1981); H. van Dyke Parunak, 'Some Axioms for Literary Architecture', *Semitics* 8 (1982), pp. 1–16; idem, 'Transitional Techniques in the Bible', *JBL* 102 (1983), pp. 525–48; Peter D. Miscall, *The Workings of Old Testament Narrative* (Philadelphia: Fortress, 1983); Adele Berlin, 'Point of View in Biblical Narrative', in Stephen A. Geller (ed.), *A Sense of Text: The Art of Language in the Study of Biblical Literature* (Winona Lake: Eisenbrauns, 1983), pp. 71–113.

2   By 'related hermeneutical trajectories', I am referring to developments such as reader-response criticism, performance criticism, postmodern criticism and postcolonial criticism. The reception of narrative criticism within academic biblical studies helped pave the way for these hermeneutical methods to emerge over the past two decades. For more on the different expressions of narrative criticism within NT scholarship, see Mark Allan Powell, 'Narrative Criticism: The Emergence of a Prominent Reading Strategy', in Kelly R. Iverson and Christopher W. Skinner (eds), *Mark as Story: Retrospect and Prospect* (SBLRBS, 65; Atlanta: Society of Biblical Literature, 2011), pp. 19–43.

Anatomy of the Fourth Gospel,[3] which, along with Rhoads' and Michie's *Mark as Story* (1982),[4] helped usher in a new era in NT scholarship.[5] The resulting paradigm shift forced students of the NT narratives to consider the text in its final form before (and in some cases, apart from) the historical-critical questions that too often led to a fragmented reading of the text.[6] Though the past three decades have yielded a girth of scholarly contributions to the study of numerous aspects of the NT narratives, comparatively little has been done in the area of characterization until very recently.[7]

Never before in the history of NT scholarship has there been such a panoply of possibilities for approaching the NT narratives – a prospect which holds implications for narrative criticism in general, as well as the more narrow field of character studies. The present volume is concerned with current directions in both the theory and exegesis of Johannine characters. This essay aims to trace major movements in character studies in research on the Fourth Gospel from the mid-1970s to the current day, with a view to situating the other essays in this volume.

<hr/>

3   R. Alan Culpepper, *Anatomy of the Fourth Gospel: A Study in Literary Design* (Philadelphia: Fortress, 1983). For contemporary reflections on Culpepper's achievement 25 years after the book's initial publication, see Tom Thatcher and Stephen D. Moore (eds), *Anatomies of Narrative Criticism: The Past, Present, and Futures of the Fourth Gospel as Literature* (SBLRBS, 55; Atlanta: Society of Biblical Literature, 2008).

4   David Rhoads and Donald Michie, *Mark as Story: An Introduction to the Narrative of a Gospel* (Philadelphia: Fortress, 1982). The second edition, with contributions from a third author – Joanna Dewey – was published in 1999; the book is now available in a third edition (2012). For contemporary reflections on this book's achievements 30 years after its initial publication, see Iverson and Skinner (eds), *Mark as Story: Retrospect and Prospect* (2011).

5   These two studies were followed by narrative-critical analyses of Luke and Matthew, respectively. See Robert C. Tannehill, *The Narrative Unity of Luke-Acts: A Literary Interpretation* (2 vols; Minneapolis: Fortress, 1986–89); and Jack Dean Kingsbury, *Matthew as Story* (Minneapolis: Augsburg Fortress, 1988).

6   A common early criticism of the narrative approach is that the discipline tends to be ahistorical, and in some cases, anti-historical, and therefore has the potential to lead to endless speculation and subjectivity. On this point, I cite the wisdom of my *Doktorvater*, Prof. Francis J. Moloney, who consistently insisted to his doctoral students that it is both disingenuous and intellectually dishonest to ask literary questions without also asking the requisite historical questions. In other words, narrative criticism at its very best is aided by the questions that are raised by historical-critical inquiry. The two disciplines, historical criticism and narrative criticism, must therefore work in concert with and complement one another.

7   Outside of Johannine scholarship, studies of character have been more common in recent Markan scholarship than in research on Matthew or Luke-Acts. Major treatments include, Elizabeth Struthers Malbon, *In the Company of Jesus: Characters in Mark's Gospel* (Louisville: Westminster John Knox, 2000), idem, *Mark's Jesus: Characterization as Narrative Christology* (Waco, TX: Baylor University Press, 2009); Joel F. Williams, *Other Followers of Jesus: Minor Characters as Major Figures in Mark's Gospel* (JSNTSup, 102; Sheffield: Sheffield Academic Press, 1994); Susan Miller, *Women in Mark's Gospel* (LNTS, 259; London: T&T Clark, 2004); and Kelly R. Iverson, *Gentiles in the Gospel of Mark: 'Even the Dogs Under the Table Eat the Children's Crumbs'* (LNTS, 339; London: T&T Clark, 2007).

II. Representative Figures

The 1976 publication of Raymond F. Collins' study of 'representative figures' in John marked an important development in Johannine character studies.[8] In two essays, Collins – writing from within the Roman Catholic tradition – scrutinized a burgeoning tradition among historical-critical scholars that regarded Fourth Gospel characters as symbolic or representative types rather than historical persons. Despite the overall tendency among Roman Catholic exegetes to view most of John's characters in their historical individuality, there had been a movement within the same group to regard the mother of Jesus (2.1-11; 19.25-27) as a type of the Church, a model of faith, or even an eschatological presentation of 'woman'.[9] Outside the Catholic exegetical tradition, others had argued that the Beloved Disciple (13.18-30; 18.15-18; 20.3-10; 21.20-23) represented either the disciple *par excellence* or an ideal response of faith to Jesus. Some scholars even argued that the Beloved Disciple represented the Johannine church in its superiority over the Petrine tradition.[10] Still others had seen Nicodemus, the Samaritan woman, Nathanael and Thomas, among others, as performing a representative role in the Gospel. Collins attempted to consider the possible merits of symbolic interpretation while also keeping his discussion in the context of historical-critical inquiry. Situating his study against the backdrop of John's *Sitz im Leben*, Collins argued:

> [W]ithin the life-situation of the Johannine church we ought to envision a series of homilies directed to enkindling faith in Jesus. In the development of these homilies, various persons were chosen from the common gospel tradition or selected from his own tradition by the homilist in order to illustrate some point about the nature of faith, or lack of it, in Jesus Christ . . . [T]hey have been selected from the homiletic tradition of the Johannine tradition to teach the evangelist's readers something about that faith in Jesus Christ which is life-giving.[11]

---

8   The articles first appeared as 'The Representative Figures of the Fourth Gospel, Part I', *DRev* 94 (1976), pp. 26–46; idem, 'The Representative Figures of the Fourth Gospel, Part II', *DRev* 94 (1976), pp. 118–32 (reprinted together as 'Representative Figures', in idem, *These Things Have Been Written: Studies on the Fourth Gospel* [Leuven: Peeters/Grand Rapids: Eerdmans, 1990], pp. 1–45). The citations that follow refer to the pagination of the reprinted version.

9   See, e.g., André Feuillet, 'Les adieux de Christ à sa mere (Jn. 19,25-27) et la maternité spirituelle de Marie', *NRT* 86 (1964), pp. 469–83; idem, 'L'heure de la femme (Jn. 16-21) et l'heure de la Mère de Jésus (Jn. 19,25-27)', *Bib* 47 (1966), pp. 169–84; idem, 'La signification fondamentale du premier miracle de Cana (Jo. II, 1-11) et le symbolisme johannique', *RevThom* 65 (1965), pp. 517–35. See also the symbolic interpretations advanced by Alfred Loisy, *Le quatrième Evangile. Les epîtres dites de Jean* (Paris: Emile Nourry, 1921), and Rudolf Bultmann, *Das Evangelium des Johannes* (Göttingen: Vandenhoeck & Ruprecht, 18th edn, 1964).

10   See, e.g., A. Kragerud, *Der Lieblingsjünger im Johannesevangelium. Ein exegetischer Versuch* (Oslo: Universitätsverlag, 1959).

11   Collins, 'Representative Figures', pp. 7–8.

According to Collins, major Johannine characters[12] embody a dominant trait that is *intended by the evangelist* to represent a certain type of faith response to Jesus. These types are further meant to function as models for the audience to emulate or reject based upon the narrative's call to believe and follow the Johannine Jesus (cf., e.g., 20.31).

Though Collins' argument is built largely upon redaction-critical criteria and the concept of 'individualism' in John, he demonstrates a sensitivity to the literary integrity of the Gospel that anticipates the rise of narrative-critical method. He writes:

> [T]*he very literary style which characterizes the Fourth Gospel should lead the interpreter and reader to question the symbolic characters of the individuals who appear within its twenty-one chapters.* I would therefore propose that the individualism of the Fourth Gospel is a key to its interpretation, not in the sense that it determines the realized eschatology which is characteristic of the Gospel . . . *but in the sense that it provides a basic insight into the meaning of the Gospel,* the tradition that lay behind it, and the purpose for which it was compiled.[13]

Perhaps unwittingly, Collins helped move Johannine character studies closer to the type of narrative analysis that would begin to take shape a few years later. The more carefully nuanced representative approach advocated by Collins also became an interpretive option for understanding the function of Fourth Gospel characters in subsequent scholarship.

For example, in 1983, Margaret Pamment published an essay exploring the role of the Beloved Disciple in John.[14] Though her article contains no citations (and therefore it is difficult to ascertain what research was informing her argument), Pamment's discussion relies heavily on a representative understanding of character. She notes that Nicodemus '*represents* the secret admirer rather than the open advocate', and that calling him 'the Pharisee who came to Jesus by night' would have 'emphasized his *representative character*'.[15] She also acknowledges that the evangelist uses names 'in cases where the *representative character* of the individual or group is important, and where naming individuals would distract from the centre of interest in Jesus'.[16] Like Collins, Pamment regards Johannine characters as archetypal figures embodying a dominant trait that symbolizes a specific, hoped-for

---

12   Collins considered 15 characters: John the Baptist (1.19-34; 3.25-30), Nathanael (1.43-51), Nicodemus (3.1-15; 7.50; 19.39), the Samaritan woman (4.3-42), the royal official (4.46-54), the lame man (5.1-18), the man born blind (9.1-34), Philip (1.43-51; 6.1-15; 12.20-36; 14.1-14), Lazarus (11.1-44; 12.1-11), Judas (6.67-71; 12.1-8), Mary (2.1-11; 19.25-27), Mary Magdalene (20.1-2, 11-18), Thomas (20.24-29), Peter (ch. 21), and the Beloved Disciple (21.2-7, 19-24).

13   Ibid., p. 4 (emphasis added).

14   Margaret Pamment, 'The Fourth Gospel's Beloved Disciple', *ExpTim* 94 (1983), pp. 363–7.

15   Ibid., p. 364 (emphasis added).

16   Ibid. (emphasis added).

response from the audience. She also seems to have an appreciation for the Gospel's literary integrity though she sets forth her argument without a specific discussion of the literary dimensions of the text.

In another essay from 1983, W. R. Domeris explores the 'Johannine Drama', finding a number of parallels between the Gospel and Greek tragedy.[17] Regarding Fourth Gospel characters, Domeris notes: 'As John introduces each of his main characters, Nathanael, Nicodemus, the Samaritan woman, Martha, Thomas, and others, we become aware . . . [that] *they serve a representative function*'.[18] Thus,

> *Nathanael represents the view of the true Israelite* (cf. 1:47), who recognizes Jesus as the messianic king and the fulfilment of the hope of the Old Testament (cf. 1:45); *Nicodemus represents the secret disciples*, who for fear of the Jews, choose to remain within the confines of the Synagogue (cf. 12:42f.); *Martha, Peter, the blind man and Thomas represent the true believers*, who come to Jesus and discover in him eternal life . . . The confessions, which occur at key points, are clearly constructed to depict *the point of view of the represented community*.[19]

Though it is outside the scope of this survey, an examination of commentaries, monographs and other literature of this period would reveal that the view advocated by Collins became an increasingly important position among scholars during the two decades that followed his essays. It should also be noted that, when it was first articulated, Culpepper's discussion of character in *Anatomy* stood squarely on the shoulders of Collins' contributions.[20] Prior to the rise of narrative criticism within Gospel studies, the representative model was one of the more important approaches to understanding Johannine characters.

More recent work on Johannine characterization has identified two inherent weaknesses in the representative approach. First, the model tends to categorize characters in a way that fails to account for the complexity that we find in many Johannine figures.[21] The work of Fred W. Burnett[22] and Cornelis Bennema[23]

---

17   W. R. Domeris, 'The Johannine Drama', *Journal of Theology for Southern Africa* 42 (1983), pp. 29–35.

18   Ibid., p. 32 (emphasis added).

19   Ibid. (emphasis added).

20   'In John's narrative world the individuality of all the characters except Jesus is determined by their encounter with Jesus. The characters represent a continuum of responses to Jesus which exemplify misunderstandings the reader may share and responses one might make to the depiction of Jesus in the gospel' (Culpepper, *Anatomy of the Fourth Gospel*, p. 104). It is not a coincidence that this comment from Culpepper is accompanied by a footnote citing Collins' essay on representative figures.

21   See the helpful critique of this weakness in James L. Resseguie, *The Strange Gospel: Narrative Design and Point of View in John* (BIS, 56; Leiden: Brill, 2001), ch. 3.

22   Fred W. Burnett, 'Characterization and Reader Construction of Characters in the Gospels', *Semeia* 63 (1993), pp. 3–28.

23   See Cornelis Bennema, *Encountering Jesus: Character Studies in the Gospel of John* (Milton Keynes: Paternoster, 2009), esp. pp. 12–15. Though he does not cite the study in the book, Bennema's theory is heavily reliant upon Burnett's foundational article.

has been particularly helpful for bringing this weakness to light. Second, there is a general lack of unanimity among scholars as to what trait the representative figures actually embody. In other words, it has proven difficult to arrive at a consensus on the *representative function* of each supposedly *representative* figure. Despite these weaknesses, however, the representative approach has not been completely abandoned in contemporary Johannine scholarship, and some have even found it compatible with a literary approach.[24]

III. Culpepper and the Rise of Narrative Criticism

It would be difficult to overstate the importance of Culpepper's *Anatomy of the Fourth Gospel* (1983) to contemporary Johannine research.[25] In the late 1970s and early 1980s, redaction criticism had become the dominant interpretive framework within which Gospel scholars were working.[26] Within Johannine studies scholars were particularly concerned with proposing various source theories, identifying concrete stages in the Gospel's development, and connecting the dots between the so-called Johannine community and John's *Sitz im Leben*. Aided by a strong awareness of contemporary literary theory as applied in everyday English courses, Culpepper undertook an analysis of the *literary design* of John's Gospel. As pedestrian as it now seems, it was ground-breaking at that time to insist that the narrative be read as a coherent story with emphasis primarily on the world *within the text*. Such an approach was truly novel in the world of scholarship obsessed with both the sources and stages

---

24   See, e.g., Arthur H. Maynard, 'The Role of Peter in the Fourth Gospel', *NTS* 30 (1984), pp. 531–47; Kevin Quast, *Peter and the Beloved Disciple: Figures for a Community in Crisis* (JSNTSup, 32; Sheffield: Sheffield Academic Press, 1989), ch. 1; Craig Koester, *Symbolism in the Fourth Gospel: Meaning, Mystery, Community* (Minneapolis: Augsburg Fortress, 2003), pp. 33–77; Jocelyn McWhirter, *The Bridegroom Messiah and the People of God: Marriage in the Fourth Gospel* (SNTSMS, 138; Cambridge, UK: Cambridge University Press, 2006), ch. 2; and Jerome H. Neyrey, *The Gospel of John* (NCBC; Cambridge, UK: Cambridge University Press, 2007), pp. 58–9, 67, 94, 134. See also, Rekha M. Chennattu, RA, 'Women in the Mission of the Church: An Interpretation of John 4' (Paper presented at the Conference on 'Mission in Asia in the Third Millennium: Models for Integral Human Liberation', Sanata Dharma University, Yogyakarta, Indonesia, 14–17 April 1999).

25   Thatcher states it well when he writes that 'the most enduring contribution of *Anatomy of the Fourth Gospel* rose from its point where the book diverged most sharply from the mainstream of its day: the thesis that John's story is inherently meaningful, regardless of its sources, composition history, or historical value. At a time when scholars were deeply absorbed in speculations about literary sources, the Johannine community, and the number of revisions leading up to the present text, Culpepper boldly declared that a close reading of the Gospel of John as a unified narrative could produce striking new insights' (Tom Thatcher, 'Anatomies of the Fourth Gospel: Past, Present, and Future Probes', in Thatcher and Moore [eds], *Anatomies of Narrative Criticism*, p. 1).

26   There is not space here to rehearse the history of redaction criticism and its relative merits and deficiencies *vis-à-vis* narrative criticism. For a helpful overview of methodological developments from source criticism to modern reader-oriented methods, see Francis J. Moloney, *The Living Voice of the Gospels* (Peabody, MA: Hendrickson, 2007), pp. 309–42.

of the Gospel's development. That said, Culpepper's chapter on characters, the second longest in the book, did not stray far from the predominant discussions taking place in literary circles at that time. Of particular importance to his treatment of Johannine characters were categories set forth in Collins' two articles as well as discussions found in the works of Seymour Chatman, E. M. Forster and W. J. Harvey.

a. Chatman's Story and Discourse

In his influential book, *Story and Discourse*,[27] Seymour Chatman addressed the dichotomy between characters as representations of reality and characters as mere plot functionaries, preferring the former. This debate over 'realist' and 'purist' approaches continues to be an important area of discussion among literary critics. The realist (or mimetic) approach argues that characters 'acquire an independence from the plot in which they occur, and that characters can be discussed apart from their literary contexts'.[28] Practically, this means that characters can be extracted from their narrative worlds and treated as real people in hypothetical situations in the real world. This approach is primarily associated with the Romantic writers of the nineteenth century,[29] and finds fewer advocates today among theoreticians.

The other side of the discussion is represented by the purist (or functional) approach, which rejects the idea that characters can be taken out of their literary contexts or viewed in hypothetical, non-literary situations as autonomous individuals. The purist view is derived from an Aristotelian understanding of character. According to Aristotle, 'action' is the most important element in any dramatic presentation; the secondary element in the drama is the agent who performs the action.[30] The Aristotelian approach to characterization almost completely subjugates the character to the action performed, and in so doing reduces the character to a formless agent. Chatman notes that 'Aristotle's general formulation of character and characterization is not appropriate to a general theory of narrative, although, as usual, he provokes questions that cannot be ignored'.[31] If Aristotle's categories raise the question of the character's importance, the modern purist approach builds on that foundation by raising the question of the character's autonomy apart from the narrative in which that character originally appears.

---

27   Seymour Chatman, *Story and Discourse: Narrative Structure in Fiction and Film* (Ithaca, NY: Cornell University Press, 1980).

28   Burnett, 'Characterization and Reader Construction of Characters in the Gospels', p. 4.

29   Colleen M. Conway (*Men and Women in the Fourth Gospel: Gender and Johannine Characterization* [SBLDS, 167; Atlanta: Society of Biblical Literature, 1999], p. 50) notes that this view 'saw characters as more or less autonomous beings who possessed motives, values, and personality, all of which were open to analysis by the critic'.

30   See the discussion of Aristotle's *Poetics* in Chatman, *Story and Discourse*, pp. 108–10.

31   Ibid., p. 110.

Culpepper acknowledged that Chatman's study, while valuable, had limited implications for the study of the Fourth Gospel, since 'most of the characters in it appear so briefly that it is difficult to form an impression of them as "autonomous beings"'.[32] Practically, this meant that, for Culpepper, most Johannine characters are reduced more to the role of plot functionaries.

b. Forster's Aspects of the Novel

In his classic work, *Aspects of the Novel*,[33] E. M. Forster asked whether characters should be viewed as human beings, historical persons, or something else altogether.[34] Prefiguring the conclusions of the purist camp, Forster concluded that characters should not be extracted from the narrative and given unconditional autonomy.[35] However, Forster's deeper concern in posing the question was to understand how characters function with respect to the other elements of the narrative. This is the context in which Forster set forth his well-known distinction between 'round' and 'flat' characters.[36] According to Forster, 'round' characters are those prominent figures in any story that display a host of potentially conflicting traits, while 'flat' characters are predictable and one-dimensional. Using these categories, one might refer to the Jesus of John's Gospel as 'round' inasmuch as he displays a host of emotional characteristics and complex motivations.[37] One might also refer to the uncomprehending characters of the Fourth Gospel as 'flat' inasmuch as they are primarily defined by their consistent misperception of the mission and message of Jesus. To do this, however, would be to overstate the case.

Though Culpepper cited Forster's categories approvingly in his discussion of character in *Anatomy*, many narrative critics today have found this dichotomy to be problematic in that it too rigidly compartmentalizes characters that seem to exist on a more expansive spectrum. For this reason, the distinction between round and flat characters, though widely referenced, has fallen out of favour with NT scholars employing a narrative approach. Strict adherence to these two categories would fail to recognize the complexity in many of the minor characters found in the canonical Gospels. Seemingly flat characters can express genuine insights and be momentarily transformed into characters with 'rounded edges'.[38] In the Fourth Gospel this is particularly true of Nicodemus, who early

---

32   Culpepper, *Anatomy of the Fourth Gospel*, p. 102.

33   E. M. Forster, *Aspects of the Novel* (New York: Harcourt, Brace and Company, 1927).

34   'What is the difference between people in a novel and people like the novelist or like you, or like me, or Queen Victoria? There is bound to be a difference. If a character in a novel is exactly like Queen Victoria – not rather like but exactly like – then it actually is Queen Victoria, and the novel, or all of it that the character touches, becomes a memoir' (Forster, *Aspects of the Novel*, p. 71).

35   Ibid., p. 100.

36   Ibid., pp. 103–25.

37   For instance, Jesus cleanses the temple in a fit of anger (2.1-22), weeps at the death of his friend Lazarus (11.35), and is continually driven by the Father's will (5.16-44; 6.35-51; 8.16-29; 10.14-18; 12.27-50).

38   Shlomith Rimmon-Kenan (*Narrative Fiction: Contemporary Poetics* [London:

in the narrative displays an inability to understand Jesus' message and mission (3.1-15) but later appears as a follower of (or at least sympathizer with) the crucified Jesus (19.38-42). His seemingly 'flat' characteristic of misperception is 'rounded' by the narrator to indicate not just a new characteristic (i.e., belief) but rather a genuine, thoroughly Johannine transformation. Burnett expresses this concept well when he writes that it 'seems best to speak of *degrees of characterization* in biblical texts, and to plot textual indicators on a continuum for any particular text, from words at one pole to "persons" at the other pole'.[39] This continuum must include at least three categories: (1) *agents*, which have little or no development and function essentially to advance the plot; (2) *types*, which have differing levels of character development and typically reveal a prominent, mainly static trait; and (3) *full-blown characters* with differing levels of direct and indirect characterization. Each of these individual categories must also be understood to exist on a continuum.

c. *Harvey's* Character and the Novel

In *Anatomy*, Culpepper also referenced W. J. Harvey's classification of characters into protagonists, intermediate characters (e.g., cards and *ficelles*), and background characters. [40] Harvey's categories – particularly protagonist and *ficelle* – seemed to fit in nicely with Culpepper's classification of Johannine characters. Jesus is the clear protagonist of the story, while most of the other characters function as *ficelles* – 'typical characters easily recognizable by the readers. They exist to serve specific plot functions, often revealing the protagonist, and may carry a great deal of representative or symbolic value.'[41]

These basic categories (mimetic vs functional, round vs flat, protagonist vs *ficelle*) were the building blocks of Culpepper's brief exposition of characterization. From there he provided character analyses of Jesus and three groups of characters – the disciples, the 'Jews', and other minor characters[42] – with little further discussion devoted to a theory of character. For a considerable period after the publication of *Anatomy*, little work was done toward the development of a comprehensive theory of character, though studies of individual characters proliferated.

Methuen & Co., 1983], p. 61) comments: 'A trait may be implied both by one-time (or non-routine) actions . . . One-time actions tend to evoke the dynamic aspect of character, often playing a part in a turning point in the narrative. By contrast, habitual actions tend to reveal the character's unchanging or static aspect, often having a cosmic or ironic effect, as when a character clings to old habits in a situation which renders them inadequate.'

39   Burnett, 'Characterization and Reader Construction', p. 19 (emphasis added).

40   See W. J. Harvey, *Character and the Novel* (Ithaca, NY: Cornell University Press, 1965), pp. 52–73.

41   Culpepper, *Anatomy of the Fourth Gospel*, p. 104.

42   Culpepper's discussion of minor characters includes: John the Baptist, Jesus' mother, Nicodemus, the Samaritan woman, the royal official, the lame man, the brothers of Jesus, the blind man, Mary, Martha and Lazarus, and Pilate. See *Anatomy*, pp. 132–44.

As narrative criticism continued its move into mainstream biblical scholarship, more publications on Johannine characters and characterization began to appear. The period between 1989 and 2003 saw the publication of numerous individual studies of Johannine characters including the mother of Jesus,[43] Nicodemus,[44] the Samaritan woman,[45] Peter,[46] Judas,[47] Lazarus,[48] Mary and Martha,[49] 'the Jews',[50] God,[51] various women,[52] and minor characters.[53] This period also saw the publication of numerous monographs focused on issues of character in the Fourth Gospel: Robert G. Maccini's *Her Testimony is True* (1996),[54] David

43   Judith M. Lieu, 'The Mother of the Son in the Fourth Gospel', *JBL* 117 (1998), pp. 61–77.

44   Jouette M. Bassler, 'Mixed Signals: Nicodemus in the Fourth Gospel', *JBL* 108 (1989), pp. 635–46; Debbie Gibbons, 'Nicodemus: Character Development, Irony and Repetition in the Fourth Gospel', *Proceedings: Eastern Great Lakes and Midwest Bible Societies* 11 (1991), pp. 116–28.

45   Stephen D. Moore, 'Are There Impurities in the Living Water that the Johannine Jesus Dispenses? Deconstruction, Feminism and the Samaritan Woman', *BibInt* 1 (1993), pp. 207–27; cf. also, ch. 5, entitled 'The Samaritan Woman', in Frances Taylor Gench, *Back to the Well: Women's Encounters with Jesus in the Gospels* (Louisville: Westminster John Knox, 2004), pp. 109–35.

46   Arthur J. Droge, 'The Status of Peter in the Fourth Gospel: A Note on John 18:10-11', *JBL* 109 (1990), pp. 307–11.

47   Tom Thatcher, 'Jesus, Judas, and Peter: Character by Contrast in the Fourth Gospel', *BSac* 153 (1996), pp. 435–48.

48   Wilhelm Wuellner, 'Putting Life Back into the Lazarus Story and Its Reading: The Narrative Rhetoric of John 11 as the Narration of Faith', *Semeia* 53 (1991); Raimo Hakola, 'A Character Resurrected: Lazarus in the Fourth Gospel and Afterwards', in David Rhoads and Kari Syreeni (eds), *Characterization in the Gospels: Reconceiving Narrative Criticism* (JSNTSup, 184; Sheffield: Sheffield Academic Press, 1999), pp. 223–63.

49   Francis J. Moloney, 'The Faith of Mary and Martha: A Narrative Approach to John 11,17-40', *Bib* 75 (1994), pp. 471–93; idem, 'Can Everyone Be Wrong? A Reading of John 11.1–12.8', *NTS* 49 (2003), pp. 505–27.

50   Francis J. Moloney, '"The Jews" in the Fourth Gospel: Another Perspective' *Pac* 15 (2002), pp. 16–36.

51   Marianne Meye Thompson, '"God's Voice You Have Never Heard, God's Form You Have Never Seen": The Characterization of God in the Gospel of John', *Semeia* 63 (1993), pp. 177–204.

52   Turid Karlsen Seim, 'Roles of Women in the Gospel of John', in L. Hartman and B. Olsson (eds), *Aspects on the Johannine Literature* (ConBNT, 18; Uppsala: Almqvist & Wiksell, 1987), pp. 56–73; Ingrid R. Kitzberger, 'Mary of Bethany and Mary of Magdala – Two Female Characters in the Johannine Passion Narrative: A Feminist Narrative-Critical Reader-Response', *NTS* 41 (1995), pp. 564–85; idem, 'Synoptic Women in John: Interfigural Readings', in Ingrid R. Kitzberger (ed.), *Transformative Encounters: Jesus and Women Re-viewed* (Leiden: Brill, 1999), pp. 77–111; Leticia A. Guardiola-Saenz, 'Border-Crossing and Its Redemptive Power in John 7:53–8:11: A Cultural Reading of Jesus and *the Accused*', in Kitzberger (ed.), *Transformative Encounters*, pp. 267–91. See also, ch. 6, 'A Woman Accused of Adultery', in Gench, *Back to the Well*, pp. 136–89.

53   Colleen M. Conway, 'Speaking Through Ambiguity: Minor Characters in the Fourth Gospel', *BibInt* 10 (2002), pp. 324–41.

54   Robert G. Maccini, *Her Testimony is True: Women as Witnesses according to John* (JSNTSup, 125; Sheffield: Sheffield Academic Press, 1996).

Beck's *The Discipleship Paradigm* (1997),[55] Adeline Fehribach's *The Women in the Life of the Bridegroom* (1998),[56] Colleen Conway's *Men and Women in the Fourth Gospel* (1999),[57] Peter Dschulnigg's *Jesus begegnen* (2002),[58] Stan Harstine's *Moses as a Character in the Fourth Gospel* (2002),[59] Susanne Ruschmann's *Maria von Magdala im Johannesevangelium* (2002),[60] and Margaret Beirne's *Women and Men in the Fourth Gospel* (2003).[61] Though character studies were advancing during this period, little was done to promote a comprehensive theory of character that would help to explain how characters function in the Fourth Gospel. This trend, however, has been reversed during the past decade, another productive period in which methods for approaching character studies have been at the forefront of scholarly deliberations.

IV. Characters and Theories (2003–Present)

Over the past decade, there has been a surge of interest in the characters of the Fourth Gospel,[62] and in the past six years alone, no less than eight monographs

---

55   David R. Beck, *The Discipleship Paradigm: Readers and Anonymous Characters in the Fourth Gospel* (BIS, 27; Leiden: Brill, 1997).

56   Adeline Fehribach, *The Women in the Life of the Bridegroom: A Feminist Historical-Literary Analysis of the Female Characters in the Fourth Gospel* (Collegeville, MN: Liturgical, 1998).

57   Cf. n. 29 above for full bibliographic information.

58   Peter Dschulnigg, *Jesus begegnen: Personen und ihre Bedeutung im Johannesevangelium* (Münster: Lit, 2002).

59   Stan Harstine, *Moses as a Character in the Fourth Gospel: A Study of Ancient Reading Techniques* (JSNTSup, 229; Sheffield: Sheffield Academic Press, 2002).

60   Susanne Ruschmann, *Maria von Magdala im Johannesevangelium: Jüngerin—Zeugin—Lebensbotin* (2002).

61   Margaret M. Beirne, *Women and Men in the Fourth Gospel: A Genuine Discipleship of Equals* (JSNTSup, 242; Sheffield: Sheffield Academic Press, 2003).

62   See the following essays (in order of appearance): James M. Howard, 'The Significance of Minor Characters in the Gospel of John', *BSac* 163 (2006), pp. 63–78; Humphrey Mwangi Waweru, 'Jesus and Ordinary Women in the Gospel of John: An African Perspective', *Swedish Missiological Themes* 96 (2008), pp. 139–59; Andrew T. Lincoln, 'The Lazarus Story: A Literary Perspective', in Richard Bauckham and Carl Mosser (eds), *The Gospel of John and Christian Theology* (Grand Rapids: Eerdmans, 2008), pp. 211–32; Marianne Meye Thompson, 'The Raising of Lazarus in John 11: A Theological Reading', in Bauckham and Mosser (eds), *The Gospel of John and Christian Theology*, pp. 233–44; Ruben Zimmerman, 'The Narrative Hermeneutics of John 11: Learning with Lazarus How to Understand Death, Life, and Resurrection', in Craig Koester and Reimund Bieringer (eds), *The Resurrection of Jesus in the Gospel of John* (WUNT, I/222; Tübingen: Mohr Siebeck, 2008), pp. 75–101; Steven A. Hunt, 'Nicodemus, Lazarus, and the Fear of the "the Jews" in the Fourth Gospel', in Gilbert van Belle, Michael Labahn and P. Maritz (eds), *Repetition and Variation in the Fourth Gospel: Style, Text, Interpretation* (Louvain: Peeters, 2009), pp. 199–212; William M. Wright IV, 'Greco-Roman Character Typing and the Presentation of Judas in the Fourth Gospel', *CBQ* 71 (2009), pp. 544–59; Cornelis Bennema, 'The Character of John in the Fourth Gospel', *JETS* 52 (2009), pp. 271–84; idem, 'The Identity and Composition of οἱ Ἰουδαῖοι in the Gospel of John', *TynBul* 60 (2009), pp. 239–63.

have appeared, most of which advance a specific method for approaching Johannine characters.

In 2006, Philip Esler and Ronald Piper drew on social-identity theory to examine the siblings of Bethany.[63] They found that Lazarus, Mary and Martha function as important prototypes or ideal characters for the audience of the Fourth Gospel. In 2007, Judith Hartenstein's Marburg dissertation, *Charakterisierung im Dialog*, used a narrative approach to examine Mary Magdalene, Peter and the mother of Jesus both in the Fourth Gospel and in other early Christian texts (including the Synoptics and the *Gospel of Thomas*).[64] She sees John's presentation of characters as more complex than is usually suggested but notes that characters change very little throughout the story. Also appearing in 2007 was Bradford Blaine's revised dissertation, *Peter in the Gospel of John*.[65] Like Hartenstein, Blaine also employs a narrative-critical approach that takes seriously both the Gospel's sources and its historical setting. Blaine's study is driven by the concern to refute the common opinion that the Fourth Gospel presents Peter in a substantially negative light.

Three more monographs on Johannine characterization were published in 2009. The first to appear was my revised dissertation, *John and Thomas: Gospels in Conflict?*,[66] which sought to analyse Johannine characters with a view to evaluating the thesis that the Fourth Gospel contains an 'anti-Thomas polemic'. After looking at Thomas, Peter, Nicodemus, the Samaritan woman, Mary, Martha, Philip, Judas (not Iscariot), and the disciples as a representative group, I concluded that the Johannine presentation of Thomas is part of a wider literary pattern within the story where characters misunderstand the mission and message of Jesus, and thus the charge of an 'anti-Thomas polemic' is unfounded. I also contend that misunderstanding should be one of the primary foci guiding our understanding of John's characters. The next book to appear in 2009 was Susan Hylen's *Imperfect Believers*.[67] Hylen examines Nicodemus, the Samaritan woman, the disciples, the Jews, Martha, Mary, Peter and the Beloved Disciple, and draws out an important element of their characterization: ambiguity. She argues that it is difficult to discern whether John's characters exercise a satisfactory belief in Jesus. Many characters seem to grasp important insights about Jesus but fail to believe or understand in other key areas. Thus, ambiguity is the lens through which we should view John's characters. Cornelis Bennema's book, *Encountering*

---

63   Philip Esler and Ronald Piper, *Lazarus, Mary and Martha: A Social-Scientific and Theological Reading of John* (London: SCM, 2006).

64   Judith Hartenstein, *Charakterisierung im Dialog: Maria Magdalena, Petrus, und die Mutter Jesu im Johannesevangelium* (NTOA, 64; Göttingen: Vandenhoeck & Ruprecht, 2007).

65   Bradford B. Blaine, Jr, *Peter in the Gospel of John: The Making of an Authentic Disciple* (AcBib, 27; Atlanta: Society of Biblical Literature, 2007).

66   Christopher W. Skinner, *John and Thomas: Gospels in Conflict? Johannine Characterization and the Thomas Question* (PTMS, 115; Eugene, OR: Wipf & Stock, 2009).

67   Susan Hylen, *Imperfect Believers: Ambiguous Characters in the Gospel of John* (Louisville: Westminster John Knox, 2009).

Jesus,[68] also appeared in 2009, and that work more than any of the aforementioned volumes demonstrates a concern for an overarching theory of character. Bennema considers nearly all of John's characters using a method that categorizes characters into one of four categories: agent (or actant), type (or stock character), character with personality, or individual (or person). In addition to his classification system, Bennema's discussion of each character is accompanied by a chart that plots the character's appearances, identity, speech and actions, character classification, degree of characterization, and response to Jesus. More than any other recent scholar, Bennema has demonstrated a concern for developing a comprehensive theory of character – a topic to which he returns in this volume.

In his 2010 dissertation, Nicolas Farelly used narrative analysis to examine the faith and comprehension of five Johannine disciples – Peter, Judas, the Beloved Disciple, Thomas and Mary Magdalene.[69] Farelly asserts that the disciples have genuine faith and life from a very early point in the narrative, but thereafter struggle to come to terms fully with Jesus' identity, words and mission. Also appearing in 2010 was Michael Martin's dissertation, *Judas and the Rhetoric of Comparison.*[70] Martin situates the negative depiction of Judas in the Fourth Gospel in the context of the ancient practice of *genus syncrisis,* or the comparison of types. This practice compares two real-world groups by comparing ideal or extreme representatives from each group. This practice, argues Martin, creates a two-level drama in which it is possible to both see the superiority of one literary type and apply this superiority to the group that the character in question represents. These more recent studies have given way to a concern for developing a theory of character as it applies to the characters of the Fourth Gospel, which is one major concern of the present volume.

Though not a movement within narrative criticism *per se,* Richard Bauckham's theory of eyewitness testimony in the Gospels also deserves mention in our survey. In his 2008 monograph, *Jesus and the Eyewitnesses,*[71] Bauckham argued that the canonical Gospels are best understood against the background of ancient historiography in which the best historical practice was to rely on eyewitness testimony (αὐτοψία). Challenging the form-critical position that the Gospel material about Jesus circulated in oral form for a lengthy period in the Church before it was recorded by the evangelist, Bauckham asserts that the Gospels were based largely on eyewitness testimony; he also contends that John was actually composed by an eyewitness – John the elder rather than one of the Twelve.[72] Bauckham's thesis has implications for character studies inasmuch

---

68   Cf. n. 23 above for full bibliographic information.

69   Nicolas Farelly, *The Disciples in the Fourth Gospel* (WUNT, II/290; Tübingen: Mohr Siebeck, 2010).

70   Michael W. Martin, *Judas and the Rhetoric of Comparison in the Fourth Gospel* (NTM, 25; Sheffield: Sheffield Phoenix Press, 2010).

71   See Richard Bauckham, *Jesus and the Eyewitnesses: The Gospel as Eyewitness Testimony* (Grand Rapids: Eerdmans, 2008).

72   See his argument in ibid., pp. 358–83.

as eyewitness testimony would suggest that specific Gospel characters reflect a historical individuality rather than a carefully crafted narrative creation. For these reasons, and because Bauckham's argument has proven influential among a segment of scholars, it needs to be discussed here.

Bauckham's work on eyewitness testimony in the Gospels is characteristically brilliant, but his thesis has proven to be problematic. He insists that reliance on eyewitnesses played a determining role in securing reliable Jesus tradition in the first decades of the early Church. Narrative-critical approaches to the Gospels of the NT stand on the shoulders of the substantive contributions of source, form and redaction criticisms. Thus, it is commonly affirmed that the canonical Gospels developed over time as part of a lengthy process of compiling written and oral material (source and form criticism), editorial activity (redaction criticism), and creative shaping of the received stories (narrative criticism). This process results in a set of theologically stylized narratives with historical roots; these narratives reflect sophisticated storytelling, internal unity, and a theology unique to the individual account. If, as Bauckham contends, eyewitnesses are responsible for the content of the Gospels, this would rob the individual evangelists of the creativity that seems to be a characteristic element of each canonical account of Jesus. For example, in the Gospel of John, characters consistently misunderstand the mission and message of Jesus. Whereas this is a component elsewhere in the Synoptic tradition, it is a driving motif in Fourth Gospel characterization. From a narrative-critical standpoint, this appears to be a fairly obvious literary theme, woven into the narrative as part of the evangelist's intentional theological presentation. Against this backdrop, Bauckham's theory would suggest that such an obvious element of literary design derives from the life and vocation of the historical Jesus, rather than from the final stage of the Gospel's composition. A great deal more could be said about Bauckham's interesting work, but space limitations preclude such a discussion. However, in several of the essays that follow, Bauckham's theory will be engaged from sympathetic and disagreeing points of view.

V. Characters and Characterization in the Gospel of John (2013)

Our survey brings us to the contributions of the present volume. The essays in this volume seek to articulate theories of character, provide interaction with and critique of contemporary views, and offer fresh analyses of Johannine characters. The book is divided into two sections. The first section is methodological and explores various theories about characterization and models for reading character. The second section is exegetical and consists of character studies from diverse perspectives within a narrative-critical framework.

In Chapter 1, James Resseguie provides an elegant primer on a narrative-critical approach to characters and characterization showing how rhetoric, point of view, setting, and master-plot contribute to our interpretation of characters in the Fourth Gospel. In Chapter 2, R. Alan Culpepper reflects upon the surge of interest in Johannine characterization and uses recent research as a launching point to discuss how characters impact the thematic development and rhetorical plan of the Gospel. In Chapter 3, Cornelis Bennema follows up on his recent work on methodology by proposing what he calls, 'a comprehensive, non-reductionist theory of character' as it applies to the Gospel of John. Chapter 4 features a discussion of characters, eyewitnesses and current psychological research. In 2010, Judith Redman published a critique of Richard Bauckham's eyewitness thesis that was set in the context of contemporary psychological research on eyewitness testimony.[73] In her essay for this book, Redman returns to Bauckham's theory using contemporary research on eyewitness testimony, this time set within the framework of a narrative hermeneutic. In Chapter 5, Raymond F. Collins takes a closer look at the roles comparison and contrast play in several character groups and how this contributes to the rhetorical scheme of the narrative. In Chapter 6, Susan Hylen returns to the theme of ambiguity and shows how three elements – historical context, the implied reader and the nature of faith – impact on our reading of John's characters. In the final chapter of the first section, I discuss the Prologue (1.1-18) as a reader-elevating device that places the reader in a position of privilege; this provides the reader with a greater awareness of and appreciation for the role of misunderstanding in the Gospel story and is a key component of the Gospel's approach to characterization.

Stan Harstine begins the second section of this volume with a study of God as a character in the Fourth Gospel from a rhetorical perspective. In Chapter 9, Sherri Brown examines John the Baptist against the backdrop of the Prologue with specific emphasis on the Baptist's role as witness. In Chapter 10, Craig Koester uses the concept of 'theological complexity' to explore Nicodemus' role as a figure that provides readers with glimpses of how the revelatory work of God is done in the world. Turning to the Samaritan woman in Chapter 11, Mary Coloe examines her narrative and theological significance, and highlights her role as a vehicle of the evangelist's ideological point of view. In Chapter 12, Dorothy Lee surveys the Lukan and Johannine portraits of Martha and Mary as understood in history, sacred literature and art. Drawing on his previous work on anonymity and discipleship, David Beck looks at the Beloved Disciple's relationship to the related themes of belief and witness in John. In the book's final chapter, Cornelis Bennema looks at Pilate from a historically informed narrative approach. Emphasizing Pilate's response to Jesus and his impact on the development of the Gospel's plot, he concludes that the common portrait of the Johannine Pilate as weak and vacillating is incorrect.

Taken together, these chapters combine substantive insights on method and individual characters from leading interpreters of the Fourth Gospel. These reflections are meant to provide a comprehensive interaction with

---

73   Judith C. S. Redman, 'How Accurate are Eyewitnesses? Bauckham and the Eyewitnesses in the Light of Psychological Research', *JBL* 129 (2010), pp. 177–97.

contemporary models of approaching character in a way that will influence the direction of future conversations of Johannine characters and characterization.

PART ONE

METHODS AND MODELS
FOR READING JOHANNINE CHARACTERS

Chapter 1

A NARRATIVE-CRITICAL APPROACH TO THE FOURTH GOSPEL

James L. Resseguie

I. Introduction

A narrative-critical approach to the Fourth Gospel focuses on the literariness of the Gospel, the qualities that make it work as a piece of literature.[1] The 'what' (its content) and the 'how' (its rhetoric and structure) of the Gospel are viewed as a complete tapestry, an organic whole in which form and content are an indissoluble unit. A narrative analysis attends to the words on a page, the formal features of the Gospel in its finished form such as narrative structure, rhetorical devices, settings, narrator's role in shaping the narrative, point of view, and master-plot or universal story that underlies the narrative and shapes its conflicts. This essay develops and elaborates five aspects of John's narrative – point of view, rhetorical devices, settings, characters and characterization, and master-plot – that contribute to its literariness and are especially important for close readings. Close readings are the detailed, often painstaking analysis of the words on a page that bring out the nuances and ambiguities of words, images and metaphors, and other formal features of the text.

II. Point of View

Point of view is 'the way a story gets told'.[2] It is both the mode or angle of vision from which characters, dialogue, actions, setting and events are observed, and the narrator's attitude towards or evaluation of characters

---

1   On introductions to narrative criticism see James L. Resseguie, *Narrative Criticism of the New Testament: An Introduction* (Grand Rapids: Baker Academic, 2005); Mark Allan Powell, *What Is Narrative Criticism?* (Minneapolis: Fortress, 1990); Daniel Marguerat and Yvan Bourquin, *How to Read Bible Stories: An Introduction to Narrative Criticism* (London: SCM, 1999); Elizabeth Struthers Malbon, 'Narrative Criticism: How Does the Story Mean?', in Janice Capel Anderson and Stephen D. Moore (eds), *Mark & Method: New Approaches in Biblical Studies* (Minneapolis: Fortress, 1992), pp. 23–49; David Rhoads, Joanna Dewey and Donald Michie, *Mark as Story: An Introduction to the Narrative of a Gospel* (Minneapolis: Fortress, 2nd edn, 1999).

2   M. H. Abrams, *A Glossary of Literary Terms* (New York: Harcourt Brace College Publishers, 7th edn, 1999), s.v. 'Point of View'.

and events. The angle of vision, sometimes called 'objective' point of view, focuses on the relationship between the narrator and the narrative.[3] What is the position from which the narrator views the narrative? Is the narrator outside the story or a character within the story? If the narrator is outside, does she or he have privileged access to the characters' thoughts, motivations and feelings? The narrator of the Fourth Gospel is a third-person omniscient narrator who tells the story from outside and refers to the characters by name or by 'he', 'she', or 'they'. Similar to a moving camera creating a montage, this narrator roams from character to character, event to event, delving into the thoughts of some, elaborating the motivations of others, commenting on characters, and so forth. Occasionally, the narrator of the Fourth Gospel abandons the third-person narrative approach and resorts to first-person narration as seen in the Prologue. 'And the Word became flesh and lived among *us*, and *we* have seen his glory, the glory as of a father's only son, full of grace and truth' (John 1.14). This first-person narration lends authority to what is written since the narrator is presumably a witness to the events (cf. also John 21.24b, 25).

First-person or third-person narration, however, is not the way persons on the street understand point of view when asked, for instance, for their point of view on global warming. This aspect of point of view goes beyond the mode or angle of vision – the narrator's stance in relationship to the narrative in an 'objective' sense – and moves to a subjective stance that focuses on the narrator's response to and evaluation of characters, dialogue, actions, setting and events. Susan Sniader Lanser calls this the 'subjective point of view',[4] and Wallace Martin refers to it as point of view 'in its most common meaning – a set of attitudes, opinions, and personal concerns that constitute someone's stance in relation to the world'.[5] Other critics use various terms to designate subjective point of view, such as 'conceptual',[6] 'ideological',[7] or 'evaluative'.[8] David Rhoads, Joanna Dewey and Donald Michie prefer the term 'standards of judgment', which they define as 'a system of beliefs and values implicit in the point of view from which the narrator judges and evaluates the characters in the story'.[9]

The ideological point of view (the preferred term in this essay) is the most important aspect of point of view for biblical narrative analysis, since it explores the worldview – the norms, values and beliefs – that the implied author wants the implied reader to adopt. The implied author is the persona

---

3   See Susan Sniader Lanser, *The Narrative Act: Point of View in Prose Fiction* (Princeton, NJ: Princeton University Press, 1981), p. 16.

4   *The Narrative Act*, p. 16.

5   *Recent Theories of Narrative* (Ithaca, NY: Cornell University Press, 1986), p. 147.

6   Seymour Chatman, *Story and Discourse: Narrative Structure in Fiction and Film* (Ithaca, NY: Cornell University Press, 1978), p. 152.

7   Boris Uspensky, *A Poetics of Composition: The Structure of the Artistic Text and Typology of a Compositional Form* (trans. V. Zavarin and S. Wittig; Berkeley: University of California Press, 1978).

8   Powell, *What Is Narrative Criticism?*, p. 24.

9   *Mark as Story*, pp. 44–5.

that the real author creates while the implied reader is the reader that the implied author creates, a reader who can take the clues of the narrative and correctly interpret it. Biblical narratives are written to persuade the implied reader to adopt a perspective that is in line with the narrative's norms, values and beliefs. This perspective is the ideological point of view.

But how is the ideological point of view of a story made known in the story? In some narratives this perspective is on the surface and easily available, which Susan Sniader Lanser calls 'explicit ideology'.[10] In other narratives the ideological point of view is embedded in the deep structures of the text and is more difficult to mine.[11] The Fourth Gospel is more explicit in its ideology, stating its perspective in the Prologue: 'the Word became flesh (σάρξ, *sarx*) and lived among us, and we have seen his glory (δόξα, *doxa*), the glory as of a father's only son, full of grace and truth' (John 1.14).[12] The glory is seen in the flesh, a point of view that is a stumbling block for some characters while others resolve the paradox. The ideological perspective shapes the primary dilemma of the story that the characters must resolve. Some characters see only flesh, Jesus' humanness, when they look at his actions and dialogue and are blinded to the glory; other characters see the glory in the flesh.

The conflicting responses to the narrative point of view surface in the religious authorities' conflicts with Jesus and in Jesus' encounters with other characters in the Gospel. In John 7 and 8, for example, Jesus accuses the authorities of judging by 'appearances' (7.24) and 'by human standards' (literally, 'according to the flesh', 8.15), whereas he judges with 'right judgement' (7.24). 'Appearance' judgement or judgement 'according to the flesh' hinders them from seeing the glory in the flesh. Again in John 9 the religious authorities see only flesh because they judge by appearances and conclude that since Jesus violates the Sabbath laws, he must be a sinner. The man born blind, on the other hand, does not judge by appearances and concludes that Jesus must be 'from God' (9.33). He sees the glory in the flesh.

III. Rhetorical Devices

A narrative analysis pays close attention to rhetorical devices and the way they function in a narrative. The Fourth Gospel uses simile, metaphor, irony, *double entendres* and misunderstandings, to name a few, to expand its

---

10   *The Narrative Act*, p. 216.

11   Lanser, *The Narrative Act*, pp. 216–17. Uspensky, *Poetics of Composition*, p. 8, concludes that the ideological point of view is 'the most basic aspect of point of view' but also 'the least accessible to formalization, for its analysis relies, to a degree, on intuitive understanding'.

12   See Rudolf Bultmann, *The Gospel of John: A Commentary* (trans. G. R. Beasley-Murray; Philadelphia: Westminster, 1971), p. 63: 'The δόξα is not to be seen *alongside* the σάρξ nor through the σάρξ as through a window; it is to be seen in the σάρξ and nowhere else. If man wishes to see the δόξα, then it is on the σάρξ that he must concentrate his attention, without allowing himself to fall a victim to appearances.'

narrative ideology and to expose the thinking of those who rely on judgement by appearances or according to the flesh.

Irony, for instance, is an alluring and effective weapon to dissemble superficial judgements. It is 'a mode of discourse for conveying meanings different from – and usually opposite to – the professed or ostensible ones',[13] and its effectiveness relies on the exploitation of the distance between words and events and their contexts. Douglas Colin Muecke identifies three basic features of all irony. First, irony depends on a double-layered or two-story phenomenon for success. 'At the lower level is the situation either as it appears to the victim of irony (where there is a victim) or as it is deceptively presented by the ironist.'[14] The upper level is the situation as it appears to the implied reader or the ironist. Second, the ironist exploits a contradiction, incongruity, or incompatibility between the two levels. Third, irony plays upon the innocence of a character or victim. 'Either a victim is confidently unaware of the very possibility of there being an upper level or point of view that invalidates his own, or an ironist pretends not to be aware of it.'[15]

The irony of unknowing knowing shapes the encounter of Jesus and the Pharisees in John 9. At the lower level are the religious leaders who play the role of *alazons*, self-deceived braggarts who claim to know more than they actually know. Muecke defines an *alazon* as 'the man who blindly assumes or asserts that something is or is not the case, or confidently expects something to happen or not to happen; he does not even remotely suspect that things might not be as he supposes them to be, or might not turn out as he expects them to'.[16] The Pharisees' *alazony* emerges in their first-person discourse that leaves them vulnerable to ironic dissimulation by the man born blind. In reference to Jesus, they say 'We know that this man is a sinner' (9.24), and later they claim that 'We know that God has spoken to Moses, but as for this man, we do not know where he comes from' (9.29). The man born blind unravels their overconfident judgement with the truth. 'Here is an astonishing thing! You do not know where he comes from, and yet he opened my eyes' (9.30).

The narrator and implied reader share the upper level of Muecke's diagram, and the man born blind plays the role of *eiron*, a dissembler who unravels the logic of the religious leaders who know yet are unknowing and see yet are unseeing. When the Pharisees want to hear a second time about the blind man's healing, he lashes back with biting sarcasm that uncovers their orotundity: 'Why do you want to hear it again? Do you also want to become his disciples?' (9.27). The irony then turns tragic at the end when Jesus reveals that his mission is to enable the blind to see and the sighted to become blind

13   Roger Fowler (ed.), *A Dictionary of Modern Critical Terms* (London: Routledge & Kegan Paul, rev. edn, 1987), p. 128. On irony in the Fourth Gospel see Paul Duke, *Irony in the Fourth Gospel* (Atlanta: John Knox, 1985) and Gail R. O'Day, *Revelation in the Fourth Gospel: Narrative Mode and Theological Claim* (Philadelphia: Fortress, 1986).

14   Douglas Colin Muecke, *The Compass of Irony* (London: Methuen & Co., 1969), p. 19.

15   Ibid., p. 20.

16   Ibid., p. 30.

(9.39). Still unaware of an upper level and a point of view that undermines their own point of view, the Pharisees ask if they are blind: 'Surely we are not blind, are we?' (9.40). The negative answer that they expect is what Jesus offers. 'If you were blind, you would not have sin. But now that you say, "We see", your sin remains' (9.41). Blindness can be cured; sightless seeing remains incurable.

An ironic reading of John 9 is not only necessary to fathom Jesus' mission in 9.39 ('I came into the world for judgement so that those who do not see may see, and those who do see may become blind'). It is necessary to understand how God works in this world and the way superficial judgements hinder the understanding of God's actions. The religious authorities illustrate the tragedy of the sighted blind, for Jesus does not fit their conventions of how God works in this world. How can one heal on the Sabbath and yet be from God? The more they insist on the clarity of their vision, the further they descend into spiritual darkness.

Metaphors also are effective rhetorical devices to disrupt familiar patterns of thought in the Fourth Gospel. A metaphor ascribes an action or quality of one thing to a second by way of identity.[17] I. A. Richards uses the concepts of *vehicle*, an image that illumines the subject of the metaphor, and *tenor*, the subject of the metaphor, to analyse metaphors.[18] The reader must discover the implied analogy or implicit comparison between the vehicle and tenor. For example, when Jesus says, 'I am the bread of life', bread is the vehicle that is applied to the tenor, Jesus. The metaphor invites the reader to explore the way (or ways) in which Jesus is life-sustaining bread.

An entire narrative may hinge on an ambiguous metaphor and its potential for misunderstanding. Consider, for instance, the metaphor of born 'again' or 'from above' (ἄνωθεν, *anōthen*) in Jesus' encounter with Nicodemus. 'Very truly, I tell you, no one can see the kingdom of God without being born from above [or again]' (John 3.3). The vehicle refers either to being born 'from above' or to being born 'again'; the tenor is the kingdom of God. But the ambiguity of the vehicle makes the point of comparison uncertain. Did Nicodemus apply a literal interpretation to the metaphor and envision a rebirth in a physical sense (born 'again') while Jesus intended a spiritual birth (born 'from above')? This would seem to account for his amusing question: 'How can anyone be born after having grown old? Can one enter a second time into the mother's womb and be born?' (John 3.4). Did he believe that rebirth is a self-improvement project that he can bring about rather than a new origin that comes from God, as Bultmann suggests?[19] Or did Nicodemus get one-half of the equation correct but miss the full potential of the metaphor? Are both meanings intended by the ambiguous vehicle: a person must be born

---

17   See Resseguie, *Narrative Criticism*, pp. 62–4.
18   I. A. Richards, *The Philosophy of Rhetoric* (New York: Oxford University Press, 1936), pp. 119–27.
19   Bultmann, *The Gospel of John*, pp. 136–7.

'again' *and* born 'from above' to enter the kingdom of God?[20] Not only are both meanings likely, but both are needed to understand the ideological point of view of the narrative. Jesus certainly means that the origin of the new birth is from above, i.e., from God, which the Pharisee misunderstands. But Nicodemus's understanding of rebirth contains an element of truth that the narrative both develops and 'makes strange' at the same time.[21] Entering the kingdom of God is not just an act from above; it is also a second birth, i.e., the making of a new creation. The metaphor of born 'again' or born 'from above' foregrounds the spiritual act of rebirth against the background of physical birth, thereby making strange the notion that salvation can somehow be achieved by human efforts.[22]

Similarly, the ambiguity of the metaphor 'living water' (ὕδωρ ζῶν, *hydōr zōn*) in John 4 makes strange what humankind calls 'living water'.[23] The Samaritan woman misunderstands Jesus' offer of 'living water' and assumes that he knows of a mundane source – perhaps a running stream – that will make her task of fetching water easier. Jesus, however, uses the metaphor in its nonliteral, spiritual sense. In this instance, the woman attaches the wrong tenor to the metaphor and assumes Jesus is talking about ordinary, everyday water. The metaphor not only shapes the dialogue between Jesus and the woman; it allows the reader to explore the similarities and dissimilarities between the tenor the woman imagines and the tenor Jesus intends, which are developed in John 4.13-14: 'Everyone who drinks (ὁ πίνων, *ho pinōn*) of this water will be thirsty again, but those who drink (ὃς δ' ἂν πίῃ, *hos d' an piē*) of the water that I will give them will never be thirsty. The water that I will give will become in them a spring of water gushing up to eternal life.' Everyday water quenches thirst for a short while only and requires repeated trips (ὁ πίνων, *ho pinōn* = present ongoing action) to a diminishing source, whereas the water that Jesus provides is a one-time action that slakes thirst once for all (ὃς δ' ἂν πίῃ, *hos d' an piē* = momentary action). The metaphor makes strange what humankind calls 'living water' that slakes thirst momentarily; by contrast the thirst-quenching water Jesus offers is indeed 'living'.

---

20   In this instance the metaphor is a *double entendre* in which both meanings are intended. See the section on 'Double Entendre and Misunderstanding' in *Narrative Criticism of the New Testament*, pp. 64–7.

21   'Making strange' or defamiliarization is the technique of making the familiar seem strange so that the familiar is seen anew. Defamiliarization suspends, twists, turns on its head the familiar or everyday way of looking at the world by substituting a new, unfamiliar frame of reference. See Resseguie, *Narrative Criticism*, pp. 33–8.

22   See James L. Resseguie, *The Strange Gospel: Narrative Design and Point of View* (BIS, 56; Leiden: Brill, 2001), pp. 52–3.

23   Cf. Bultmann, *The Gospel of John*, p. 181: 'the water which men call "living" is not really "living water" at all'.

IV. Setting

Settings are more than colourful backdrops of the story world. They are saturated with meaning. Setting contributes to the mood of a narrative,[24] or delineates the traits of a character, or contributes to the development of plot conflicts. Setting may develop a character's mental, emotional, or spiritual landscape; it may be symbolic of choices to be made; it provides structure to the story and may develop the central conflict in a narrative.[25]

A setting may be geographical (Samaria, Judaea, Galilee), topographical (sea, mountain, desert), architectural (temple, courtyard, sheepfold, tomb, well, praetorium, garden), or religious (Passover, Preparation, Booths). It may be temporal (night, day), spatial (above, below), political (kingdom of God, Rome), social or cultural (meals, Samaritan, Centurion, clean, unclean). Props such as a water jar, clothing, perfumed spices, charcoal fire, judge's bench, or an un-torn net may be saturated with meaning. Minor characters – what Seymour Chatman calls 'walk-ons'[26] – may also be a part of the setting (crowd, soldiers, passers-by).

Temporal settings in the Fourth Gospel may indicate the 'kind of time' in which an action takes place,[27] and may be symbolic. Darkness in the Gospel may symbolize opacity or represent separation from the light. When Judas leaves the Last Supper to hand Jesus over to the authorities, 'it was night' (John 13.30). Night represents a kind of time; Judas goes out into the darkness to join the powers of darkness. Nicodemus comes to Jesus 'by night', which defines one of his traits: he comes to Jesus uncomprehending and unseeing (John 3.2; cf. 19.39). Mary Magdalene came to the tomb 'early on the first day of the week, while it was still dark' (John 20.1). Mary, who is 'in the dark' about the risen Jesus, arrives at the tomb while it is still dark. The contrast between night and day is the setting for Jesus' appearance to the seven disciples in John 21. They fished all night but caught nothing; just after daybreak – an opportune time for awakenings – Jesus appears and the abundance of fish threatens their nets (John 21.3-6).

Other settings in the Fourth Gospel tie together diverse narratives, inviting the implied reader to interpret the narratives in light of each other. A prop such as a charcoal fire (ἀνθρακιά, *anthrakia*), which occurs only twice in the New Testament, links together Peter's denial and defection in the courtyard with his restoration beside the Sea of Tiberias (John 18.18; 21.9). The courtyard in 18.15 and the sheepfold in 10.1, 16 are the same words in Greek (αὐλή, *aulē*) and suggest a relationship between the two settings. In John 10, Jesus tells a parable of the sheepfold, an enclosed space open to the sky[28] that protects the sheep from outside threats such as brigands and thieves who lurk outside the

---

24   Chatman, *Story and Discourse*, p. 141.
25   Rhoads, Dewey and Michie, *Mark as Story*, p. 63.
26   Chatman, *Story and Discourse*, pp. 138–9.
27   Powell, *What Is Narrative Criticism?*, p. 73.
28   BDAG, s.v. αὐλή.

pen and attempt to enter by subterfuge and steal the sheep (10.1). Wolves also attack the sheep from the outside (10.12). A gatekeeper (θυρωρός, *thyrōros*) opens the gate (θύρα, *thyra*) of the sheepfold for the shepherd (10.1, 2), and the sheep, who hear the shepherd's voice, follow him outside. The courtyard scene in John 18 recalls this architectural setting,[29] for not only is the word the same for both, but also a gatekeeper is present in both (10.3; 18.16, 17); characters or sheep go in and out through a gate in both (10.1, 2; 18.16); and the good shepherd is present in both. There are differences, of course. Jesus is the gate for the sheepfold (cf. 10.7) but not in the courtyard scene. The anonymous disciple is the mediating character who goes in and out of the courtyard whereas Jesus fulfils that role in the parable of the sheepfold. Nevertheless, the similarities between the two scenes suggest that they may mutually interpret each other.

In the parable of the sheepfold, the role of the good shepherd contrasts with the hired hands. At the first sign of danger hired hands run away, while the good shepherd remains, even laying down his life for the sheep. The sheep run away at 'the voice of strangers' and respond only to the voice of the good shepherd (10.5). In the courtyard scene, both Simon Peter and the unnamed disciple (perhaps the Beloved Disciple) follow Jesus to the high priest's courtyard. Yet only the anonymous disciple, who is known to the high priest, enters while Peter stands 'outside at the gate' (18.16a). With Peter outside, the other disciple speaks to the gatekeeper and brings Peter into the courtyard. (It is also possible that the gatekeeper brings Peter inside.) Mark Stibbe suggests that the similarity between the parable of the good shepherd and the courtyard scene lies in the distinction between the good shepherd and the hired hand. The good shepherd is the anonymous disciple who goes in and out of the courtyard, 'whilst Peter functions as the hired hand who flees in the hour of danger (though Peter's flight is a metaphorical flight from confession, not a literal desertion). Peter is not yet a shepherd like his master, willing to lay down his life for the sheep.'[30] The hired hand analogy is possible but not likely. Peter does not flee; he enters the courtyard with the aid of the anonymous disciple and then proceeds to reveal his true colours. Rather, the actions of Peter and the unnamed disciple clarify the difference between the sheep who hear the master's voice and follow obediently and the sheep who regard the master as a total stranger and deny him. In John 10, the sheep hear the shepherd's voice, follow him, and refuse to listen to the voice of a stranger (10.4, 5). Similarly, in the courtyard scene the anonymous disciple follows Jesus into danger as Peter lags behind, outside the gate. When Peter enters and is given the opportunity to show that he is a follower of Jesus, he treats Jesus as a total stranger. Thus the architectural settings of the sheepfold and courtyard mutually interpret each other, accenting the distinction between the faithful disciple who follows Jesus at all costs and the follower who treats his master as a stranger.

---

29   See Mark W. G. Stibbe, *John as Storyteller: Narrative Criticism and the Fourth Gospel* (SNTSMS, 73; Cambridge, UK: Cambridge University Press, 1972), pp. 102–3, for similarities in the two passages. Cf. also Resseguie, *Strange Gospel*, pp. 64–71.

30   Stibbe, *John as Storyteller*, p. 104.

V. Characters

Characters are known by their speech (what they say and how they say it), by their actions (what they do), by their gestures and posture (how they present themselves), and by their clothing (what they wear).[31] Characters are also known by what other characters say about them, by the narrator's comments, and by the environment or setting in which they appear. Characters may develop within a narrative and undergo an important change for either the better or the worse. These are dynamic characters. Or characters may be the same at the end of the narrative as at the beginning. These are static characters. The character traits that enable a character to rise to success or fall to disaster are important in the development of characters. The reader learns both from the success of characters that overcome obstacles and from the errors of judgement that lead others to disaster. Changes in characters elaborate and develop a narrative's meaning. Since character and plot are intricately bound,[32] a change or development in a character often provides a clue to the direction and meaning of the plot and theme. As Laurence Perrine says, the way a protagonist responds to a crucial situation in his or her life will 'likely be the surest clue to the story's meaning'.[33] And 'to state and explain the change [in a character] will be the best way to get at the point of the story'.[34]

Two generally recognized narrative techniques of characterization are *showing* and *telling*. In showing, which is also called the *dramatic method* or *indirect presentation*, 'the author simply presents the characters talking and acting and leaves the reader to infer the motives and dispositions that lie behind what they say and do'.[35] Generally, the Fourth Gospel prefers showing to telling, indirect presentation to direct presentation. In telling, which is also called *direct presentation*, the narrator intervenes to comment directly on a

---

31   On characterization in literature see Baruch Hochman, *Characters in Literature* (Ithaca, NY: Cornell University Press, 1985); Thomas Docherty, *Reading (Absent) Character: Towards a Theory of Characterization in Fiction* (Oxford: Clarendon, 1983); Chatman, *Story and Discourse*; James Phelan, *Reading People, Reading Plots: Character, Progression, and the Interpretation of Narrative* (Chicago: University of Chicago Press, 1989); Walter J. Harvey, *Character and the Novel* (Ithaca, NY: Cornell University Press, 1965); Mieke Bal, *Narratology: Introduction to the Theory of Narrative* (Toronto: University of Toronto Press, 1985), pp. 79–93; Shlomith Rimmon-Kenan, *Narrative Fiction: Contemporary Poetics* (London: Routledge, 1983).

32   Cf. Henry James, 'The Art of Fiction', in *The Art of Fiction and Other Essays by Henry James*, ed. Morris Roberts (New York: Oxford University Press, 1948), pp. 3–23 (13): 'What is character but the determination of incident? What is incident but the illustration of character?'

33   Thomas R. Arp, *Perrine's Story and Structure* (Fort Worth: Harcourt Brace College Publishers, 9th edn, 1998), p. 80. Some narrative critics regard biblical characters as flat and static characters that do not change or develop. See, for example, Rhoads, Dewey and Michie, *Mark as Story*, p. 100. Others, however, offer a more nuanced understanding of ancient characterization, seeing more complexity in biblical characterization. See, for example, Susan E. Hylen, *Imperfect Believers: Ambiguous Characters in the Gospel of John* (Louisville: Westminster John Knox, 2009), pp. 3–4, 15.

34   Arp, *Perrine's Story and Structure*, p. 80.

35   Abrams, *A Glossary of Literary Terms*, s.v. 'Character and Characterization'.

character, singling out a trait for the reader to notice or making an evaluation of a character and his or her motives and disposition. Judas, for instance, is consistently portrayed in a negative light through narrative commentary. In his first appearance in the Gospel, the narrator tells the reader that '[Judas] was going to betray [Jesus]' (John 6.71). Later, when Judas objects to the waste of a costly perfume, saying that it should have been sold and the money given to the poor, the narrator tells the reader of his motivation. 'He said this not because he cared about the poor, but because he was a thief; he kept the common purse and used to steal what was put into it' (John 12.6).[36] In John 13, the narrator again intrudes into the story and tells the reader of Judas's motivation: 'The devil had already put it into the heart of Judas son of Simon Iscariot to betray [Jesus]', and 'after [Judas] received the piece of bread, Satan entered into him' (13.2, 27).

Names, titles and epithets that a narrator gives to a character may be meaningful in the development of a character or the telling of a story. Consider, for instance, the names given to Peter as he and the Beloved Disciple set out on a footrace to make a new discovery in John 20.2-10. The narrator's normal pattern of introducing Peter into a narrative is to use his full name, Simon Peter, and then to refer to him subsequently by his abbreviated name, Peter.[37] When Mary Magdalene runs to the two disciples to tell them of her discovery, the narrator refers to Peter in the expected way, 'Simon Peter' (John 20.2). Then the shortened name is used to describe the race to the tomb: 'Then Peter and the other disciple set out . . . but the other disciple outran Peter and reached the tomb first' (John 20.3-4). The usual pattern, however, is broken at the moment of Peter's discovery and the narrator expands the disciple's name. 'Then Simon Peter came following him, and went into the tomb. He saw the linen wrappings lying there, and the cloth that had been on Jesus' head, not lying with the linen wrappings but rolled up in a place by itself' (John 20.6-7). At the moment of discovery the narrator resorts to unexpected fullness of Peter's name, an expanded name that corresponds to an expanded or important discovery. Similarly, the Beloved Disciple is given an expanded description at the moment of his discovery. He is introduced into the narrative as 'the other disciple, the one whom Jesus loved' and then simply referred to as 'the other disciple' (John 20.2, 3, 4). But at the moment he enters the tomb and believes, the narrator lengthens his description to 'the other disciple, who reached the tomb first' (John 20.8). Peter's expanded name and the Beloved Disciple's expanded description emphasize the importance of the two disciples' discoveries.

---

36   William Klassen believes that John is guilty of 'bearing false witness, slander, and calumny' because of these narrative intrusions. See *Judas: Betrayer or Friend of Jesus?* (Minneapolis: Fortress, 1996), p. 146.

37   See J. K. Elliot, 'Κηφᾶς: Σίμων Πέτρος: Ὁ Πέτρος: An Examination of New Testament Usage', *NovT* (1972), pp. 241–56 (243): 'The rule is that Πέτρος is written only after the name Σίμων Πέτρος has occurred: the latter always appears first in the context by way of introducing the disciple.'

Changes in names may signal a change in a character. Mary Magdalene's development as a character in John 20 parallels the names given her. The narrator calls her by her full name, Mary Magdalene, in 20.1 and 18, and by her shortened name in 20.11. The characters within the narrative, however, call her 'woman', except at an important moment that signals a change. Both the angels in the tomb and Jesus call her 'woman' and both ask identical questions: 'Woman, why are you weeping?' (John 20.13, 15). Her disconsolation is further reinforced by her speech, which is filled with loss. 'They have taken away my Lord, and I do not know where they have laid him' (John 20.13; cf. 20.2, 15). But when Jesus calls her 'Mary' (John 20.16; cf. John 10.3) not only is she awakened to a risen Jesus; she becomes the first character in the Gospel to learn a new language, the language of the resurrection. 'I have seen the Lord' (John 20.18; cf. 20.25; 1 Cor. 9.1). Her development as a character who sees what others have not seen and speaks what others could not utter is signalled by a change in names.

Speech patterns are important in identifying character traits or for tracing the development of a character. The first words a character speaks are often significant. The disciples' first words, for example, are a desire to abide or remain with Jesus ('Rabbi . . . where are you staying?', the two disciples in John 1.38); or lofty confessions of faith ('We have found the Messiah', Andrew in John 1.41; 'We have found him about whom Moses in the law and also the prophets wrote', Philip in 1.45; 'you are the Holy One of God', Peter in 6.69); or a willingness to die with Jesus ('Let us also go, that we may die with him', Thomas in 11.16). On the other hand, Judas's first (and only) words in John are an objection to the anointing of Jesus by Mary: 'Why was this perfume not sold for three hundred denarii and the money given to the poor?' (John 12.5). Whereas the other disciples' language is filled with lofty confessions of faith or a desire to follow Jesus, Judas's language is characterized by po-faced deceit.

The speech patterns of the man born blind parallel his development as a character in John 9. In his first appearance in John 9.1-7, he is mute, a waif at the margins of society, and an object lesson to solve a theological problem ('who sinned, this man or his parents, that he was born blind?', 9.2). After his healing, his speech patterns develop like a child learning a new language. When his neighbours ask if he is the man born blind or someone else, he repeatedly says 'I am' (NRSV: 'I am the man', 9.9). No longer an object, he is a subject and a predicate, even mimicking the divine 'I am'. Although he does not take on the identity of the divine, he finds his voice and his identity in an encounter with the divine.[38] As the man develops in the narrative his speech patterns become emboldened, blending the serious with the sarcastic. He takes over the role of interrogator from the Pharisees ('Why do you want to

---

38   See Jonathan Bishop, 'Encounters in the New Testament', in Kenneth R. R. Gros Louis (ed.), *Literary Interpretations of Biblical Narratives*, Vol. 2 (Nashville: Abingdon, 1982), pp. 285–94 (288).

hear it again? Do you also want to become his disciples?', 9.27) and proceeds to lecture the authorities on the way God works in this world (9.30-33). His speech even gets him expelled from the synagogue (9.34b), and he learns to say what the authorities are unable to utter ('Lord, I believe', 9.38). By contrast, the speech patterns of the religious authorities become more rigid as they descend into disaster. Initially they are divided as to Jesus' identity; some say he is a sinner while others say a sinner could not perform such signs (9.16). But the first person plural overtakes their language and expresses the tragic flaw of unknowing knowing: 'We know that this man is a sinner' (9.24). At the end they confirm their character flaw as their speech turns ironical: 'Surely we are not blind, are we?' (9.40). Throughout the narrative, the authorities remain static, 'flat' characters that are convinced that they know but are without understanding.[39]

VI. Master-plot

Master-plots are 'recurrent skeletal stories, belonging to cultures and individuals that play a powerful role in questions of identity, values, and the understanding of life'.[40] They deal with universal stories such as the quest for meaning in life (where are we going?), questions of origins (where did we come from?), the quest for identity (who are we?), the quest to find our way home (alienation and reconciliation), and questions of free will and determinism (is our destiny determined or are we free agents?). An examination of a narrative's master-plot shifts the emphasis from traditional ways of looking at plot – unity of action, causation, conflict, discovery and reversal, all of which are very good questions to ask of a narrative – to an examination of the overarching, universal story that shapes the narrative and its conflicts.

An example of a master-plot in Greek literature is the Oedipus narrative, which develops the conflict between a person's free will and fate.[41] Can persons escape the constraints of life, such as heredity, looks, status, or societal values, to find their destiny apart from these constraints? Or is the outcome unavoidable because life's constraints cannot be changed? Does Oedipus have free will to determine his future or is his fate already established? In biblical literature, the master-plot of the book of Revelation is the quest for the people of God to find their way to the new promised land, the new

---

39   A 'flat' character is two-dimensional, constructed around a single idea or quality; they can be summed in a single phrase or sentence. A flat character lacks hidden complexity or depth and is incapable of surprising the reader. The opposite of a flat character is a 'round' character. A round character is three-dimensional, possessing several complex traits. This character type is lifelike and capable of surprising the reader in a convincing way. See E. M. Forster, *Aspects of the Novel* (New York: Harcourt, Brace and Company, 1927), pp. 69–78.

40   H. Porter Abbott, *The Cambridge Introduction to Narrative* (Cambridge, UK: Cambridge University Press, 2002), p. 192; see also Resseguie, *Narrative Criticism*, pp. 203–4.

41   See Resseguie, *Narrative Criticism*, pp. 203–4.

Jerusalem. Similar to the story of the Israelites and their exodus from Egypt, the people of God in Revelation are pursued and persecuted by a new pharaoh, a seven-headed dragon and his earthly incarnations, the beast from the sea and the beast from the land. As with the Israelites, the people of God are given refuge in the wilderness and are nourished during the in-between times ('time, and times, and half a time', Revelation 12.14). This familiar replay of the Exodus story shapes and develops the conflicts within the Apocalypse. Will the people of God, for example, follow the Lamb to the new promised land or will they be side-tracked by the blandishments of Babylon and make 'the great city' their homeland (Revelation 11.8)?[42] Will they 'come out' of Babylon to join the pilgrimage to the new Jerusalem or will they assimilate to Babylon's norms and values, forgoing the journey to the new promised land (Revelation 18.4)? The master-plot also shapes the conflicts that occur on this journey to the new promised land, such as the defeat of the dragon and his representatives, the necessity of a messianic repair to a fractured cosmos and how it will be repaired, and the dangers of compromise and assimilation with the contemporary culture.

The master-plot of the Fourth Gospel deals with basic questions of identity and the way God works in this world. It is closely aligned with the ideological point of view of the Gospel and Jesus' stated mission of enabling the blind to see and those who see to become blind (John 9.39). The Fourth Gospel's master-plot develops the paradox of the glory in the flesh, the divine in the ordinary, and shapes the dilemma that the characters must resolve: is Jesus from God or not? If the glory is revealed in the flesh, why do some characters see this mystery while others see only flesh? What are the character traits of those who fail to see the glory in the flesh? What tragic flaw causes them to stumble? Is there a recognition scene in which the characters move from ignorance to knowledge, or do they remain ignorant and spiral downward to disaster? And what can be learned from the success of those who see the glory in the flesh and from the failure of those who do not?

The blind man of John 9 sees because he is persuaded that Jesus is from God and that a sinner could not open the eyes of the blind. He sees the glory in the flesh. The Pharisees, on the other hand, are unseeing because they remain convinced that Jesus is a sinner. Their tragic flaw is their unknowing knowing, their insistence that Jesus cannot be from God because he violates Sabbath conventions, which blinds them even more to the glory in the flesh.

The tragic flaw of the Jerusalemites and the reason they do not see the glory in the flesh is that they exegete at the surface and miss the deeper significance of events and persons. They judge 'according to the flesh' or according to 'appearances', not with 'right judgement' as Jesus judges (John 8.15; 7.24). Their vision is limited because they are 'from below' and 'of this world', which hinders them from seeing the way Jesus sees, which is a perspective

---

42   See James L. Resseguie, *The Revelation of John: A Narrative Commentary* (Grand Rapids: Baker Academic, 2009), pp. 46–7.

'from above' and 'not of this world' (8.23). Rather than seeing the glory in the flesh, they see only flesh and conclude that Jesus is a sinner, not from God. The plot conflicts thus centre on matters of interpretation and the way God works in this world. Is it possible for someone to heal on the Sabbath and be without sin or does the Sabbath healing make Jesus sinful (cf. John 5.1-18 and John 9)? Those who judge according to the flesh or by appearances conclude that he is a sinner and see only flesh. Those who judge with right judgement and not by appearances or according to the flesh conclude that Jesus is from God. They see the glory in the flesh.

The Beloved Disciple is able to see what other disciples are unable to see. He exegetes at a deeper level and represents the ideal point of view of the Gospel: one who is able to see the glory in the flesh (cf. John 1.14). He looks in the tomb and sees what Peter sees but his insight is greater, resulting in belief in the resurrection (John 20.8). At the Sea of Tiberias, he sees what the other disciples see, but again he sees in a different way and concludes that 'It is the Lord!' on the shore (John 21.7).

Nicodemus and the Samaritan woman add to the master-plot with their interpretations of being born 'again'/'from above' and 'living water'. Will they adopt a surface exegesis that understands rebirth and 'living water' in a literal, physical way, or will they move to a deeper, spiritual understanding? In other words, will Nicodemus and the Samaritan woman see the glory in the flesh in their encounters with Jesus or will they see only flesh? Pilate also adds to the master-plot with his shuttling back and forth between the crowd outside the praetorium and Jesus inside the palace (John 18.28–19.16a). Will Pilate listen to the voice of Jesus or to the dissonant, unappeasable voices outside? Pilate's 'to-ing' and 'fro-ing' illustrates the impossibility of bringing conflicting views of Jesus – Jesus' revelation inside and his rejection outside – into rapprochement. Unable to solve the paradox of the glory revealed in the flesh, Pilate adopts a compromising stance that fails to resolve the dilemma of Jesus' identity.

Mary Magdalene's encounter with Jesus in the garden advances the master-plot of Jesus' identity and the way God works in the world. In the recognition scene in the garden, Mary awakens to a new Jesus, the risen Lord (John 20.16), but the Jesus of her expectations is not the Jesus that stands before her. Mary assumes that the Jesus she sees is the Jesus she knew and seeks to cling to the old Jesus – or at least, to the earthly Jesus she thought she saw (John 20.17). The glory in the flesh, however, is now more clearly defined as a transcendent, resurrected Jesus.

The master-plot of the Fourth Gospel centres on Jesus' identity and the paradox of the way God works in the world. The characters in the Gospel struggle to recognize his identity, to see the glory in the flesh, and to move to a deeper, spiritual exegesis. Some resolve the dilemma of Jesus' identity, while others fail. Some exegete at the surface and judge by appearances, while others exegete at a deeper level and judge with right judgement. Whether the characters see the glory in the flesh or remain blinded by their own expectations of the way God should work in this world, the implied reader learns from both their successes and failures.

VII. Conclusion

A narrative-critical approach to the Fourth Gospel complements traditional methods of interpretation – for instance, the historical-critical method – by asking a new set of questions concerning the way a text communicates its meaning as a self-contained unit, a literary artefact, an undivided whole. Whereas traditional forms of criticism seldom focus on point of view, the narrative-critical approach not only develops and elaborates the ideological point of view of a narrative, but also explores the way point of view shapes the conflicts within the story and the effects it has on the implied reader. If point of view is the way a story is told, then the basic questions of interpretation become: What ideological perspective does the implied author want the implied reader to adopt? Why does the implied author tell this particular story in this way (and not in some other way)? And how is the implied reader changed in the reading of this story?

The narrative-critical approach is also attentive to the 'how' of a text. How does the narrative construct its meaning, and what are the formal features of the text that contribute to its literariness? Narrative critics do close readings of texts that pay attention to the words on a page. These detailed, often painstaking analyses focus on rhetorical devices, setting, characters and their development, and master-plot. Close readings also make the familiar seem strange by deforming familiar narratives so that they are seen in new, fresh ways. Narratives that seem too familiar and staid are enlivened through close readings and seen anew once more.

Chapter 2

THE WEAVE OF THE TAPESTRY: CHARACTER AND THEME IN JOHN

R. Alan Culpepper

I. Introduction

In retrospect, the most significant insights about characterization in *Anatomy of the Fourth Gospel* are probably twofold, first that in aggregate the characters offer a spectrum of responses to Jesus, and second that the depiction of these responses serves the stated purpose that 'these things are written that you may believe . . .' (20.31). By encountering the range of responses to Jesus represented by the various characters, the reader is able to examine their responses and misunderstandings while the implied author manoeuvres the reader toward a response of faith.

In 1983, I commented that:

> [I]t is surprising that the art of characterization has not yielded more to analysis than it has. Literary critics can draw upon relatively precise and sophisticated analyses of time and point of view, for example, but when they come to characterization they are likely to find W. J. Harvey's judgement confirmed: 'Modern criticism, by and large, has relegated the treatment of character to the periphery of its attention, has at best given it a polite and perfunctory nod and has regarded it more often as a misguided and misleading abstraction.'[1]

At the time, the most significant work on characterization in John was in the two articles by Raymond F. Collins on the Johannine characters as representative figures.[2] Theory and analysis of characterization had not moved much beyond Aristotle's four principles in the representation of characters: (a) 'first and foremost, the character represented should be morally good'; (b) 'the characters represented should be suitable'; (c) 'they should be life-

---

1 R. Alan Culpepper, *Anatomy of the Fourth Gospel: A Study in Literary Design* (Philadelphia: Fortress, 1983), p. 101, quoting W. J. Harvey, *Character and the Novel* (London: Chatto & Windus, 1965), p. 192.

2 See Raymond F. Collins, 'The Representative Figures of the Fourth Gospel, Part I', *DRev* 94 (1976), pp. 26–46; idem, 'The Representative Figures of the Fourth Gospel, Part II', *DRev* 94 (1976), pp. 118–32 (reprinted as 'Representative Figures', in idem, *These Things Have Been Written: Studies on the Fourth Gospel* [Leuven: Peeters/Grand Rapids: Eerdmans, 1990], pp. 1–45).

like'; and (d) 'they should be consistent' (Aristotle, *Poetics*, 1454a); the formalist and structuralist approaches to characters as plot functionaries; E. M. Forster's typology of characters as flat or round;[3] Seymour Chatman's view of characters as autonomous beings distinguished by their traits;[4] and W. J. Harvey's description of *ficelles* as intermediate characters (in contrast to the protagonist) as 'the vehicles by which all the most interesting questions are raised; they evoke our beliefs, sympathies, revulsions; they incarnate the moral vision of the world inherent in the total novel'.[5]

Viewing the Gospels as coherent narratives was itself a significant step beyond historical criticism, in which the characters were seen as simply the historical personages whom Jesus encountered. The Gospel of John is no doubt based on historical tradition, and the historicity of many of its characters can be documented from other sources. Nevertheless, in John they are more than simply part of the historical tradition, or interesting, colourful figures whom Jesus met.

II. Characterization in Recent Johannine and Gospels Scholarship

Once the shift was made from a historical to a literary perspective, work on characterization in the Gospels, and John in particular, has advanced at a dizzying pace. The literature is much too extensive to be reviewed here, but the following notes (and of course the other essays in this volume) offer some indication of the directions this work has taken.

In 2009 Cornelis Bennema proposed a new approach to the characters in the Gospel, showing that many characters are more complex, round and developing than most scholars would have us believe. In the introductory chapter he surveys the literature on characterization in the Gospel of John, offering brief summations and critiques of Eva Krafft (1956), Raymond Collins (1976, 1995), Culpepper (1983), Davies (1992), Stibbe (1992, 1993, 1994), Tolmie (1995), Maccini (1994, 1996), Fehribach (1998), Resseguie (2001), Conway (1999, 2002), Koester (2003), Edwards (2003), Beirne (2003) and Brant (2004). Since his survey is readily available, I will not go back over the same ground here.[6] Suffice it to say that he might have added as well Bonney (2002); Dschulnigg (2002); Harstine (2002); Ruschmann (2002); Esler and Piper (2006); Blaine (2007); Gench (2007); Skinner (2009);

---

3   See, E. M. Forster, *Aspects of the Novel* (New York: Harcourt, Brace and Company, 1927), pp. 54–84.

4   See Seymour Chatman, *Story and Discourse: Narrative Structure in Fiction and Film* (Ithaca, NY: Cornell University Press, 1978), pp. 107–33.

5   Harvey, *Character and Novel*, p. 56.

6   See Cornelis Bennema, *Encountering Jesus: Character Studies in the Gospel of John* (Milton Keynes: Paternoster, 2009), pp. 1–21.

Hylen (2009); and Farelly (2010).[7] The literature on characterization is now vast!

In response to earlier work on characterization Bennema calls for an approach that is comprehensive, non-reductionist and text-centred. A theory of characterization 'must explain how all the responses [to Jesus] fit into John's dualistic worldview'.[8] Bennema discards the simplistic categorization of characters as 'flat', 'round', or '*ficelles*', recognizing instead 'degrees of characterization' that move from 'type', to 'personality', to 'individual'. These classifications are based on an analysis of the place of each character on three continua or axes: complexity (from a single trait to a complex web of traits), development (from no development to movement or change), and penetration into the inner life (from those who remain opaque to those into whose mind the narrator gives the readers a glimpse).[9] Here Bennema follows the work of Joseph Ewen,[10] summarized by Shlomith Rimmon-Kenan.[11] Bennema then analyses and classifies the characters' responses to Jesus, reducing them to either adequate or inadequate based on the Gospel's dualistic norms.[12] These scales and classifications are summarized and tabulated in the book's concluding chapter. Bennema also perceptively distinguishes between the complexity of the characters and their belief-responses. As a result, a complex character (a personality or individual) may still exhibit a response that functions as a type. Further, some are '"representative figures" in that they have a symbolic value or paradigmatic function beyond the narrative',[13] while others are not.

---

7   The full bibliographic information for these volumes is as follows: William Bonney, *Caused to Believe: The Doubting Thomas Story as the Climax of John's Christological Narrative* (BIS, 62; Leiden: Brill, 2002); Peter Dschulnigg, *Jesus begegnen: Personen und ihre Bedeutung im Johannesevangelium* (Münster: Lit, 2002); Stan Harstine, *Moses as a Character in the Fourth Gospel: A Study of Ancient Reading Techniques* (JSNTSup, 229; London: Sheffield Academic Press, 2002); Susanne Ruschmann, *Maria von Magdala im Johannesevangelium: Jüngerin—Zeugin—Lebensbotin* (NTAbh, 40; Münster: Aschendorff, 2002); Philip Esler and Ronald A. Piper (eds), *Lazarus, Mary and Martha: A Social-Scientific and Theological Reading of John* (London: SCM, 2006); Bradford B. Blaine, Jr, *Peter in the Gospel of John: The Making of an Authentic Disciple* (AcBib, 27; Atlanta: Society of Biblical Literature, 2007); Frances Taylor Gench, *Encounters with Jesus: Studies in the Gospel of John* (Louisville: Westminster John Knox, 2007); Christopher W. Skinner, *John and Thomas: Gospels in Conflict? Johannine Characterization and the Thomas Question* (PTMS, 115; Eugene, OR: Pickwick, 2009); Susan Hylen, *Imperfect Believers: Ambiguous Characters in the Gospel of John* (Louisville, Westminster John Knox, 2009); and Nicolas Farelly, *The Disciples in the Fourth Gospel: A Narrative Analysis of their Faith and Understanding* (WUNT, II/290; Tübingen: Mohr Siebeck, 2010).

8   Bennema, *Encountering Jesus*, p. 12.

9   Ibid., p. 14.

10   Joseph Ewen, 'The Theory of Character in Narrative Fiction', *Hasifrut* 3 (1971), pp. 1–30.

11   See Shlomith Rimmon-Kenan, *Narrative Fiction: Contemporary Poetics* (New York: Methuen & Co., 1983).

12   Ibid., pp. 14–15.

13   Ibid., pp. 20–1.

In another recent monograph devoted to characterization, Susan Hylen has provided compelling analyses of a number of John's characters while advancing the thesis that 'John's characters are ambiguous and complex'.[14] Hylen defines her approach over against earlier studies in four areas. (1) Characters in ancient narratives, especially the Hebrew Bible, are not always flat, static and opaque, so Hylen explores the way characters function in the Gospel rather than what they represent. (2) Hylen works with the paradox that while John describes people in dualistic categories it portrays characters that do not fit neatly into these categories. She therefore reads the characters as metaphors rather than symbols, and observes the way they interact with the metaphors used to portray Jesus. (3) Hylen resists reducing the plot of the Gospel to the conflict over responses to the revelation in Jesus (belief or unbelief) and instead pays close attention to 'the particularity and substance of John's metaphors'.[15] (4) Hylen employs a two-part method, observing first the direct and indirect modes of characterization in the text and then interacting with the decisions other interpreters have made about each character.

Work in the other Gospels, especially Mark, also offers new perspectives that can be fruitful in the study of characterization in John. In 1999 Petri Merenlahti contended that 'Characters are constantly being reshaped by ideological dynamics.'[16] He followed Scholes and Kellogg in saying that 'In antiquity, characters had not so much "personality" in the modern sense, as *ethos*—a static, unchanging set of virtues and vices',[17] but in the Gospels,

> characters are most often not yet complete. In the event of being read, some of them will increase, while others decrease. Which way it will go, depends on how each character relates to the ideology of each Gospel and to the ideology of its readers . . . This makes all static, comprehensive and harmonious interpretations of these characters problematic.[18]

Literary critics are nevertheless bent on finding ways to integrate the biblical characters into the narrative and find narrative unity. As Mark Allan Powell observed in *What Is Narrative Criticism?*, 'Narrative critics are interested in characterization, that is, the process through which the implied author provides the implied reader with what is necessary to reconstruct a character from the narrative.'[19]

---

14   Hylen, *Imperfect Believers*, p. 15.
15   Ibid., p. 12.
16   Petri Merenlahti, 'Characters in the Making: Individuality and Ideology in the Gospels', in David Rhoads and Kari Syreeni (eds), *Characterization in the Gospels: Reconceiving Narrative Criticism* (JSNTSup, 184; Sheffield: Sheffield Academic Press, 1999), p. 50.
17   Ibid., p. 51.
18   Ibid., p. 71.
19   Mark Allan Powell, *What Is Narrative Criticism?* (GBS; Minneapolis: Fortress, 1990), p. 52.

Elizabeth Malbon's work on characterization in Mark has been both sustained and fruitful. Malbon advanced the discussion in her *In the Company of Jesus* by observing that, 'The richness of Markan characterization is in the interplay, comparisons, and contrasts *between* these characters and in their reaching out to the hearers/readers, both ancient and contemporary.'[20] Malbon's *Mark's Jesus*[21] rigorously examines the way the basic elements of characterization (what the character does, what others say, what the character says in response, what the character says instead, and what others do) are employed in the characterization of Jesus in Mark. Her careful analysis of the various narrative layers of Mark's Christology enables her to distinguish points of view more clearly than previous studies. In particular, she concludes that the point of view of the Markan Jesus and the Markan narrator do not always coincide. The key to the argument is that the narrator is assertive, ascribing to Jesus the titles Christ and Son of God in Mark 1.1, while Jesus is reticent, deflecting honour to God. Parenthetically, the distinction between the narrator and Jesus in John may not be as dramatic as in Mark because both the Johannine narrator and the Johannine Jesus are more assertive than Mark's narrator and the Markan Jesus. The Johannine narrator makes explicitly retrospective statements (2.22; 12.16) and states the purpose of writing the Gospel in John 20.30-31, and the Johannine Jesus uses Father-Son language throughout and speaks explicitly of his having been sent and of his future role (e.g., 14.18-24) – but that is fodder for another conversation.

In her recent contribution to *Mark as Story: Retrospect and Prospect*,[22] Malbon relocates the study of characterization once more, this time by means of a new appreciation that 'Narrative criticism seeks to understand and interpret the narrative process, from implied reader to implied audience, and this includes dwelling imaginatively among the characters of the story world.'[23] She also came to realize in the course of working on this essay that 'in Mark's Gospel, minor characters can play major roles; discipleship is more significant than disciples, and characterization is more than characters'.[24]

After a period of general neglect and dormancy, it appears, therefore, that the study of characterization is finally receiving the kind of focused theoretical and methodological reflection that will enable us to better describe the roles and functions of John's characters. While interpreters have moved to appreciate

---

20   Elizabeth Struthers Malbon, *In the Company of Jesus: Characters in Mark's Gospel* (Louisville: Westminster John Knox, 2000), p. x.

21   Elizabeth Struthers Malbon, *Mark's Jesus: Characterization as Narrative Christology* (Waco: Baylor University Press, 2009).

22   Elizabeth Struthers Malbon, 'Characters in Mark's Story: Changing Perspectives on the Narrative Process', in Kelly R. Iverson and Christopher W. Skinner (eds), *Mark as Story: Retrospect and Prospect* (SBLRBS, 65; Atlanta: Society of Biblical Literature, 2011), pp. 45–69.

23   Ibid., p. 58.

24   Ibid., p. 61.

the complexity and ambiguity of the Gospel's more developed characters, as the following comments by Sheridan, Hylen and Bennema illustrate, we are still striving to understand the ways in which the character functions in relation to the Gospel's plot, themes and metaphors. Ruth Sheridan, for example, critiques the approach to characterization in *Anatomy of the Fourth Gospel* for claiming that 'the Johannine characters simply fulfil a role in the narrative'.[25] Hylen offers the perceptive observation that 'characterization and metaphor interact on a complex level when a character's actions or words are read in relationship to the metaphors used to understand Jesus',[26] and Bennema notes briefly that because 'a story consists of events and characters, held together by a plot', it is important to outline 'the story within which the characters operate',[27] and it is to the relationship between story and character that we now turn. The title of this essay signals its aim of examining the relationship between characterization and theme development in John: as a noun, 'weave' means 'the pattern, method of weaving, or construction of a fabric'.[28]

III. Character and Theme in John's Major Sections

Studies of characterization and the characters in John typically proceed from an examination of the various characters individually – as I did in *Anatomy of the Fourth Gospel* – and our survey of recent literature shows that increasingly the characters are being read as developing characters and/or as ambiguous or unfinished. Here, I propose to take a different, and perhaps somewhat contrarian, approach to show that characterization in John is closely related to the development of the Gospel's themes. That is not to say that the characters are purely plot functions, agents, or foils, or that some of them are not richly evoked, ambiguous, or developing. Perhaps a modest advance can be made by surveying the ways John's characters operate not merely in the Gospel as a whole but within its major sections.

Commentators have noted that every outline of the Gospel is artificial and that some transitional sections both conclude the previous section and introduce the following one.[29] Nevertheless, allowing for this important

---

25   Ruth Sheridan, *Retelling Scripture: 'The Jews' and the Scriptural Citations in John 1:19–12:15* (BIS, 110; Leiden: Brill, 2012), p. 79.

26   Hylen, *Imperfect Believers*, p. 8.

27   Bennema, *Encountering Jesus*, pp. 15–16.

28   *The American Heritage Dictionary* (New York: Hougton Mifflin, 3rd edn, 1993), p. 2023.

29   See the discussion of organization and themes in George Mlakuzhyil, *The Christocentric Literary Structure of the Fourth Gospel* (AnBib, 117; Rome: Editrice Pontificio Istituto Biblico, 1987), esp. pp. 103–6; Raymond E. Brown, *An Introduction to the Gospel of John* (ed. Francis J. Moloney; ABRL; New York: Doubleday, 2003), pp. 298–315; and Robert Kysar, 'John, The Gospel of', *ABD*, Vol. 3, pp. 913–14.

caveat the following general divisions of the Gospel are widely accepted: John 1, 2–4, 5–10, 11–12, 13–17, 18–20, and 21. For the purposes of this essay, I will consider chapter 21 with chapters 18–20. The approach taken here will be to survey the plot development and major themes of each section and then examine how each of the active characters (Bennema's term for those characters who make some belief-response to Jesus)[30] function in that section of the Gospel. The argument is necessarily circular: characters contribute to a narrative's themes, so it is artificial to summarize the theme of a section and then find that the characters in that section are related to its themes. In this case, however, the circularity does not undermine the significance of the clear and close relationship between characterization and theme development in John that this exercise reveals. We will be particularly interested in identifying instances where characterization transcends the contribution of the character to John's themes.

a. John 1

The first chapter consists of the Prologue and narrative introduction to Jesus and his mission. The Prologue sets the stage for the opening of the narrative, and introduces Jesus as the incarnation of the pre-existent *Logos* who was the creative agency of the cosmos and the revealer in Israel's history. The opening phrase, 'In the beginning', echoes the opening words of Genesis. The reference to Moses and the law foreshadow coming references in which Jesus is presented as greater than Moses, and the law is said to testify to Jesus (5.45-46; 7.19). The Prologue introduces Jesus from the perspective of the scriptures. The *Logos* became incarnate in Jesus to reveal the Father (1.18). The rest of the chapter offers additional definition to Jesus' identity by means of his first words, declarations about his mission (to 'take away the sin of the world', v. 29), and a series of Christological confessions. The first chapter is therefore appropriately introductory and anticipatory, providing the reader with reliable information about Jesus' identity and clues to the significance of his work. It closes with the assurance, 'You will see greater things than these' (1.50).

The narrative proper starts in v. 19 with the witness of John the Baptist (much like the Gospel of Mark), picking up the references to the Baptist in vv. 6-8 and 15.[31] The active characters in John 1 are John the Baptist (vv. 19-36); the Jews (1.19); the priests (the only time priests, as opposed to chief priests, appear in John) and Levites (the only time Levites appear in John) sent from Jerusalem (v. 19); the Pharisees (v. 24); two of John's disciples, one anonymous, one Andrew (vv. 35-42); Philip (vv. 43-46); and Nathanael (vv. 45-51). Each of them, though they make different responses to Jesus, advances

---

30   Cf. Bennema, *Encountering Jesus*, p. 18.
31   See Tom Thatcher's provocative thesis that these verses constitute the core of the Prologue in his essay, 'The Riddle of the Baptist and the Genesis of the Prologue: John 1:1-18 an Oral/Aural Media Culture', in Anthony LeDonne and Tom Thatcher (eds), *The Fourth Gospel in First-Century Media Culture* (LNTS, 426; London: T&T Clark, 2011), pp. 29–48.

the introductory and anticipatory functions of the opening chapter with its concentration on introducing Jesus as the fulfilment of the scriptures. John the Baptist testifies that Jesus is the one who 'comes after me [but] ranks ahead of me because he was before me' (vv. 15, 30), that Jesus is 'the Son of God' (v. 34) and 'the Lamb of God!' (vv. 29, 36), and that he will baptize with the Holy Spirit (v. 33). The introduction of the Jews, the priests and Levites, and the Pharisees as those who cross-examine John anticipates their role as Jesus' antagonists later in the Gospel. Their question for John, as it will be for Jesus, is 'Who are you?' (v. 22), which is the theme of this introductory chapter.

The first disciples come to Jesus with confessions and declarations that continue to echo the scriptures:

Andrew: 'We have found the Messiah' (which is translated Anointed) (v. 41).
Philip: 'We have found him about whom Moses in the law and also the prophets wrote' (v. 45).
Nathanael: 'Rabbi, you are the Son of God! You are the King of Israel!' (v. 49).

And Jesus responds with another allusion to the scriptures: 'Very truly, I tell you, you will see heaven opened and the angels of God ascending and descending upon the Son of Man' (v. 51).

In John 1, therefore, the characters serve the plot function of introducing Jesus by means of confessions and declarations that echo or reference the scriptures and by referring to his role as one who will baptize with the Holy Spirit, take away the sins of the world, and serve as the Messiah, King of Israel, and eschatological Son of Man. While both the Jewish groups and the disciples (with the exception of Nathanael, who is mentioned later only in passing in 21.2) will reappear in later scenes and receive a higher degree of characterization, it is clear from this chapter that their roles are tightly integrated with the plot development.

b. John 2–4

The theme of these three chapters is the life that Jesus mediates to those who believe in him. The theme of life is announced in the Prologue, 1.4, and presented in John 2–4 first by way of symbolism, as an abundance of fine wine at a marriage feast, then through an allusion to Jesus as the new temple, and finally through his resurrection. Reception of the new life from above requires a new birth, through water and the Spirit. Jesus will be lifted up, just as Moses lifted up the serpent on a pole in the wilderness, so that those who looked to it might live (3.14). In the same way, Jesus was sent to bring eternal life to those who believe in him (3.16), and this summary of the Gospel is repeated at the end of the discourse in John 3 (v. 36). John 4 takes up the same theme. Jesus is the source of 'living water' that conveys eternal life, and the chapter closes with a healing that repeats the words, 'live', 'believe', 'live', 'believe'. Through this sequence of different episodes in Cana, Jerusalem, Aenon near Salim, Samaria, and Cana once again, and through dialogues with various characters, discourses, and narrative asides and summaries, John 2–4 examines various facets of the theme of life.

The characters play individual roles, but in these chapters they each serve the theme of life in the Johannine sense. Jesus' mother is introduced briefly at the wedding at Cana, with the hint that her real role will become clear when Jesus' 'hour' has come (2.4). 'The Jews' don't understand that Jesus' body, that will be resurrected, will replace the temple (2.20-21), and Jesus would not entrust himself to those who believed simply because of the signs he did (cf. 2.11, 23-25). Nicodemus comes to Jesus at night, a Pharisee and leader of the Jews, but also as a representative of those who saw the signs and knew that Jesus was a teacher 'who had come from God' (3.2). The conversation with Nicodemus offers the implied author a chance to introduce the difficulty of being born anew and receiving the life Jesus offers. To this point the reader may have assumed it is as simple as the calling of the first disciples in the first chapter. Nicodemus steps forward as one for whom the revelation is not clear and the birth pangs are very real. Jesus' allusions to being born of water, and to that which is from above, are explored in the remainder of the chapter through Jesus' discourse on the crisis of his coming into the world, which brings both judgement and life, and through John's exchange with his followers who are concerned that Jesus and his disciples are baptizing more than John: 'John answered, "No one can receive anything except what has been given from heaven"' (3.27) – a line that clarifies Nicodemus's struggle.

The Samaritan woman has often been compared and contrasted with Nicodemus. For our present purposes it is sufficient to note that they offer contrasting responses to Jesus on the same issue, namely, receiving the life that he offers. With Nicodemus the issue was new birth, of water and the spirit. With the Samaritan woman the invitation is framed around the invitation to ask Jesus for the 'living water' that he offers her. In contrast to Nicodemus, she exhibits remarkable character development in the course of their dialogue, parrying his challenges but moving from one level of address to another with each exchange until finally she says, 'Sir, I see that you are a prophet' (4.19), leaves her bucket at the well, and returns to the village saying, 'He cannot be the Messiah, can he?' (4.29). The Samaritans complete the Christological development in the discourse by confessing that Jesus is 'the Saviour of the world' (4.42).

In the final episode of this section, a royal official comes to Jesus with the urgent request that Jesus come to Capernaum, where the man's son is at the point of death (4.47). Jesus declares that if he did not see signs he would not believe (4.48), and the man repeats his plea for help 'before my little boy dies' (4.49). It is a life or death issue. Jesus responds, 'Go; your son will live' (4.50); the royal official believes him and starts home. On the way he is met by bearers of 'glad tidings': his son has recovered; he is alive. When the official ascertains that his son has recovered at the exact hour when Jesus said he would live, he and his whole household believe (4.53). The repetition and intertwining of the references to believing and living make the point that the life from above that Jesus promised to Nicodemus and offered to the Samaritan woman is given to those who believe.

This section illustrates how the Gospel develops a central theme through a succession of episodes. Each character is distinct and has his or her own integrity, but they serve a larger purpose. While they illustrate different responses to Jesus that are juxtaposed for the reader to compare and contrast, as I observed in *Anatomy of the Fourth Gospel*, it is also true that they serve thematic and rhetorical purposes that weave them into the narrative. Nicodemus can introduce complications not evident in earlier responses to Jesus. John the Baptist can say something that clarifies Nicodemus's response (3.27). The Samaritan woman's incredulous question as to whether Jesus is greater than their father Jacob bounces off of the Prologue, John's testimony to Jesus in the first chapter, and the closing verses of the third chapter. The villagers' confession caps off the dialogue between Jesus and the Samaritan woman, and the healing of the royal official's son settles the issue of receiving life by returning to the importance of believing (see 1.12; 2.23-25; 3.16, 36). In this section too, therefore, the narrative is tightly scripted, and while it is episodic, it weaves together the episodes with their respective characters around larger, overarching themes.

c. John 5–10

This is the longest and arguably the most complicated section of the Gospel. In these chapters 'the Jews' are depicted as Jesus' antagonists, who plot to kill him and make various attempts to do so. Conflict escalates, Jesus withdraws from Judaea, and when Jesus returns to Jerusalem the conflict escalates further. The drama revolves around the Jewish festivals, and at each one Jesus shows that he is the fulfilment of what the festival celebrates. Jesus continues to do 'signs', each of which is greater than the previous ones. The signs now lead to dialogues and discourses that unpack the meaning of the signs, and the more clearly Jesus reveals himself, the sharper the cleavage becomes between those who receive his revelation and those who do not. All the while, Jesus names and responds to the objections and impediments to receiving his revelation.

Because the characters play across a broader canvas in this section, they serve in the advancement of multiple themes. To illustrate their functions, one inevitably becomes guilty of reductionism. Closer examination of each character will allow additional thematic and rhetorical functions to be identified. Our purpose here is not to be exhaustive but to illustrate how the characters serve these thematic functions.

John 5 introduces the conflict between Jesus and the religious authorities that has remained in the background until this point, only hinted at in the first four chapters. In the first chapter the authorities in Jerusalem sent priests and Levites to question John. In the second chapter Jesus confronted 'the Jews' in the temple, and Nicodemus, a leader of the Jews, came forward to meet with Jesus in John 3. 'A Jew' raised questions with John's disciples about purification (3.25), perhaps another investigation, and when Jesus heard that the Pharisees had heard that he was making more disciples than John, he retreated to Galilee, going through Samaria (4.1-3).

With the healing of the man at the pool of Bethesda, the issues between Jesus and the Jewish authorities are exposed. Jesus healed on the Sabbath, and he made himself equal to God (5.18). The festival is not identified, so the conflict does not revolve around Jesus as its fulfilment. Instead, it introduces the conflict that will escalate during the coming festivals. The issue is Jesus' identity and his violation of the Sabbath because of this healing. The sequence of five one-on-one exchanges in 5.1-18 progresses with a sense of inevitability to a confrontation between Jesus and 'the Jews':[32]

vv. 5-9	Jesus and the man who had suffered for 38 years
vv. 10-13	The man who had been healed and 'the Jews'
v. 14	Jesus and the man who had been healed
v. 15	The man who had been healed and the Jews
vv. 16-18	Jesus and the Jews

The discourse that follows (5.19-30) returns to the theme of life. The authorities seek to kill Jesus for healing (i.e., giving life) on the Sabbath (cf. Mark 3.4). Jesus declares that the Father has given him authority to give life and that the tombs will be opened and the dead will rise. The second part of the discourse (5.31-47) employs the trial motif in which Jesus cites a variety of witnesses (John, the works the Father gave him to do, the Father himself, the scriptures, and Moses).

The reference to Moses triggers the story of the feeding of the 5,000 in Galilee at the time of the Passover celebration. Andrew and Philip bring Jesus a boy's lunch, and Jesus tests Philip. The narrator reports that 'When the people saw the sign that he had done, they began to say, "This is indeed the prophet who is to come into the world"' (6.14). The import of the feeding is then explained in the discourse that follows in the rest of John 6. Jesus is himself the bread from heaven, the bread that gives life. Those who eat his body and drink his blood will have the life he promised. He is himself, therefore, the embodiment of God's delivering and life-giving work at the Exodus. He did what Moses did, but it was not Moses but his Father who fed the people in the wilderness. The themes of fulfilment of scripture, giving of life, fulfilment of the festivals, and division following Jesus' revelation are all advanced in this chapter. 'The Jews' murmur and then argue. Many of Jesus' disciples turn away, and Peter confesses, 'You have the words of eternal life' (6.68). The scene advances the characterization of Peter, but it also advances the theme of life that dominates John 2–4.

Jesus' brothers do not believe in him (7.5), but they too play a role in clarifying the various kinds of time at work in the Gospel and the kinds of

---

32   See R. Alan Culpepper, 'John 5:1-18: A Sample of Narrative-Critical Commentary', in Mark W. G. Stibbe (ed.), *The Gospel of John as Literature* (Leiden: Brill, 1993), pp. 193–207; and Francisco Lozada, Jr, *A Literary Reading of John 5: Text as Construction* (Studies in Biblical Literature, 20; New York: Peter Lang, 2000), pp. 69–87.

expectations placed on Jesus. The division in the crowd in John 6 continues with division among the pilgrims in Jerusalem in John 7, and the debate between those who hold different estimates of Jesus clarifies the assumptions at work in the expectations of the Messiah. The hostile response escalates, and as it does the division within the crowd, and even the authorities, deepens. Those sent to arrest Jesus marvel at his speech, and Nicodemus calls his peers to follow the law, give Jesus a hearing, and find out what he is doing (7.50-51). Although Nicodemus appeared earlier (in John 3), his appearance in John 7 fits the developing dynamics of division and debate in this part of the Gospel, which reaches an acrimonious climax in John 8.

The blind man in John 9 is caught between Jesus and the authorities, but in contrast to the man at the pool in John 5, with whom he is often compared, he moves step by step to an affirmation of faith in Jesus. This artfully crafted story in seven scenes further clarifies the bases of the division among the people in response to Jesus. It is no coincidence, therefore, that the story of the blind man occurs at just this point in the Gospel. Character and theme – in this case seeing and believing, blindness and sin, accepting and rejecting Jesus, the disciples of Moses and the disciples of Jesus – are beautifully developed through the blind man, the Pharisees, and the supporting cast of disciples, neighbours and parents.

With no apparent break the story yields to Jesus' discourse on the sheep, the thief, the shepherd and the hirelings in John 10. Here the reader encounters the cast of an embedded story that interprets characters in the primary story. And again, fitting the themes of John 5–10, the issue is the identity of the good shepherd and the response of his sheep, and not incidentally the difference between the good shepherd and the hirelings. Once again (cf. 8.59; 10.31) 'the Jews' take up stones against Jesus, and the chapter ends with the comment that although John the Baptist did no signs, everything he said about Jesus was true. John is a true witness, as he was in John 1, and what has happened in the intervening chapters has confirmed that his testimony was true.

Although these chapters develop a variety of themes, especially escalating division and hostility in response to Jesus, fulfilment of the Jewish scriptures and festivals, and recognition of Jesus as the Messiah, and some of the characters serve more than one theme, each character in this section is closely related to its themes.

d. John 11–12

The themes of Jesus' public ministry come together in John 11–12. We traced the theme of life in John 2–4 and the theme of the acceptance and rejection of Jesus in John 5–10. The themes of these preceding sections coalesce and climax in the story of the raising of Lazarus, with its interpretive dialogues between Jesus and his disciples, Thomas, Martha and Mary before the actual sign, and the responses of the crowd afterwards. With Thomas and Martha, Jesus talks of the transient nature of death and the assurance of life now and after death for those who believe in him (11.25-27). After the raising of Lazarus many of the Jews believe in him (11.43), others report what he had done to the Pharisees and chief priests (11.44), who call a meeting of the council to plot against Jesus. The reasons for the rejection of Jesus have been fully interpreted, the hostility against Jesus has escalated in waves, and now the authorities take steps to do away with the blasphemer who is jeopardizing Rome's fragile tolerance of their worship. Caiaphas counsels political realism in words that ironically give voice to a higher truth. Mary and Martha's response is to celebrate Lazarus's return with a banquet, and Mary anoints Jesus with expensive ointment. Jesus rebukes Judas's criticism of Mary's extravagant gift and says that she has anointed his body for burial. The coming of the Greeks serves as a further sign for Jesus that his hour has come (12.20-24). A voice comes from heaven, and some in the crowd say it is thunder, while others say an angel had spoken (12.28-29). The division is deep; even some of the synagogue leaders believe in Jesus but will not confess him for fear of 'the Jews' (12.42). Jesus' closing soliloquy at the end of John 12 sums up these themes: 'Whoever believes in me . . .' (12.44), 'The one who rejects me . . .' (12.48), and 'I know that his commandment is eternal life' (12.50).

The themes of Jesus' public ministry are clearly adduced in these chapters, and once again the primary themes are developed through the characters that appear in these chapters. The characters are not free agents who lend incidental colour or interest to the narrative. They are an important feature of the narrative's rhetorical and thematic development.

e. John 13–17

John 13 narrates the foot-washing and Jesus' prediction of Judas's betrayal and Peter's denials, and the interactions between Jesus and the disciples often turn on what Jesus knows and the disciples do not yet know.[33] The narrator describes Jesus' laying aside his garments and then taking them up again, using the same terms Jesus used in John 10 to relate the authority of the good shepherd to lay down his life and take it up again (10.18; 13.4, 12). This repetition of terms underscores that Jesus' washing the disciples' feet foreshadowed the meaning of his coming death, laying down his life for them. In the rest of this section, commonly called the Farewell Discourse, Jesus reflects on the meaning of his life and ministry and what the disciples (and by extension the Gospel's readers) can expect after his death, including Jesus' continued presence with the disciples through the *Paraclete*, and the hostility they will experience from 'the world'. In John 17 Jesus consecrates himself for his coming death and prays for the disciples and those who will come after them.

Most of this section is extended discourse, so the disciples have a relatively less significant role than they do in the narrative sections of the Gospel. Aside from references to the Father, the devil, the Jews, and the world, only Jesus and the disciples appear in this section, and the only disciples who have speaking

---

33   See R. Alan Culpepper, 'The Johannine *hypodeigma*: A Reading of John 13', *Semeia* 53 (1991), pp. 133–52.

roles are Peter (13.6-10, 36-38), the Beloved Disciple (13.23-25), Thomas (14.5), Philip (14.8), and Judas (not Iscariot, 14.22). The disciples speak as a group in 16.29-30. Judas Iscariot is prominent in 13.2 and 26-30, but he does not speak.

Peter does not understand the meaning of the foot-washing. Later he denies that he will deny Jesus, and in the scene in the garden in John 18 it becomes evident that he does not understand the necessity of Jesus' death. The disciples' lack of understanding, indeed obtuseness, in this section sets them up as foils for Jesus' discourse on the events that lie ahead. They have not grasped the ethic of servanthood that is ultimately expressed in laying down one's life for one's 'friends' (15.13-14). In response, Jesus gives them the 'new commandment' to love one another as he has loved them (13.34; cf. 13.1; 15.12).

Once the discourse begins, Jesus is interrupted three times in John 14 and once at the end of the discourse. Thomas voices the disciples' ignorance about his 'departure' (i.e., his death): 'Lord, we do not know where you are going. How can we know the way?' (14.5). Philip does not understand that Jesus himself is the revelation of the Father: 'Lord, show us the Father and we will be satisfied' (14.8; cf. 1.18). Then, Judas (not Iscariot) does not understand how Jesus will reveal himself to them and not to the world (14.22), prompting Jesus to tell them of the coming of the *Paraclete*. Almost as if in an interview or staged press conference, the disciples pitch 'softballs' at Jesus – questions that allow him to 'stay on message'. Their interjections are directly related to the themes of the Farewell Discourse. At the end of the discourse they exclaim, 'Now we know . . .' (16.30), but of course they do not, and cannot yet understand. After Jesus' death they will all be scattered.

As in earlier sections of the Gospel, the role of the characters in John 13–17 is tightly scripted; the disciples do not do or say anything that is not closely related to the major themes of this section of the Gospel.

f. John 18–21

The closing chapters of the Gospel are usually divided into two sections: John 18–20 and John 21. This division is based primarily on the apparent conclusion of the Gospel at the end of John 20, casting John 21 as a later addition. While this may reflect how the Gospel was composed, it separates the resurrection appearances into two units. Alternatively, one could divide these chapters by subject, with the arrest, trial, death and burial of Jesus in John 18–19 and the discovery of the empty tomb and the resurrection appearances in John 20–21. In order to prioritize the finished Gospel over a theory regarding its composition, and continuity over segmentation, John 18–21 is treated here as a unit within which one can recognize subsections. Like John 5–10, it is a long narrative section with several major themes and numerous characters.

The major concerns of this section are Jesus' identity and the meaning of his death and resurrection for his followers. The narrative of Jesus' arrest develops further Jesus' identity as the light of the world (in contrast to the night, lamps and torches) and the good shepherd who lays down his life for his sheep. The trial of Jesus sets up further clarification that Jesus' death will be his 'lifting up' (3.14; 8.28; 12.32), his exaltation as king, but one whose kingdom is not 'of this world' (18.36). The events surrounding Jesus' death convey to the attentive reader that through his 'exaltation' Jesus as 'king' will draw all people to himself (12.32), and they will constitute a new family as 'children of God' (1.12; 11.52).[34] Jesus' death, therefore, fulfils 'all things': the scriptures, all that the Father gave him to do, and his mission to reveal the Father and take away 'the sins of the world' (1.29, 36).

The discovery of the empty tomb and the resurrection appearances focus even more explicitly on the 'narrative future', the future of Jesus' disciples and the work they will do. Jesus is going to his Father. He consecrates the disciples and sends them, just as the Father had sent him. Finally, the work of the disciples is characterized by three metaphors: fishing, shepherding and bearing witness.

These chapters are richly populated by characters who advance the action of this part of the story: Judas (18.2-5), the disciples (18.2; 20.18, 19-23, 24-29; 21.1), soldiers and police (18.3-12, 18, 22; 19.2, 6, 23-24, 32-34), Peter (18.10-11, 16-18, 25-27; 20.2-10; 21.2-22), Malchus (18.10), Annas (18.13, 19-24), Caiaphas (18.13-14, 23, 28), the 'other disciple' (18.15-16), a female slave (18.17), slaves of the high priest (18.10, 18, 26), Pilate (18.28–19.16; 19.19-22, 31, 38), 'the Jews' (18.36, 38; 19.7, 12, 14-15, 20, 31; 20.19), Barabbas (18.40), chief priests (19.6, 15-16, 21), Jesus' mother (19.25-27), Mary the wife of Clopas (19.25), Mary Magdalene (19.25; 20.1-2, 11-18), the Beloved Disciple (19.26-27, 35[?]; 20.2-10; 21.7, 20, 23-24), Joseph of Arimathea (19.38-42), Nicodemus (19.39-42), Thomas (20.24-29; 21.2-14), the Twelve (20.24), Nathanael, the sons of Zebedee (21.2-14), and the 'we' of 21.24 and the 'I' of 21.25. As examples of character development, the most significant of these are Peter, Pilate, Nicodemus, Mary Magdalene and Thomas, and appropriately the last section of the Gospel is where we meet the most fully developed and ambiguous of the Gospel's characters.

Peter appears in several key scenes. At the arrest he takes the sword, showing that he has not understood Jesus or the necessity of his death. In the courtyard he denies Jesus, serving as a foil by saying, 'I am not' in contrast to Jesus' repeated 'I am'. He also denies his discipleship and tries to hide, while Jesus avows that he has spoken openly and those who have heard him will testify in his defence. Peter then runs with the Beloved Disciple to the tomb, where he apparently does not understand until the Beloved Disciple tells him the significance of what they see there. After he and the others 'returned to their homes' (20.10), he takes a group of the disciples fishing. Again, he does not recognize that the stranger on the shore is the risen Lord until the Beloved Disciple tells him. In the narrative's symbolic imagery, Peter is the image of

---

34   See R. Alan Culpepper, 'The Theology of the Johannine Passion Narrative: John 19:16b-30', *Neot* 31 (1997), pp. 21–37; and Jean Zumstein, 'Johannes 19, 25-27', *ZTK* 94 (1997), pp. 131–54.

the missionary apostle, dragging the net full of fish to the risen Lord, where the disciples share a meal with the Lord.[35] In the conversation that follows, Jesus asks Peter three times if Peter loves him and three times commissions him to be a shepherd.[36] Finally, when Peter asks about the fate of the Beloved Disciple, Jesus rebukes him once more: 'What is that to you? You follow me' (21.22). Peter will serve as a shepherd and die a martyr's death, but the Beloved Disciple is consistently closer to Jesus and more perceptive than Peter. At the end, he is already following Jesus (21.20) when Peter is challenged to do so, and he will bear a true witness (21.24). While these scenes no doubt evoke Peter as arguably the most complex character in the Gospel, he serves as a foil for Jesus at the arrest and trial before Caiaphas, he serves as a contrast to the Beloved Disciple where they are together, and he represents the future missionary and pastoral role of the disciples. His rehabilitation as a disciple in John 21 moves beyond theme development, however, and evinces a clear interest in Peter as a character and the need (also evident in Mark 16.7, 'go and tell his disciples and Peter') to complete the story of his development.

Pilate represents imperial power, both officially and symbolically. He is also yet another character who struggles to understand Jesus' enigmatic claims and challenges. He appears to grow in sympathy toward Jesus, pronouncing him innocent and seeking to release him, but he also has Jesus beaten, and allows the soldiers to mock him. He taunts the chief priests by saying, 'Shall I crucify your King?' (19.15), eliciting from them the blasphemous confession, 'We have no king but Caesar' (19.15), before handing Jesus over to them. The question for interpreters is whether the wording of the *titulus* and Pilate's refusal to alter it is a final taunting of both Jesus and the Jews, or whether it represents a dawning awareness that Pilate is not willing to confess openly (see Pilate's question in 18.33, 'Are you a king?', his pronouncements of Jesus' innocence, and the narrator's statement that Pilate is 'the more afraid' when 'the Jews' tell him that Jesus deserves to die because 'he made himself the Son of God', 19.7). Regardless of one's interpretation of Pilate, he is a complex character who moves back and forth between Jesus and the accusing crowd both literally and figuratively, wrestling with the competing demands of his office, justice, loyalty to Rome, his desire to both appease and demean the Jewish religious authorities, and Jesus' unyielding challenges to him to recognize Jesus' true identity. Clearly, Pilate plays an important role in the thematic and plot development of the Gospel, but he also emerges as a much more fully rounded and complex figure in John than in any of the other Gospels.

---

35   R. Alan Culpepper, 'Designs for the Church in the Imagery of John 21:1-14', in Jörg Frey, Jan G. van der Watt and Ruben Zimmermann (eds), *Imagery in the Gospel of John: Terms, Forms, Themes and Theology of Figurative Language* (WUNT, 200; Tübingen: Mohr Siebeck, 2006), pp. 369–402.

36   R. Alan Culpepper, 'Peter as Exemplary Disciple in John 21:15-19', *PRSt* 37 (2010), pp. 165–78.

Nicodemus is probably the most ambiguous character in the Gospel.[37] At the burial of Jesus he is identified with Joseph of Arimathea, a secret believer, and he brings a lavish quantity of spices. While some interpreters contend that Nicodemus's appearance in this scene marks his public identification with Jesus, others point out that he remains 'one of them' (7.50) and one 'who came to him the first time at night' (19.39). Nicodemus's development is ambiguous, and at best he represents Jews who, while not disciples, are sympathetic to Jesus.[38] Like Pilate, he is one who struggles with his response to Jesus but never professes Jesus publicly. Both Pilate and Nicodemus may therefore play an important role in the rhetoric of the Gospel by offering readers character studies of those who struggle to embrace Jesus and in the end do not do so. Alternatively, the ambiguity surrounding their responses may prompt readers to find ways to construct for them a more positive response than the Gospel attests.

Mary Magdalene, by contrast, serves the thematic role of clarifying Jesus' 'whither', in contrast to Nathanael, who did not understand Jesus' 'whence'. As Paul Minear observed, her refrain is 'I don't know where . . .' (20.2, 13; cf. 20.15).[39] She does not understand Jesus' resurrection or his exaltation. When the risen Lord appears to her in the garden and calls her name, she is 'weeping' (20.11). 'Turning' (20.16), which signals a change in her perspective, she holds him (still not understanding), but then she goes to the disciples, 'proclaiming' (20.18).[40] Like Mary Magdalene, Thomas too seems to undergo a change, voicing the Gospel's climactic confession when the risen Lord appears and invites him to touch his wounds (20.28).

The last four chapters of the Gospel contain a wide range of characters, some of whom appear only incidentally, while others exhibit the greatest complexity, development and ambiguity of any of the characters who encounter Jesus. As in earlier sections of the Gospel, most of the characters either simply fulfil plot functions or advance the Gospel's themes. This final section of the Gospel, however, also offers examples of characterization where development of the character transcends plot and theme functions, especially in the cases of Peter, Pilate and Nicodemus.

---

37   On this assertion, see Hylen, *Imperfect Believers*, pp. 23–40. Cf. also, Raimo Hakola, 'The Burden of Ambiguity: Nicodemus and the Social Identity of the Johannine Christians', *NTS* 55 (2009), pp. 438–55.

38   Rainer Metzner, *Die Prominenten im Neuen Testament. Ein prosopographischer Kommentar* (NTOA 66; Göttingen: Vandenhoeck & Ruprecht, 2008), p. 305; cf. p. 339.

39   See Paul S. Minear, '"We Don't Know Where . . ." John 20:2', *Int* 30 (1976), pp. 125–39.

40   Sandra M. Schneiders, *Written That You May Believe: Encountering Jesus in the Fourth Gospel* (New York: Herder & Herder, 1999), p. 192.

IV. Conclusions

This survey of the function of characters in relation to plot and theme suggests that it is inadequate to treat the characters individually, in isolation from one another, or simply as representative responses to Jesus that form a spectrum of responses. There is much to be gained from studying the ways each character is evoked, and their role in the Gospel. Many of the characters appear in only one scene, chapter or section of the Gospel, but even some of these characters manifest degrees of change and development in their response to Jesus (e.g., the Samaritan woman and the man born blind). The group characters (the Jews, the Pharisees, the crowd, the disciples) typically appear in more than one section of the Gospel, as do John the Baptist, Jesus' mother, Nicodemus, Peter, Andrew, Philip, Thomas, the Beloved Disciple and Caiaphas. Part of their complexity is constructed by their role in the development of various themes in more than one section of the Gospel. Here again Peter stands out for the prominence of his role across the Gospel from the first chapter to the last.

While it is true that John's characters illustrate various responses to Jesus and move the reader toward a response of believing in Jesus (20.30-31), they also have specific functions within the thematic development and rhetorical plan of the Gospel. The more richly evoked characters transcend their ties to thematic functions. Yet, in a sense, each of the characters is a 'plot functionary', and it is important to take note of the ways characterization, theme development and the rhetorical design of the Gospel narrative are all intertwined.

Chapter 3

A COMPREHENSIVE APPROACH TO UNDERSTANDING CHARACTER
IN THE GOSPEL OF JOHN

Cornelis Bennema

I. Introduction

In the last thirty-odd years there has been an increased interest in the Bible as
literature and story. Literary methods have been applied to the Gospel of John
(with great success), taking the Gospel to be the story of Jesus Christ – a story
with a plot, events and characters. While much has been written on events and
plot, character appears to be the neglected child. There is no comprehensive
theory of character in either literary theory or biblical criticism, and therefore
no consensus on how to analyse and classify characters.[1] Too often scholars
perceive character in the Hebrew Bible (where characters can develop) to be
radically different from that in ancient Greek literature (where characters are
supposedly consistent ethical types). Many also sharply distinguish between
modern fiction with its psychological, individualistic approach to character
and ancient characterization where characters lack personality or individuality.
When it comes to John's Gospel, most if not all Johannine characters are
regarded as 'flat' or 'types', showing little complexity or development.

I have challenged these views and proposed a different approach to character
in the Gospel of John, arguing that the differences in characterization in the
Hebrew Bible, ancient Greek literature and modern fiction are differences
in emphases rather than kind.[2] It is therefore better to speak of degrees of

---

1   Nevertheless, the study of character has recently received attention in literary and
media theory: Jens Eder, Fotis Jannidis and Ralf Schneider (eds), *Characters in Fictional
Worlds: Understanding Imaginary Beings in Literature, Film, and Other Media* (Revisionen,
3; Berlin/New York: De Gruyter, 2010). Regarding biblical criticism, the most recent work on
understanding character comes from Sönke Finnern, *Narratologie und biblische Exegese: Eine
integrative Methode der Erzählanalyse und ihr Ertrag am Beispiel von Matthäus 28* (WUNT,
II/285; Tübingen: Mohr Siebeck, 2010), pp. 125–64.

2   Cornelis Bennema, 'A Theory of Character in the Fourth Gospel with Reference to
Ancient and Modern Literature', *BibInt* 17 (2009), pp. 375–421. Although I differ from her,
Colleen M. Conway also criticizes scholars' tendency to 'flatten' the Johannine characters
('Speaking through Ambiguity: Minor Characters in the Fourth Gospel', *BibInt* 10 [2002], pp.
324–41).

characterization along a continuum. I then outlined a comprehensive approach to understanding character in the Gospel of John, consisting of three aspects. First, I study character in text and context, using information from the text and other sources. Second, I analyse and classify the Johannine characters along three dimensions (complexity, development, inner life), and plot the resulting character on a continuum of degree of characterization (from agent to type to personality to individuality). Third, I evaluate the characters in relation to John's point of view, purpose and dualistic worldview. In a separate work, I have applied this theory to John's Gospel, showing that only eight out of twenty-three characters are 'types'.[3]

Although I have not changed my views on how to understand Johannine characters, I wish to return to the subject for two reasons. First, the publication of my twofold work on Johannine characters coincided with that of Susan Hylen's *Imperfect Believers: Ambiguous Characters in the Gospel of John*,[4] and Christopher W. Skinner's *John and Thomas: Gospels in Conflict? Johannine Characterization and the Thomas Question*.[5] Both Hylen and Skinner provide a theoretical framework for analysing Johannine character.[6] Although we each attempt to provide correctives to the trend among scholars to view most Johannine characters as one-dimensional or 'flat', we also differ. While I suggest that Johannine characters be analysed along the continua 'complexity of traits', 'character development' and 'inner life', Hylen appears to use a continuum of ambiguity and Skinner one of misunderstanding.[7] This raises the question whether our approaches are conflicting, mutually exclusive or complementary. Could I, for example, enhance my theory by adding a fourth continuum of ambiguity or misunderstanding? Second, in reviewing my work, Richard Rohrbaugh, an authority on the social and cultural world of the New Testament, questions the legitimacy of applying modern literary methods to analyse characters in ancient texts. He alleges that I naïvely use modern trait-names for understanding ancient characters, and questions how I

---

3   Cornelis Bennema, *Encountering Jesus: Character Studies in the Gospel of John* (Milton Keynes: Paternoster, 2009). Besides the two essays in this volume, I have been invited to contribute to other works on the subject: essays on Judas, the chief priests and the crowd in S. A. Hunt, R. Zimmermann and D. F. Tolmie (eds), *Character Studies in the Fourth Gospel* (WUNT, I; Tübingen: Mohr Siebeck, forthcoming 2013), on character analysis in relation to the Markan miracle stories in B. Kollmann and R. Zimmermann (eds), *Hermeneutik der frühchristlichen Wundererzählungen* (WUNT; Tübingen: Mohr Siebeck, forthcoming 2013), and on the Johannine characters as moral agents in L. D. Chrupcała (ed.), *Rediscovering John: Essays in Honour of Frédéric Manns* (AnBib; Rome: Biblical Institute Press, forthcoming 2013).

4   Louisville: Westminster John Knox, 2009.

5   PTMS, 115; Eugene, OR: Wipf & Stock, 2009. Frances Taylor Gench has also studied some Johannine characters recently but she does not provide a theoretical foundation (*Encounters with Jesus: Studies in the Gospel of John* [Louisville: Westminster John Knox, 2007]).

6   Hylen, *Believers*, ch. 1; Skinner, *John and Thomas*, ch. 2.

7   It is unclear whether Hylen and Skinner view ambiguity and misunderstanding as a character trait (which they contend most Johannine characters possess) or as a continuum (even if they do not use the term).

infer a character's traits from the text.[8] By engaging with these views, I aim to explain and sharpen my argument rather than merely repeating what I said in 2009, hopefully stimulating further discussion.

II. Theoretical Prolegomena regarding the Study of Character in Antiquity

In this section, I will revisit two pertinent hermeneutical issues: (i) the legitimacy of applying modern literary methods to study ancient characters; and (ii) the appropriateness of the method of inference to reconstruct characters from a text. Is it hermeneutically viable and valid to compare ancient and modern characterization or are we comparing apples and oranges? I will draw on my earlier work to show that while there are differences in characterization in the Hebrew Bible, ancient Greek literature and modern fiction, these are differences in emphases rather than kind.[9] I will seek to address Richard Rohrbaugh's criticism of my alleged anachronism and ignorance, arguing that it is not only legitimate but also necessary to draw on modern labels to infer a character's traits.

Regarding the *nature* of character, most people sharply distinguish between modern fiction and its psychological, individualistic approach to character and ancient characterization where character lacks personality or individuality. And within ancient literature, the common perception is that while character in the Hebrew Bible can develop and be 'round', character in ancient Greek literature is static or 'flat' – based on Aristotle's well-known view on character as fixed ethical types (cf. his *Poetics* 6.7-21). Many biblical scholars assume that the Aristotelian view of character was representative of all ancient Greek literature and also influenced the Gospels. I have found these distinctions to be untrue. I have sought to demonstrate that from the fifth century BCE to the second century CE, from classical tragedy to comedy to biography, historiography and novel, there are significant instances where character can be complex, change, have inner life and even show personality.[10] The notion that all characters in ancient Greek literature are flat, static and one-dimensional, which many scholars have derived from Aristotle's thought, appears therefore to be a caricature. Characterization in ancient Graeco-Roman literature was more complex and varied, and capable of approaching modern notions of character at times. Consequently, we can no longer uphold that, in contrast to modern fiction, ancient literature has no psychological interest in character or that characters cannot move towards personality or even individuality.[11] We must, however, remain aware that characterization in ancient

8   Richard L. Rohrbaugh's review in *BTB* 41 (2011), pp. 110–11.

9   Bennema, 'Theory of Character', pp. 379–98.

10   Ibid., pp. 383–9. I referred for example to Sophocles' *Ajax* and *Antigone*; Euripides' *Medea, Electra, Orestes* and *Antiope*; Plutarch's *Lives*; Tacitus's *Annals*; Chariton's *Chaereas and Callirhoe*; Heliodorus's *Aethiopica*; Apuleius's *Golden Ass*; and Tatius's *Leucippe and Clitophon*.

11   See especially the essays in C. B. R. Pelling (ed.), *Characterization and Individuality in Greek Literature* (Oxford: Clarendon, 1990).

and modern literature is not identical but has different emphases: the ancients did not give character as much individual and psychological emphasis as the moderns do in the Western world. Hence, differences in characterization in ancient and modern literature are differences in *emphases* rather than kind, and it is better to speak of *degrees* of characterization along a continuum.[12] Both ancient and modern literature portray flat and round, static and dynamic characters, although in modern fiction character is much more developed and 'psychologized'.

Regarding the *method* of character reconstruction, the main difficulty is that one can rarely read character from the surface of the text. Many scholars have recognized that in ancient literature characterization is often indirect – information about a character is conveyed primarily through the character's speech and actions rather than the narrator's statements – and the reader is thus obliged to reconstruct the character through *inference* or 'filling the gaps'.[13] But the practice of inference is employed in modern literature too – it is unavoidable. Seymour Chatman, for example, argues that we reconstruct character by inferring traits from the information in the text.[14] In fact, as Chatman asserts, to curb 'a God-given right to infer and even to speculate about characters' would be 'an impoverishment of aesthetic experience'.[15] Thus, in both ancient and modern literature, character is reconstructed from the information provided in the text. The only difference is that in ancient literature there is *less* direct characterization and one has to resort to the device of inference or gap-filling *more* than in modern fiction.

How then should we respond to Rohrbaugh's stated aversion to using modern literary methods to study ancient characters and to using a method of inference that has inherent tendencies to be speculative, imaginative and ignore cultural differences? Should the sparse portrayal of character lead us

---

12   Fred W. Burnett has excellently argued this case ('Characterization and Reader Construction of Characters in the Gospels', *Semeia* 63 [1993], pp. 3–28 [6–15]). Skinner supports Burnett's view (*John and Thomas*, p. 29).

13   See especially Robert Alter, *The Art of Biblical Narrative* (New York: Basic Books, 1981), ch. 6; Adele Berlin, *Poetics and Interpretation of Biblical Narrative* (Sheffield: Almond Press, 1983), pp. 33–42; Meir Sternberg, *The Poetics of Biblical Narrative: Ideological Literature and the Drama of Reading* (Bloomington: Indiana University Press, 1985), ch. 6; Shimon Bar-Efrat, *Narrative Art in the Bible* (JSOTSup, 70; Sheffield: Almond Press, 1989), ch. 2. Bar-Efrat points out that in real life too we usually infer people's character from what they say and do (*Art*, p. 89).

14   Seymour Chatman, *Story and Discourse: Narrative Structure in Fiction and Film* (Ithaca/London: Cornell University Press, 1978), pp. 119–20. Cf. Shlomith Rimmon-Kenan, *Narrative Fiction: Contemporary Poetics* (London/New York: Routledge, 2nd edn, 2002), pp. 36, 59, 128–30; Uri Margolin, 'Individuals in Narrative Worlds: An Ontological Perspective', *Poetics Today* 11 (1990), pp. 843–71 (847–9); Jonathan Culpeper, 'Reflections on a Cognitive Stylistic Approach to Characterisation', in G. Brône and J. Vandaele (eds), *Cognitive Poetics: Goals, Gains and Gaps* (Applications of Cognitive Linguistics, 10; Berlin/New York: De Gruyter, 2009), pp. 139–49. The reader's need to infer character traits from the information dispersed in the text goes back to Wolfgang Iser, 'The Reading Process: A Phenomenological Approach', *New Literary History* 3 (1972), pp. 279–99 (284–5).

15   Chatman, *Story*, p. 117.

to despair in reconstructing character or abandon the task altogether? No, but caution is demanded. I contend that there is reasonable evidence that character in ancient Hebrew and Greek literature could be complex, change and even show personality, suggesting that character in ancient and modern literature rather than being distinct is to be viewed on a continuum. It would then be legitimate to use insights from modern fiction to study character in ancient literature. I maintain that we can apply aspects from modern literary methods to study character in ancient narratives as long as we take the necessary precautions. The interpreter must be aware, for instance, that by applying such methods she or he fuses the modern and ancient horizon, and uses modern terminology to understand characters in ancient literature. That is, in the reconstruction of characters, the interpreter merges two horizons and bridges a vast cultural gap.[16] I must explain why this is legitimate and even inevitable.

Commenting on the Bible's reticence in characterization, Robert Alter for example asserts that '[w]e are compelled to get at character and motive . . . through a process of inference from fragmentary data, often with crucial pieces of narrative exposition strategically withheld, and this leads to multiple or sometimes even wavering perspectives on the characters'.[17] Nevertheless, Sternberg emphasizes that the reader's task of gap-filling is legitimate and by no means an arbitrary process since any hypothesis must be validated by the text.[18] Even though readers reconstruct characters differently from the same text, just as scholars differ on the meaning of a text, this does not nullify the task of inference. Any interpretation involves an element of speculation because the reader-interpreter tries to make sense of the text in the absence of the author. In this process, the interpreter does not merely repeat the author's *ipsissima verba* but engages in the task of understanding the meaning of the text – whether that meaning be 'behind', 'in' or 'in front of' the text. In other words, the hermeneutical task involves a level of abstraction or aggregation – the interpreter explores the meaning of the text and this includes acts of analysis, comparison, extrapolation, inference, and so on. At the same time, rules of syntax and genre, relation to the wider text and knowledge of the socio-cultural setting of the text provide the necessary hermeneutical parameters to control the process of interpretation. Thus, the modern interpreter must aim to speak about the meaning of the text within its original literary and socio-historical context.[19]

16　This so-called 'new hermeneutic', rooted in the work of philosophers Martin Heidegger and Hans-Georg Gadamer, is developed extensively by Anthony C. Thiselton in *The Two Horizons* (Exeter: Paternoster, 1980) and *New Horizons in Hermeneutics* (San Francisco: HarperCollins, 1992).

17　Alter, *Art*, p. 126.

18　Sternberg, *Poetics*, pp. 188–9.

19　I consider myself a 'critical realist'. On the one hand, I do not claim to understand the Johannine characters as a first-century Jewish or Graeco-Roman reader would (that is impossible); on the other hand, my understanding of the Johannine characters is not an uncritical twenty-first-century Western reading of the text. As I carefully seek to consider the linguistic, literary and socio-cultural aspects of the Johannine narrative, I maintain that my understanding of the Johannine characters is nevertheless a *Johannine* understanding.

But what about the use of modern labels to name a character's traits? If we accept Chatman's definition of character as a 'paradigm of traits' in which traits have to be inferred from the deep structure of the text, it would be natural that the trait-names we assign are derived from what we know of real people in the real world. This means we would use contemporary language to describe a character. It is inevitable, for example, when we infer a character's traits from the deep structure of an ancient text that we use trait-names that are familiar to our modern world. Chatman thus argues that because the trait is not often named explicitly in the text but must be inferred, readers will usually rely upon their knowledge of the trait-name in the real world, so traits are culturally coded.[20] We must also remember that the names for traits are 'socially invented signs . . . Trait-names are not themselves traits.'[21] Chatman forcefully asserts that 'characters as narrative constructs do require terms for description, and there is no point in rejecting those out of the general vocabulary of psychology, morality and any other relevant area of human experience'.[22] This holds true for the study of character both in modern literature and in ancient narratives. Using modern terminology to analyse and describe characters in ancient literature is acceptable provided we remember that we sometimes use terms or categories unknown to the ancient authors and audiences. Simon Goldhill, for example, points out that '[s]ince the description of character necessarily involves the mobilisation of (at least) implicit psychological models, it is unlikely that the criticism of Greek tragedy can expect wholly to avoid an engagement with psychological and psychoanalytic theory'.[23] Robert Tannehill likewise defends the use of insights from modern fiction to ancient biblical narratives:

> [T]here are qualities which all narratives share and further qualities which various narratives may share, even when some make use of historical fact, if the author has a strong, creative role. Because of the importance of the novel in modern literature, qualities of narrative are often discussed in terms of the novel. With proper caution the biblical scholar can learn from this discussion.[24]

As long as we are vigilant about the differences between a collectivist, ancient Mediterranean culture and an individualistic, modern Western culture,

---

20   Chatman, *Story*, pp. 123–5.

21   G. W. Allport and H. S. Odbert, *Trait-Names: A Psycholexical Study*, *Psychological Monographs* 47 (Princeton, NJ, 1936), p. 17, cited in Chatman, *Story*, p. 124.

22   Chatman, *Story*, p. 138. Stressing that we need 'substantive rules of inference', Margolin claims that these can be borrowed from any actual-world model of readers if the text world coincides with it in its broader outline or is at least compatible with it ('Individuals', pp. 852–3).

23   Simon Goldhill, 'Modern Critical Approaches to Greek Tragedy', in P. E. Easterling (ed.), *The Cambridge Companion to Greek Tragedy* (Cambridge, UK: Cambridge University Press, 1997), p. 343.

24   Robert C. Tannehill, 'The Disciples in Mark: The Function of a Narrative Role', *JR* 57 (1977), pp. 386–405 (387).

I maintain that it is possible to speak of an individual in antiquity without transposing a modern individualistic notion of identity onto the text. We can do so by using the concept of a 'collectivist identity' or 'group-oriented personality', where the individual's identity is *embedded* in a larger group or community.[25] As Burnett asserts, there is evidence that there was a move from the typical to the individual in the ancient Greek and Roman world, allowing for the reader to construct a character's individuality.[26] Similarly, Patricia Easterling notes that even though the Greeks were not interested in the individual's unique private experience found in modern literature, they had an interest in individuals as part of a community.[27] In the same way, Louise Lawrence argues that even the primarily collectivist Graeco-Roman and Jewish cultures testify to the existence of individualistic traits.[28]

So, on the one hand, I unequivocally agree with Rohrbaugh that knowledge of the social and cultural world of the New Testament is essential for understanding the personality, motive and behaviour of ancient characters. On the other hand, since ancient characterization is often indirect, we are compelled to infer aspects of character from the sparse information in the text with the assistance of modern terminology. And this is where the tension lies. I contend that the usage of modern trait-names to identify the traits of ancient character must be governed by knowledge of the first-century world. This is precisely why the first aspect of my theory is the study of character in text *and context*, where the latter refers to the socio-cultural first-century environment (cf. section III.a, below).[29]

25   Cf. Bruce J. Malina, *The New Testament World: Insights from Cultural Anthropology* (Louisville: Westminster John Knox, 3rd edn, 2001), pp. 60–7.

26   Burnett, 'Characterization', pp. 11–12.

27   Patricia E. Easterling, 'Character in Sophocles', *Greece and Rome* 24 (1977), pp. 121–9 (129).

28   Louis J. Lawrence, *An Ethnography of the Gospel of Matthew: A Critical Assessment of the Use of the Honour and Shame Model in New Testament Studies* (WUNT, II/165; Tübingen: Mohr Siebeck, 2003), pp. 249–59.

29   Ironically, based on his belief in the validity of cultural continuity, Malina concedes that he uses anthropological models of *contemporary* Mediterranean culture to understand cultures in the first century (*New Testament World*, p. xii; cf. also Bruce J. Malina and Richard L. Rohrbaugh, *Social-Science Commentary on the Gospel of John* [Minneapolis: Fortress, 1998], pp. 19–20). But how do we know that nothing has fundamentally changed in the last two millennia or the extent to which modern Spanish and Italian societies are comparable to first-century Palestinian society? Who then engages in anachronism, I dare ask? Although elsewhere Richard Rohrbaugh addresses the issue of extending sociological models diachronically (e.g., he uses the concept of sacred space in relation to the temple before and after 70 CE), he only refers to a time continuum of 50 years ('Models and Muddles: Discussions of the Social Facets Seminar', *Forum* 3.2 [1987], pp. 23–33 [28–30]). Of course, at higher levels of abstraction one can always find correspondence – sacred space, purity, honour/shame, and so on exist in every culture and time – but the question is whether we can assume, for example, that the purity system in modern Italy is an appropriate model for that in first-century Palestine.

III. A Comprehensive Approach to Understanding Johannine Character

Having clarified that the nature of character in ancient and modern literature is more alike than not and that to infer character from indicators in the text is both legitimate and inevitable, we can start to think of a comprehensive, non-reductionist theory for analysing character in the Johannine narrative. I propose a three-dimensional approach.

a. Character in Text and Context

On the one hand, characters do not have 'lives' beyond the text and hence we reconstruct character from the information in the text. With regard to John's Gospel, the author primarily employs indirect characterization, so we must infer character from the character's speech and actions, and what other characters say about that character, rather than the narrator's speech.[30] On the other hand, since John's Gospel claims to be a non-fictional narrative and therefore refers to events and people in the real world, we must fill the gaps from our knowledge of the socio-historical context of the first-century Mediterranean world (rather than our imagination). Narrative critics tend to limit themselves to the text, but I shall demonstrate the need to go occasionally *beyond* the text for the reconstruction of character.

John's Gospel claims to be a non-fictional narrative by a reliable eyewitness to the events recorded (19.35; 21.24). This implies that the Johannine characters have historical referents and must be interpreted within the socio-historical context of first-century Judaism and not just on the basis of the text itself. In other words, the *dramatis personae* in the Johannine story are also composites of real historical people. This demands that we also look outside John's Gospel at other sources that can assist us in reconstructing the Johannine characters. The historical data available to us from other (literary and non-literary) sources should supplement the data that the text provides about a character. Frank Kermode has said that in constructing character we (should) augment the text 'by inferring from the repertoire of indices characteristics not immediately signalled in the text, but familiar from other texts and from life'.[31] Marianne Meye Thompson argues similarly: '"Actual readers" of the gospels may well have access to the characters in the narrative in other ways, whether through oral or written tradition, and these other "narratives" surely influence the way they read.'[32]

---

30   Occasionally the author provides direct characterization. For example, the narrator's information about Judas's betrayal of Jesus and being a thief in 12.4, 6 reveals traits of disloyalty and dishonesty.

31   Frank Kermode, *The Genesis of Secrecy: On the Interpretation of Narrative* (Cambridge, MA: Harvard University Press, 1979), p. 78.

32   Marianne Meye Thompson, '"God's Voice You Have Never Heard, God's Form You Have Never Seen": The Characterization of God in the Gospel of John', *Semeia* 63 (1993), pp. 177–204 (181).

In comparing fictional and non-fictional narratives, Petri Merenlahti and Raimo Hakola state that in the case of the latter, (i) the author vouches for the veracity of the narrative and assumes that the reader believes it; and (ii) the narrator represents the author and his point of view and therefore there is continuity between 'reality' and the narrative world.[33] Indeed, the Johannine author (or a later editor speaking for the author) explicitly states that his story is true and therefore can be believed (19.35; 21.24), and since there is no real distinction between the author and narrator in John's Gospel, the narrator reliably represents the author's voice and view.[34] Merenlahti and Hakola then state why non-fictional narratives must be seen *in context*:

> Because a non-fictional narrative claims to refer to events and circumstances of the 'real' world, it is natural that the readers try to fill any gaps the narrative may have, making use of all available information about the events and circumstances in concern. What readers of a non-fictional narrative think of a character depends not only on what the narrator reveals but also on what else the readers may know about the person who is portrayed as a character in the narrative . . . The natural way to read a Gospel would be to make connections between character groups of the story and the 'real' groups which those characters intend to portray . . . An 'intrinsic', text-centered approach does not seem to match properly the nature of the Gospels as non-fictional narratives.[35]

These arguments readily apply to John's Gospel. One cannot simply assume, for example, that 'the Jews' in John's Gospel are a monolithic group – either in composition or in its response to Jesus. So it is essential to study the 'referent' of 'the Jews', which relates to the group's identity as real people in the time of Jesus or the author.[36] As for the character of Pilate, we must examine the works of Josephus and Philo since many scholars contend that these sources portray Pilate differently from John's Gospel. Besides, we should also look at the Synoptic portrayal of Pilate, especially since a good case can be made that the Johannine author knew Mark's Gospel.[37] This invites a comparison of how the various sources portray Pilate.

---

33   Petri Merenlahti and Raimo Hakola, 'Reconceiving Narrative Criticism', in David Rhoads and Kari Syreeni (eds), *Characterization in the Gospels: Reconceiving Narrative Criticism* (JSNTSup, 184; Sheffield: Sheffield Academic Press, 1999), pp. 35–8.

34   Cf. Culpepper, *Anatomy*, pp. 42–3. Jeffrey L. Staley, however, argues that the Johannine narrator is not consistently reliable, resulting in the entrapment or victimization of the reader (*The Print's First Kiss: A Rhetorical Investigation of the Implied Reader in the Fourth Gospel* [SBLDS, 82; Atlanta: Scholars, 1988]), but his case has not won much support.

35   Merenlahti and Hakola, 'Narrative Criticism', pp. 40–3.

36   I have undertaken this study elsewhere, arguing that the referent of the term 'the Jews' *cannot* be resolved entirely narratologically (Cornelis Bennema, 'The Identity and Composition of οἱ Ἰουδαῖοι in the Gospel of John', *TynBul* 60 [2009], pp. 239–63).

37   Cf. Richard Bauckham, 'John for Readers of Mark', in idem, *The Gospels for All Christians: Rethinking the Gospel Audiences* (Grand Rapids: Eerdmans, 1998), pp. 147–71; Paul N. Anderson, *The Riddles of the Fourth Gospel: An Introduction to John* (Minneapolis: Fortress, 2011), pp. 126–9. In my analysis of the Johannine Pilate elsewhere in this volume, I shall therefore also refer to the Markan Pilate. This does not mean that I will read the Johannine Pilate

At the same time, John may have 'fictionalized' or embellished aspects of his characters by leaving out, changing or adding certain details from his sources – as historians and biographers often do. For example, John (the Baptist) appears in this Gospel as an eloquent witness to Jesus while the Synoptics present him as a rough-hewn figure preaching a baptism of repentance. The so-called Beloved Disciple was either as perfect as this Gospel portrays him or may have been somewhat 'idealized'. If the Gospels belong to the genre of the ancient Graeco-Roman biography (as many scholars contend today),[38] they need not be historically accurate in every detail.[39] In fact, no serious scholar claims that the Gospels contain the *ipsissima verba Jesu*. The authors may have used literary 'creativity' but what matters is that the reader does not disbelieve their credibility. As Merenlahti and Hakola explain, while not everything in non-fictional narratives is necessarily historical, this does not make them fictional narratives since they do claim to describe the real world; what counts is that the reader does not doubt the author's explicit or implicit truth claims.[40]

This is an important shift in narrative criticism. Too often, narrative critics restrict themselves to the text of the Gospel and the narrative world it evokes, effectively reading the Gospel as a fictional narrative that is disconnected from reality.[41] Instead, we need a form of *historical narrative criticism* that takes a text-centred approach but examines aspects of the world outside or 'behind' the text if the text invites us to do so.[42] In other words, we should reconstruct

---

through a Markan lens, but that I assume that John knew Mark's characterization of Pilate and either confirms or augments his portrayal.

38   The compelling case for this has been made by Richard A. Burridge, *What Are the Gospels? A Comparison with Graeco-Roman Biography* (Grand Rapids: Eerdmans, 2nd edn, 2004; orig. SNTSMS, 70; Cambridge, UK: Cambridge University Press, 1992), pp. 213–32.

39   Cf. Andrew T. Lincoln, *Truth on Trial: The Lawsuit Motif in the Fourth Gospel* (Peabody, MA: Hendrickson, 2000), pp. 369–97.

40   Merenlahti and Hakola, 'Narrative Criticism', p. 38. Sternberg argues similarly for the Hebrew Bible as historiography: 'history-writing is not a record of fact—of what "really happened"—but a discourse that claims to be a record of fact. Nor is fiction-writing a tissue of free inventions but a discourse that claims freedom of invention. The antithesis lies not in the presence or absence of truth value but of the commitment to truth value' (*Poetics*, pp. 24–35 [quotation taken from p. 25]). Thus, the historicity of the characters in John's Gospel does not exclude the possibility that the author used a legitimate degree of artistic freedom to portray his characters. Besides, the Gospel authors were theologians; they wrote from a post-Easter perspective and interpreted the pre-Easter events with a specific (theological) agenda in mind. The primary concern of the Johannine author is to assure his readers that his story of Jesus is a true and reliable testimony (cf. 19.35; 21.24).

41   Although James L. Resseguie presents a more 'mature' form of narrative criticism, stating that the narrative critic should be familiar with the cultural, linguistic, social and historical assumptions of the audience envisioned by the implied author, he nevertheless contends that this information must be obtained *from the text itself* rather than from outside the text (*Narrative Criticism of the New Testament: An Introduction* [Grand Rapids: Baker Academic, 2005], pp. 32, 39).

42   Almost twenty years after *Narrative Fiction* was first published, Rimmon-Kenan points to new forms of narratology, including a cultural and historical narratology that is context-orientated,

the Johannine characters from the information that the text of John's Gospel provides *and* supplement it with relevant information from other sources.[43]

b. Character Analysis and Classification

One of the earliest and most well-known classifications in literary criticism, by E. M. Forster, categorizes characters as 'flat' and 'round'. Flat characters or types are built around a single trait and do not develop, whereas round characters are complex characters that have multiple traits and can develop in the course of action. Forster's criterion for deciding whether a character is round or flat is its capacity to surprise the reader.[44] Differently, W. J. Harvey uses the categories of protagonists (the central characters in the narrative), cards (characters who support and illuminate the protagonists), *ficelles* (typical characters who serve certain plot functions) and background characters (characters who serve a mechanical role in the plot or act as chorus).[45] Where Forster classifies characters according to traits and development, Harvey classifies them according to narrative presence or importance.[46] Thus, Harvey's classification does not improve our understanding of the characters themselves but only of how active they are in the plot. If we accept Chatman's definition of character as a paradigm of traits, Forster's 'psychological' classification has scope but is still too reductionistic since not every character would fit neatly into either one of his categories.[47] This has prompted some people to refine Forster's classification. Adele Berlin, for example, uses the categories of full-fledged character (Forster's round character), type (Forster's flat character) and agent (the plot functionary), but she considers these categories to be *degrees* of characterization rather than fixed categories.[48] Some biblical

---

and historical and diachronous in orientation (*Narrative Fiction*, pp. 140–2). Cf. Finnern, who labels it 'postclassic narratology' (*Narratologie*, pp. 35–6).

43   Cf. John A. Darr, who proposes an extratextual approach (*Herod the Fox: Audience Criticism and Lukan Characterization* (JSNTSup, 163; Sheffield: Sheffield Academic Press, 1998), pp. 89–91. Mark W. G. Stibbe also asserts that 'characters in the gospels need to be analysed with reference to history, and not according to the laws of fiction' (*John as Storyteller: Narrative Criticism and the Fourth Gospel* [SNTSMS, 73; Cambridge, UK: Cambridge University Press, 1992], p. 24). Martinus C. de Boer provides the best defence for a combined historical and narratological approach to John's Gospel ('Narrative Criticism, Historical Criticism, and the Gospel of John', *JSNT* 47 [1992], pp. 35–48). I do not go as far as Raymond E. Brown, who identifies seven historical groups of people behind the representative figures within the Gospel (*The Community of the Beloved Disciple* [New York: Paulist, 1979], pp. 59–91).

44   E. M. Forster, *Aspects of the Novel* (New York: Harcourt, Brace and Company, 1927), pp. 73–81.

45   W. J. Harvey, *Character and the Novel* (London: Chatto & Windus, 1965), pp. 52–73.

46   Cf. Daniel Marguerat and Yvan Bourquin, *How to Read Bible Stories: An Introduction to Narrative Criticism* (London: SCM, 1999), p. 60.

47   For a critique of Forster, see Rimmon-Kenan, *Narrative Fiction*, pp. 40–1; Stibbe, *John as Storyteller*, p. 24; D. François Tolmie, *Jesus' Farewell to the Disciples: John 13:1–17:26 in Narratological Perspective* (BIS, 12; Leiden: Brill, 1995), pp. 122–3. However, even Forster admits that a flat character could acquire 'roundness' (*Aspects of the Novel*, pp. 74–5, 112–13).

48   Berlin, *Poetics*, pp. 23, 32.

scholars hold the same position. Meir Sternberg and Shimon Bar-Efrat, for example, perceive biblical characters as moving along a continuum rather than existing as two contingencies, either flat or round.[49] Similarly, Fred Burnett concludes that 'it would seem wise to understand characterization, for any biblical text at least, on a continuum. This would imply for narratives like the Gospels that the focus should be on the *degree* of characterization rather than on characterization as primarily typical.'[50]

The classification of characters as points along a continuum is a significant development but the question of how such a continuum should look has not been resolved. I suggest using the non-reductionist model of Jewish scholar Joseph Ewen to analyse the Johannine characters. He advocates three continua or axes upon which a character may be situated:

- *Complexity*: characters range from those displaying a single trait to those displaying a complex web of traits, with varying degrees of complexity in between.
- *Development*: characters may vary from those who show no development to those who are fully developed.
- *Penetration into the inner life*: characters range from those who allow us a peek inside their minds to those whose minds remain opaque.[51]

While Ewen's classification is a big step forward, I suggest we go a step further. After analysing the character along the three continua, I classify or plot the resulting character on *a continuum of degree of characterization* as (i) an agent, actant or walk-on; (ii) a type, stock or flat character; (iii) a character with personality; or (iv) an individual or person.[52]

We have dealt with the first aspect of Ewen's model of character classification – complexity – in section II, saying that we must infer the character's traits from the text. Now I must elaborate on the other two aspects of Ewen's model. Regarding the second aspect, development is *not* simply that the reader becomes aware of an additional trait later in the narrative or a character's progress in his or her understanding of Jesus.[53] Instead, development occurs when a new trait replaces an old one or does not fit neatly into the existing set of traits, implying that the character has changed.[54] This coheres with Forster's criterion of a character's ability to surprise the reader. We can therefore speak of development when tension becomes apparent within a character's set of

---

49   Sternberg, *Poetics*, pp. 253–5 (cf. his chs 9–10); Bar-Efrat, *Art*, pp. 86–91.

50   Burnett, 'Characterization', p. 15 (original emphasis).

51   Ewen's works are only available in Hebrew but his theory is summarized in Rimmon-Kenan, *Narrative Fiction*, pp. 41–2.

52   In classifying ancient characters, the categories 'personality' and 'individual/person' are not used in the modern sense of an autonomous individual but refer to a 'collectivist identity' or 'group-oriented personality' where the individual identity is *embedded* in a larger group or community.

53   *Pace* Resseguie, *Narrative Criticism*, p. 153.

54   Cf. Rimmon-Kenan, *Narrative Fiction*, p. 39.

traits. Speaking of penetration into the inner life, it appears at first that we are not privy to the inner thoughts, emotions or motivations of the Johannine characters – only Jesus' inner life is well portrayed.[55] François Tolmie, for example, concludes that no inner life of the Johannine characters is revealed.[56] This is, however, a mistaken notion; John's Gospel portrays the inner life of many characters.[57] Evidence of inner life is one aspect that moves a character towards roundness or individuality. The inner life of characters gives the reader insight into their thoughts, emotions and motivations, and is usually conveyed by the narrator and sometimes by other characters.[58]

I do not necessarily restrict myself to Ewen's model of three continua; the number of continua to analyse characters could well be extended. For example, Baruch Hochman uses no less than eight continua upon which a character may be located.[59] At this point, I return to Susan Hylen and Chris Skinner whom I mentioned in the Introduction. Hylen presents an alternative

---

55   Jesus is zealous about his Father's affairs (2.17); has insight into people's lives (2.24-25); can be tired (4.6), agitated (11.33, 38), sad (11.35), troubled (12.27; 13.21), and joyful (11.15; 15.11; 17.13); he loves people (11.5; 13.1, 23, 34); he knows his betrayer (6.70; 13.11, 21). Cf. Stephen Voorwinde, *Jesus' Emotions in the Fourth Gospel: Human or Divine?* (LNTS, 284; London: T&T Clark, 2005).

56   Tolmie, *Jesus' Farewell*, p. 142. Except for Jesus and the disciples, whose inner life is revealed 'a little' (without providing examples), he considers the inner life of all other characters as 'none'. Part of Tolmie's problem is that he only examines a section of the narrative (Jn 13–17) to reconstruct characters. If he had considered the entire Johannine narrative, his analysis would undoubtedly have rendered different results. Similarly, Culpepper, who only mentions what the *narrator* conveys about the characters' inner life, regards these inside views as 'brief' and 'shallow', concluding that the author shows 'no interest in exploring the more complex psychological motivations of his characters' (*Anatomy*, pp. 22–6 [quotation from p. 26]). However, despite many inside views being brief, they convey profound understanding of a character. The brief insights about Judas's dishonesty and that he is influenced by the devil can hardly be called shallow. We can obviously not expect the same elaboration and kind of inner life as in a modern novel. For a more sustained critique of Tolmie and Culpepper's method of character classification, see Bennema, 'Theory of Character', pp. 408–10.

57   See Bennema, 'Theory of Character', pp. 405–7; idem, *Encountering Jesus*, pp. 203–4, showing that 16 out of 23 characters reveal aspects of their inner life.

58   Berlin, *Poetics*, p. 38. Cf. Bar-Efrat, who provides numerous examples of the inner life of characters in the Hebrew Bible (*Art*, pp. 58–64).

59   Baruch Hochman, *Character in Literature* (Ithaca, NY: Cornell University Press, 1985), pp. 86–140. David B. Gowler, for example, utilizes Hochman's model in his character study of the Pharisees in Luke-Acts, although he admits that this model is not entirely adequate to evaluate character in ancient narrative (*Host, Guest, Enemy and Friend: Portraits of the Pharisees in Luke and Acts* [ESEC, 2; New York: Peter Lang, 1991], pp. 53–4, 306–17, 321). Although Colleen M. Conway refers to Hochman's classification, she does not utilize it herself (*Men and Women in the Fourth Gospel: Gender and Johannine Characterization* [SBLDS, 167; Atlanta: Society of Biblical Literature, 1999], p. 58). Based on Jens Eder's work on character in film, Finnern proposes multiple *Gegensatzpaare* ('opposite/contrasting pairs') to analyse characters (*Narratologie*, pp. 157–61). However, it is unclear whether he intends to use them as binary categories (e.g. a character is either static or dynamic) or as continua (e.g. a character can be positioned on a spectrum of development that ranges from static to dynamic). Moreover, Finnern does not clarify what he will do with the results.

strategy for understanding characters in John's Gospel. Rather than viewing many Johannine characters as 'flat' or one-dimensional, she argues that John's characters display various kinds of ambiguity.[60] Although Hylen does not use the term 'continuum' in relation to ambiguity (she views ambiguity as a trait), since she contends that all Johannine characters possess this trait, ambiguity effectively functions as a continuum on which she positions the various Johannine characters. Although I applaud her endeavour to resist treating the Johannine characters in a reductionist way, I also have a few critical observations. First, I am uncertain how Hylen differs from Colleen Conway, who also criticizes the 'flattening' of Johannine characters, arguing that the Johannine characters portray varying degrees of ambiguity, causing instability and resulting in responses to Jesus that resist or undermine the Gospel's binary categories of belief and unbelief.[61] Second, Hylen often observes (correctly in my view) that certain characters are not perfect in their belief and understanding, and this 'imperfection' she labels as 'ambiguity'. However, can imperfect faith not still be adequate (i.e. sufficiently authentic) without being called ambiguous? And does an ambiguous action immediately make one an ambiguous character? Since no one is perfect, holds perfect beliefs and is completely consistent throughout life, everyone would be ambiguous. Thus, the concept as Hylen uses it loses its meaning. Third, I wonder whether Hylen attributes the Johannine characters with more ambiguity than the author intended. Would the author have intentionally built ambiguity into each of his characters? We should not confuse diversity in modern interpretations with the author's (supposedly) intended ambiguity. Otherwise we could conclude that the entire Bible is intentionally ambiguous. Ambiguity, as witnessed in the variety of interpretations, may be more the result of modern hermeneutical enterprises than the author's intentional design.

Regardless of my evaluation of Hylen's work, I accept that many (if not all) Johannine characters show various degrees of ambiguity and I did therefore consider whether we could use a continuum of ambiguity. Along with the other three continua, should I perhaps have extended Ewen's model to include a *continuum of stability* (to use a positive category) on which to position the various Johannine characters? I eventually decided against this move. To me, plotting various characters on a continuum of stability will not translate or correspond linearly to the degree of characterization. Let me explain. While a higher degree of complexity, development or inner life results in a higher degree of characterization (moving the character towards individuality), we cannot say the same regarding stability. A greater degree of stability (or lesser degree of ambiguity) does not necessarily point towards personality or individuality. Conversely, a greater degree of instability or ambiguity does not necessarily point in the direction of the character being a type. For example, both Peter and the man born blind have a high degree of characterization

---

60   Hylen, *Imperfect Believers*, ch. 1.
61   Conway, 'Speaking through Ambiguity', pp. 324–41. For my own critique of Conway, see Bennema, *Encountering Jesus*, pp. 210–11.

(individual and personality respectively).[62] But whereas Peter is unstable on many occasions – he grasps Jesus' identity at a crucial time (6.68-69) but otherwise often misunderstands Jesus; he denies Jesus, contrary to his earlier bold claims; he defects but is restored later – the blind man shows a remarkably high degree of stability under relentless pressure from his interrogators. Similarly, many types appear stable (often because the text simply dispenses little information about them), but Thomas displays instability, fluctuating between courage/commitment (11.16) and misunderstanding (14.5), between unbelief (20.24-25) and belief a week later (20.28). Thus, although I assume we can plot the various characters on a continuum of stability or ambiguity, such a continuum will *not* contribute to our understanding of character and its degree of characterization.

The same would apply to Skinner's approach of looking at the Johannine characters through the lens of misunderstanding. While Skinner does not use the term 'continuum', he contends that every Johannine character is uncomprehending to a degree.[63] Considering the Johannine Prologue as the greatest source of information about Jesus, Skinner states:

> Each character in the narrative approaches Jesus with varying levels of understanding but no one approaches him fully comprehending the truths that have been revealed to the reader in the prologue. Thus, it is possible for the reader to evaluate the correctness of every character's interaction with Jesus on the basis of what has been revealed in the prologue.[64]

Agreeing with Skinner that all Johannine characters show misunderstanding, I also considered creating a *continuum of understanding* (to use a positive category). However, plotting characters on a continuum of understanding would be difficult if not impossible because it is hard to measure the *degree* of a character's understanding. Does Thomas, for example, misunderstand Jesus to a greater extent than Peter? Besides, even if we could plot characters on a continuum of understanding, it would, again, not contribute to the degree of characterization. For example, while characters such as Thomas, the crowd and Peter frequently misunderstand, they have different degrees of characterization – Thomas is a type, the crowd has personality and Peter is an individual. Conversely, both the Beloved Disciple and Thomas have a low degree of characterization ('type'), but the former exhibits near perfect understanding while the latter often misunderstands.[65]

---

62   Cf. Bennema, *Encountering Jesus*, p. 204.
63   Skinner, *John and Thomas*, p. 40.
64   Skinner, *John and Thomas*, p. 37.
65   Bennema, *Encountering Jesus*, pp. 203–5. When it comes to evaluating a character's response to Jesus (see section III.c), misunderstanding may be an inadequate response but misunderstanding itself does not determine whether the character's overall response is adequate or inadequate – other aspects are responsible for that. For instance, the crowd's frequent misunderstanding of Jesus taken *together with* being divided, fearful, dismissive and unbelieving cause the overall response to be inadequate. Conversely, the Twelve frequently misunderstand

In sum, although we could turn a trait that most Johannine characters possess (whether ambiguity, misunderstanding or something else) into a continuum, I question whether it would contribute to our understanding of character and the degree of characterization.[66] In fact, the choice to use a continuum of complexity in terms of a character's traits virtually excludes the use of individual traits to create other continua. I suggest therefore, that we first analyse and classify a character along Ewen's three continua (complexity, development, inner life), and then plot the resulting character on a continuum of degree of characterization (from agent to type to personality to individual). The results of the character analysis can be aggregated in the following table:[67]

Character	Complexity	Development	Inner Life	Degree of Characterization
Character 1	0	0	0	Agent
Character 2	–	0	0	Type
Character 3	–/+	0	–	Personality
Character 4	+	+	–	Personality
Character 5	++	+	+	towards Individual
Character 6	++	++	+	Individual

Key: 0 = none, – = little, + = some, ++ = much.

c. Character Evaluation

Besides analysing and classifying the Johannine characters, we must also *evaluate* them from the author's ideological point of view. Any meaningful communication, whether verbal or non-verbal, has a specific message that the sender wants to get across to the receiver. Authors thus have an agenda, implicit or explicit, and the author of John's Gospel belongs to the latter category. As 20.30-31 indicates: 'Now Jesus did many other signs in the presence of his disciples, which are not written in this book. But these are written *so that* you

---

Jesus but remain at his side; the Samaritan woman and the man born blind struggle to understand but are open-minded and eventually reach sufficient understanding to make an adequate belief-response to Jesus.

66   Both Hylen and Skinner's works have made me consider expanding my model with further continua and my decision not to do so is in no way a negative appraisal of their study. The social sciences are perhaps better suited to providing appropriate continua to extend Ewen's model. Although it is impossible to explore here, additional continua could include 'status (in the Johannine group)' or 'degree of testimony'. See further Jerome H. Neyrey, *The Gospel of John* (NCBC; Cambridge, UK: Cambridge University Press, 2007), pp. 7–9, 313–15, 321–4.

67   For the actual results of my analysis of most Johannine characters, see Bennema, *Encountering Jesus*, pp. 203–4. At present, I position a character on each continuum in comparison to other characters, but such an intuitive approach may need refinement towards more precise criteria for what constitutes 'little' or 'much'.

may (come to or continue to) believe that Jesus is the Messiah, the Son of God, and that through believing you may have [eternal] life in his name.'[68] Driven by this salvific purpose, the author tells his story from a particular perspective called '*point of view*'.[69] Stephen Moore defines point of view as 'the rhetorical activity of an author as he or she attempts, from a position within some socially shared system of assumptions and convictions, to impose a story world upon an audience by the manipulation of narrative perspective'.[70] James Resseguie states that point of view is 'the *mode* or *angle of vision* from which characters, dialogue, actions, setting and events are considered or observed. But also point of view is the narrator's *attitude towards* or *evaluation of* characters, dialogue, actions, setting and events.'[71] Consequently, a narrative is not neutral because it has an *inbuilt* perspective that is communicated to the reader, and in the case of John's Gospel we must evaluate the characters in the light of the author's evaluative point of view.[72]

In evaluating a character, we must know what we are evaluating and how – we require guidelines or criteria for evaluation. For instance, what is the central theme against which we might evaluate characters? In the case of John's Gospel, I recommend that we must evaluate the characters primarily in terms of their *response* to Jesus.[73] The author's purpose in writing his Gospel – to evoke and strengthen belief in Jesus among his readers – indicates that what counts is the *reader's* response to Jesus. The author's strategy for achieving his purpose is to put various characters on the stage and show their interaction with Jesus. He wants his readers to evaluate the characters' responses to Jesus, join his point of view and make an adequate belief-response themselves. It also follows that in order to evaluate the character's (belief-)response to Jesus according to the *author's* point of view, the reader must understand the author's concept of what constitutes adequate belief. I have defined the author's concept of an adequate belief-response to Jesus as a sufficiently true, Spirit-provided understanding of Jesus in terms of his identity, mission and relationship with his Father, resulting

---

68   For a discussion of the textual variant πιστεύ[σ]ητε in 20.31, see any major commentary.

69   Others use the term 'focalization' (Rimmon-Kenan, *Narrative Fiction*, p. 72; Tolmie, *Jesus' Farewell*, p. 170).

70   Stephen D. Moore, *Literary Criticism and the Gospels: The Theoretical Challenge* (New Haven, CT: Yale University Press, 1989), p. 181.

71   James L. Resseguie, *The Strange Gospel: Narrative Design and Point of View in John* (BIS, 56; Leiden: Brill, 2001), p. 1 (original emphasis).

72   I observe that many scholars who have studied the Johannine characters have not discussed the ideological or evaluative point of view of John's Gospel, with the result that the characters' responses to Jesus have not been evaluated. For a critique of the few who do connect the Johannine characters with the Gospel's worldview and evaluative point of view (Alan Culpepper, James Resseguie, Colleen Conway, Jo-Ann Brant), see Bennema, 'Theory of Character', pp. 412–14.

73   With regard to Mark's Gospel, for example, I suggest that we evaluate the characters in the light of *discipleship* – one of the Gospel's central themes. So, the reader must discern the extent to which the various characters exemplify true discipleship, as the author defines it in his Gospel.

in a personal allegiance to Jesus.[74] It is impossible, however, to quantify such a belief-response, i.e., I cannot determine how much authentic understanding is adequate. Instead, I seek to determine whether or not a character's response is adequate by discerning the author's (implicit or explicit) evaluation of this response, which relates to his evaluative point of view. Once we know what, for the author, constitutes an adequate belief-response, we can evaluate the character's response to Jesus. For this we must also take into account the author's worldview. The author of John's Gospel operates with a dualistic worldview where, ultimately, people either accept or reject Jesus. This implies that for the author the characters' responses are either adequate or inadequate. In short, *we must evaluate the Johannine characters in terms of their response to Jesus, in keeping with the author's evaluative point of view, purpose, concept of belief and dualistic worldview*. Let me explain this further.

As we analyse the Johannine characters, we must be conscious of the author's evaluative point of view, which is his appraisive commentary on the story that operates at the level of narrative. As the Johannine characters interact with Jesus, the author evaluates their responses according to his ideology and point of view, and communicates this to the reader with the intention that the reader should embrace it.[75] Since the author has written his Gospel with a specific purpose in mind (20.31), his evaluative point of view is directly related to the purpose and worldview of the Gospel. Stephen Moore succinctly captures the dynamic between purpose and point of view in John's Gospel:

> Johannine characterization . . . is entirely christocentric. Jesus is a static character in the Fourth Gospel . . . The functions of the other characters are to draw out various aspects of Jesus' character by supplying personalities and situations with which he can interact, and to illustrate a spectrum of alternative responses to him . . . Such characterizations are strategically oriented toward the reader, pushing him or her also toward a decisive response to Jesus.[76]

Similarly, Mark Stibbe asserts that

> The narrator works obviously . . . to coax the reader round to the point of view or ideological stance which he embraces. That point of view is the enlightened post-resurrectional understanding of Jesus as the Messiah, the Son of God, and it is this understanding which undergirds the narrator's rhetorical strategy expressed in John 20.31.[77]

---

74   Cornelis Bennema, *The Power of Saving Wisdom: An Investigation of Spirit and Wisdom in Relation to the Soteriology of the Fourth Gospel* (WUNT, II/148; Tübingen: Mohr Siebeck, 2002), pp. 124–33; idem, 'Christ, the Spirit and the Knowledge of God: A Study in Johannine Epistemology', in Mary Healy and Robin Parry (eds), *The Bible and Epistemology: Biblical Soundings on the Knowledge of God* (Milton Keynes: Paternoster, 2007), pp. 119–20.

75   Cf. Culpepper, *Anatomy*, pp. 32–3, 89, 97–8.

76   Moore, *Literary Criticism*, p. 49.

77   Stibbe, *John as Storyteller*, p. 28.

The author tries to persuade his readers by communicating and recommending his values and norms to the reader, particularly in the way he portrays his characters and evaluates them. Through his portrayal of various characters, the author encourages the reader to identify with those characters or responses that are worthy of imitation and to dissociate from characters or responses that are not. The reader, therefore, must evaluate both the characters and the extent to which each character's response to Jesus is adequate. As the reader identifies with the characters, he or she must also evaluate his or her own belief-response. The author reveals his point of view in the narrative rhetoric and demands from the reader a self-evaluation and response, recommending one that corresponds to the purpose of his Gospel stated in 20.30-31.[78] As Culpepper aptly concludes:

> The affective power of the plot pushes the reader toward a response to Jesus. The characters, who illustrate a variety of responses, allow the reader to examine the alternatives. The shape of the narrative and the voice of the narrator lead the reader to identify or interact variously with each character . . . readers may place themselves in the role of each character successively while searching for the response they will choose. Through the construction of the gospel as narrative, therefore, the evangelist leads the reader toward his own ideological point of view, the response he deems preferable.[79]

The author's evaluative point of view thus corresponds to the soteriological purpose of the Gospel – to elicit faith in Jesus as the Messiah in order to have eternal life – and to his dualistic worldview in which there is scope for only two responses: acceptance or rejection. The author's evaluative point of view thus has two options – adequate and inadequate. In other words, the characters' responses to Jesus are part of a larger soteriological framework that is informed by the purpose and worldview of John's Gospel. But there is a tension. On the one hand, the author's dualistic worldview only allows for acceptance or rejection of Jesus, and hence for all responses to be either adequate or inadequate. On the other hand, the characters' responses to Jesus in John's Gospel are varied and form a broad spectrum. So how do they correspond with the dualistic scheme that John's Gospel presents? Can such diverse responses fit into the binary categories of belief and unbelief, adequate and inadequate?[80] I suggest that the characters' responses can (and should) fit into the dualistic worldview of John's Gospel as follows: the Johannine characters reflect the *human* perspective, representing the whole gamut of responses that people make in life, while from a *divine* perspective these responses are ultimately

---

78   For this paragraph I depended on Tannehill, 'Disciples', pp. 387–96. Conway also notes that John's Gospel 'pushes the reader toward a decision' ('Ambiguity', p. 324).

79   Culpepper, *Anatomy*, p. 148.

80   While Conway does not believe that the dualism of John's Gospel can contain such a range of responses ('Ambiguity', pp. 328–41), Jo-Ann Brant contends that we should not even try to fit this spectrum of responses into it (*Dialogue and Drama: Elements of Greek Tragedy in the Fourth Gospel* [Peabody, MA: Hendrickson, 2004], pp. 225–6, 259–60). For my reply to Brant, see Bennema, 'Theory of Character', p. 414.

evaluated as acceptance or rejection. The divine reality is that the world and its people are enveloped in darkness and do not know God – they are 'from below' (cf. 1.5; 8.23). In order to dispel people's darkness or lack of divine knowledge, Jesus came to the world to reveal God and to bring people into an everlasting, life-giving relationship with himself and God. People who encounter Jesus may either reject or accept him, and consequently remain part of the world below or enter the world above through a spiritual birth. The reality is that human responses to Jesus vary – they may be instant or gradual, positive or negative, consistent or haphazard, ambiguous or evident. Faced with this reality we must attempt to evaluate what John thinks would qualify someone for the new birth that brings a person into the realm of God, what kind of responses would bring and keep someone in a life-giving relationship with Jesus.[81] While evaluating the various responses as either 'adequate' or 'inadequate', I refrain from plotting the characters' responses along a continuum of faith because that would assume some sort of rating. Who can decide whether testifying about Jesus, following him or remaining with him is closer to the ideal, or whether antipathy is worse than apathy?[82]

After this rather elaborate explanation for why a character's response to Jesus is the first criterion for character evaluation, I briefly introduce a second criterion for evaluating the Johannine characters, namely their relation to the plot.[83] If 'plot' is the logical and causal order of events in a narrative, the plot of John's Gospel evolves around the revelation of the Father and Son in terms of their identity, character, mission and relationship, and people's response to this revelation.[84] The Gospel's plot is shaped by the author's aim of persuading

---

81   For an overview of my evaluation of the responses of the Johannine characters to Jesus, see Bennema, *Encountering Jesus*, pp. 204–6. In a recent review, David Ball criticizes my theory, saying it is 'weakened by categorizing all belief responses as "adequate" or "inadequate". This does not effectively account for the complexity of characters such as Nicodemus' (*JSNT* 33.5 [2011], p. 70). Unfortunately, Ball has misunderstood me on this point. We must distinguish between what happens at the story level and the narrative level. At the story level, the author does not resolve whether Nicodemus makes an adequate belief-response – while he is clearly attracted to Jesus, Nicodemus neither accepts nor rejects him, remaining ambiguous throughout. At the narrative level, however, the author informs his reader that as a belief-response such an attitude is not an option. The author is not negative about Nicodemus *per se* but about his response; he wants his readers to evaluate the character's *response* to Jesus rather than the character. Hence, the categories adequate/inadequate have nothing to do with the character's complexity (or lack of it) but with the representative value of his response for the reader. For an analysis of Nicodemus, see Bennema, *Encountering Jesus*, pp. 83–4.

82   This is the difficulty we have with Culpepper's taxonomy, ranking the various belief-responses of the characters (*Anatomy*, pp. 146–8).

83   I am grateful to David Ball for drawing my attention to this in his review of my book (*JSNT* 33.5 [2011], p. 70). For brief discussions on the relation between character and plot, see Bennema, 'Theory of Character', pp. 389–90; Nicolas Farelly, *The Disciples in the Fourth Gospel: A Narrative Analysis of their Faith and Understanding* (WUNT, II/290; Tübingen: Mohr Siebeck, 2010), pp. 164–7.

84   Cf. Culpepper, *Anatomy*, pp. 79–98; Andrew T. Lincoln, *The Gospel According to Saint John* (BNTC, 4; London: Continuum and Peabody, MA: Hendrickson, 2005), pp. 11–12; Farelly, *Disciples*, pp. 168–76.

the reader to believe that Jesus is the Christ and the source of everlasting life
or salvation (20.31).[85] Hence, the extent to which the Johannine characters for
instance reveal Jesus' identity and respond to him also indicates the extent to
which they advance the plot.

Once we have evaluated the Johannine characters in terms of their response
to Jesus and their role in the plot, we must determine each character's
significance for today. Since the author of John's Gospel seeks to win his
readers over to his point of view using a broad array of characters that interact
with Jesus, we must reflect on how these characters and their responses have
representative value for readers in other contexts and eras. It was Raymond
Collins who, in 1976, dubbed the characters in John's Gospel as 'representative
figures'. He argued that John has definitely typecast the various characters
(they have characteristic traits) in order to represent a particular type of
belief-response to Jesus.[86] Culpepper significantly advanced the paradigmatic
function of Johannine characters, producing an extensive continuum of
belief-responses.[87] Although Collins and Culpepper have rightly noticed the
representative value of the Johannine characters, they have wrongly concluded
that the author reduces his characters to their belief-responses and hence to
types.[88] I propose that a character's typical belief-response need not reduce
the character to a type. I believe I have amply demonstrated in my book that
many Johannine characters are complex, able to change and show personality
or even individuality. Yet, while many Johannine characters cannot be reduced
to 'types', their belief-responses can – it is the character's *response* to Jesus
that is 'typical'.[89] I contend that the author has presented an array of responses
to Jesus that can be found in any time and context – they are human responses.
Even so, I contend that the representative value across cultures and time lies in
the *totality* of each character – traits, development *and* response.

Hence, we must carefully distinguish between evaluating the character's
response and gauging the representative value of the total character. On the one
hand, the author urges the reader to evaluate the character's typical response
to Jesus as either adequate or inadequate rather than the character itself. The
author is not warning us to dissociate from Nicodemus as a character as much

85   Cf. Culpepper, *Anatomy*, p. 98.
86   Raymond F. Collins, 'Representative Figures', in idem, *These Things Have Been
Written: Studies on the Fourth Gospel* (Louvain: Peeters/Grand Rapids: Eerdmans, 1990), pp.
1–45 (8).
87   Culpepper, *Anatomy*, pp. 101–48.
88   Many still subscribe to the views of Collins and Culpepper. Neyrey, for example,
writes that '[i]t is now accepted wisdom to examine the Johannine characters as representative of
some trait important to the group or along some continuum of responses to Jesus or according to
the choices made concerning Jesus' (*Gospel*, p. 6).
89   We must note that a typical response is not necessarily restricted to one character –
characters displaying completely different traits may have the same response: e.g., defection is
seen in some disciples in 6.60-66 but also in Peter and Judas; and misunderstanding occurs with
both the Twelve and the crowd. Conversely, a character is not limited to one response: e.g., Peter
responds both adequately and inadequately.

as from his response to Jesus. Nor are we to judge Peter harshly. Peter is far from perfect, shifting between adequate responses (his confessions in 6.68-69 and 21.15-17) and inadequate ones (his misunderstandings in 13.6-10 and 18.10-11; his denial; his petulant query about the Beloved Disciple in 21.20-22), but he is (and remains) firmly at Jesus' side (cf. his restoration in 21.15-19 after his temporary defection). Admittedly, in the cases of Judas and 'the Jews' it would be difficult to differentiate between character and response since both are negative or inadequate throughout the Gospel with little hope of change. Thus, we cannot always clinically separate characters from their responses – a character's response corresponds with who that character is.[90] On the other hand, the Johannine characters are representative figures in that they have a symbolic or illustrative value beyond the narrative but not in a reductionist, 'typical' sense. The reader is invited to identify with (aspects of) one or more of the characters, learn from them and then make his or her own response to Jesus – preferably one that the author approves of. Conversely, the reader may already have made a response to Jesus and can now evaluate that response against those of the characters.[91]

IV. Conclusion

The lack of scholarly consensus on how to study characters has led me to develop a comprehensive, non-reductionist theory of character. Underlying my theory of character is the belief that character in ancient and modern literature is more alike than different and hence, with proper caution, we can use modern literary methods to analyse character in ancient narratives. I have suggested a three-dimensional approach to understanding the Johannine characters. First, I study character in text and context, using information in the text and other sources. Second, I analyse and classify the Johannine characters along three continua (complexity, development, inner life), and plot the resulting character on a continuum of degree of characterization (from agent to type to personality to individuality). Third, I use two criteria for character evaluation. I evaluate the characters in terms of their response to Jesus, in keeping with the author's point of view, purpose, concept of belief and dualistic worldview. I also evaluate the characters regarding their role in the Gospel's plot. After having arrived at a comprehensive understanding of the Johannine characters, I seek to determine their representative value for today. Although I have

90   In a recent work, Ruth Sheridan wonders whether I might have 'cordoned off' too neatly the characters' responses from the characters themselves (*Retelling Scripture: 'The Jews' and the Scriptural Citations in John 1:19–12:15* [BIS, 110; Leiden: Brill, 2012], p. 82). This is not my intention. What I suggest is that we approach characters wholistically, and if there is anything 'typical' it is their response rather than their totality – the latter is in most cases too complex to typify.

91   For an attempt to indicate the contemporary representative value of the various Johannine characters, see Bennema, *Encountering Jesus*, pp. 209–10.

related this theory to John's Gospel thus far, I contend it can be extended to the Synoptic Gospels and Acts.

The study of Johannine characters is not merely a cognitive task but also involves the volitional and affective aspects of the reader's personality because these characters resemble people. Using their choices, the author urges the reader also to choose. Besides, the representative value of the Johannine characters for today challenges and affects the contemporary reader at various levels. Like the Johannine characters, people present a broad spectrum of responses to Jesus, but in keeping with the Johannine author's dualism, their responses will eventually (probably only at the Parousia) be distilled or crystallize to two basic categories – acceptance and rejection. For the Johannine author, people have either accepted or rejected Jesus, they are either 'from below' or 'from above', they belong either to God's family or to the devil's. At the same time, life is complex, unstable and ambiguous, and so are people. Even those who have an adequate belief-response to Jesus and enter into a saving relationship with him and God rarely have consistent or stable belief-responses throughout their lives. People have doubts, struggles, fluctuations or lapses in faith, and may even defect. In real life, a believer's relationship with Jesus rarely shows neat, linear development. The complexity (and sometimes apparent absurdity) of life causes people to shift or change, perhaps by acquiring new traits, adding to or replacing existing ones. A person's faith is often not consistent or progressive; circumstances may generate critical questions, create doubt and cause a shift in faith. Yet, I contend that ambiguity, polyvalence and shifting in a person's character and faith can take place within a world of absolutes that allows only light or darkness, acceptance or rejection, belief or unbelief. The Twelve, for example, are firmly on Jesus' side from the beginning, but they often misunderstand him and fail to grasp important aspects of discipleship. While Peter also remains on Jesus' side, he is unstable, shifting between adequate and inadequate responses. Since characters resemble people, the array of Johannine characters and their responses to Jesus correspond to people and their choices in real life in any generation and culture. The Johannine author thus seeks to challenge the Gospel's readers, past and present, about where they stand in relation to Jesus. So, even today, the reader of John's Gospel, like the characters in the story, will encounter this Jesus – and must respond.

Chapter 4

EYEWITNESS TESTIMONY AND THE CHARACTERS IN THE FOURTH GOSPEL

Judith Christine Single Redman

I. Introduction

'No character in a book is a real person. Not even if he is in a history book and his name is Ulysses S. Grant'[1] or she is in a history book and her name is Margaret Thatcher. It is, however, clear that some characters are pure fiction, some are quite accurate representations of reality and others still are somewhere in between. This essay examines the contributions made by theories of character and characterization and the work of psychologists on eyewitness testimony and human memory to our understanding of where along this continuum the characters in the Gospel according to John might fall.

It is clear that the author of the Fourth Gospel is a much more gifted storyteller than are the authors of the Synoptics.[2] In its pages, characters come alive. We are not just told that the man born blind had an encounter with the Jewish authorities. We learn that he had a mischievous sense of humour that caused him to ask them 'Why do you want to hear it again? Do you also want to become his disciples?' (9.27).[3] Martha tells Jesus not just that her brother has been dead for four days, but 'already there is a stench' (11.39).

The Fourth Gospel contains the claim (in 21.24 and slightly more obliquely in 19.35) that its author is the disciple Jesus loved, an eyewitness to the events it sets out, and that his testimony is true. If we accept this at face value, what does it mean? A recent article by James Charlesworth demonstrates that there is a returning confidence among scholars that the Fourth Gospel contains historically accurate material as well as theological reflections about Jesus.[4] Richard Bauckham says that the eyewitnesses to Jesus life and ministry 'remained the living and active guarantors of the traditions' in whose name

---

1   Robert Scholes, *Elements of Fiction* (New York: Oxford University Press, 1968), p. 17.
2   The author will be referred to as John, but no attempt will be made to determine his identity.
3   The English translation used throughout is the New Revised Standard Version.
4   James H. Charlesworth, 'The Historical Jesus in the Fourth Gospel: A Paradigm Shift?', *JSHJ* 8 (2010), pp. 3–46.

they were transmitted,[5] and that '[t]estimony offers us . . . a theological model for understanding the Gospels as the entirely appropriate means of access to the historical reality of Jesus'.[6]

This essay looks at what level of historical reality of Jesus we might access through the Fourth Gospel. In doing so, it will examine the depth of characterization and purpose of the characters in the Gospel; first-century understandings of historical method and how the Fourth Gospel fits with them; eyewitness testimony as an accurate tool for understanding events; and the possible role of eyewitnesses in early Christian communities.

II. Characters and Characterization

R. Alan Culpepper's 1983 *Anatomy of the Fourth Gospel*[7] clearly demonstrated that it is both possible and worthwhile to use the techniques of narrative criticism on the Fourth Gospel. Richard Burridge's contention that it belongs with the Synoptics in a specific sub-genre of the Graeco-Roman βίος – βίος Ἰησοῦ[8] seems to have gained general acceptance, but how the characters are to be understood is still a matter of discussion.[9] There is debate around the degree of characterization of the various characters and about which characters represent acceptable and unacceptable belief-responses to Jesus, but agreement that they do represent belief-responses. I intend to argue that while this is how the Church has tended to use them, it was not the intention of the Fourth Gospel's author. Rather, the author intended to show the implied reader that the heroes and heroines of the early Christian movement were ordinary, fallible human beings, empowered to do extraordinary things by their encounters with and belief in Jesus and that the reader can also access the belief in Jesus that results in life.

a. Character Theory and the Fourth Gospel

Much of the theory around character and characterization was developed with reference to novels of the past several centuries, and although it has now been

---

5   Richard Bauckham, *Jesus and the Eyewitnesses: The Gospels as Eyewitness Testimony* (Grand Rapids: Eerdmans, 2006), p. 290.

6   Bauckham, *Jesus*, p. 5.

7   R. Alan Culpepper, *Anatomy of the Fourth Gospel: A Study in Literary Design* (Philadelphia: Fortress, 1983).

8   Richard A. Burridge, *What Are the Gospels? A Comparison with Graeco-Roman Biography* (Grand Rapids: Eerdmans, 2004), pp. 213–32, see especially 231–2.

9   See Cornelis Bennema, *Encountering Jesus: Character Studies in the Gospel of John* (Milton Keynes: Paternoster, 2009), pp. 2–12 and Christopher W. Skinner, *John and Thomas: Gospels in Conflict? Johannine Characterization and the Thomas Question* (PTMS 115; Eugene, OR: Pickwick, 2009), pp. 19–41, for summaries of the various analyses to 2006–07. Bennema's own theory is presented in 'A Theory of Character in the Fourth Gospel with Reference to Ancient and Modern Literature', *BibInt* 17 (2009), pp. 375–421.

applied to a range of other types of texts, including biblical texts,[10] Gospels differ from the novels on which the theory was based in several important ways. First, the Gospels were written when narrative focused on action rather than character;[11] second, they are significantly shorter than novels; and third, they are presented as truth, not fiction. These factors influence our understanding of the methods and levels of characterization used by John.

The *action-focused narrative tradition* combined with the *relative shortness of the texts* resulted in an initial underestimation of the complexity of characters in the Fourth Gospel. Because of the minimal descriptions provided in the text, early analyses of biblical characters generally characterized them as 'flat' (following E. M. Forster's typology[12]), that is, characters who exhibit one or two characteristics and do not develop during the course of the narrative. Culpepper's work on the Fourth Gospel is no exception. He says that Jesus is the protagonist and most of the characters in the Fourth Gospel are *ficelles*,[13] typical characters existing to serve a specific plot function and possibly carrying a great deal of representative or symbolic value. The rest are background characters.[14]

Fred Burnett maintains that the reading conventions for character construction in ancient literature create problems for the modern critic, who equates indirect characterization from the actions, words and relationships with flatness. It is, he says, nevertheless possible to infer character from these.[15] Adele Berlin uses examples from Hebrew scripture to illustrate how character is sketched using indirect techniques[16] and her methodology can be extended to the Gospel narratives. It should also be noted that Gospels are much closer in length to a short story than a novel, so we should expect narrative in which characters are sketched rather than drawn in fine detail because the author 'cannot afford the space for leisurely analysis and sustained development of character'.[17] A good sketch can nevertheless bring its subject to life.

---

10   For application to biblical texts, see, for example, Robert Alter, *The Art of Biblical Narrative* (New York: Basic Books, 1981); Adele Berlin, *Poetics and Interpretation of Biblical Narrative* (Sheffield: Almond Press, 1983), and also Adele Berlin and Elizabeth Struthers Malbon (eds), *Semeia 63: Characterization in Biblical Literature* (Atlanta: Society of Biblical Literature, 1993).

11   Fred W. Burnett, 'Characterization and Reader Construction of Characters in the Gospels', *Semeia* 63 (1993), pp. 3–28, summarizes the Greek, Roman and Jewish literary traditions of the times.

12   E. M. Forster, *Aspects of the Novel* (New York: Harcourt, Brace and Company, 1927), pp. 75–7.

13   W. J. Harvey, *Character and the Novel* (Ithaca, NY: Cornell University Press, 1965), pp. 62–8.

14   Culpepper, *Anatomy of the Fourth Gospel*, pp. 103–4, 145.

15   Burnett, 'Characterization', pp. 4–19.

16   Berlin, *Poetics*, pp. 34–42.

17   Meyer Howard Abrams and Geoffrey Galt Harpham, *A Glossary of Literary Terms* (Boston: Wadsworth Cengage Learning, 2009), p. 332.

Burnett maintains that when examining biblical texts it is more helpful to think of degrees of characterization along a continuum, rather than of fixed categories. He uses as markers the three points proposed by Berlin: the agent, about whom nothing is known that is not essential for the plot; the type, who possesses limited and stereotypical traits and who represents a class of people with these traits; and the (fully-fledged) character, whose range of traits is broader, not necessarily representative of his/her class and about whom we know more than is necessary for the progress of the plot.[18]

Building on the work of Burnett and Berlin and that of Jewish scholar Joseph Ewen as summarized by Shlomith Rimmon-Kenan,[19] Bennema develops a tool that is potentially very useful for plotting degree of characterization along a continuum that takes into consideration three sub-continua: the degree of complexity; the level of development; and how much the reader is able to penetrate into the character's inner life. Each of these is rated on a scale from 'none' (0), through 'little' (-) and 'some' (+) to 'much' (++). His continuum has four points: (i) agent, actant or walk-on; (ii) type, stock or flat character; (iii) character with personality; and (iv) individual or person; and he provides a table that indicates which levels of each dimension are required for a character to be scored as being at each of the four points.[20] He uses tables to set his conclusions out very clearly, but they suggest a greater level of objectivity than is actually achieved, since the upper ends of his three axes are open to subjective interpretation. The highest level of complexity is described as 'displaying a complex web of traits'; the highest level of development is 'fully developed . . . when a newly found trait replaces another or does not fit neatly into the existing set of traits, implying that the character has changed'; and the highest level of penetration into the inner life is those who 'allow us a peek inside their minds'.[21] Bennema rates Judas as ++ for both character development and inner life and Peter as ++ for development, but others might disagree.

Bennema himself is not always consistent in the way he applies his criteria, as can be seen from the fact that he rates Lazarus at 0 for complexity, development and inner life but still lists him as a type, whereas his table indicates that he should be a walk-on.[22] In addition, Bennema acknowledges the difficulty of assessing penetration into the inner life because inner life is not often directly presented in either Hebraic or Hellenic literature and only Jesus' inner life is well portrayed in the Fourth Gospel. He maintains quite credibly, however, that both the narrator and Jesus give the reader insight into the thoughts, emotions and motivations of various characters and that we occasionally receive clues from characters themselves.[23]

18   Berlin, *Poetics*, p. 23; Burnett, 'Characterization', pp. 11–15.
19   Shlomith Rimmon-Kenan, *Narrative Fiction: Contemporary Poetics* (London/New York: Methuen, 1983), pp. 41–2. Ewen's work is only available in Hebrew.
20   Bennema, *Encountering Jesus*, p. 14.
21   Ibid., p. 14.
22   Ibid., p. 203.
23   Bennema, 'Theory', pp. 405–7.

Although the descriptors used and specific conclusions reached vary, there is now general consensus that some of the characters are more complex than Culpepper originally suggested. Nicodemus acts out of type for a Pharisee by coming to see Jesus privately and by asking perceptive questions that are not designed to trick Jesus (3.1-10). He leaves without making a belief commitment and we expect to hear no more of him, but he later tries to convince the other Jewish leaders to give Jesus a hearing before condemning him (7.50-52) and then appears with one hundred pounds of spices to give Jesus' body a proper burial (19.38-42). The man born blind, whom we would expect to be uneducated, is able to engage the Pharisees in a cogent theological argument (9.1-34). The Samaritan woman acts out of type by engaging with Jesus in theological discussion in which she moves from highlighting the differences between the beliefs of her people and his and finishes by becoming a successful evangelist (4.1-42). We follow these and a number of other characters, including Peter, as their belief matures over time as a result of their encounters with Jesus and we also see how Judas turns from disciple to betrayer, despite being presented with the evidence that brought others to life-giving belief. They clearly fit better along a continuum of development than in discrete categories.

The third factor, that *Gospels are non-fiction*, is important in an analysis of the Fourth Gospel, because it places limitations on the author that are not present for the writer of fiction. Fictional characters are written so that they do what is necessary for the development of the plot and the author can imagine any events and any ending s/he wishes. The presence of eyewitnesses to historical events means this is not possible in non-fiction. What this means will be dealt with in detail later in the essay.

b. Characters in the Fourth Gospel – Representations or Real People?

In applying his theory of character to the Fourth Gospel, Culpepper concludes that the characters in the Fourth Gospel serve two primary functions: to draw out characteristics of Jesus; and to represent various responses to Jesus so that readers can see their inherent problems. He then outlines seven paradigmatic responses.[24] Bennema affirms that the Johannine characters have a representative value 'but it is the totality of the character – traits, development *and* response – that is representative across cultures and time. We cannot separate characters from their responses – a character's response corresponds to who that character is.'[25]

Bennema argues that it is these belief-responses, rather than the characters, that are reducible to types and that since the characters in the Fourth Gospel operate within a dualistic framework, the responses need to be viewed as either adequate or inadequate. Once again, he provides summaries of his assessments in tabular form, noting that characters do not necessarily have

---

24   Culpepper, *Anatomy of the Fourth Gospel*, pp. 145-8.
25   Bennema, *Encountering Jesus*, p. 208 (emphasis in original).

only one belief-response.[26] Again, however, there are no objective criteria provided for assessing whether or not a response is to be considered adequate or inadequate. He says: 'saving belief is not merely an initial adequate belief-response; it demands an ongoing belief expressed in discipleship. A person is not simply required to enter into a life-giving relationship with Jesus but also to remain in that relationship.'[27] Not all the types of adequate response that he lists could be said to do this, especially hearing Jesus' voice; being intimate with Jesus; seeking; and sympathy.[28]

Beck offers a third possibility: that the only characters whose response is adequate are those who are anonymous.[29] He highlights the fact that it is unusual for an author to provide extended narrative about anonymous characters and contends that this is done in the Fourth Gospel in order to allow readers to identify more closely with those who exhibit appropriate belief-responses. He offers two criteria for assessing an appropriate response. At the beginning of the book he states that the character whose belief-response is appropriate bears witness to the power of Jesus' words.[30] In the conclusion he offers a modification: 'Genuine discipleship in the Fourth Gospel consists of an active faith response to Jesus' word, without the prerequisite of a "sign" or any visible demonstration.'[31]

His arguments are unconvincing at a number of levels. First, the notion of allowing readers to identify more closely with appropriate belief paradigms comes from the psychology of today and would not have been part of the mindset of the first-century author. Closer identification may well be a *result* of anonymity but it is highly unlikely to have been a conscious motive. Second, the author of the Fourth Gospel states that the purpose of the book is that the reader may 'come to believe that Jesus is the Messiah, the Son of God, and that through believing . . . may have life in his name' (John 20.31). There is no textual evidence for the extra criteria that Beck imposes in order to fit the anonymous characters into his theory. Third, of the named characters, at least Mary Magdalene fits the criterion of bearing witness,[32] while Nicodemus's help with the burial and provision of 100 pounds of spices could be cast as an active faith response as might those of both Mary and Martha of Bethany. Fourth, Beck's cases for including the lame man and the woman taken in adultery as paradigms for life-giving responses are not convincing. All that we know about the woman's response is that she was able to tell Jesus that

---

26   Ibid., pp. 204–7.

27   Ibid., p. 17.

28   Ibid., pp. 206–7.

29   David R. Beck, *The Discipleship Paradigm: Readers and Anonymous Characters in the Fourth Gospel* (BIS, 27; Leiden/New York: Brill, 1997). See especially ch. 8.

30   Ibid., p. 5.

31   Ibid., p. 137.

32   Beck's *idée fixe* reaches the heights of misogyny when he states that Mary Magdalene's 'was a necessary, yet temporary role of eye-witness to the risen Jesus. There is no possibility nor need for a continuation of this role by modern readers or even later first-century readers' (cf. Beck, *Discipleship Paradigm*, p. 139).

no one was left to condemn her, while the Gospel records the man's testimony as simply that it was Jesus who healed him. Neither of these statements is evidence that the speaker achieves the stated purpose of the Gospel: believing that Jesus is the Messiah, the Son of God.

In fact, none of the anonymous characters meets Beck's criterion as stated in the conclusion. The man born blind and the lame man were both healed, Jesus told the Samaritan woman everything she had ever done and the disciple whom Jesus loved saw many signs (and more that he did not record).

It is far more likely that the anonymous characters were not named because they were not known, even by reputation, to members of the Gospel's intended audience so their names were not important. The author does not narrate in the fashion of the tedious elderly relative who insists that his or her audience keep track of the names of total strangers but instead identifies them by characteristics which are of interest to the hearer/reader and so more memorable. This makes sense of the aside to the reader in 11.2 that Mary of Bethany is the one who anointed Jesus' feet with perfume. Mary was known by reputation to members of the implied audience, but the three siblings were not personally known to them, so needed to be introduced.

Culpepper, Beck and Bennema all conclude that the characters serve representative functions, but they do not agree on what they are or on which are adequate for life-giving belief. In this, they are not alone. As Colleen Conway notes: 'Even a brief survey of the history of interpretation reveals little agreement among readers as to what each character typifies or represents. One is soon led to suspect that the proposed types are found not so much in the text, as they are in individual interpretations of the text.'[33] She maintains there is no clarity regarding what the characters represent because 'they do not line up on either side of the belief/unbelief divide'.[34] Thus, while believers down the centuries have certainly found value in casting the characters as representatives of various types of response to Jesus, it seems highly unlikely that this was the intention of the Gospel's author. If it was, he did not succeed, which is surprising in a writer of his ability.

Bennema responds to Conway by suggesting that the characters reflect the human perspective, but their responses are ultimately evaluated from the divine perspective and are considered to be either acceptance or rejection of Jesus, so it is at that point that they fit into binary categories. He argues that the Fourth Gospel 'seeks to challenge its readers, past and present, about where they stand in relation to Jesus'.[35]

What criteria within the text, though, allow readers to evaluate reliably where they stand? The text tells us that the Gospel is written so that the reader may believe that Jesus is the Messiah, the Son of God, and the Jesus of the Fourth Gospel continually exhorts people to believe, asks them if they believe

---

33   Colleen M. Conway, 'Speaking through Ambiguity: Minor Characters in the Fourth Gospel', *BibInt* 10 (2002), pp. 324–41 (328).

34   Ibid., p. 340.

35   Bennema, *Encountering Jesus*, pp. 210–11.

and records that people believed. The reader therefore simply needs to ask 'do I believe this?' and answer 'yes' or 'no', although there *is* a need to understand what it means for Jesus to be Messiah and Son of God.

Skinner argues that:

> The prologue sets the theological and literary agenda for the remainder of the Fourth Gospel. The implied reader of the Fourth Gospel is able to comprehend the meaning of Jesus's origin and mission in a way that the characters in the narrative cannot. This allows the reader to interpret and evaluate the various responses to Jesus.[36]

He concludes that belief in Jesus requires an understanding of the truths that Jesus is the Christ, the Son of God, who has come from above to reveal the Father and to be glorified on the cross and at the tomb.[37] The rest of the text seems to support this, but does it help to determine who fits into which category?

Within the text itself, only Martha (11.27) proclaims Jesus to be both Messiah and Son of God, while Andrew (1.41) and some members of the crowd (7.31) proclaim him to be the Messiah and the Samaritan woman asks if he might be (4.29) but in a way that expects the answer 'no'. John the Baptist (1.34) and Nathaniel (1.49) proclaim him to be the Son of God, Thomas calls him 'my Lord and my God' and the man born blind believes in him as ὁ υἱὸς τοῦ ἀνθρώπου – the Son of Humankind.

Thus, if we understand the criteria in John 20.31 as both/and, the only person who qualifies as having life-giving belief is Martha. If we understand them as either/or, an odd collection of others is added, none of them known leaders of the early Church. Using Skinner's criteria no one can be demonstrated as having achieved life-giving belief before the end of the narration period, although clearly the author of the Gospel has achieved this status by the time of writing, yet he is such an undeveloped figure that he surely cannot be the only example of life-giving faith. Some of the others must surely also qualify.

Since (almost) everyone in the Gospel fails the orthodox belief test as defined by the Gospel, it would seem that John did *not* intend the characters in the Gospel to be representations of effective and ineffective belief-responses against which readers could judge either themselves or anyone else. It is more likely that his purpose really was, as stated in the text, to provide an account of Jesus' life for his audience so that each of them might 'come to believe that Jesus is the Messiah, the Son of God, and that through believing [they might] have life in his name' (John 20.31).

The text informs the reader that he was eyewitness to the events he recounts and that they are true, so we can understand that we have true stories about real people. They are both men and women from a range of walks of life, who did extraordinary things (both bad and good) in response to encounters with Jesus. They demonstrate that a belief that leads to life does not necessarily happen in

36   Skinner, *John and Thomas*, p. 39.
37   Ibid., p. 231.

an instant or remain constantly strong in the face of difficult life circumstances. They show that even the heroes of the movement made mistakes along the way – including being so afraid for their own safety that they denied their faith – but that most were able to recover.

John's implied audience had readily available knowledge about what happened to most of the named characters after the Gospel ends, so there is no need for him to say which of the characters came to and continued in life-giving belief – but I contend that he never intended them to be used as yardsticks. Unlike modern authors, he is unlikely to have conceptualized his work as speaking across cultures and time. Instead, the characters demonstrate to the reader that he or she can also attain life in Jesus, and reading about them would have encouraged believers and would-be-believers living in a time of persecution. Rather than being representations of belief-responses, they serve as examples for you, the reader, of what the life that comes with belief in Jesus might involve.

The characters are not flat because their stories are those of real live people and real live people are not flat. They do not necessarily behave in ways that sit comfortably within a plot outline, and the writer of historical narrative cannot easily dispose of the problematic behaviours because other people know they happened. They are characterized along a continuum because of the needs of the author to include more or less of their stories in order to highlight those aspects of Jesus' life, death and resurrection that will enable the reader to enter into, or continue in, life-giving belief.

c. Narrative Technique and Historical Accuracy

As indicated above, dealing with historical characters and events places some restrictions on what can and cannot be done. Adele Berlin reminds us, however, that narrative is a form of representation and the characters in biblical narrative are no more actual historical individuals than a painting of an apple is an actual piece of fruit. We can make a transfer from a representation to the real object it represents if we know the conventions of the medium, but this is not always easy to know when working with ancient literature.[38] Because of the conventions used, '*representations of reality do not always correspond in every detail to reality*'[39] and all we can know about the events reported is a subset of what actually happened – those details the author chooses to tell us. Numerous interpreters of the Gospels nevertheless seem to work on the premise that we know everything there is to know about the event and can thus form an accurate picture of it from the text.

A further problem in accessing historically accurate information from the Gospels is that the picture that the author has when writing a given text is not necessarily the one that the reader obtains from reading it. As Chatman reminds us, the reader provides 'any number of additional details' about the characters,

---

38   Berlin, *Poetics*, p. 13.
39   Ibid., p. 14 (emphasis in original).

based on the material provided for us by the author, because a narrative can never provide the same level of detail that is contained in a photograph or film or even the level of information that one gleans from being present at an event.[40] How we fill in the details depends to a significant extent on who we are and what our life experience has been – our extratexts.[41] Clearly, twenty-first-century extratexts are very different from those of the author of the Gospel or the intended audience of the book, so the details we add and the assumptions we make from them have the potential to differ greatly to those intended by the author or made by his implied audience. Thus, even a narrative that is intended to portray historical events accurately will not result in the reader forming a full, accurate understanding of what happened.

III. The Fourth Gospel as Eyewitness Testimony

a. Eyewitness Testimony?

The Fourth Gospel ends with the statement that 'This [viz., the disciple whom Jesus loved] is the disciple who is testifying to these things and has written them, and we know that his testimony is true' (21.24). The foregoing analysis indicates that the most sensible way to understand the characters in the text is as real people, often known at least by reputation to the implied audience, who encountered Jesus on real occasions. Can we believe, however, that the Gospel really is eyewitness testimony rather than a compilation of community traditions or largely the product of an author's imagination?

Compared to the Synoptic accounts of Jesus' life, the Fourth Gospel contains significantly fewer events, but these are narrated in significantly more detail, using dialogue and discourse to provide the reader with information. The narrator is omniscient and omni-communicative, providing detail that could not have been available to any of the characters within the narrative: both inside views of the characters – their thoughts and feelings – and information that cannot credibly be put into the mouths of the characters.[42] Although the identity of the narrator/author is unknown, some of the words presented as direct speech could not possibly have been heard by anyone who might conceivably be 'the disciple whom Jesus loved'. For example, there were no disciples present when Jesus first met the woman at the well, or when the man born blind or his parents were confronted by the Jewish authorities. Some of the information provided by the narrator raises other problems. For example, we are told that the parents of the man born blind were afraid of the Jewish authorities who 'had already agreed that anyone who confessed Jesus to be the Messiah would be put out of the synagogue' (9.22, see also 12.42 and 16.2),

---

40   Seymour Chatman, *Story and Discourse* (Ithaca, NY: Cornell University Press, 1978), pp. 29–30.

41   Beck, *Discipleship Paradigm*, pp. 3–4.

42   For examples, see Culpepper, *Anatomy*, pp. 18–26; Skinner, *John and Thomas*, pp. 38–9.

something that is highly unlikely to have happened until some significant time after Jesus' death.[43] These kinds of issues are easier to explain if the text is conceptualized as something other than eyewitness testimony recorded by, or at the dictation of, the eyewitnesses concerned. They could, however, be understood as minor editorial additions provided by, say, the scribe and added to a substantially eyewitness account.

In a paper published in 2010, James Charlesworth traces scholarly assessment of the likely historicity of the accounts of Jesus in the Fourth Gospel.[44] He notes that in 1832, Friedrich Schleiermacher held that it was the best source for reconstructing the life and teaching of Jesus Christ, but very soon afterwards scholarly opinion began to move towards a general consensus that it was almost devoid of any historical information. This view held sway for the vast part of the twentieth century, but in the 1990s and the first decade of this century, a number of scholars began to question this. Charlesworth cites the works of John P. Meier, Gerd Theissen and Annette Merz, Richard Bauckham, Paul N. Anderson, and D. Moody Smith as five influential opinions that offer a new paradigm which does not ignore the content of the Fourth Gospel in the search for historical information about Jesus.[45] He provides ten reasons for reassessing the putative consensus: John is theologically shaped, but he is not the only evangelist with a theology; John is not clearly dependent upon the Synoptics; John's traditions do not always postdate the Synoptics; the Synoptics are not intrinsically superior to John for historical data; the Synoptic chronology is not obviously superior to John's chronology; the Synoptic geography may intermittently presuppose John's emphasis on Judaea; John's traditions of Jesus' speeches may be grounded in pre-Synoptic traditions; Jesus' authority and high esteem are not uniquely Johannine; names and anonymity – no rules govern the transmission of traditions; and John has knowledge of pre-70 CE Judaism that is superior to the Synoptics.[46]

---

43   Raymond E. Brown, *The Gospel According to John* (AB, 29; New York: Doubleday, 1966), p. 380; Adele Reinhartz, 'The Gospel According to John', in Amy-Jill Levine and Marc Zvi Brettler (eds), *The Jewish Annotated New Testament: New Revised Standard Version Bible Translation* (Oxford/New York: Oxford University Press, 2011), pp. 152–7 (156–7).

44   Charlesworth, 'Historical Jesus'.

45   Paul N. Anderson, *The Fourth Gospel and the Quest for Jesus: Modern Foundations Reconsidered* (London: T&T Clark, 2006); Richard Bauckham, *The Testimony of the Beloved Disciple: Narrative, History, and Theology in the Gospel of John* (Grand Rapids: Baker Academic, 2007), pp. 93–112; John P. Meier, *A Marginal Jew: Rethinking the Historical Jesus* (ABRL; New York: Doubleday, 1991); D. Moody Smith, *The Fourth Gospel in Four Dimensions: Judaism and Jesus, the Gospels and Scripture* (Columbia, SC: University of South Carolina Press, 2008); Gerd Theissen and Annette Merz, *The Historical Jesus: A Comprehensive Guide* (Minneapolis: Fortress, 1998). For Bauckham, see also Bauckham, *Jesus*, pp. 358–471; idem, 'Historiographical Characteristics of the Gospel of John', *NTS* 53 (2007), pp. 17–36; idem, 'Eyewitnesses and Critical History: A Response to Jens Schröter and Craig Evans', *JSNT* 31 (2008), p. 221; idem, 'In Response to My Respondents: *Jesus and the Eyewitnesses* in Review', *JSHJ* 6 (2008), pp. 225–53.

46   Charlesworth, 'Historical Jesus', pp. 13–34.

A detailed evaluation of the above authors' arguments is outside the scope of this essay. They are, however, sufficiently cogent to make it worth asking 'If the Fourth Gospel contains significant historical material, what kind of historical material is it and how might we evaluate its accuracy?' Bauckham's answer to 'what kind of material?' is 'traditions [that] were originated and formulated by named eyewitnesses, in whose name they were transmitted and who remained the living and active guarantors of the traditions'.[47] He regularly uses the term 'eyewitness testimony' to describe the accounts of Jesus' life as they appear in all four canonical Gospels,[48] but what exactly does this mean? Eyewitness testimony is used as evidence in courts of law and popularly held to be accurate. Does understanding the Fourth Gospel as eyewitness testimony necessarily indicate that the truth being claimed by the text is the same as historical accuracy as understood by a twenty-first-century reader? Can we consider that in the dialogue and discourse we have the actual words of Jesus, or a good Greek translation of the original Aramaic conversations?

b. Jesus' Actual Words?

Bauckham's *Jesus and the Eyewitnesses* is a large book and in it he covers a huge amount of ground,[49] which makes it challenging for the reader to keep all the facets of his argument in view at once. 'Historiographical Characteristics of the Gospel of John' provides a more concise and coherent view of what he is actually claiming about the historicity of the Fourth Gospel. Drawing heavily on the work of Samuel Byrskog,[50] he argues that because of the Gospel's various characteristics, first- and second-century readers would have recognized its genre as biography – an accepted form of historiography. He uses various ancient sources to demonstrate that they would therefore expect that the author was providing them with eyewitness testimony either from the author's own experience or, where that was not possible, by interviewing eyewitnesses to the actual events and recording them. They would also have expected the author to be selective about the details provided, concentrating on the important matters and skimming over or omitting entirely those things that were unimportant. It was accepted that recording speeches was generally impracticable or impossible and that the task of the historian was to supply words that the speaker in question would have said in the given circumstances.[51]

---

47   Bauckham, *Jesus*, p. 290.
48   In addition to extended passages in *Jesus*, he also deals with it in Bauckham, 'Historiography', pp. 29–30; Bauckham, 'Eyewitnesses and Critical History, pp. 223–8; idem, 'The Fourth Gospel as the Testimony of the Beloved Disciple', in Richard Bauckham and Carl Mosser (eds), *The Gospel of John and Christian Theology* (Grand Rapids: Eerdmans, 2008), pp. 120–39; idem, 'In Response', *passim*; idem, 'The Transmission of the Gospel Traditions', *Revista Catalana de Teología* 33 (2008), pp. 377–94 (384–7).
49   It contains over 500 pages of argument.
50   Samuel Byrskog, *Story as History – History as Story: The Gospel Tradition in the Context of Ancient Oral History* (WUNT, 123; Tübingen: Mohr Siebeck, 2000).
51   See especially Bauckham, 'Historiography', pp. 30–1.

In other words, in saying that the Fourth Gospel is historiography, Bauckham is arguing that it is as historically accurate as other texts from the period, not that it is word-for-word infallible. In response to David Catchpole's review of *Jesus and the Eyewitnesses* he says: 'Eyewitnesses and others exercised the ordinary freedom allowed in the ancient world to anyone who told a story, the freedom, that is, to tell a good story effectively and to vary the details around a stable core. Historians and biographers did this all the time.'[52] This method has much in common with what the author of fiction does in providing characters with thoughts, words and actions that contribute to the furtherance of the plot. With respect to the discourses and dialogues, Bauckham is suggesting that the gist is likely to be accurate, but not necessarily the details, let alone the words themselves.

Bauckham further maintains that many of Jesus' sayings were remembered either as independent aphorisms and parables or attached to short narratives in the form of *chreiai* or pronouncement stories, but that these were 'carefully composed distillations of his teaching, put into memorable form for hearers to take away with them' rather than the entire content of any teaching session.[53] When the Synoptics talk about Jesus teaching a crowd, as for example in Mark 4.1, it is likely his teaching was more discursive than the three parables that Mark attributes to him. The presentation of a small number of aphorisms and/ or parables is a particular way of representing Jesus' teaching. Bauckham contends that John has chosen to represent Jesus' teaching in the form of discourses and dialogues, which provide a more realistic representation of the way Jesus taught but are still artificial in their own way and require the author to put far more words into Jesus' mouth.[54]

c. Access to the Historical Jesus through Eyewitness Testimony

We have built a picture of text that provides information about Jesus that is as historically accurate as we can expect from material of the time, telling us about the real activities of real people. We are aware that the words of the characters are very unlikely to be the actual words spoken by them, but that they would be in keeping with what they are likely to have said. What can be said about the remainder of the information? At what level can it be said to be historically accurate?

In a second paper published since *Jesus and the Eyewitnesses*, Bauckham argues that the Gospel writers were writers of oral history, rather than recorders and users of oral tradition, and that the early Christian movement was interested in preserving the traditions about Jesus faithfully, although not necessarily verbatim. He says that 'in the case of narratives, what was expected to remain constant was the main structure and core elements, while inessential detail

---

52   Bauckham, 'In Response', p. 236.
53   Bauckham, 'Historiography', p. 32.
54   Ibid., pp. 32–3.

could vary, resulting, among other things, in shorter or longer versions'.[55] He argues for two roles for eyewitnesses: they provided the information contained in the tradition, and they also acted as 'accessible sources and authoritative guarantors' of these traditions throughout their lives. In other words, if the versions in circulation throughout the communities began to vary at the level of main structure and core elements, the eyewitnesses would correct them. Bauckham says that as well as the major eyewitnesses such as the disciples, who were able to testify about Jesus as people having been with him from the beginning, there were many minor eyewitnesses who had been part of one encounter with Jesus, each concerned with ensuring that the pieces of the tradition to which they were eyewitnesses remained accurate.[56] He concludes: 'we should not envisage the Gospels as separated from the eyewitnesses by a long period of anonymous community tradition, but as based on the testimony of the eyewitnesses, often directly, rarely at more than two stages of transmission removed. The Gospels are oral history based on and even incorporating the testimony of eyewitnesses to the events.'[57]

We, therefore, need to examine the question of how accurately eyewitnesses remember the events they witness both in the short and long term. My own survey of the psychological literature on eyewitness testimony and human memory, summarized in 'How Accurate are Eyewitnesses?',[58] indicates that despite the popular conception that eyewitness testimony is accurate, this is only true within some fairly restrictive parameters. Robert McIver's recent book *Memory, Jesus and the Synoptic Gospels* provides more detailed coverage of much of the material, although he is somewhat more optimistic about the end result.[59]

Daniel Schacter lists seven problems that can lead to inaccuracy in memory over time: transience, absent-mindedness, blocking, misattribution, suggestibility, bias, and persistence.[60] McIver argues that transience, suggestibility and bias have the greatest potential to affect the accuracy of Gospel accounts.[61] I would add that both absent-mindedness and misattribution can make significant contributions in some situations.

1. Absent-mindedness is a problem that occurs when information is being encoded, or stored in memory. In any situation, the amount of information available is too great for it all to be stored in our memories, so we select, usually unconsciously, what we will remember. If information is not encoded initially, it cannot be recalled. Normally the stimuli that we encode are those

---

55   Bauckham, 'Transmission', pp. 383–4.

56   Ibid., pp. 384–9.

57   Ibid., p. 393.

58   Judith Christine Single Redman, 'How Accurate are Eyewitnesses? Bauckham and the Eyewitnesses in the Light of Psychological Research', *JBL* 129 (2010), pp. 177–97.

59   Robert K. McIver, *Memory, Jesus, and the Synoptic Gospels* (Atlanta: Society of Biblical Literature, 2011).

60   Daniel L. Schacter, *The Seven Sins of Memory: How the Mind Forgets and Remembers* (Boston: Houghton Mifflin, 2001), pp. 1–11, provides an overview.

61   McIver, *Memory*, p. 22.

that are noticeable, sudden, surprising, interesting; those that are potentially important; and those that are continuous with what has already happened.[62] Unfortunately, they do not always include mundane but useful information such as where we put our car keys or reading glasses. What qualifies as interesting, surprising and potentially important varies with the personalities and interests of witnesses and with their life experiences,[63] and what witnesses expect to see or hear can affect the way they perceive an event.[64] What a witness expects to see or hear can be shaped by culture, stereotypes, past experience, or personal prejudice.[65] Thus, what is stored in the memory about a particular event will vary from person to person. Among a group of eyewitnesses there might be a number of different but accurate memories of the same event, in the same way that there might be a number of different but equally accurate maps of the same locale.[66] Thus, to borrow from the courtroom, while what we remember may well be the truth, it will never be the whole truth. There is also no guarantee that it will be nothing but the truth.

Once stored, memories are subject to deterioration and change over time, both during storage and retrieval. The remaining problems occur during the storage and retrieval period.

2. Transience refers to the fact that over time the amount of detail that can be recalled about a particular event declines. The decline is very rapid in the short term, with measurable loss occurring within a few days or even hours of an event. The rate of loss slows and after several years almost flattens. The total loss and the point at which it flattens varies depending on the type of information and what kind of memory support is provided. Lists of nonsense words are forgotten more rapidly than words that make sense, and material that is rehearsed regularly over a learning period is, in general, remembered better than that which is only experienced once.[67]

One exception to this is for events that, while experienced once, have a profound effect on the life of the person concerned. The original research

---

62   Ralph Norman Haber and Lyn Haber, 'Experiencing, Remembering and Reporting Events', *Psychology, Public Policy, and Law* 6 (2000), pp. 1057–97 (1060–62); Elizabeth F. Loftus, *Eyewitness Testimony* (Cambridge, MA: Harvard University Press, 1979), pp. 25–7.

63   Haber and Haber, 'Experiencing', pp. 1059–64; Ulric Neisser, 'Memory: What are the Important Questions?', in Ulric Neisser (ed.), *Memory Observed: Remembering in Natural Contexts* (San Francisco: W. H. Freeman, 1982), pp. 3–19 (16).

64   Jerome S. Bruner and Leo Joseph Postman, 'On the Perception of Incongruity: A Paradigm', *Journal of Personality* 18 (2) (1949), pp. 206–23.

65   Gordon W. Allport and Leo Joseph Postman, *The Psychology of Rumor* (New York: Henry Holt and Co., 1947), pp. 97, 102; Bruner and Postman, 'Perception'; Albert H. Hastorf and Hadley Cantril, 'They Saw a Game: A Case Study', *Journal of Abnormal and Social Psychology/Journal of Abnormal Psychology* 49 (1) (1954), pp. 129–34; Loftus, *Eyewitness Testimony*, pp. 37–42.

66   Sue Campbell, 'Our Faithfulness to the Past: Reconstructing Memory Value', *Philosophical Psychology* 19 (2006), pp. 361–80 (365).

67   McIver, *Memory*, pp. 21–40, provides a detailed summary of research in this area, together with graphs of rates of information loss over time.

in this area was done by Brown and Kulik,[68] who examined the very vivid and long-lasting memories of the circumstances in which people first learned about very surprising and consequential or emotionally arousing events and coined the term 'flashbulb memory' to describe them. David Pillemer maintains that personal trauma, critical incidents and moments of insight can also generate this kind of memory, which he calls personal event memories.[69] These are memories of an event that took place at a specific time in a specific location; contain a detailed account of the person's own circumstances; are verbal accounts accompanied by sensory images; are from a short rather than an extended period; and are believed to be truthful by the person remembering them.[70] Research is inconsistent about whether or not these memories *are* retained more effectively than normal memories, probably because research that finds that the deterioration level over time is similar to that for ordinary events has not distinguished between genuine flashbulb-style memories (those meeting the five criteria) and ordinary event memories for extraordinary events.[71] Memory enhancement in these circumstances is likely to happen because those who experience these kinds of dramatic events tend to rehearse them frequently in the time close to the event, either by talking about them with others or by turning them over in their minds. The Johannine encounters with Jesus would surely engender personal event memories, for which detail is more likely to be remembered for longer.

Typically, what is remembered fifty years on is not much less than what is remembered five years on, but the loss in detail in the first few years is significant. Thus, the time between Jesus' ministry and the writing of the Fourth Gospel does not necessarily indicate that the memory of eyewitnesses consulted for it would have been significantly less accurate than those consulted when the Synoptics were written some years earlier.

3. *Suggestibility* refers to changes that can occur as a result of questions asked and suggestions made when a person is trying to recall information. It is a function of a person being part of a community. Talking to other people who also witnessed the event may change how each individual recalls it, and it is unbelievable that groups of people touched by Jesus' ministry did not talk to each other about it. A group of people working together will be able to retrieve more details of a particular event than any one member of the group working alone, and group memory appears to be more stable over time than individual memory.[72] Sometimes, however, things that did not happen may be incorporated

68   Roger Brown and James Kulik, 'Flashbulb Memories', *Cognition* 5 (1977), pp. 73–99.

69   David B. Pillemer, *Momentous Events, Vivid Memories* (Cambridge, MA: Harvard University Press, 1998), pp. 25–62.

70   Pillemer, *Momentous Events*, pp. 50–1.

71   Antonietta Curci and Olivier Luminet, 'Follow-up of a Cross-National Comparison on Flashbulb and Event Memory for the September 11th Attacks', *Memory* 14 (2006), pp. 329–44.

72   Mary Susan Weldon and Krystal D. Bellinger, 'Collective Memory: Collaborative and Individual Processes in Remembering', *Journal of Experimental Psychology: Learning, Memory, and Cognition* 23 (1997), pp. 1160–75; Mary Susan Weldon, 'Remembering as a Social Process', *The Psychology of Learning and Motivation: Advances in Research and Theory* 40 (2000), pp. 67–120.

because one person in a group made a mistake but talks about it in a confident way.[73] Memory can also be changed because of the way someone is questioned. Questions that ask when, where, or how something happened or that anticipate a particular answer may elicit answers that provide more detail, but the detail is not necessarily accurate.[74] Finally, if only some aspects of an incident are retold, the aspects that are not retold are much more likely to be forgotten. In conversation, speakers may well wish to catch and maintain the interest of their audience, fill in gaps in their memories so that the story flows more smoothly, or to justify their actions, and they will alter their accounts accordingly.[75] Research indicates that 'what people remember about events may be the story they last told about those events'[76] and what they last told may well be only those aspects that they thought their audience wanted to hear. Thus, the effects of suggestibility would have both positive and negative consequences for accuracy of the eyewitness testimony that formed the Fourth Gospel.

4. Bias comes about because of the effect that our current knowledge and beliefs has on how we remember our pasts. Schacter says 'we often edit or entirely rewrite our previous experiences—unknowingly and unconsciously—in the light of what we now know or believe. The result can be a skewed rendering of a specific incident, or even of an extended period in our lives, which says more about how we feel *now* than about what happened *then*.'[77] In addition, most people, most of the time, are not concerned about preserving an accurate record of what happened in their past. Memories help people to make sense of the world and of themselves and the stories they tell tend to focus on what happened to them and what that event meant to them.[78] The fact that all the Gospels were written from a post-resurrection perspective may have had a significant effect on the eyewitness testimony before it became stabilized.

---

73   Robert Buckhout, 'Eyewitness Testimony', in Ulric Neisser (ed.), *Memory Observed: Remembering in Natural Contexts* (San Francisco: W. H. Freeman, 1982), pp. 116–25 (122); Gerald Echterhoff, William Hirst and Walter Hussy, 'How Eyewitnesses Resist Misinformation: Social Postwarnings and the Monitoring of Memory Characteristics', *Memory & Cognition*, 33 (5) (2005), pp. 770–82; Loftus, *Eyewitness Testimony*, pp. 56–8, 72–4; Helen M. Paterson and Richard I. Kemp, 'Comparing Methods of Encountering Post-Event Information: The Power of Co-Witness Suggestion', *Applied Cognitive Psychology* 20 (2006), pp. 1083–99; Henry L. Roediger, Michelle L. Meade and Erik T. Bergman, 'Social Contagion of Memory', *Psychonomic Bulletin and Review* 8 (2001), pp. 365–71; Daniel B. Wright, Gail Self and Chris Justice, 'Memory Conformity: Exploring Misinformation Effects When Presented by Another Person', *British Journal of Psychology* 91 (2000), pp. 189–202.

74   Julian A. E. Gilbert and Ronald P. Fisher, 'The Effects of Varied Retrieval Cues on Reminiscence in Eyewitness Memory', *Applied Cognitive Psychology* 20 (2006), pp. 723–39; Loftus, *Eyewitness Testimony*, pp. 94–7; Schacter, *Sins*, pp. 112–37; Rachel Sutherland and Harlene Hayne, 'The Effect of Postevent Information on Adults' Eyewitness Reports', *Applied Cognitive Psychology* 15 (2001), pp. 249–63.

75   Haber and Haber, 'Experiencing', pp. 1067–8.

76   Elizabeth J. Marsh, 'Retelling is Not the Same as Recalling: Implications for Memory', *Current Directions in Psychological Science* 16 (2007), pp. 16–20.

77   Schacter, *Sins*, p. 5.

78   Haber and Haber, 'Experiencing', pp. 1065–6.

5. Misattribution results in attributing a memory to the wrong source. People are not very accurate in their ability to remember whether a memory is of something they experienced or something they were told about.[79] There is also evidence that many people do not remember previously held attitudes or beliefs when they come to a new position.[80] While this is not of major concern when considering the general gist of stories about Jesus, it provides a further reason to mistrust detail and could well explain some of the variation between accounts of what must surely be the same events in different Gospels.

Thus, as with the words of the dialogues and discourses, so too with the details of the narrative. If we take the claims of the text at face value, we cannot rely on the details not to have been supplied from the imagination of either John, to improve the flow of the story, or his informants in an effort to please, although the ongoing presence of the eyewitnesses is likely to have ensured that they remained consistent with what actually happened.

IV. Drawing the Threads Together

The author of the Fourth Gospel is an expert storyteller, able to make his characters come alive and grab the imagination of the reader. If we accept what the text tells us, his life of Jesus is written so that you, the reader, can believe in Jesus as the Messiah, the Son of God, and that in believing you may have life in his name. It is the testimony of the disciple whom Jesus loved and is attested as truth by his community. Numerous attempts have been made to fit the characters in it into the binary world of darkness and light with which the Gospel begins, but none of them are particularly convincing, because the characters behave like real people, unable to be contained in binary categories.

I have argued that it was not the author's intent in writing to provide the reader with yardsticks against which to judge people's belief, whether their own or others', but rather to provide examples for the reader of what a belief in Jesus that brings life might look like in real life. In order to do so, the author selected from among the information available that which best served his case.

Recently, a number of scholars, including Richard Bauckham, have begun to rehabilitate the Fourth Gospel as a source of historically accurate material within the theologized. Bauckham has provided evidence that the methodology used by John would have been very similar to that of secular historians of his time and has looked at eyewitness testimony as a method of accessing historically accurate material about the life of Jesus. By his own admission, however, this can only ever be argued at the level of main structure and core

---

79   See, for example, Haber and Haber, 'Experiencing', pp. 1068–70; Loftus, *Eyewitness Testimony*, pp. 54–79; Paterson and Kemp, 'Comparing'; Schacter, *Sins*, pp. 88–111.

80   George R. Goethals and Richard F. Reckman, 'Recalling Previously Held Attitudes', *Journal of Experimental Social Psychology* 9 (1973), pp. 491–501; Marcia K. Johnson, Shahin Hashtroudi and D. Stephen Lindsay, 'Source Monitoring', *Psychological Bulletin* 114 (1993), pp. 3–28.

elements, because the technique of the historian of the time was to select from among the information available that which s/he thought most important and to use his or her narrative skill to tell it engagingly. Narrative theory also suggests that all we can access from narrative is a representation of historical people, not real persons.

The notion of accuracy comes from a forensic understanding of testimony where the testimony is used as evidence on which to judge whether a person is innocent or guilty. If the characters of the Fourth Gospel are intended to serve as examples of lives of faith rather than as yardsticks against which to judge belief, then perhaps the testimony is not intended as forensic testimony but as inspirational testimony? The telling of people's stories is a time-tested effective technique for changing what people believe. While we can, indeed, access accurate historical information from the Gospel, and while we can trust that there is no deliberate intent to mislead on the part of the author or his informants, we have no reliable way of separating what is accurate from what is just consistent with what really happened or from what helps the author or his informants to make sense of the world in which they were living, unless it is corroborated by external evidence. While people of faith will continue to accept it as truth, the research to date brings us no closer to being able to demonstrate that it is the whole truth and nothing but the truth, much though some Christians would like to be able to do so.

V. Conclusion

Mark's Gospel has been likened by the form critics to a haphazard collection of beads on a string, although Morna Hooker suggests that the beads might have been strung together in a deliberate order.[81] John's Gospel is more like a heavy necklace which features various precious stones held in place by a series of wires woven through and around them. Jesus is the main, central stone to which the setting draws attention. The other stones are the other characters, each displayed so that they provide the amount of information needed to present Jesus in a way that can generate life-giving belief in the reader. The wires are the narrative that provides the reader with information that is necessary if the reader is to develop life-giving faith, but which cannot be credibly provided by any of the characters. The wires themselves form part of the intricate pattern, but are background, not foreground, and the whole design is three-dimensional, although some parts are in higher relief than others. In the same way as a jeweller uses only enough wire to ensure that the stones that are the focus of the necklace are set securely and displayed to their fullest advantage, and selects, shapes and polishes the number of smaller stones necessary to achieve the desired effect, the author of John's Gospel only

81   Morna D. Hooker, *The Gospel According to St. Mark* (Peabody, MA: Hendrickson, 1993), p. 10.

develops each character or character group as far as is necessary to display to their fullest advantage the points that he wants to highlight. The eyewitnesses authenticated the genuineness of each stone as it was incorporated, but we must assume that none of them is the same raw material with which the author began to craft his necklace.

Chapter 5

'WHO ARE YOU?'
COMPARISON/CONTRAST AND FOURTH GOSPEL CHARACTERIZATION

Raymond F. Collins

I. Introduction

Every parent has experienced a toddler's saying 'no'. Many a parent is annoyed at hearing this word come from the mouth of a two-year-old. Toddlers, as the National Network for Child Care reminds us, have difficulty separating themselves from their parents and other people who are important to them. They try to assert themselves by saying no. Their 'no' is their way of affirming their identity as individual human beings. The affirmation of their otherness is a way of saying 'yes' to who they are.

What is true of toddlers is in some ways true of adult human beings. It is often true of literary figures as well, as the Johannine author reminds us when he describes the figure of John, witness to Jesus. The first interrogating group asks 'Who are you?' The author's John replies, 'I am not the Messiah.' 'What then? Are you Elijah?' . . . 'I am not.' 'Are you the prophet?' . . . 'No.' Then, 'Who are you?' Then, and only then, does John say, 'I am the voice of one crying out in the wilderness, "Make straight the way of the Lord".'[1]

The second interrogating group asks about the reason for John's activity if he is neither the Messiah, nor Elijah *redivivus*, nor the prophet. Responding to their questioning, John contrasts his activity of baptizing with water with the activity of one who will come after him, baptizing with the Holy Spirit. As the narrative continues, John witnesses to the one who was to come after him, declaring, 'Here is the Lamb of God' (1.29, 36).

The author of the Fourth Gospel effectively uses comparison and contrast to develop the literary profile of John the witness. The technique is an important literary device[2] not only in the Johannine author's characterization of John but

---

1   Cf. John 1.19-23. English-language texts of biblical citations are taken from the New Revised Standard Version.

2   Given the brevity of this article I will not enter into a discussion of comparison and contrast in contemporary literary theory nor will I attempt to cite every instance of its use in the Johannine narrative.

also in his portrayal of other figures throughout the Gospel. We will begin with two examples where contrast enters into the setting of the scene.

II. The Sisters of Bethany

The story of Mary, Martha and their brother Lazarus is beautifully told in 11.1–12.8.[3] The three siblings are introduced in 11.1, where Mary and Martha are introduced as sisters, that is, Martha is introduced as the sister of Mary.[4] The explicit characterization of Mary continues in the following verse which speaks of Mary as the one who anointed Jesus' feet, anticipating 12.1-8 and suggesting that Mary's action was well known in the Johannine community. It was the trait by which she was known to them. Just as Martha is introduced as Mary's sister in v. 1, so Lazarus is introduced as Mary's brother in v. 2b. Only by implication is he likewise the brother of Martha. It is Mary who has a sister and a brother.

The sisters, but not the brother, send a message to Jesus saying that the one whom you love[5] is ill. The narrative subsequently clarifies that all three siblings were loved by Jesus (11.5).[6] Martha comes to the fore in this corrective observation. Not only is she listed first among the siblings but Mary is referenced as 'her sister' without the use of her proper name.

After a discussion between Jesus and his disciples, the scene shifts to Bethany (11.17-18). To the extent that the Fourth Gospel can be seen as a drama, the shift of locale to the siblings' home village represents the beginning of a new scene in the drama. Jesus arrives in the village where many of the Jews were attempting to console the sisters, Martha and Mary, sorrowing because their brother had died. On news of Jesus' arrival, a physical separation of Martha and Mary occurs.[7] Martha goes out to meet Jesus somewhere in the

---

3   Commentators generally consider this unit to be a single narrative, as well they should. Tradition history considerations reveal that Lazarus's presence at the meal is the third element in the miracle story scheme. It is the proof of the reality of Lazarus's resurrection (cf. Mark 5.43; Luke 8.55, 24.41-43; John 21.12-13).

4   Martha's being introduced as the sister of Mary rather than as the sister of Lazarus would be contrary to the dominant cultural norms. Cf. Jo-Ann A. Brant, *John* (Paideia; Grand Rapids: Baker, 2011), p. 172. Some scholars hold that the way that Martha is introduced in v. 1 is an indication that the Martha material in the narrative is a late addition to the story. For a discussion of the pros and cons of this approach, see Urban C. von Wahlde, *The Gospel and Letters of John*, Vol. 2 (ECC; Grand Rapids: Eerdmans, 2010), pp. 512–15. The discussion is, of course, beyond the scope of a narrative reading of the text.

5   Cf. 11.36.

6   Despite 11.5, von Wahlde (*The Gospel and Letters*, Vol. 2, p. 485) writes, 'Apart from the BD . . . Lazarus is the only other figure said to be loved by Jesus.'

7   This separation belies Hylen's contention that 'John makes no explicit contrast between the two women'. Cf. Susan E. Hylen, *Imperfect Believers: Ambiguous Characters in the Gospel of John* (Louisville: Westminster John Knox, 2009), p. 87. She is, however, quite right in excluding any comparison with Luke 10.32-42, a comparison unfortunately introduced by J. Ramsey Michaels, *The Gospel of John* (NICNT; Grand Rapids: Eerdmans, 2010), p. 613 and *passim*.

The comparison has often been made throughout the years. See, for example, Barnabas

neighbourhood; Jesus had not yet arrived in the village itself (11.30). Martha's action is a token of great respect. Social custom would suggest that she continue to sit *shiva*. Mary stays home, where she continues to be consoled by the visiting Jews (11.20, 31).[8]

From v. 5, Martha is the focus of the evangelist's attention. The dialogue between Martha and Jesus in vv. 21-27 clarifies the reason. Martha takes the initiative in speaking with Jesus. Addressing Jesus as κύριε, she says, 'If you had been here, my brother would not have died' (v. 21) and affirms her trust in God and in Jesus. The purpose of the present essay precludes the necessity of any detailed exegesis of the passage. Let it only be noted that the passage employs Johannine misunderstanding, incorporates a self-revelatory ἐγώ εἰμι saying of Jesus,[9] and concludes with a formal confession of faith by Martha.

The focus on Martha that has predominated thus far in the narrative of the sisters changes in vv. 28-29. There is also a change of scene. Martha takes the initiative by calling her sister Mary,[10] who had stayed at home where she was being consoled by some Jews.[11] Preserving her privacy,[12] she tells Mary that the teacher[13] had been calling for her. This narrative detail adds an element that had previously been lacking in the narrative, namely, that Jesus had been calling for Mary.

Having told her sister that Jesus wants to see her, Martha virtually disappears from the narrative. Her movements are not mentioned. Did she lead Mary to Jesus so that Mary would know where he was? The author does not tell us. Martha reappears in the narrative at Lazarus's tomb, where she seemingly objects to the removal of the stone. 'Lord,' she says, 'already there is a stench because he has been dead for four days' (11.39). Jesus responds with a mild rebuke about her lack of sufficient faith (11.40). Martha again disappears from the narrative until she reappears as the server at the celebratory dinner in honour of Jesus six days before Passover (11.2).

On hearing from Martha that Jesus wanted to see her, Mary acts quickly (11.29, 31). Hastily she goes to Jesus, who is still somewhere beyond the confines of the village. But Mary is not alone. The Jews who have been

---

Lindars (*The Gospel of John* [NCB; London: Oliphants, 1972], pp. 385, 393); C. K. Barrett (*The Gospel According to John* [Philadelphia: Westminster, 2nd edn, 1978], p. 394), and von Wahlde (*The Gospel and Letters*, Vol. 2, pp. 526, 535).

8   Conway notes the distinction between the two sisters but observes that one must read further into the narrative to find reasons why the sisters are distinguished. Cf. Colleen M. Conway, *Men and Women in the Fourth Gospel: Gender and Johannine Characterization* (SBLDS, 167; Atlanta: Society of Biblical Literature, 1999), pp. 139–40.

9   This is the only double-predicate ἐγώ εἰμι saying in the Fourth Gospel.

10   Cf. 11.5.

11   Cf. 11.31.

12   Keener suggests that the privacy motif 'likely indicates her wish to protect Jesus; his hour had not yet come'. Cf. Craig S. Keener, *The Gospel of John*, Vol. 2 (Peabody, MA: Hendrickson, 2003), p. 845. Michaels opines that the privacy of the conversation owes to the presence of Jews in the house (cf. Michaels, *John*, p. 634).

13   Cf. 1.38; 3.2; 8.4; 13.13, 14; 20.16.

consoling her follow her, thinking that the sorrowful woman is going to the tomb. Mary has not told them where she is going. She speaks only to Jesus. On seeing Jesus she says, 'Lord, if you had been here, my brother would not have died' (11.32). The words are identical to those spoken by Mary when she arrived in Jesus' presence (11.21). At this point in the narrative, Mary seems to be on the same page as Martha. What Mary says to Jesus is the same thing as what Martha said, without, however, the profession of trust in God and Jesus that Martha had made.

The evangelist draws attention to Mary's physical demeanour in the presence of Jesus, something that he had not done in the case of Martha. He tells the reader that Mary spoke her opening words – in fact, the only words uttered by Mary in the entire narrative (11.1–12.8) – while she was kneeling at Jesus' feet. She was also weeping, as were the Jews who had followed her (11.33a). The presence of the Jews makes the encounter between Mary and Jesus a public event in a way that is different from the encounter between Martha and Jesus. The evangelist leaves the reader to wonder as to whether or not the disciples have observed either encounter.[14]

Mary appears for the second time in the final scene of the Lazarus story[15] (12.1-8). Once again the setting is the home at Bethany. The three siblings are mentioned but their relationship is not cited in the scene.[16] First named is Lazarus, apparently the owner of the home. The dwelling is identified as 'the home of Lazarus'. Lazarus is identified as the one whom Jesus had raised from the dead (12.1).[17] Martha served the dinner; Lazarus is one of those at table with Jesus. All eyes are now on Mary. Where is she? What is she doing? In response to the reader's unasked question, the still taciturn Mary appears bearing a pound of costly perfume. As a good hostess, she anoints Jesus' feet and, in an unusual gesture, dries them with her hair. Her gesture is one of humility and respect. As in 11.32, Mary is at Jesus' feet. Judas Iscariot objects to what she has done but Jesus defends Mary: 'Leave her alone. She bought it so that she might keep it for the day of my burial' (12.7).

The two women are often compared and contrasted with other figures in the Gospel narrative. Thus, Martha has been compared to Nicodemus and the Samaritan woman. The three of them initially misunderstand what Jesus says

---

14   The disciples were last mentioned in v. 16, when Thomas said to his fellow disciples 'Let us also go, that we may die with him.' The evangelist does not indicate whether or not the disciples followed through on Thomas's suggestion. They do not reappear in the narrative, though it is possible that the evangelist did not want to exclude them from the crowd present at the tomb (11.42).

15   The story is, in fact, more about the sisters than it is about Lazarus.

16   Cf. 11.1, 2, 3, 5, 19, 21, 23, 28, 32, 39.

17   Mention of this characterizing fact might appear to be superfluous. Certainly the reader of the Gospel knows that Jesus raised Lazarus from the dead. However a great amount of material has intervened, describing the plot against Jesus (11.45-57), since the description of the life-giving miracle, and a probative finale to the miracle story has not yet been given. Prior to the dinner the reader was left with Jesus' command that the dead man be unwrapped (11.44).

to them.[18] Mary has been seen as the counterpart of Judas, the true female disciple in contrast with the unfaithful male disciple.[19]

More often, however, a comparison is made between the two sisters. Frequently cited in the exegetical literature is a comment made by Alan Culpepper, who writes, 'Of the two sisters, Martha is the one with discerning faith. Mary . . . represents the response of devotion and uncalculatingly, extravagant love, and in contrast to her sister never verbalizes her faith in Jesus.'[20] More recently, Cornelis Bennema has written, 'Both sisters show similarities and dissimilarities. Both are loved by Jesus, serve Jesus, and belong to him, but where Martha shows more cognitive progress and insight, Mary seems more emotional and affective.'[21]

I would note that these comparisons of the two sisters are somewhat simplistic and tend to overlook the comparative-contrasting elements in the Johannine narrative itself, including what is perhaps the dominating element in the author's portrayal of the two sisters. That is the very fact of their being sisters. Four times the narrative describes one of the women as being sister to the other;[22] once it mentions 'the sisters' in the plural.[23] As with all kinship language, the word 'sister' (ἀδελφή) is a relational term that both links and separates two characters. The one character is not the other. She is sister to the other. Use of a relational term like 'sister' inevitably invites comparison and contrast.

The evangelist highlights the contrast throughout the narrative, especially in the dramatic physical separation of the two in 11.20. The sisters had acted in concert in v. 3. In concert they have been loved by Jesus (v. 5) and have been consoled by the Jews (v. 19) but in verse 20 their respective actions contrast them with one another. Martha goes to meet Jesus while Mary stays home.

Further contrasts are to be seen in the evangelist's description of their respective meetings with Jesus. They are similar insofar as both sisters use the same words to mildly chastise Jesus for not being present and preventing Lazarus's death (vv. 21, 32). Thereafter the similarities end.

---

18   See, for example, Francis J. Moloney, *Signs and Shadows: Reading John 5–12* (Minneapolis: Fortress, 1996), pp. 162–3.

19   Thus, Elisabeth Schüssler Fiorenza, 'A Feminist Interpretation for Liberation: Martha and Mary: Lk. 10:38-42', *Religion and Intellectual Life* 3 (1986), pp. 21–36 (32).

20   R. Alan Culpepper, *Anatomy of the Fourth Gospel: A Study in Literary Design* (Philadelphia: Fortress, 1983), pp. 141–2.

21   Cornelis Bennema, *Encountering Jesus: Character Studies in the Gospel of John* (Milton Keynes: Paternoster, 2009), p. 155. Bennema acknowledges Kitzberger for his psychologizing approach to Mary. Cf. Ingrid Rosa Kitzberger, 'Mary of Bethany and Mary of Magdala – Two Female Characters in the Johannine Passion Narrative: A Feminist, Narrative-Critical Reader-Response', *NTS* 41 (1995), pp. 564–86 (578). Scholes and Kellogg have, however, shown that ancient narratives are not concerned with the interior psychological state of a character. That is a modern concern. Cf. Robert Scholes and Robert Kellogg, *The Nature of Narrative* (New York: Oxford University Press, 1966).

22   11.1, 5, 23, 39.

23   11.3.

Martha's encounter with Jesus is apparently a private affair; Mary's is public. It takes place in the presence of the Jews. Martha is the garrulous one; Martha, the silent one. Jesus speaks to Martha but he does not speak to Mary; rather he speaks to the Jews. The evangelist focuses on Martha's words, especially her confession of faith (v. 27). He focuses on Mary's actions, her kneeling at Jesus' feet (v. 32) and her visible tears (v. 33). After her encounter with Jesus, Martha goes to call her sister. Prior to meeting up with Jesus, Mary is followed by Jews.

Martha's confession of faith in Jesus is explicit and titular, especially in the rich formulation of verse 27, where Martha acknowledges Jesus as Lord,[24] Messiah, Son of God, and 'the one coming into the world'. The last three named epithets are part of a formal confession of faith, 'I believe that you are the Messiah, the Son of God, the one coming into the world.'[25] To Martha's fourfold expression of faith in Jesus in v. 27 can be added her acknowledgement that he is 'the Teacher' (v. 28). Mary's acknowledgement of the dignity of Jesus is, apart from the respectful 'Lord' in v. 32, implicit, to be construed from her gesture of kneeling (v. 32) and her being again at Jesus' feet to perform the hostess's and servant's gesture of anointing the feet of an honoured guest welcomed into a home at the end of a journey.

In each of her two meetings with Jesus, outside the city and at the tomb, Martha is mildly rebuked by Jesus (vv. 25-26, 40). Rather than being rebuked by Jesus, Mary is defended by him (12.7). Johannine misunderstanding is a feature of the evangelist's portrayal of each of the sisters, but in keeping with his characterization of each sister, Martha misunderstands Jesus' words (11.23-24). Mary is seemingly oblivious to the real meaning of her own action, anointing Jesus' feet. Jesus clarifies the meaning of his words to Martha (11.25-26); he explains the significance of Mary's action (12.7). As a prelude to the Johannine 'passion narrative'[26] or as part of the passion narrative more broadly construed, the evangelist's Martha material focuses on resurrection and life, the Mary material on death and grieving. There can be little doubt that the evangelist wanted his readers to understand that the two sisters were different from one another.

---

24   See also the vocative κύριε in v. 21.

25   In form, Martha's confession of faith parallels that of Simon Peter (6.69) but the triple designation is fuller than Peter's confession. He acknowledges Jesus to be 'the Holy One of God'. Martha's confession is echoed in the Gospel's finale, 'But these are written so that you may come to believe that Jesus is the Messiah, the Son of God, and that through believing you may have life in his name' (John 20.31).

26   Cf. Raymond F. Collins, 'John's Gospel: A Passion Narrative?', in *The Bible Today* 24 (1986), pp. 181–6; reprinted as 'A Passion Narrative?', in Collins, *These Things Have Been Written* (LTPM, 2; Leuven: Peeters, 1990), pp. 87–93.

III. The Resurrection Diptych

A pair of appearance narratives, 19.19-23 and 19.26-28, form a literary diptych which serves as a narrative conclusion to 'this book', that is, the Fourth Gospel without the epilogue of John 21. The hinge element of the diptych, 20.24-25, is a transitional passage which introduces the figure of Thomas and features a dialogue between the disciples and Thomas.

The evangelist employs contrast to good effect in his portrayal of 'Doubting Thomas'. The disciples and Thomas are well-known figures in the evangelist's narrative. Culpepper observes that the evangelist uses the term 'disciples' some 78 times.[27] That is, in fact, a count of the number of times that the Greek μαθητής, 'disciple', appears in the Fourth Gospel. Not all of the evangelist's uses of the noun are in the plural nor is the term always used in reference to the disciples of Jesus. As a designation of the disciples of Jesus, the Greek term is used 14 times in the singular and 57 times in the plural.[28]

'The disciples' are a corporate character in the Fourth Gospel.[29] They act, speak and are spoken to as a group and accordingly, says Hylen, 'warrant their own designation as a character'.[30] They are surely more complex than von Wahlde's simple description of them as 'perfect models for the perfect response to the witness of the Father'.[31] The complexity of 'the disciples' as a corporate character is evident in the way that the evangelist mentions their speaking to one another[32] and writes about 'one of the disciples'[33] and the 'other disciples'.[34] Although a corporate character, they are not a homogeneous group.

Thomas first appears in the Johannine narrative in the midst of the Lazarus narrative where he says, with a bit of bravado, 'Let us also go, that we may die with him [Jesus]' (11.16). Abruptly introduced into the narrative, Thomas is identified for the benefit of the Johannine reader as one 'who was called the Twin'. The descriptive phrase recurs in the Johannine narrative to 'introduce'

---

27   See Culpepper, *Anatomy*, p. 115.

28   Included in this count are the four occurrences of the singular and the five occurrences of the plural in the epilogue. Cf. 21.7, 20, 23, 24, for the singular, and 21.1, 2, 8, 12, 14 for the plural.

29   Cf. Raymond F. Collins, 'From John to the Beloved Disciple: An Essay on Johannine Characters', *Int* 49 (1995), pp. 359–69 (360), reprinted in Jack Dean Kingsbury (ed.), *Gospel Interpretation: Narrative-critical & Social-scientific Approaches* (Harrisburg, PA: Trinity Press International, 1997), pp. 200–11. In his survey of 23 characters in the Fourth Gospel, among which are the Jews, the crowd, and the Twelve, Bennema does not present the almost omnipresent disciples as a literary character to be studied and analysed.

30   Hylen, *Imperfect Believers*, p. 60.

31   Urban C. van Wahlde, 'The Witnesses to Jesus in John 5.31-40 and Belief in the Fourth Gospel', *CBQ* 43 (1981), pp. 385–404 (399, 404). More nuanced descriptions of the disciples are found in Culpepper, *Anatomy*, pp. 115–25, and Hylen, *Imperfect Believers*, pp. 59–76.

32   Cf. 4.33; 13.22; 16.17; 18.15.

33   Cf. 6.6; 12.4; 13.27; 18.17, 25.

34   Cf. 21.2, 8. See also 11.16, where the word συμμαθητής, *hapax legomenon* in the New Testament, appears in the plural.

Thomas on two of the three other occasions in the Fourth Gospel when he appears in the story.[35] The exception is 14.5 where Thomas appears in the narrative in *deus ex machina* fashion,[36] saying to Jesus, 'Lord, we do not know where you are going. How can we know the way?' The reader will, of course, note the inconsistency between Thomas's words in 11.16 and those in 14.5 but that is not the point of this essay.

When Thomas is first introduced into the narrative at 11.16, his words are addressed to his co-disciples (συμμαθηταῖς). In this fashion the evangelist implicitly characterizes Thomas as one of Jesus' disciples. The implicit characterization of Thomas as one of the disciples is echoed in 21.2 where Thomas, identified as the Twin, is part of a group of five on the shore of the Sea of Tiberias along 'with two others of his disciples'. Of the four passages in the Johannine story in which Thomas appears, 21.2 is the sole passage in which he has nothing to say.

In the hinge unit of the appearance diptych (20.24-25) Thomas[37] is formally introduced as one of the Twelve (εἷς ἐκ τῶν δώδεκα) and as one who was called the Twin.[38] The Twelve[39] constitute another corporate character in the Johannine narrative but they make only two appearances, namely, in 6.66-71 and 20.24-25.[40] As a group designation, 'the Twelve' appears only four times in the Fourth Gospel (6.67, 70, 71; 20.24), that is, with far less frequency than the term is used in the Synoptic Gospels. The Twelve have been chosen by Jesus (6.70). Three of the group are named: Simon Peter, implicitly, as their spokesperson (6.67-68), Judas son of Simon Iscariot, and Thomas, explicitly, each of them being designated 'one of the Twelve' (6.70-71; 20.24).

The evangelist also identifies Thomas as one who is called the Twin, *Didymus*. The Greek term is a translation of the Aramaic 'Thomas', which means twin. The Greek epithet is proper to the Fourth Gospel; it is not used in the Synoptics. The Fourth Evangelist says that Thomas is called the Twin. The evangelist does not say that Thomas is a twin[41] nor does he mention that Thomas had any siblings, let alone one who was born almost simultaneously. Thus the reader is left to ponder as to whether the sobriquet indicates the

---

35   Cf. 11.24; 21.2.

36   Adding an 'incidental' detail to further advance the story line is one of the evangelist's literary techniques. Cf. 5.9; 9.14.

37   Keener discusses a number of different issues related to the historicity of the Thomas tradition. See Keener, *John*, Vol. 2, pp. 1208–9.

38   The NRSV reverses the sequence of the two elements in the evangelist's formal introduction of Thomas.

39   Keener notes that a group could retain its numerical label even if not numerically accurate. Cf. Keener, *John*, Vol. 2, p. 1208, n. 367.

40   See Raymond F. Collins, 'The Twelve, Another Perspective: John 6,67-71', *Melita Theologica* 90 (1989), pp. 95–109, reprinted as 'The Twelve: Another Perspective', in Collins, *These Things*, pp. 68–86; 'Characters Proclaim the Good News', *Chicago Studies* 37 (1998), pp. 47–57 (49–52); Bennema, *Encountering Jesus*, pp. 164–70.

41   The third-century gnostic *Acts of Thomas* identifies Thomas as the twin brother of Christ whose appearance is like that of Christ. Cf. *Acts Thom.* 11, 31, 39.

circumstances of Thomas's birth, whether it is his proper name, or whether it is perhaps a nickname.[42]

The evangelist explicitly tells his readers two things about Thomas in v. 24. He then adds an element of indirect characterization to his twofold direct characterization,[43] namely, that Thomas was not with them, the 'other disciples' (21.25), when the risen Jesus came to them. Physical absence from the group serves to distinguish Thomas from the other disciples. As in the case of Martha and Mary (11.20), the evangelist uses physical separation to contrast the two literary figures.

The evangelist's use of 'other' (ἄλλοι) to describe the group that had seen Jesus implies that Thomas is a disciple, even though the evangelist does not explicitly so designate him, neither here nor elsewhere in his narrative. Thomas rejoins the group of disciples in the second panel of the evangelist's diptych, in a short scene that takes place a week after the parallel scene in 20.19-22.[44]

As was the case with the evangelist's presentation of the contrasting characters Martha and Mary, so now the parallel narratives begin with a portrayal of similarity. Six elements stand out in a setting of a scene that will highlight the contrast between Thomas and the other disciples. These are the time, the place, the locked doors,[45] the presence of the disciples, to whom Jesus comes and among whom he stands, and Jesus' words, 'Peace be with you.'

Thereafter the contrast between Thomas and the other disciples, first suggested by the former's physical absence from them on the occasion of Jesus' first appearance, is unpacked. The evangelist's unfolding of the contrast can suggest that his 'one of the twelve' in reference to Thomas (20.24) might be somewhat more than an element of explicit characterization. It might help to set him apart from the other disciples. The phrase might possibly suggest that Thomas was absent *even though* he was one of them.[46] The Twelve are less than idealized disciples in the Fourth Gospel. As a group they seem to have been in danger of joining those disciples who turned away from Jesus (11.66-67). One of the Twelve was, in Jesus' words, a devil (διάβολος, 6.70). That was Judas, son of Simon Iscariot, who was going to betray him. And the other one of the Twelve, identified by name, is Thomas, the one who is about

42   Cf. Helmut Koester, 'ΓΝΩΜΑΙ ΔΙΑΦΟΡΟΙ', in Helmut Koester and James M. Robinson, *Trajectories through Early Christianity* (Philadelphia: Fortress, 1971), pp. 114–57; John Y. H. Yieh, 'Thomas', *NIDB*, Vol. 5, p. 582; von Wahlde, *John*, Vol. 2, p. 487.

43   'Show and tell' sums up the difference between indirect and direct characterization. Hylen notes that explicit characterization is rarely found in the Fourth Gospel (cf. Hylen, *Imperfect Believers*, p. 13).

44   The use of narrative parallelism is a familiar phenomenon in the Fourth Gospel. In addition to the Martha//Mary parallel in 11.20-27//11.28-37, see also 1.19-23//1.24-27; 9.13-23//24-34.

45   The phrase τῶν θυρῶν κεκλεισμένων appears in both v. 19 and v. 26. The NSRV's translation of v. 19 is 'the doors of the house . . . were locked'; the translation of the same phrase in v. 26 is 'although the doors were shut'.

46   Cf. Michaels, *John*, p. 1015.

to demonstrate his incredulity when the other disciples say, 'We have seen the Lord' (20.25).[47] He was, as Jesus will imply, a doubter (20.27).[48]

The Johannine narration contrasts Thomas and the other disciples in a number of other ways. To begin with, absent from the group on the occasion of Jesus' first appearance to them, Thomas is not missioned nor is he the recipient of the gift of the Spirit as the other disciples had been (20.21b-23). The evangelist's description of the second appearance does not indicate that Thomas was compensated for that lacuna.

The Lord showed the other disciples his hands[49] and his side. Thereupon the disciples rejoiced, an appropriate response to the vision and the Lord's welcoming 'Peace be with you.'[50] The customary greeting, repeated again in v. 21, achieved its gift-giving effect. At peace, the disciples experienced joy in the Lord's presence. Mention of Jesus' side is a uniquely Johannine feature,[51] present in each of the parallel narratives as well as in the hinge verses (20.24-25) which echo 19.34.

In the Thomas episode, rather than simply showing his hands and his side, the Lord tells Thomas to do what he had claimed would lead to his belief, namely, touch the wounds in the Lord's hands with his finger and put his hand in the hole in the Lord's side (20.25, 27). The text is silent as to whether or not Thomas obeyed the Lord's command[52] but it is not silent with regard to the rebuke that Jesus addressed to Thomas: 'Do not doubt but believe' (20.27c). Instead of experiencing joy at the Lord's presence, Thomas is rebuked. The rebuke directly addresses Thomas's boastful, 'Unless I see the mark of the nails in his hands, and put my finger in the mark of the nails and my hand in his side, I will not believe' (20.25).

Thomas got the message. He immediately responds with a strong Christological confession that proclaims not only Jesus' lordship but also, and explicitly, his divine status. Thomas's words constitute the only confessional attestation to Jesus' divinity in the Fourth Gospel. His utterance of the Gospel's climactic confession of faith[53] shows that he has become a believer.

47   20.25, an 'echo' of Mary's 'I have seen the Lord' (20.18).

48   Brant (*John*, p. 272) characterizes Thomas as the killjoy in the story.

49   With Luke (cf. 24.39), the Johannine narrative assumes but has not previously stated that Jesus has been nailed to the crossbeam. Unlike the Lukan account, the Fourth Gospel does not mention Jesus' feet but it does mention Jesus' side. In Roman crucifixion the victims were often tied to the crossbeam with rope, but sometimes nails were driven through the wrists or forearms. Cf. Pliny, *Natural History* 28.11.46; Livy, *History of Rome* 1.26.6.

50   These words of greeting contrast with the 'Do not be afraid' of other appearance stories. Cf. Matt. 28.5, 10; John 6.20.

51   Cf. Luke 24.39.

52   Commentators differ among themselves as to how this silence is to be interpreted. 'Instead of taking advantage of the offer', says Michaels (*John*, p. 1018), 'Thomas responds immediately and emphatically to the invitation "be no longer faithless but faithful"', while von Wahlde (*John*, Vol. 2, p. 871) writes, 'it seems that the author intends us to understand that Thomas has actually touched the hands and sides of Jesus'.

53   On the climactic nature of Thomas's confession in the Johannine story line, see Keener, *John*, Vol. 2, p. 1211.

No such confession is found on the lips of the other disciples to whom Jesus had appeared. Their belief is attested in their giving witness to Thomas that, 'We have seen the Lord' (20.25). With his confession Thomas has rejoined the group of believing disciples from whom he had been separated at the time of Jesus' first appearance to them.

Nevertheless, Jesus has the last word. The sole beatitude in the Fourth Gospel (John 20.29)[54] can be seen as yet another rebuke of Thomas and as a preparation for the Gospel's statement of purpose (20.31).

The contrast between the other disciples and Thomas explicitly attested by the evangelist's hinge narrative is implicit throughout the three scenes of the eleven verses (20.19-29). The narrative contrast is highlighted in two parallel and remarkably similar scenes which have many traits in common.

In the first appearance scene, the disciples are passive characters. Jesus appears to them, greets them, not once but twice, shows them his hands and side, gives them the gift of the Holy Spirit, commissions them as he himself had been commissioned, and empowers them to forgive sins. The disciples are speechless throughout the scene. Their sole activity is rejoicing at the sight of the Lord.

They become active in the hinge unit when they tell Thomas, 'We have seen the Lord.' Thereafter they fall into silence once again and are passively present at the periphery of the second appearance account. Thomas is anything but silent. His dramatic refusal to believe is his first utterance. His response to the disciples' announcement that they had seen the Lord does not even acknowledge that the one of whom they were speaking is the Lord. Thomas refers to Jesus simply as 'him' (αὐτοῦ).[55] Thomas will speak again when, after Jesus' command and first rebuke, Thomas acknowledges him as 'my Lord', adding the climactic 'and my God'.

The other disciples rejoice, are sent into mission, receive the gift of the Spirit, and are empowered to forgive. They are a gifted group, the beneficiary of being given Jesus' mission, the Holy Spirit, and the power to forgive. In contrast, Thomas is not said to rejoice nor is he gifted. Even the beatitude that is addressed to him, blesses not him but those who are unlike him, those who come to belief without having seen.

In contrast with the other disciples whose encounter with the risen Lord is entirely positive, Thomas's experience of the Lord is rather negative. His bluff is called.[56] He is questioned. He is rebuked. Whereas the modern reader might have expected Jesus to respond to Thomas's full-blown expression

---

54   Cf. Raymond F. Collins, '"Blessed Are Those Who Have Not Seen": John 20:29', in Rekha M. Chennattu and Mary L. Coloe (eds), *Transcending Boundaries: Contemporary Readings of the New Testament* (Biblioteca di Scienze Religiose 187; Rome: Libreria Ateneo Salesiano, 2005), pp. 173–90.

55   The pronoun is twice used, as a qualifier of 'hands' (ταῖς χερσὶν) and 'side' (τὴν πλευρὰν).

56   A psychological reading of the text would undoubtedly call for a mention of Thomas's embarrassment but, as has been noted above (n. 18), prying into the psyche of literary characters is a modern technique absent from ancient literary works.

of faith with some words of congratulations, the congratulatory formula[57] is pronounced on behalf of others.

In a word, although Thomas is clearly one of the disciples, he is very different from the others.

IV. Nicodemus and the Samaritan Woman

In her analysis of the Johannine account of Jesus' encounter with the Samaritan woman, Susan Hylen indicates that the reader of the Fourth Gospel should read the story of the Samaritan woman in tandem with the story of Nicodemus. She speaks of the contrast between these two ambiguous characters.[58] Similarly, I once wrote that, 'The story of Jesus' encounter with the woman of Samaria (4.1-42) creates a diptych with the story of Jesus' meeting with Nicodemus, the panels of which, notes Herman Servotte, depict the same theme in different tonality.'[59] Contrast is an important feature of the characterization of these two figures to whom the evangelist devotes a considerable part of his narrative. In fact, Margaret Mary Pazdan, who holds that contrasts highlight the unity of the diptych, subtitles her study of the pair as one of 'contrasting models of discipleship'.[60] The contrast merits further exploration.

As was the case with the evangelist's use of contrast to profile the literary figures of Martha and Mary and of the other disciples and Thomas, the evangelist's use of contrast is all the more effective because of the similarities in the narrative accounts. As far as Nicodemus and the Samaritan woman are concerned, biblical motifs are significant features of the background of each story. Dialogue about water is an important feature of Jesus' dialogue with Nicodemus as it is in the story of Jesus' meeting the Samaritan woman. Misunderstanding is a feature of both accounts. Nicodemus, for example, does not understand how a mature man can be born again (3.3)[61] while the Samaritan does not understand how a man without a bucket can give living water (4.10). In each case, their misunderstanding is expressed in the form of a pair of questions that the interlocutor addresses to Jesus (3.4; 4.11-12). Both Nicodemus (3.3) and the Samaritan woman are beneficiaries of Jesus' revelation, in her case, of Jesus' self-revelation (4.26).

---

57   In terms of their literary form, beatitudes are expressions of praise or congratulation. Cf. Raymond F. Collins, 'Beatitudes', *ABD*, Vol. 1, pp. 629–31 (629).

58   See Hylen, *Imperfect Believers*, p. 43.

59   Collins, 'Johannine Characters', p. 363. The reference is to Herman Servotte, *According to John: A Literary Reading of the Fourth Gospel* (London: Darton, Longman and Todd, 1994), p. 22.

60   See Margaret Mary Pazdan, 'Nicodemus and the Samaritan Woman: Contrasting Models of Discipleship', *BTB* 17 (1987), pp. 145–8 (146).

61   The misunderstanding bears upon the ambiguity of the evangelist's ἄνωθεν, whose meaning can be either 'from above', as in the NRSV translation, or 'anew'. Cf. Hylen, *Imperfect Believers*, pp. 29, 32. On Nicodemus's misunderstanding, see especially Marinus de Jonge, 'Nicodemus and Jesus: Some Observations on Misunderstanding and Understanding in the Fourth Gospel', *BJRL* 53 (1971), pp. 337–59; reprinted in de Jonge, *Jesus, Stranger from Heaven and Son of God* (Missoula, MT: Scholars, 1977), pp. 29–47.

Such similarities provide the context within which the evangelist pairs and contrasts Nicodemus and the Samaritan woman. The contrast is most evident in the temporal setting of each scene. Nicodemus came to Jesus by night (3.2), a not incidental feature of the story which the evangelist echoes in 19.39.[62] Nicodemus is a nocturnal character. On the other hand,[63] the Samaritan came to Jesus about noon (4.6). She approaches him in broad daylight.

It is probable that these temporal indications have a function in the Johannine narrative beyond merely providing a temporal element in the setting of the scene. In the Fourth Gospel, night is not a good time. Productive things don't happen at night.[64] Most likely, the nocturnal characterization of Nicodemus associates him with those who walk in darkness.[65] The light is not in him.[66] Some might argue that the nocturnal setting portrays Nicodemus as someone who acts in secrecy, perhaps out of fear.[67] In which case, Nicodemus would be contrasted with Jesus who speaks publicly and acts in the open.[68] I would, however, suggest that this is a less fruitful way to approach the night-time appearance than that which sees Nicodemus as being removed from the light.

That Jesus[69] would be tired after his journey and craving a drink of water in the mid-day heat is not an unlikely scenario. That a solitary woman should come to a well at noon is, however, far from likely. Groups of women would typically draw water in the relative cool of the morning hours or later in the day, towards dusk. This leads some commentators to suggest that the noon-time setting is an indication that the solitary Samaritan was not welcome among the other women, that she was perhaps some sort of a pariah because of her sexual history.[70] To the extent that this line of reasoning is valid, her solitary presence at the well would type her as a well-known sinner in contrast to Nicodemus who was, at least presumably, a law-abiding Pharisee.

In the setting of the respective scenes, the evangelist uses time to contrast Nicodemus and the Samaritan woman but he also uses space for the same purpose. The Nicodemus story is set in Jerusalem, the holy city of pious Jews

---

62   Cf. 7.50.

63   Hylen *(Imperfect Believers,* p. 43) sees the contrasting time frames as a major reason for reading the two stories in tandem.

64   Cf. 9.4; 13.30; 21.3.

65   Cf. Adele Reinhartz, 'The Gospel of John', in Elisabeth Schüssler Fiorenza (ed.), *Searching the Scriptures. Vol. 2: A Feminist Commentary* (New York: Crossroad, 1994), pp. 571–600 (570).

66   Cf. 11.10; 12.35-36.

67   Cf. Hylen, *Imperfect Believers*, pp. 34–5.

68   Cf. 7.26; 18.30.

69   Thus far in this episode, the emphasis is on Jesus alone. The evangelist writes in the third person singular. The disciples do not appear on scene until 4.27. The disciples are absent, having gone to the city to buy food (4.8).

70   See Mark F. Whitters, 'Discipleship in John: Four Profiles', *WW* 18 (1998), pp. 422–7 (424); Keener, *John*, Vol. 1, pp. 593–5; Hylen, *Imperfect Believers*, p. 171, n. 6. Brant, referencing Day, observes that the Samaritan's morality is nowhere at issue in the narrative but that does not mean that she lives without shame. With neither husband nor children, she is without family honour. Cf. Brant, *John*, p. 82; Janeth Norfleete Day, *The Woman at the Well: Interpretation of John 4:1-42 in Retrospect and Prospect* (BIS, 61; Leiden: Brill, 2002), pp. 170–1.

(2.23). The geographic setting of the scene is sometimes omitted from studies of Nicodemus because of the chapter break after 2.25. The break is the work of Stephen Langton, an early thirteenth-century archbishop of Canterbury, not the work of the evangelist. The evangelist has, in fact, linked the Nicodemus story to its Jerusalem setting by means of the catchword 'man' (ἄνθρωπος), the last word of 2.25 and the third word of the following sentence. Unfortunately the NRSV renders the link almost indiscernible with its translation, '. . . for he himself knew what was in everyone. Now there was a Pharisee (ἐν τῷ ἀνθρώπῳ. Ἦν δὲ ἄνθρωπος) . . .' (2.25b–3.1a).

In contrast, the story of Jesus' encounter with the Samaritan woman takes place in a Samaritan city called Sychar (4.5), a city which was on Jesus' way to Galilee from Judaea. The narrator's brief account of the journey (4.3-5a) serves to separate Jerusalem from Sychar geographically but the contrast between the two cities was not only geographical, it was also geopolitical. In first-century Palestine a Samaritan city was a world apart from the Judaean capital. Indeed, divine intervention was needed in order for Jesus to bridge the divide between the two worlds and make the journey from Jerusalem to Sychar. Such would seem to be the import of the evangelist's ἔδει, 'he had to' go through Samaria (4.4).[71]

Geography and culture separate Sychar from Jerusalem but so, too, does their literary and historical notoriety. Jerusalem is the location of many episodes in the Fourth Gospel; Sychar serves as the site only of Jesus' encounter with the Samaritan. The evangelist mentions Jerusalem (Ἱεροσόλυμα) a dozen times;[72] only once does he refer to Sychar (Συχάρ), namely in 4.5. Not only is the name of the Samaritan city a *hapax legomenon* in the Fourth Gospel, it is also *hapax* in the entire Greek Bible. Neither the city nor Jacob's well appears elsewhere in the biblical story, whereas Jerusalem appears in the biblical narrative scores of times.

Nicodemus is formally introduced into the narrative at 3.1, 'Now there was a Pharisee (ἄνθρωπος ἐκ τῶν Φαρισαίων) named Nicodemus, a leader of the Jews.' The woman of Samaria is introduced simply as 'a Samaritan woman' (γυνὴ ἐκ τῆς Σαμαρείας) in 4.7.[73] He is a man; she is a woman. He is a Pharisee; she is a Samaritan. He is named and has a social position; she is anonymous and may well be shunned. He will appear again in John's story, as a learned lawyer in discussion with other Pharisees (7.50-52) and as a companion of Joseph of Arimathea, who appears to have had an inroad with

---

71   Michaels cites Brown, Morris, Moloney, and himself at a previous point in time, as supporting the interpretation of ἔδει as an indication of theological necessity. Cf. Michaels, *John*, p. 235, n. 12. Keener (*John*, Vol. 1, p. 590) supports this view as does Okure, a view from which both von Wahlde (*John*, Vol. 2, p. 170) and Michaels, in his recent commentary (*John*, pp. 234–5), demur. The way in which the evangelist uses δεῖ seems to favour the theological connotation of the necessity that constrained Jesus to pass through Samaria. See, especially, Teresa Okure, *The Johannine Approach to Mission: A Contextual Study of John 4:1-42* (WUNT, II/32; Tübingen: Mohr [Siebeck], 1988), pp. 83–6.

72   1.19; 2.13, 23; 4.20, 21, 45; 5.1, 2; 10.22; 11.18, 55; 12.12.

73   Cf. 4.9a.

Pilate (19.38-42).[74] After 4.1-42, she disappears completely from the Gospel story.

Nicodemus's gender[75] is not a focus of the evangelist's attention. That the woman at the well is a woman and a Samaritan woman at that is important for the narrative sequence that follows. When the disciples return to Jesus after buying provisions in town, they are astonished that he is talking with a woman (μετὰ γυναικός, 4.27). That she is a Samaritan woman, γυναικὸς Σαμαρίταδος οὔσης (4.9), phraseology that emphasizes her Samaritan origins even more than the initial presentation of her in 4.7, allows the evangelist to suggest that Jesus ought to have nothing to do with her because Samaritans have nothing in common with Jews.

Both Nicodemus and the Samaritan woman approach Jesus, he directly, she indirectly as she approaches the well near which Jesus is sitting. Then the narratives diverge. Nicodemus speaks to Jesus and Jesus answers (3.2-3). Jesus speaks to the Samaritan; she is the one who answers (4.7b, 9).

Nicodemus speaks to Jesus reverentially, assigning him the title 'Rabbi', an epithet that echoes the disciples in 1.38. He also calls Jesus 'teacher',[76] anticipating the disciples' acknowledgement of Jesus as teacher (13.13).[77] Nicodemus also recognizes Jesus as coming from God and says that this is because of the signs that Jesus does (3.2). This last element of Nicodemus's multi-faceted recognition of Jesus places him among those who believe on the basis of signs, those to whom Jesus would not entrust himself (2.23-24). The plural of Nicodemus's 'we know' (οἴδαμεν, 3.2) types him as a spokesperson for this group.[78]

In contrast, the Samaritan speaks in her own name and is dismissive of Jesus: 'How is it that you, a Jew, ask a drink of me, a woman of Samaria?' (4.9). Whereas Nicodemus's opening gambit included a plethora of Christological titles which are not reprised in the subsequent narrative, titles flow repeatedly from the Samaritan's lips once she and Jesus enter into engaged conversation. She addresses Jesus as κύριε (4.11), the first person in the Gospel to do so. The next person to do so is the man who was healed at the pool of Bethzatha (5.7).[79]

---

74   The social importance of Joseph of Arimathea is explicitly mentioned in the Synoptic accounts of Jesus' burial (Matt. 27.57-60; Mark 15.42-46; Luke 23.50-53) but it can only be inferred from the Johannine narrative.

75   Conway (*Men and Women*, p. 87) suggests that in 3.1 ἄνθρωπος may have been intended to be gender-specific. This is a possibility (cf. LSJ, s.v.), perhaps reinforced by the connotation of ἄνθρωπος in 4.29.

76   The title is a key element in the reversal of roles between Nicodemus and Jesus. Cf. 3.10.

77   Cf. 1.38; 20.16.

78   Cf. Francis J. Moloney, *The Gospel of John* (SP, 4; Collegeville, MN: Liturgical, 1998), p. 97.

79   The title comes from disciples in 6.68; 9.36, 38; 11.3; 12.21, 27, 32, 34, 39; 13.6, 9, 25, 36, 37; 14.5, 8, 22. Moreover, the risen Jesus is addressed five times as κύριε by Simon Peter (21.15, 16, 17, 20, 21).

The Samaritan woman again calls Jesus κύριε in 4.15, 19.[80] She recognizes that Jesus is a prophet. Acknowledging her insight, the evangelist portrays her as saying, 'Sir, I see (θεωρῶ) that you are a prophet' (4.19).[81] Although a Samaritan,[82] she ponders the possibility of Jesus' messianic identity[83] and shares this thought with the townspeople (4.25, 30). In response, Jesus reveals himself to her as the revealer. She is the first person in the story who hears Jesus say ἐγώ εἰμι.

The Samaritan's discipleship is confirmed in her abandonment of the task at hand, drawing water,[84] in order to go to the city and bear witness to Jesus. Coming from Samaria, she is an unlikely disciple but a disciple she is. She has received the word spoken to her by Jesus and bears witness to the revealer. Nicodemus, in contrast, is one whose 'faith' is based on signs. It is not based on Jesus' revelation, let alone his self-revelation. The reader is left to ponder whether he might possibly be a secret disciple. The matter is disputed but, in my estimation, Nicodemus remains a sympathetic character but a nocturnal character nonetheless, certainly at this point in the Johannine narrative.[85]

Nicodemus's final words to Jesus, 'How can these things be?' (3.9), indicate that he does not get it. The Johannine Jesus comments on his failure to understand (3.10). Thereafter Jesus begins a monologue to which Nicodemus has nothing to say. And his failure to be a witness to Jesus is evident in its absence from the John 3 narrative.

V. Simon Peter and the Beloved Disciple

In each of the pairs of contrasting characters that we have considered thus far, a mention of geographic distance is part of the evangelist's contrasting technique. This is not the case with regard to Simon Peter and the Beloved Disciple, arguably the most important characters in the evangelist's story about Jesus other than the protagonist himself. Perkins observes that, 'The contrast between Peter and the Beloved Disciple highlights the irony with which the Fourth Evangelist treats Jesus' disciples.'[86] A detailed study of the contrast between these two characters would unduly lengthen the present essay. Hence, I will present only a quick overview of the scenes in which they appear together.[87]

---

80   On the connotation of the term, see Michaels, *John*, pp. 241–2.

81   Cf. 1.21, 25.

82   See Collins, *These Things*, p. 17, n. 50.

83   Cf. 1.41.

84   Cf. Mark 1.18, 20; 2.13, and parallels.

85   See 7.50-52.

86   Pheme Perkins, *Peter: Apostle for the Whole Church* (Studies on Personalities of the New Testament; Columbia, SC: University of South Carolina Press, 1994), p. 96.

87   The only scene in the Fourth Gospel in which the Beloved Disciple appears when Simon Peter is absent is the scene at the foot of the cross (19.25-27).

The Beloved Disciple appears for the first time in the Johannine narrative at 13.23-25. Twice he is described as reclining next to Jesus, on his chest.[88] Simon is reclining at a less privileged place at table. The Beloved relays Simon Peter's question to Jesus (13.24-25). A cameo of the scene is reprised in 21.20.

The two disciples appear together again in the court of the high priest (18.15-16)[89] and in the race to the tomb, when the Beloved outruns Simon Peter but defers to him at the entrance of the tomb (20.3-10). In the epilogue to the Fourth Gospel, the two disciples appear together on the shores of the Sea of Tiberias. During the third appearance of the risen Jesus to his disciples, the Beloved recognizes Jesus and, for the benefit of Peter (21.7) and the other disciples, identifies as 'Lord' the figure they have seen.

The final pairing of the two appears in the last scene of the Fourth Gospel. The Beloved is described in language that echoes the Last Supper scene (21.20). He is the object of Peter's concern. The previous pericope has featured a two-part conversation between Jesus and Peter. On seeing the Beloved Disciple, Peter asks Jesus, 'What about him?' (21.21). Jesus dismisses Peter's concern, challenging him to attend to his own discipleship: 'If it is my will that he remain until I come, what is that to you? Follow me' (21.22).

Repeating Jesus' words, the evangelist says that the fate of the Beloved is none of Peter's business: 'If it is my will that he remain until I come, what is that to you?' (21.23). The difference between the Beloved and Peter could not be clearer than it is in the evangelist's repetition of Jesus' words. For one final time, he has employed contrast to characterize his literary figures.

---

88   The Greek of v. 23 reads ἐν τῷ κόλπῳ τοῦ Ἰησοῦ; that of v. 25 as ἐπὶ τὸ στῆθος τοῦ Ἰησοῦ.

89   Frans Neirynck convincingly argued that the 'other disciple' in this scene is to be identified with the Beloved Disciple. See Neirynck, 'The "Other Disciple" in Jn 18, 15-16', in Neirynck, *Evangelica: Gospel Studies—Etudes d'Evangile* (BETL, 60; Leuven: University Press, 1982), pp. 335–64.

Chapter 6

Three Ambiguities: Historical Context, Implied Reader, and the Nature of Faith

Susan E. Hylen

I. Introduction

Interpreters often recognize that John's characters have varying – and sometimes conflicting – attributes. The Jews believe in Jesus (8.31; 11.45; 12.11) and seek to kill him (8.59; 19.14-15). The disciples believe in him (2.11) but often misunderstand his words (e.g., 4.32-34; 11.11-13). Part of the interest and difficulty in reading John is deciding what to do with this variation in the portrayal of characters.

Scholars now see greater complexity in John's characters than did scholars of the last century.[1] In earlier periods, John's characters were often understood as 'flat'.[2] Each character was confronted with a simple choice between two options: belief in Jesus or disbelief. This either/or choice was largely determinative of character. By contrast, many recent studies recognize greater complexity in John's characters. Cornelis Bennema argues that some of John's characters show development over time.[3] Christopher Skinner traces evidence of belief and disbelief in the characters of Thomas, Peter and

---

1   For example, books published in the last five years include: Cornelis Bennema, *Encountering Jesus: Character Studies in the Gospel of John* (Milton Keynes: Paternoster, 2009); Bradford B. Blaine, Jr, *Peter in the Gospel of John: The Making of an Authentic Disciple* (AcBib, 28; Atlanta: Society of Biblical Literature, 2007); Nicholas Farelly, *The Disciples in the Fourth Gospel: A Narrative Analysis of their Faith and Understanding* (WUNT, 290; Tübingen: Mohr Siebeck, 2010); Susan E. Hylen, *Imperfect Believers: Ambiguous Characters in the Gospel of John* (Louisville: Westminster John Knox, 2009); Michael W. Martin, *Judas and the Rhetoric of Comparison in the Fourth Gospel* (Sheffield: Sheffield Phoenix Press, 2010); Christopher W. Skinner, *John and Thomas: Gospels in Conflict? Johannine Characterization and the Thomas Question* (PTMS, 115; Eugene, OR: Pickwick, 2009); Tan Yak-hwee, *Re-Presenting the Johannine Community* (New York: Peter Lang, 2008).

2   Drawing on literary theories of characterization by E. M. Forster and W. J. Harvey: E. M. Forster, *Aspects of the Novel* (New York: Harcourt, Brace and Company, 1927); W. J. Harvey, *Character and the Novel* (London: Chatto & Windus, 1965). For application of these theories, see especially R. Alan Culpepper, *Anatomy of the Fourth Gospel: A Study in Literary Design* (Philadelphia: Fortress, 1983), 101–48.

3   E.g., Bennema, *Encountering Jesus*, 203–4.

other disciples.[4] John's characters emerge as something of a mixed bag. They display misunderstanding alongside remarkable statements of faith.

In *Imperfect Believers* I argued not only that John's characters are complex but also that they are ambiguous. Many characters believe in Jesus; at the same time they display misunderstanding of his identity. Characters may change over the course of the Gospel, but there is not a clear trajectory from misunderstanding to belief. Even at the end, John characterizes the disciples as both believing and questioning Jesus' identity. In the case of at least one character, Nicodemus, it seems impossible to determine his final level of belief. While other interpreters argue that all characters must choose between belief and unbelief, I have argued instead that the ambiguity in John's characters need not be resolved.[5]

I argue for this reading of John's characters in full recognition that the dualistic reading is a possible and even a good interpretation of John. It accounts for the language of the text and situates it within a plausible first-century context. My intention is not to displace all other readings of John but to offer a different way of seeing the text. Interpreting John's characters as ambiguous requires the reader to make a number of assertions about the act of interpretation that contradict the weight of twentieth-century scholarship. In *Imperfect Believers* I began to name and unpack these interpretive decisions. In this essay I explore three such elements of Johannine interpretation. I hope to show some of the assumptions interpreters of John's characters have shared as a way of making room for readers to work with different assumptions.

The first interpretive decision I discuss below is the relationship between the literary text and the historical context. Historical-critical scholarship prepared readers to view the text as a window into the historical situation of the author (and/or editors) who produced it. Because this way of viewing John is well developed and dominates many scholarly readings, shifting to a literary approach to character presents a series of hurdles. I find the Jews to be the most difficult of John's characters to approach as a literary character, because I have imbibed the common notion that this character speaks directly to a historical situation of conflict with Judaism. It is difficult to imagine another way of reading in which the Jews do not simply map onto late first-century opponents of Christianity. Nevertheless, I find it fruitful to try and explain how the discontinuities in the Jews as a corporate character might make sense apart from redaction theories and a historical context of separation from Judaism.

Second, I discuss the interpreter's construction of the implied reader. The scholarly consensus has been that John creates an implied reader who is an 'insider' in a Gospel with a sharp dichotomy between insider and outsider. As insiders, readers already understand Jesus' identity, and thus may look down upon the unwitting characters in the Gospel who encounter him without such perfect knowledge. This view relies on the idea that the reader may easily

---

4   Skinner, *John and Thomas*, chs 4 and 5.

5   Hylen, *Imperfect Believers*. For Nicodemus, see ch. 2; for the disciples, see ch. 4.

discern and classify characters according to their belief or unbelief, and that characters often grossly misunderstand Jesus, taking his metaphorical language literally. My reading of John's characters suggests instead that many characters understand a good deal about Jesus, including his metaphorical speech. But characters may be difficult to classify because they understand some things and not others, and also because John does not always give the reader sufficient means to determine a character's faith. As a result, the implied reader is one who searches for knowledge and must evaluate complex speech and actions in light of the Gospel's standards for faith.

A third consideration for interpreters of John's characters is a theological determination of the goal of the Gospel: faith. Many interpreters, following Rudolf Bultmann's lead, have portrayed John's message as a stark decision between belief and unbelief. This perspective emphasizes the moment of decision as transformative and the resulting faith as enabling an entirely new way of being. By contrast, understanding John's characters as ambiguous makes the most sense against the background of a different understanding of the Gospel's message. While faith is still important, it is not a singular, all-or-nothing decision, and does not require complete or perfect knowledge.

Throughout this essay I draw on classic examples of these interpretive choices like Rudolf Bultmann and J. Louis Martyn. These are not the most recent examples of these arguments, but are formative of the way later readers interpret the text. I hope that readers will recognize the influences on their own understandings of John, and that seeing these assumptions will make possible other ways of reading the Gospel.

II. Historical Context

For two centuries, one of the defining goals of New Testament studies has been to explore the history of the production of the NT writings. The texts are read as historical data to identify the theological viewpoints and religious practices of the earliest Christians, to situate them in their cultural context, and to describe how the texts as we know them came into being. Scholars reading John's Gospel with this goal often see the Gospel as evidence of stages of composition, of developments in Christian belief, and of a sharp divide between Christianity and Judaism.[6]

Interpreters who share this historical goal often recognize a good deal of variety and complexity in John's characters, but they divide the language according to its historical referent. When the reader notes apparent variety in John's wording about a character or theological topic, these different verses

---

6   For example, see the landmark works of Raymond E. Brown and J. Louis Martyn: Raymond E. Brown, *The Community of the Beloved Disciple* (New York: Paulist, 1979); J. Louis Martyn, *History and Theology in the Fourth Gospel* (Nashville: Abingdon, 2nd edn, 1979). Other works, like Martin's more recent study of Judas, situate the Gospel in a situation of intra-Christian rivalry: Martin, *Judas*, ch. 4.

are assigned to a different layer of redaction. The layers each have a historical location that explains the variety.

Scholarly treatment of John's terminology, *hoi Ioudaioi* (οἱ Ἰουδαῖοι, 'the Jews'), is one example of this approach. The division of John's use of *hoi Ioudaioi* into positive, neutral and hostile references makes sense in a scholarly context where John is viewed as the product of multiple stages of composition. For example, John Ashton explains the assertion that 'salvation is from the Jews' (4.22) by arguing that here *hoi Ioudaioi* means 'Judaean', which was considered Jesus' country of origin. However, 'by the time the Gospel was completed, the word Ἰουδαῖοι had acquired, all too evidently, much more sinister connotations'.[7] Ashton and others attribute different uses of *hoi Ioudaioi* to layers of editing.

Another classic representative of this approach is the 'two-level drama' of J. Louis Martyn's *History and Theology in the Fourth Gospel*. Martyn understood some of John's language to represent Judaism positively, and attributed this to a period before the decisive break when Christians still understood themselves as Jews.[8] Evidence of this positive relationship includes the statement that 'salvation is from the Jews' (John 4.22) and the notion that John understands Jesus as continuous with Jewish scripture (5.46).[9] Martyn sees much to suggest that John understands Jesus as a 'prophet like Moses'.[10] Viewed from his perspective, these elements of the Gospel reflect an earlier period before Johannine Christianity and Judaism were forcibly separated.

Martyn argues that other elements of John portray a negative view of Judaism. He sees John's use of *hoi Ioudaioi* and the hostile exchange of John 8 as evidence of an ultimate discontinuity between the Christian community and the synagogue. He understands the references to those who confess Christ being put out of the synagogue (ἀποσυνάγωγος γένηται, *aposynagōgos genētai*, 9.22; cf. 12.42; 16.2) as references to the historical location of the author, in which Christians had already experienced a forced separation from Judaism. To identify the historical background, Martyn described the *birkat ha-minim* as a late first-century proclamation from Jamnia that systematically excluded Christians from synagogue worship.[11] In light of this, the Pharisees' statement to the blind man, 'You are his disciple, but we are disciples of Moses' (9.28), is a reflection of the opinion of Jews known to the author.[12] It suggests that the Jews understand allegiance to Moses and Jesus as an either/or choice.

---

7   John Ashton, 'The Identity and Function of the ΙΟΥΔΑΙΟΙ in the Fourth Gospel', *NTS* 27 (1985), p. 53. Cf. p. 54, where Ashton argues that the similarity between the Jews and the crowd in John 6 comes from a different time period.

8   Martyn, *History and Theology*, p. 65.

9   Ibid., pp. 16, 39.

10   Ibid., pp. 118–20.

11   Ibid., pp. 50–62.

12   Ibid., pp. 39, 99. All NT quotations are from the NRSV.

Although there has been wide criticism of important elements of Martyn's thesis, his solution remains highly influential. Subsequent interpreters note significant problems with Martyn's use of the *birkat ha-minim* as evidence of a social situation in which Jews have cast out Christians.[13] Later scholars have modified Martyn's claim of widespread persecution by Jews to suggest sporadic and localized excommunication.[14] However, the methodological framework remains important: scholars use varieties in John's characters as a springboard to describe the historical development of Christianity.

Martyn's decision to read John 9 as evidence of the author's historical situation strongly shapes his treatment of John's characters. Martyn notices a good deal of variety in John's wording regarding characters. Some aspects portray Judaism positively, while others seem to reject elements of Jewish tradition or to portray Jews in a negative light. Martyn solves the problem of this variety by assigning elements to different historical situations, creating a narrative of the Johannine community's relationship to its Jewish neighbours. Thus, the characters in John never become multi-faceted because nuances in the language cause the interpreter to assign the verses to a different stage in production.

Methodologically, attention to an individual character shifts the interpreter's focus and makes connections across elements of the text that have been considered separately. The reader sets out each detail relating to a particular character and then assesses the evidence.[15] When the aim of reading for historical information is suspended, the variety that Martyn and others have noticed may become evidence of complex characters, rather than evidence of historical development. The Jews believe in Jesus and seek to kill him. They are the source of salvation and a group that other characters respond to in fear. Focusing on characterization has the potential to shift the way the reader understands John.

Characterization also opens up a new way of looking at the relationship between John and history because it underscores the notion that characters are not people. To situate John in its historical context, many readers have taken

13   Reuven Kimelman, '*Birkhat Ha-Minim* and the Lack of Evidence for an Anti-Christian Jewish Prayer in Late Antiquity', in E. P. Sanders (ed.), *Jewish and Christian Self-Definition*, Vol. 2 (Philadelphia: Fortress, 1981), pp. 226–44. Kimelman argued convincingly that in the early formulation of the benediction, *minim* referred to Jewish heretics or schismatics. The later inclusion of *nosrim* was aimed at Jewish Christians. Additionally, Christians seem to have been welcomed rather than excluded from the synagogue. Cf. Steven T. Katz, 'Issues in the Separation of Judaism and Christianity after 70 C.E.: A Reconsideration', *JBL* 103 (1984), pp. 43–76.

14   See the discussion by Adele Reinhartz: 'The Johannine Community and its Jewish Neighbors: A Reappraisal', in Fernando F. Segovia (ed.), *What is John?*, Vol. 2 (Atlanta: Scholars, 1998), pp. 111–38. In light of Kimelman's work, Reinhartz revises Martyn's thesis to suggest that the language of John arises from the Christian self-understanding that separation from the synagogue is necessary for those who confess Christ.

15   Alan Culpepper noted this many years ago when he argued that interpreters of *hoi Ioudaioi* must ask how the various uses of the term are related. See the discussion by Culpepper: R. Alan Culpepper, 'The Gospel of John and the Jews', *RevExp* 84 (1987), p. 276.

John's characters as 'representative': characters represent actual historical individuals or groups of people, and thus may be understood as evidence of the historical situation. Yet, from a literary perspective, characters are created by the process of writing and reading, and cannot easily be equated with historical people. Authors and readers will bring their knowledge of people, culture and history to bear in comprehending literary characters. Yet characters – even characters based on historical people – are not real people.[16] The literary reader may ask what a character expresses rather than searching for its historical referent.

When characters are understood to represent history they must be relatively narrowly construed. The interpreter must assign the character a discrete set of features that map directly onto a historical reality. There is a one-to-one correspondence between elements of the narrative and historical experiences, although the narrative need not record history but only 'represent' it in some way. The approach does not allow for much ambiguity in character, because if characters are indeterminate it is hard to narrow down what they represent and give them a concrete identity.

Literary characters can be ambiguous because they need not be identifiable as historical groups or individuals. Ambiguity in a character may contribute to the production of meaning. Conflicting elements of character may suggest a conflicted character, rather than one composed in stages reflective of historical change.

For example, John's portrait of the Jews in chapter 6 connects them explicitly with the Israelites in Exodus, who 'complained' against Moses and God about the provision of food (e.g., Exod. 16.2, 8, 9; 17.3; cf. John 6.41, 43; 7.12). In connecting the two characters, John creates a positive association between the Jews and the Israelites, who in Exodus are a people God cares for and leads, although they struggle to be faithful. The allusion to Exodus creates a connection between the complaint of the Israelites and that of the Jews in John.[17] The parallel suggests that the Jews' complaint, like Israel's, manifests a lack of faith. Read this way, the elements of belief and disbelief in the Jews' character suggests a complexity that is already familiar from scripture. An implication of this interpretation is that the complaints of the Jews actually reinforce Jesus' identity by showing how he fits the pattern of scripture. Just as the manna was sent from God despite the people's complaints, so also was Jesus.

Reading characters in this way is historical in the sense that it draws on evidence of the way that Jews in John's time understood the Exodus story.

16   As Gail O'Day argues, 'Literary works have characters, not persons; the world has persons, but not characters': Gail R. O'Day, 'The Citation of Scripture as a Key to Characterization in Acts', in Patrick Gray and Gail R. O'Day (eds), *Scripture and Traditions: Essays on Early Judaism and Christianity in Honor of Carl R. Holladay* (Leiden: Brill, 2008), p. 211. See also my discussion in Hylen, *Imperfect Believers*, pp. 4–6.

17   See Susan Hylen, *Allusion and Meaning in John 6* (BZNW; Berlin: Walter de Gruyter, 2005), pp. 146–52.

But it does not search the text for evidence of a historical referent for each character. When the Gospel is read in this way, the interpreter seeks a literary rationale for the various disjunctions in the text. This does not mean that such readings are ahistorical. The language of the story – including elements like *aposynagōgos* and *hoi Ioudaioi* – must make sense as a product of its time. The vocabulary and syntax, allusions to scripture and cultural norms may all be situated in conversation with a likely historical context. However, the point is not to narrow down the context to a specific location but to present a range of historical options in which such characters might make sense.

Reading the Jews as ambiguous makes sense within the context of first-century Jewish–Christian relationships. Interpreting the Jews as simple enemies of Jesus necessitates a historical context in which John understands Christians to be forced out of the Jewish community. Yet the argument by Kimelman and other scholars about the *birkat ha-minim* suggests that Jewish expulsions of Christians were not a widespread phenomenon in the first century. Steven Katz argues that the kind of separation for which there is evidence in the first century did not involve permanent expulsion from Judaism, and still understood the expelled person as Jewish.[18] This calls into question whether persecution as John envisions it would necessarily define John's community as non-Jewish. In recent years, scholars have continued to contest the relationship between Judaism and Christianity in the first century, without a clear consensus.[19] There is consensus, however, that both Christianity and Judaism were diverse movements. The wide range of possibilities may be a cue to look more broadly for historical contexts in which the language of John's Gospel makes sense.

For example, John's characters can also make sense within a historical context in which persecution of Christians was known but not systemic, and where even expelled Christians could still consider themselves Jewish. One character, the man born blind, is driven out by the Pharisees (9.34). Instead of a clear division between Christians and Jews, the narrative after this point expresses competition over who is the rightful leader or shepherd of God's flock (10.1-18). The Jews are divided about Jesus (10.19) and try to arrest him (10.39). Yet the Jews subsequently appear in a supportive relationship

---

18   Katz, 'Separation of Judaism and Christianity', pp. 49–50.

19   For diverse views, see for example: Daniel Boyarin, *Border Lines: The Partition of Judaeo-Christianity* (Philadelphia: University of Pennsylvania, 2004); Adela Yarbro Collins, 'How on Earth Did Jesus Become a God? A Reply', in David B. Capes, April D. DeConick, Helen K. Bond and Troy A. Miller (eds), *Israel's God and Rebecca's Children: Christology and Community in Early Judaism and Christianity* (Waco: Baylor University Press, 2007), pp. 55–66; Raimo Hakola, 'The Johannine Community as Jewish Christians? Some Problems in Current Scholarly Consensus', in Matt Jackson-McCabe (ed.), *Jewish Christianity Reconsidered: Rethinking Ancient Groups and Texts* (Minneapolis: Fortress, 2007), pp. 181–201 (185); Judith Lieu, *Neither Jew Nor Greek: Constructing Early Christianity* (New York: T&T Clark, 2002); Eyal Regev, 'Were the Early Christians Sectarians?', *JBL* 130 (2011), pp. 771–93; Adiel Schremer, *Brothers Estranged: Heresy, Christianity, and Jewish Identity in Late Antiquity* (Oxford: Oxford University Press, 2010); Yaakov Y. Teppler, *Birkat haMinim: Jews and Christians in Conflict in the Ancient World* (trans. Susan Weingarten; Tübingen: Mohr Siebeck, 2007).

with Mary and Martha, whom Jesus loves (11.5, 31).[20] Many believe in Jesus (11.45) and others plot his death (11.46-53). This variety in the character of the Jews might make sense to readers in a context in which there was not one monolithic Jewish perspective, or a single Jewish response to Christianity.

Although John's use of the terms *aposynagōgos* and *hoi Ioudaioi* are unique, John need not be read as representing a specific relationship with Judaism. Interpreters who see the blind man as representative take Jesus' words of 16.2, 'They will put you out of the synagogues', as a prediction of a widespread future reality. Yet all four Gospels predict the later persecution of Jesus' believers (cf. Matt. 24.9-14; Mark 13.9-13; Luke 21.12-19; John 15.18–16.4). The persecution of Jesus' followers is not necessarily any more prominent historically in the life of John's community than in Matthew, Mark, or Luke's. Like the Synoptics' apocalyptic teachings, John's *aposynagōgos* language creates an expectation of and rationale for persecution, but does not require that persecution was an ongoing or widespread experience for early Christians.

Instead of representing later Christians forcibly separated from the synagogue, the blind man may be seen as a character whose persecution confirms Jesus' identity as Israel's leader. In John 9, the Pharisees seek to uphold the Sabbath but miss the activity of God manifest in Jesus. John turns the expulsion of the man born blind into evidence of the Pharisees' spiritual blindness. Read in this way, the story of the blind man underscores the Pharisees' illegitimacy as leaders while confirming Jesus' identity as shepherd. Thus, John's language may be seen to invite readers to interpret persecution in a particular way, rather than providing historical evidence for widespread excommunication of Christians.

For readers interested in pursuing this angle of vision, it may be useful simply to recognize the power that historical-critical interpretation has on our conception of John. Many scholarly readers, trained in historical-critical methods, naturally consider the role of various sources or the location of the Johannine community. This is not an incorrect way to view the Gospel, but it is also not the only way. It is a dominant mode that has captured our imaginations, such that it is difficult to view the Gospel any other way. Reading John's characters as ambiguous may require a new perspective on the use of the Gospel as a source of direct evidence for the history of John's community. Gaps in the text are not read as evidence of historical layers but produce meaning that can be situated within a plausible first-century context.

III. Implied Reader

For many interpreters, John projects an implied reader who is part of a community of insiders, those who have knowledge of Jesus and who stand

---

20   See Reinhartz, 'Johannine Community', pp. 127–8.

apart from 'the world'. For example, Wayne Meeks argues that the Gospel 'is a book for insiders', those who have already arrived at faith in Jesus. Through this faith readers are transferred 'to a community which has totalistic and exclusive claims'.[21] Similarly, Paul Duke writes that the author and reader 'form a community of superior knowledge'.[22] The implied reader then stands apart from non-believers, and is invited to feel superior to others who lack the knowledge of the inside group.

Reading John dualistically is fundamental to this understanding of the implied reader. If the Gospel presents only two alternatives and categorizes all people as 'from above' or 'from below', then it makes sense that readers would align themselves with the better side of this polarity. John's polarized worldview is an essential part of Meeks's interpretation. Jesus comes from above, and those who understand his revelation form a group sharply separated from those who do not understand. 'We have in the Johannine literature a thoroughly dualistic picture: a small group of believers isolated over against "the world" that belongs intrinsically to the things below.'[23] Dualistic categories make this isolation appear natural, because there are only two choices, above and below, with a wide chasm in between.

Another important element in this construction of the implied reader is the perception that John's characters often misunderstand Jesus. When a character like Nicodemus misunderstands Jesus' words, the reader feels superior to the character in the story, and thus is aligned with the narrator's 'inside' perspective.[24] The narrator often supplies information that the characters in the story do not have, and this reinforces the expectation that readers will understand themselves as the chosen elite, in contrast to those who misunderstand even Jesus' simplest claims. This reinforces the perception of the implied reader as all-knowing, one who understands the self-revelation of Jesus.

It is also possible to read John in a way that constructs an implied reader who is an explorer and learner. John does assume the reader has some knowledge that characters on the level of the story could not have – for example, that Jesus will die. The Prologue also positions the reader to understand Jesus' divine origin. When the question of Jesus' origin arises repeatedly in the narrative (6.42; 7.15, 27, 41-42, 52), the reader understands what the characters do not. However, the implied reader also has much to learn from John's characters. John expresses knowledge about Jesus through metaphors. Many of these metaphors are acted out or discussed on some level in the story. For example, Jesus' trial centres on the question of his kingship. Many interpreters understand Nicodemus's final appearance, in which he brings a huge quantity of spices to anoint Jesus' body, in light of this metaphor. Nicodemus gives

---

21   Wayne A. Meeks, 'The Man from Heaven in Johannine Sectarianism', *JBL* 91 (1972), pp. 70–1.

22   Paul D. Duke, *Irony in the Fourth Gospel* (Atlanta: John Knox, 1985), p. 29.

23   Meeks, 'Man from Heaven', p. 68.

24   See Culpepper, *Anatomy*, p. 135; Meeks, 'Man from Heaven', p. 53.

Nicodemus & Samaritan Woman

Jesus a royal burial. His actions convey significant understanding of Jesus' identity. John never explicitly states Nicodemus's understanding, however. Some readers infer that Nicodemus understands Jesus' identity by using the kingship metaphor to make sense of this character's actions. John may construct an implied reader who draws on details of the story to develop their understanding of the identity of Jesus.

The reader can also explore many of the conversations between Jesus and other characters in search of both understanding and misunderstanding. Within a dualistic reading of John, it makes sense to say that characters have only two options: understanding and misunderstanding. Thus, many characters are said to misunderstand Jesus' metaphorical language, either through simple incomprehension or through outright resistance. However, I have argued that it is not always necessary to assume the character's ignorance of metaphorical language that was culturally conventional. Instead, granting the character at least partial understanding may allow the reader further insights into the metaphorical subject matter.

The Samaritan woman is an example of a character often interpreted as misapprehending Jesus. When Jesus offers her 'living water' (4.10), she mistakes his offer for one of physical, moving water. Her reference to the bucket and well in v. 11 shows that she has not understood the metaphor and still hopes Jesus will give her literal water. Yet the idea that the woman understands Jesus' reference to 'living water' as a metaphor is plausible historically and on the narrative level. 'Living water' is already a biblical metaphor,[25] and probably one that was as easy to understand in Jesus' time as in our own. Instead of ignoring the metaphorical tenor of Jesus' words, the Samaritan may assume 'living water' is a metaphor. Read this way, her response begins to reason along with the metaphor. Her words in vv. 11-12 ask Jesus to identify the source of his 'living water'. The woman has access to her own spiritual water, symbolized by the well of Jacob, to which she refers. She wants to know why Jesus' water would be better than what she already has. Jesus' response indicates that it is better ('those who drink of the water that I will give them will never be thirsty', v. 14). In response, she requests this water ('so that I may never be thirsty', v. 15).

Understood in this way, the discussion between Jesus and the Samaritan woman becomes a discussion over the relative value of different spiritual traditions. Jesus picks up on the woman's mention of her well in v. 12 and contrasts it further with the water he offers. Most interpreters read Jesus' words in vv. 13 and 14 as a choice between physical water and spiritual nourishment ('this water', v. 13, vs 'the water that I will give', v. 14). But if both characters are already speaking metaphorically, the conversation may point more specifically to a choice between the spiritual nourishment of her Samaritan tradition and that which Jesus offers. She is attracted by

---

25   E.g., Prov. 13.14; 18.4; Isa. 35.6-7; 41.17-18; 55.1-2; 58.11; Jer. 17.7-8, 13. The stories of God's provision of water in the wilderness (Exod. 15.22-27; 17.1-7) were probably familiar to the Samaritan. See my discussion in Hylen, *Imperfect Believers*, ch. 3.

Jesus' promise of water that really satisfies and that becomes a spring within the believer 'gushing up to eternal life' (v. 14). When the Samaritan is seen as misunderstanding, she simply chooses metaphorical over literal water. When she understands, she already has metaphorical water, but perceives that Jesus' water is better. She is a character who understands and can make determinations about the relative merits of Jesus' living water *vis-à-vis* the water of Samaritan religious traditions.

Reading John's characters as ambiguous allows the reader to explore both the understanding and misunderstanding of John's characters. Even the villainized Jews of John 8 may understand something about Jesus, and thus may point the reader toward understanding the content of Jesus' identity. For example, the Jews' climactic response to Jesus in 8.59, where they pick up stones to throw at him, shows comprehension of Jesus' words. They have understood Jesus' claim in v. 58: 'before Abraham was, I am'. Jesus' words imply that he indeed precedes Abraham, and alludes to his divinity through the use of God's name, 'I AM'. The Jews understand this as blasphemy, and respond with a conventional punishment (cf. Lev. 24.13-16). Two things are often neglected in this interaction, where the Jews are characterized as simple enemies of Jesus. The first is that the Jews understand Jesus. They reject his claim as blasphemy, but they understand what Jesus is saying. The second is that John probably agrees with the Jews that blasphemy is wrong, and even deserving of punishment. Seeing the overlap between John's perspective and that of the Jews may allow the reader to see in relief the real disagreement: John understands Jesus' claim to divinity to be true and not, therefore, blasphemy. John 8 is crafted to help the reader see how Jesus' death results from the Jews' failure to see how this claim is true.

Recognizing both apprehension and misapprehension on the part of the Jews changes the possibilities for how the text might make sense to its Jewish-Christian audience. If the Jews only misunderstand, and if their perspective is only criticized as 'from below', then it makes sense to think of John's audience as one that has completely separated from Judaism. Yet if the reader recognizes similarities between John's perspective and the Jews, it becomes possible to see that John accepts and values Jewish tradition. Through conversations that involve understanding and misunderstanding, John positions the reader to see how Jesus continues Jewish tradition, while the Jews who do not understand Jesus' identity end up being the ones who blaspheme when they declare their allegiance to Caesar (19.15).

If characters can understand some things about Jesus and misunderstand others, then the implied reader is in the position of having to figure out which elements of their words express understanding and which do not. The implied reader is a listener who makes judgements about the claims of the Gospel. Yet these judgements are not necessarily to place characters in one of two groups, those from above and those from below, but to judge what elements of their speech and actions express a good understanding of Jesus' mission and identity.

The final ambiguity in the character of Nicodemus may also suggest that the reader's process of discerning what is true about Jesus' identity may be more important than her ability to judge whether a character is an insider. Nicodemus's actions at Jesus' burial may suggest either comprehension or gross misunderstanding, depending on how the reader interprets them. The narrator does not evaluate Nicodemus explicitly or give any insight into his internal state. Interpreters who understand John dualistically judge Nicodemus negatively because of his ambiguity.[26] Yet it is possible for the reader to learn something from the story even if the ambiguity is unresolved. If Nicodemus acts out of knowledge of Jesus' kingship, then his final actions would show knowledge of Jesus' identity.[27] The character of Nicodemus reinforces the reader's understanding of Jesus' kingship, regardless of Nicodemus's own level of understanding. Other interpreters have read Nicodemus's actions as displaying a fixation on Jesus' dead body. From this perspective, Nicodemus does not understand Jesus' teaching that he will be 'lifted up' (3:14).[28] Again, regardless of Nicodemus's own level of understanding, the reader compares Nicodemus's actions with Jesus' words to arrive at a deeper comprehension of the story of Jesus.

Thus, instead of seeing themselves as part of a group of insiders pitted against a hostile world, the implied readers may not always know with certainty who possesses faith. In the case of the Samaritan woman, faith comes in surprising packages. In the ultimate ambiguity of Nicodemus's character, the reader may never be able to decide what Nicodemus believes. The implied reader is not called on to make single, either/or determinations of character, but instead encounters both positive and negative elements, even among Jesus' closest followers.

IV. The Nature of Faith

Perhaps the most influential twentieth-century interpretation of John's Gospel was that of Rudolf Bultmann. Bultmann read John's language of contrasts (e.g., light and dark, above and below, etc.) as evidence that the coming of the Redeemer creates a moment of decision in which people are faced with two choices: belief and disbelief. Bultmann's argument influenced many interpreters, who continue to read characters as responding to Jesus with an either/or decision.

---

26   See Jouette M. Bassler, 'Mixed Signals: Nicodemus in the Fourth Gospel', *JBL* 108 (1989), pp. 635–46.

27   E.g., Raymond E. Brown, *The Gospel According to John* (AB, 29A; New York: Doubleday, 1966–70), pp. 959–60; Francis J. Moloney, *The Gospel of John* (SP, 4; Collegeville, MN: Liturgical, 1988), pp. 510–11.

28   Meeks, 'Man from Heaven', p. 55; Dennis D. Sylva, 'Nicodemus and His Spices (John 19.39)', *NTS* 34 (1988), pp. 148–9.

Yet Bultmann's compelling and comprehensive vision of John's message has been challenged at many points. For example, Bultmann argued that John's Gospel reflects a gnostic Redeemer myth, and portrays Jesus in similar terms.[29] Yet the evidence for a Redeemer myth came from a much later period, and this important cultural background was widely rejected. Bultmann also dissected the text of John into minute pieces, both through reordering the manuscript and by assigning verses to different stages of redaction. Recent interpretation tends to recognize the stylistic unity of the text. Although some maintain that layers of redaction are discernible, few scholars advocate reordering the text of John, and none to the extent that Bultmann proposed.[30] These elements of Bultmann's theory were foundational for his argument, yet are not widely accepted.

Part of what may be compelling about Bultmann's interpretation is the stark and transformative power of faith in this worldview. His language is often inspirational:

> Man cannot act otherwise than as what he is, but in the revealer's call there opens up to him the possibility of being otherwise than he was. He can exchange his whence, his origin, his essence, for another; he can 'be born again' (3.1ff.) and thus attain to his true being. In his decision between faith and un-faith a man's being definitively constitutes itself, and from then on his whence becomes clear.[31]

In Bultmann's expression of it, Christian faith is a decision that alters human existence and makes possible a dramatically new understanding and way of being in the world. Bultmann's convincing theological rendering of the Gospel's message is a major strength of his interpretation.

Reading John's characters as ambiguous requires revision of the overarching theological message of the Gospel. When characters are read as ambiguous, there is no single transformative moment after which characters appear to have attained the perfect level of faith Bultmann describes. Instead, believing characters remain ignorant of Jesus' true purpose, misunderstand him, and seek to kill him. To the end, his disciples retain questions about Jesus' identity alongside their knowledge of him. This complexity of character does not give the reader insight into the 'true being' brought about by faith. However, it does allow readers to see the difficulty of human discipleship reflected in the pages of the Gospel. These are disciples who have not achieved spiritual perfection and indeed still struggle with basic questions of Jesus' identity.

From this perspective, faith appears less a single existential achievement and more a lengthy process of training in God's wisdom. This notion fits with

---

29   E.g., Rudolf Bultmann, *Theology of the New Testament*, Vol. 2 (New York: Charles Scribner's Sons, 1955), pp. 12–13.

30   To get a sense of the reordering, consult the table of contents of Bultmann's commentary. Rudolf Bultmann, *The Gospel of John* (Philadelphia: Westminster Press, 1971), pp. vii–xiii.

31   Bultmann, *Theology*, Vol. 2, p. 25.

John's metaphorical presentation of Jesus. I have argued that John's notion of faith in Jesus is not creedal, a simple concept to be apprehended.[32] Instead, John portrays a multi-faceted Jesus, who can be understood profitably in a variety of ways, often with reference to scripture. Jesus is light and life. He is bread, vine and shepherd. His death occurs at the same moment as the Passover offerings are being slaughtered in the temple. He is declared 'King of the Jews'. Each of these metaphors offers a rich conceptual terrain, drawing on biblical tradition, with which readers may profitably apprehend elements of Jesus' identity. And this is not an exhaustive list. Rather than pin Jesus down to a single concept to be apprehended by faith, John invites the reader into multiple ways of seeing Jesus, each of which is complex and worthy of exploration. Reading John this way involves the expectation that the reader must return again and again to the pages of the Gospel. Likewise, the characters of the Gospel may be read as exhibiting a kind of faith that is partial and imperfect.

John's ambiguous characters are not an indication of theological relativism. The contrasting language that many understand as John's dualistic worldview can also be read as a clear statement of John's values. There is an 'above' and a 'below', 'light' and 'dark', even if characters are not neatly classified in these terms. The terms create a backdrop against which readers may evaluate the words and actions of characters. For example, many interpreters see significance in Nicodemus's approaching Jesus 'by night' (3.2). Some view Nicodemus negatively as a result, because night is associated with darkness and/or secrecy, both of which John criticizes elsewhere (e.g., 3.19; 11.10; 12.43). Others see a positive connotation. Nicodemus also 'comes to' Jesus, a metaphor John uses for faith (e.g., 5.40; 6.35, 37, 44). And because Jesus is elsewhere described as 'light' (8.12; 9.5), Nicodemus's actions have a positive connotation (as one of those who 'come to the light'; cf. 3.21), even if he does not entirely understand or agree with Jesus' words. However the reader ultimately evaluates Nicodemus, the terms the Gospel provides become necessary standards for assessing the quality of a character's actions or belief.

Although many scholars see Nicodemus's wavering as enough to push him into the negative category, maintaining his ambiguity affirms that discipleship is not an either/or endeavour. Instead, Nicodemus becomes an example of a disciple who is truly a mixed bag. He may understand some important things about Jesus, though he is reluctant to state his faith publicly. Recognizing ambiguity in characters takes the emphasis off categorizing characters in dualistic terms and places it on a more nuanced evaluation of the variety of things a character does or says.

Seeing ambiguity in John's characters may require a reassessment of the theological outlook of the Gospel. Although John still writes to engender faith (20.30-31), this may be the kind of faith that develops over time, one that always seeks understanding but never achieves it perfectly. Characters may still display a variety of responses to Jesus, but the responses do not

32   Hylen, *Imperfect Believers*, ch. 8.

exist along a single either/or continuum. Some characters understand certain things about Jesus, while other characters understand different things, but still display incomplete knowledge. The failure to understand Jesus does not point to a character's ultimate disbelief, but is evidence of the complexity of faith and the value of pursuing greater understanding. Readers may learn about specific elements of Jesus' identity through the disbelief of the characters, but they need not experience themselves as having fully arrived at perfect faith. Instead, readers may identify with and see themselves reflected in the faith and misunderstanding of the Gospel's ambiguous characters.

Chapter 7

MISUNDERSTANDING, CHRISTOLOGY, AND JOHANNINE CHARACTERIZATION: READING JOHN'S CHARACTERS THROUGH THE LENS OF THE PROLOGUE

Christopher W. Skinner

[T]he Prologue is no introduction or foreword in the usual sense of the words . . . It is far more a mystery itself, and is fully comprehensible only to the man who knows the whole Gospel. It is only when the circle is complete, and the 'Son' has returned to the δόξα which the love of the 'Father' has prepared πρὸ καταβολῆς κόσμου (17.24), only when the reader has been led back to the temporal sphere into the eternal, that he can judge conclusively in what sense the Prologue leads out of the eternal into the temporal.

Rudolf Bultmann, *The Gospel of John*[1]

I. Introduction

For all the controversies surrounding its sources[2] and theological outlook,[3] there is little dispute that the Johannine Prologue (1.1-18) sets the literary

---

1   Rudolf Bultmann, *The Gospel of John: A Commentary* (trans. George R. Beasley-Murray; Philadelphia: Westminster, 1971), p. 13.

2   See, e.g., Matthew Black, 'Does an Aramaic Tradition Underlie John 1:16?', *JTS* 42 (1941), pp. 69–70; John A. T. Robinson, 'The Relation of the Prologue to the Gospel of St. John', *NTS* 9 (1963), pp. 120–9; J. G. van der Watt, 'The Composition of the Prologue of John's Gospel: The Historical Jesus Introducing Divine Grace', *WTJ* 57 (1995), pp. 311–32; P. J. Williams, 'Not the Prologue of John', *JSNT* 33 (2011), pp. 375–86.

3   The interpretation of the Fourth Gospel in recent history has seen the emergence of four major views on the theological outlook of John's *Logos* Christology: (1) *Logos* is a concept taken over from the 'word of the LORD' traditions in the OT; (2) *Logos* is a substitute term for the concept of wisdom in the OT wisdom literature; (3) John's *Logos* is similar or nearly identical to the concept of *Logos* as it is used by Philo; and (4) *Logos* is drawn from the *memra* traditions found in the *Targumim*. For more on these views, see Peder Borgen, 'Observations on the Targumic Character of the Prologue of John', *NTS* 16 (1969), pp. 288–95; A. T. Hanson, 'John 1:14-18 and Exodus 34', *NTS* 23 (1977), pp. 90–101; Henry Mowley, 'John 1:14-18 in the

and theological agendas for the entire Gospel narrative.[4] Like an overture that rehearses the major symphonic movements in the forthcoming story, the Prologue serves as an audience-elevating device by providing privileged information to which characters in the story have no access. The Prologue thus introduces all the themes that are needed to interpret properly John's story of Jesus, and provides the audience with comprehensive inside information regarding the Gospel's developed Christology.[5] The audience's subsequent experience with misunderstanding characters – who have neither read the Prologue nor have access to the information it reveals – serves as a constant reminder of its insider knowledge of Jesus' origins and identity.

It has long been recognized that misunderstanding is a major motif in the Fourth Gospel, though little has been written on the connection between misunderstanding and character development. In my recent monograph, *John and Thomas: Gospels in Conflict?*, I argued that misunderstanding is the trait most consistently displayed by Johannine characters.[6] In fact, apart from the Beloved Disciple there is no character who fully grasps what the audience has learned from the Prologue.[7] Armed with this information, the audience is able to evaluate the different character responses to Jesus – all of which fail in one

Light of Exodus 33:7–34:35', *ExpTim* 95 (1984), pp. 135–7; John Ashton, 'The Transformation of Wisdom: A Study of the Prologue of John's Gospel', *NTS* 32 (1986), pp. 161–86; Thomas H. Tobin, 'The Prologue of John and Hellenistic Jewish Speculation', *CBQ* 52 (1990), pp. 252–69; Daniel Boyarin, 'The Gospel of the Memra, Jewish Binitarianism and the Prologue to John', *HTR* 94 (2001), pp. 243–84; T. Baarda, 'John 1:17b: The Origin of a Peshitta Reading', *ETL* 77 (2001), pp. 153–62; and most recently, John Ronning, *The Jewish Targums and John's Logos Theology* (Peabody, MA: Hendrickson, 2010).

4   This idea is hardly new or disputed. As far back as 1898, Wilhelm Baldensperger (*Der Prolog des vierten Evangeliums: sein polemisch-apologetischer Zweck* [Tübingen: Mohr, 1898]) asserted that the Prologue was the key to understanding both the Fourth Gospel and the Johannine epistles. In his tendentious but important commentary, *Le Quatrième Evangile* (Paris: Picard, 1903), Alfred Loisy also insisted that the Prologue's 'incarnation theology' was the interpretive key to the entire Gospel. See, more recently, Michael Theobald, *Die Fleischwerdung des Logos: Studien zum Verhältnis des Johannesprologs zum Corpus des Evangeliums und zu Joh 1* (NTAbh, NF 20; Münster: Aschendorff, 1988).

5   Throughout this essay I have chosen to use the term 'audience' rather than 'reader' in recognition of the predominantly oral nature of early Christian storytelling. I am indebted to Prof. Elizabeth Struthers Malbon for this insight.

6   See Christopher W. Skinner, *John and Thomas: Gospels in Conflict? Johannine Characterization and the Thomas Question* (PTMS 115; Eugene, OR: Pickwick, 2009). Most recently, Susan Hylen (*Imperfect Believers: Ambiguous Characters in the Gospel of John* [Louisville: Westminster John Knox, 2009]) has argued that ambiguity is the most prominent character trait displayed by characters in the Fourth Gospel. While I find her treatment compelling, I remain convinced that the reader-elevating Prologue provides information that highlights the subsequent partial understanding or complete misunderstanding on the part of characters who interact with Jesus.

7   That the Beloved Disciple consistently responds to Jesus in an appropriate way, apart from the information provided in the Prologue, is strong evidence that he is to be regarded as the Johannine disciple *par excellence*. As such the Beloved Disciple is the ideal character with whom the implied audience should identify and after whom the implied audience should pattern its behaviour.

way or another – and further allows the Johannine Jesus narrative space to clarify elements of his message, mission and identity.[8] In a very real sense, the Prologue fashions the implied audience by raising expectations and explaining things heretofore unknown. Moloney expresses this concept well:

> The prologue to the Fourth Gospel begins the shaping of the reader. The author acts as teacher, but the truthfulness and even usefulness of all that has been taught is yet to be tested. The author has created an implied reader with exalted notions about Jesus Christ which are tested by the story of his life. The implied reader now begins to read a narrative designed to draw the reader more deeply into the privileged experience of a community of believers which the implied author claims to represent.[9]

I would also add that one major way in which the audience tests the truthfulness of this information is by observing character interactions – specifically interactions between Jesus and uncomprehending characters.

In this essay I will attempt to draw connections between three elements of the Fourth Gospel – the role of the Prologue, John's Christology, and the motif of misunderstanding – and demonstrate their importance for approaching John's characters. The reading strategy that emerges is meant to situate the Prologue *vis-à-vis* misunderstanding characters in the overall rhetorical plan of the narrator.

II. John's Prologue: The Identity, Origins and Mission of the Logos

Numerous concepts appear in the Prologue and are reintroduced throughout the Gospel in both character interactions and lengthier theological discourses. These concepts provide the necessary foundation as the audience comes to terms with the identity, origins and mission of Jesus. There is not space here to provide a full-scale exegesis of the Prologue, though it is necessary to identify important terms and themes as they appear in its various sections. In what follows, I provide a basic exegetical sketch of the Prologue.

a. John 1.1-5: The Word – God's Agent of Creation and Light of the World

The Fourth Gospel begins its story of the *Logos* with a transparent allusion to the creation account in Genesis 1. The narrative that ensues is thus situated

---

8   I argue that there are levels of misunderstanding in the Gospel. Clearly a character like Nicodemus represents a much greater degree of incomprehension than the Samaritan woman, who subsequently goes on to evangelize her entire village. Nevertheless, the Samaritan woman and other characters who are ultimately characterized in a favourable way, display elements of misunderstanding that allow Jesus to clarify something about his message, mission, identity, origins, etc.

9   Francis J. Moloney, *Belief in the Word: Reading John 1–4* (Minneapolis: Fortress, 1993), p. 52.

within the story of the God of Israel and how that God creates, sustains and covenants with humanity. Just as the creation account takes place 'in the beginning' (ἐν ἀρχῇ, Gen. 1.1, LXX), where God 'spoke' (καὶ εἶπεν ὁ θεός, Gen. 1.3a, LXX), and created both 'light' (γενηθήτω φῶς, Gen. 1.3b, LXX), and all living creatures (cf. Gen. 1.20-31), so John's story of Jesus Christ starts 'in the beginning' (ἐν ἀρχῇ, John 1.1) with the 'word' (λόγος, John 1.1-2) who is the purveyor of both life (ζωή, 1.4) and light (φῶς, 1.4, 5). The complete realities of the God of Israel are fully present in the *Logos* (1.1c; see the helpful rendering of the NEB: 'and what God was the Word was'), and the *Logos* is also the agent through whom God created the universe (1.3). The light of the *Logos* shines forth into a darkness which can neither comprehend nor overcome it (ἡ σκοτία αὐτὸ οὐ κατέλαβεν, 1.5).[10]

The theologically significant terms 'light' (φῶς)[11] and 'life' (ζωή)[12] appear elsewhere in the Gospel, though the concepts are present in the story even when these specific terms are not used. The presence of these concepts helps to add contours to various character interactions as the story presses forward. One such example is the coming of Nicodemus to Jesus by night (Νικόδημος . . . ἦλθεν πρὸς αὐτὸν νυκτός, 3.1-2). This description not only represents Nicodemus's darkened understanding but proleptically announces his complete bewilderment at Jesus' teaching (πῶς δύναται ταῦτα γενέσθαι; 3.9). He comes to Jesus, the light of humanity, under the cover of darkness and leaves without comprehending the substance of his words. In a very real sense, the audience's first experience with Nicodemus confirms the truth of the narrator's words: 'the darkness has not *understood*' the light (cf. 1.5).

Another example can be found in chapter 18, where a delegation of temple police and Roman soldiers arrives in the garden at night to arrest Jesus. In John 18.3 the delegation is pictured with lamps (λαμπάδων) and torches (ὅπλων) – two sources of illumination – in order to take the light of humanity into custody. The group boldly seeks Jesus but when he identifies himself (λέγει αὐτοῖς· ἐγώ εἰμι, v. 5), the delegation falls back into a quasi-worship posture (v. 6) – a response that is ironic and admittedly difficult to understand apart from the audience's knowledge of Jesus' exalted status. In the end the delegation takes Jesus into custody only because he allows it to happen; he exercises control over the situation from start to finish. This second night-time passage depicts a character interaction in which the darkness does not *overcome* the light (cf. 1.5). It is up to the audience to make these subtle connections and thereby test the truthfulness of the Prologue's witness to Jesus Christ.

---

10   *Double entendre* is a prominent feature of Johannine discourse. Numerous commentators have pointed out that καταλαμβάνω can be rendered 'overcome' or 'comprehend'. Both nuances are probably intended here. See BDAG, s.v. καταλαμβάνω (p. 520).

11   Cf. 5.35; 8.12; 9.5; 12.35, 36, 46.

12   Cf. 3.15-16, 36; 4.14, 36; 5.24, 26, 29, 39, 40; 6.27, 33, 35, 40, 47, 48, 51, 53, 54, 63, 68; 8.12; 10.10, 28; 11.25; 12.25, 50; 14.6; 17.2, 3; 20.31.

b. John 1.6-13: The Logos and the World

The second section of the Prologue begins with a reference to John the Baptist (though the Fourth Gospel never refers to John using the titles ὁ βαπτίζων[13] or ὁ βαπτιστὴς[14]). The recent history of Fourth Gospel interpretation has yielded all sorts of speculation about the significance of John's insertion at this point in the Prologue. For our purposes, what is important to note is John's designation as ἀπεσταλμένος παρὰ θεοῦ (1.6b). According to the narrator, he has no special messianic status *vis-à-vis* the *Logos*, but is simply the one authorized by God to bear witness to Jesus (1.7-8). As such, John's subsequent witness to Jesus (1.29, 34, 36) will prove to be reliable.

In v. 10 the audience is introduced to the κόσμος and learns of the relationship between the *Logos* and the world. In Hellenistic Greek, κόσμος carries a range of meanings, several of which are employed by the evangelist.[15] The term is used to refer to the material reality of the created world,[16] the physical realm into which Jesus has entered,[17] and the object of God's affection and salvific intentions.[18] In 1.10 the term appears to function metonymically as a symbol for humanity. In the story that follows, there are at least eight instances where κόσμος emerges as a technical term for humanity and in those contexts it is presented with a 'distinctly pejorative meaning'.[19] In 1.10 the audience learns that the *Logos* was, 'in the world (ἐν τῷ κοσμῷ), and though the world (ὁ κόσμος) was created through him, the world (ὁ κόσμος) did not know him'. This statement further prepares the audience for humanity's rejection of Jesus in the Gospel, and again confirms the truthfulness of the *double entendre* in 1.5: the darkness has not understood/overcome the light. Throughout the story, the darkened 'world' (= humanity) consistently fails to comprehend Jesus' words and works, and at the end of the narrative, the powers of darkness do not prevail against the risen Jesus.

Verse 11 reiterates the substance of v. 10 using a slightly different concept: 'He came to *his own place* (τὰ ἴδια) and *his own people* (οἱ ἴδιοι) did not receive him.' The neuter plural use of ἴδιος in the first half of the verse is a reference to the world as the physical realm into which Jesus has entered. The

---

13   Cf. Mark 1.4.

14   Cf. Matt. 3.1.

15   See *TDNT*, 3.868–98; BDAG, s.v. κόσμος (pp. 561–3).

16   Most notably 1.10b: ὁ κόσμος δι' αὐτοῦ ἐγένετο.

17   The Fourth Gospel presents Jesus as the one who has come 'from above'. Thus, his departure from the Father represents his entrance into 'the world', the realm of 'below'. On this, see 1.9, 10a; 3.17ab, 19; 6.14.

18   See, among others, 1.29; 3.16, 17c; 4.42; 6.51.

19   '"Obscure" though its etymology remains to this day, κόσμος is still beyond doubt one of the principal concepts of Greek thought. It was, to be sure, the richness of its various meanings that fitted it for the role it played in Greco-Hellenistic philosophy . . . For in this variety of meanings lay its potential to become "one of the most important terms in Greek philosophy" and "one of the great original creations of the Greek spirit". It is, therefore, doubly puzzling that κόσμος comes to have a *distinctly pejorative meaning* in the NT, and particularly in the Gospel of John' (Stanley B. Marrow, 'Κόσμος in John', *CBQ* 64 [2002], p. 90) (emphasis added).

masculine plural use of ἴδιος in the second half of the verse simply refers to humanity. The *Logos* has come into a world he created (cf. 1.3), which is also shrouded in darkness. That darkness renders humans both unable to understand the *Logos* and hostile toward his intentions. However, despite this existential reality, there are some who will recognize the *Logos*, call upon his name,[20] and become a part of God's newly constituted family (1.12-13) – a family built solely by God's initiative. The authority to grant one status as a 'child of God' has also been granted to the *Logos*.

As above, this section of the Prologue introduces concepts that appear in subsequent character interactions. For example, the audience is told in three separate instances that the κόσμος hates Jesus and his followers (cf. 7.1-7; 15.18-21; 17.14-15). In addition, the audience witnesses 'the world's' antipathy toward Jesus in his specific interactions with both 'the Jews' (οἱ Ἰουδαῖοι)[21] and others present in 'the crowd' (e.g., 6.59-65).

c. John 1.14-18: The Incarnate Son Reveals the Father

Numerous commentators have pointed out that after the Prologue, the evangelist abandons *Logos* terminology altogether, though this should not be regarded as problematic in light of the incarnation described in 1.14: ὁ λόγος σάρξ ἐγένετο καὶ ἐσκήνωσεν ἐν ἡμῖν. The *Logos* existed prior to creation in the presence of God (1.2), but now has taken on a new form of existence by inhabiting human flesh. The contrast created by the use of εἰμί (cf. 1.1-2) and γίνομαι (1.14) underscores the significance of this incarnation. Never before has the *Logos* 'become' something. The *Logos* has always just 'been'. There is no longer a need for *Logos* language. The incarnate word will hereafter be known as Jesus Christ (1.17). The grace and truth God unveils through him will be greater than *Torah*, which God unveiled through Moses. In a final affirmation of the intimate union between Father and Son, the narrator asserts that: (1) Jesus is εἰς τὸν κόλπον τοῦ πατρὸς ('in the bosom of the Father') – a phrase that will reappear at a significant stage of the story – and (2) Jesus reveals the Father to humanity.

As in the two previous sections of the Prologue, themes are introduced here which come into play later in the story. One example is found in chapter 14, where Jesus is discussing with the disciples his imminent departure to the

---

20   While some contend that the phrase τοῖς πιστεύουσιν εἰς τὸ ὄνομα αὐτοῦ is a reference to the name 'Jesus', I think something far greater is intended here. The connection between the *Logos* and God was explicitly spelled out in 1.1c and is a major theme throughout the Gospel. Therefore, I am persuaded that the use of ὄνομα is meant as a reference to שֵׁם – a common way of referring to the divine name. As the revealer of the Father, the *Logos* shares the very name of God, YHWH.

21   Few issues within Johannine scholarship have occasioned as much discussion or controversy as the identity of 'the Jews' in the Gospel of John. Too much has been written on the topic to provide a comprehensive bibliography here. See, more recently, Reimund Bieringer, Didier Pollefeyt and Frederique Vandecasteele-Vanneuville (eds), *Anti-Judaism and the Fourth Gospel* (Louisville: Westminster John Knox, 2001).

Father. After he proclaims that no one can come to the Father apart from him (14.6), Philip proclaims, 'Lord, show us the Father and that will be enough for us' (14.8). The audience already knows that Jesus is one who reveals the Father to humanity (cf. 1.18) and is in the position to see this request as rooted in a fundamental misunderstanding of Jesus' origins and identity. Jesus goes on to explain, 'Anyone who has seen me has seen the Father' (14.9). The audience knows this, but apparently Philip and the other disciples do not.

Many more examples could be brought forward to demonstrate this theory, though space constraints preclude a lengthy examination. By way of overview, we have seen that the Prologue describes the *Logos* as existing with God and in a unique divine state before time (vv. 1-2). He is further described as the agent of all creation (v. 3), the light of humanity that enlightens those in the world (vv. 4, 9), the possessor of the authority to both appoint God's children (v. 12) and display God's glory (v. 14), in intimate union with the Father (v. 18b), and the one who reveals the Father to humanity (v. 18c). These propositions set the stage by providing the audience with information necessary to evaluate every character's response to Jesus, and thereby they become the interpretive grid through which the audience can understand the Gospel's main purpose: to engender belief in those who hear the story (cf. 20.31). In addition to these descriptive phrases, important terms in the Prologue that appear elsewhere in the Gospel include: (1) 'life' (ζωή),[22] (2) 'light' (φῶς),[23] (3) 'witness' (μαρτυρία/μαρτυρέω, 1.7, 8, 15)[24]; (4) 'the world' (κόσμος, 1.9, 10),[25] (5) 'truth'/'true' (ἀλήθεια/ἀληθινός, 1.9, 14, 17),[26] (6) 'to believe' (πιστεύω, 1.7, 12),[27] (7) 'one's own' (ἴδιος, 1.11),[28] (8) 'glory' (δόξα, 1.14),[29] and (9) the phrase εἰς τὸν κόλπον.[30] Pamment perceptively notes that 'characters use these concepts in slightly different ways, allowing the narrator to indicate their full range of meaning, and this is the purpose of the dialogues'.[31] Characters thus appear as uncomprehending to the degree that they fail to grasp these terms and themes from the Prologue.

22   See n. 12 above.

23   See n. 11 above.

24   The nominal form appears in 1.19; 3.11, 32, 33; 5.31, 32, 34, 36; 8.13, 14, 17; 19.35; 21.24. The verbal form appears in 1.32, 34; 2.25; 3.11, 26, 28, 32; 4.39, 44; 5.31, 32, 33, 36, 37, 39; 7.7; 8.13, 14, 18; 10.25; 12.17; 13.21; 15.26, 27; 18.23, 37; 19.35; 21.24.

25   See also 1.29; 3.16, 17, 19; 4.42; 6.14, 33, 51; 7.4, 7; 8.12, 23, 26; 9.5, 39; 10.36; 11.9, 27; 12.19, 25, 31, 46, 47; 13.1; 14.17, 19, 22, 27, 30, 31; 15.18, 19; 16.8, 11, 20, 21, 28, 33; 17.5, 6, 9, 11, 13, 14, 15, 16, 18, 21, 23, 24, 25; 18.20, 36, 37; 21.25.

26   ἀλήθεια appears in 3.21; 4.23, 24; 5.33; 8.32, 40, 44, 45, 46; 14.6, 17; 15.26; 16.7, 13; 17.17, 19; 18.37, 38. ἀληθινός appears in 4.23, 37; 6.32; 7.28; 8.16; 15.1; 17.3; 19.35. ἀληθής appears in 3.33; 4.18; 5.31, 32; 6.55; 7.18; 8.13, 14, 17, 26; 10.41; 19.35; 21.24. ἀληθῶς appears in 1.47; 4.42; 6.14; 7.26, 40; 8.31; 17.8.

27   See also 1.7, 12; 2.23; 3.12-18, 36; 4.50, 53; 5.24, 46-47; 6.29-47; 7.38-39, 48; 8.24, 45-46; 9.35-38; 10.37-38, 42; 11.26-27; 12.11; 13.19; 14.1-2, 11-12; 16.9; 17.21; 19.35; 20.31.

28   See also 1.41; 4.44; 5.18, 43; 7.18; 8.44; 10.3, 4, 12; 13.1; 15.19; 16.32; 19.27.

29   See also 2.11; 5.41, 44; 7.18; 8.50, 54; 9.24; 11.4, 40; 12.41, 43; 17.5, 22, 24.

30   A variation of this phrase appears in ch. 13, where the Beloved Disciple is described as ἐν τῷ κόλπῳ τοῦ Ἰησοῦ. This significance of this phrase will be discussed below.

31   Margaret Pamment, 'Focus in the Fourth Gospel', *ExpTim* 97 (1985), p. 73.

It is not a problem for the implied audience that characters have not been exposed to the truths revealed in the Prologue. This is part of the narrator's rhetorical strategy. These misunderstandings heighten the audience's awareness and understanding of Jesus' origins, mission, and identity. The narrator then uses the discourses of Jesus to shed light on the fuller meaning of these misunderstood themes and accomplishes this in contexts where Jesus is instructing or correcting a given character. Several common elements appear during these character interactions: (1) Jesus speaks or acts in the presence of another character in a manner consistent with his mission; (2) the character in question misperceives some element of Jesus' words or deeds in a way that requires instruction or correction; and (3) Jesus speaks or acts again with the purpose of instructing or correcting the character(s) in question. In these interactions, one or more themes from the Prologue appears, further revealing the depth of the character's misunderstanding, and in turn more fully elucidating the truth about Jesus to the implied audience.

Since there is not enough space in the present essay to demonstrate this theory comprehensively we will test it by examining one major character and demonstrating how that character's misunderstandings are related to the 'insider information' to which the audience is privy. Peter is an ideal test case because – aside from Jesus – he appears more often and has more words attributed to him than any other character in the narrative. Since there is little direct characterization in John's Gospel, speech and action necessarily serve as the primary means of characterization. Peter's speech and actions, especially during the scenes in which he misunderstands, will validate the theory that misunderstanding and character development point back to and arise from the implied audience's knowledge of the Johannine Prologue. The remainder of this essay will focus on the narrator's presentation of Peter in chapters 1, 6, 13, 18 and 20.[32]

III. Simon Peter: A Test Case

a. Peter in John 1.35-42

The audience meets Peter for the first time in 1.35-42 on the day following John's proclamation that Jesus is the 'Lamb of God' (1.29) and 'God's Chosen One' (1.34). In 1.36 John announces for a second time that Jesus is the 'Lamb of God', this time in the presence of two unnamed disciples. Having heard their teacher exalt Jesus three times, two of the Baptist's disciples leave him and begin to follow Jesus. After his initial conversation with Jesus (1.38-39), one of the disciples, Andrew, seeks his brother to inform him that he and the other disciple have 'found the Messiah' (1.41b). Identifying Andrew

---

32   I have chosen not to include ch. 21 for several reasons. First, the device of misunderstanding is largely absent from that chapter since the risen Jesus is now face to face with the disciples. Second, the scholarly consensus – with which I agree – is that ch. 21 is a later addition and, as such, does not constitute the original ending of the story.

by name, the narrator refers to him as the brother of Simon Peter (v. 40a). Little narrative time passes between the first mention of Simon Peter (v. 40) and the first meeting between Jesus and Simon Peter (v. 42b). This face-to-face encounter is immediately followed by the changing of Simon's name to Cephas. The narrator introduces this new character as Σίμωνος Πέτρου, after which Jesus proclaims σὺ κληθήσῃ Κηφᾶς (v. 42d). The implied audience, which knows Greek and realizes that Peter means 'rock', perceives that this name-change promises that Peter's character will hold some significance later in the story. These words are seemingly an announcement of what Peter will become. This initial interaction between Jesus and Peter is a positive sign for the early development of Peter's character. The implied audience's initial impression of Peter is a favourable one.

b. John 6.60-71

Exegetical Summary
Peter makes his second appearance in 6.68, on the day following Jesus' multiplication of loaves for the five thousand (cf. 6.1-15). John 6 narrates a series of events over a two-day span, which culminates in two mutually exclusive responses to Jesus by his 'disciples'.[33] At several turns in the 'Bread of Life' discourse preceding the present pericope, Jesus' words have led to confusion and outrage. Jesus has encouraged his audience to 'eat his flesh' and 'drink his blood' in order to have eternal life. This saying produces the two opposing responses to Jesus in vv. 60-71. One group falls away on account of this saying and the other draws closer to Jesus. Here, Peter is again presented in a substantially positive light.

Peter in John 6
In v. 60 'many disciples' react negatively to the difficult saying. A key reason why the disciples fail to grasp and accept what Jesus has said is that they have taken his words about 'eating flesh' and 'drinking blood' literally. So Jesus condemns the flesh as useless (ἡ σὰρξ οὐκ ὠφελεῖ οὐδέν) and then affirms that his words are not flesh but spirit and life (v. 63). The audience has the privileged position of knowing what the Prologue affirms about the relationship between Jesus and 'life' (ζωή; 'in him was life and that life was the light of humanity', 1.4), as well as his relationship to 'flesh' (σάρξ; though his origins are heavenly, Jesus 'became flesh' in order to dwell among his own, 1.14). The 'disciples' to whom this message is addressed do not have this insight and will ultimately depart in ignorance. The inability of the disciples to understand Jesus ultimately gives way to their unbelief, which Jesus confirms in v. 64. This is followed by a narrative aside where the reader is told that

---

33   In 6.60-71 there is an increasing specificity on the part of the narrator regarding Jesus' 'disciples'. Two groups emerge in this unit: one group simply referred to as 'many of his disciples', and another group known as 'the Twelve'. The former represents a falling away on account of Jesus' message. The latter represents an acceptance of his message, mission and person.

Jesus knew ἐξ ἀρχῆς (cf. ἐν ἀρχῇ, 1.1, 2) not only who would not believe in him but also who would betray him. This statement brings together two future realities that will culminate in the passion narrative. Jesus is going to be betrayed by one of his disciples and ultimately rejected by his own (cf. οἱ ἴδιοι αὐτὸν οὐ παρέλαβον, 1.11).

The group of bewildered disciples decides that this 'hard saying' is ultimately too difficult to accept and they depart from following him (v. 66). Drawing upon the imagery of the Prologue, Stibbe comments that the λόγος of God has himself become the σκληρὸς λόγος ('hard word', cf. 6.60) for these departing disciples and, in many ways, for the audience.[34] Aware that many 'disciples' have left, Jesus turns to 'the Twelve'[35] and asks if they intend to depart as well (v. 67). In answer to Jesus' question, Peter confesses that Jesus has the 'words of eternal life' (v. 68), recalling the truth of what Jesus has just stated in v. 63 about his words being 'spirit and life' and the prominent theme of 'belief in Jesus' word' that runs throughout 2.1–4.54.[36] This confession also affirms truths about Jesus that reflect what the audience has learned in the Prologue. Peter correctly identifies Jesus' relationship to ἡ ζωή (ἐν αὐτῷ ζωὴ ἦν, 1.4) and ὁ θεός (ὁ λόγος ἦν πρὸς τὸν θεόν, 1.1b), allowing him to stand out, temporarily, as an example of a Johannine character with spiritual insight, though his next few appearances will reveal the limitations of that insight. After his second appearance in the story, Peter remains a positive figure in the eyes of the implied audience.

c. John 13

Exegetical Summary
In an 'example' (ὑπόδειγμα)[37] that prefigures his service on the cross, Jesus washes his disciples' feet at the beginning of chapter 13. This is where Peter begins his descent into incomprehension as a series of critical misunderstandings ensues. Following the foot-washing, the disciples and Jesus share a meal, at which time Jesus predicts that he will be betrayed by one of the Twelve. When Jesus informs the disciples that he is going away and that they will be unable to follow, Peter protests that he is willing to lay

---

34   Mark W. G. Stibbe, *John's Gospel* (New Testament Readings; London: Routledge, 1994), p. 24.

35   Outside of this chapter, this designation for Jesus' closest followers occurs only one other time in the Gospel; in John 20.24, Thomas is identified as 'one of the Twelve'.

36   In that unit a handful of characters including the mother of Jesus (2.5), the Samaritans (4.39), and the royal official (4.50) believe Jesus on the basis of his word. By contrast Nicodemus (3.4, 9) fails to believe because he does not understand Jesus' words. At this stage of the narrative, Peter fits squarely within the tradition of those who believe in Jesus' word. Peter also proclaims that Jesus is the 'Holy One of God' (6.69). With these words the audience witnesses another confession to add to the growing list of Christological affirmations in the Gospel.

37   For more on the significance of ὑπόδειγμα, see R. Alan Culpepper, 'The Johannine *hypodeigma*: A Reading of John 13', *Semeia* 53 (1991), pp. 133–52.

down his own life for Jesus. Peter's naïve misunderstanding is met with Jesus' correction and a prediction of Peter's future threefold denial.

Peter in John 13.1-15

In 13.1-5, Jesus is washing and drying the disciples' feet until he comes to Peter, at which point there is an abrupt break in the foot-washing. Peter first expresses surprise (v. 6) and then registers an outright objection (οὐ μὴ νίψῃς μου τοὺς πόδας εἰς τὸν αἰῶνα) to Jesus washing his feet. The combination of οὐ μὴ and εἰς τὸν αἰῶνα underscores the intensity of Peter's protest. The use of οὐ and μή with the aorist subjunctive is the strongest way to negate something in Hellenistic Greek, denying even the potentiality of an action.[38] In response to Peter's protest, Jesus declares that if Peter rejects the foot-washing he can have no share (μέρος) with Jesus. Often translated 'part', the term μέρος probably refers to a portion of an inheritance – a concept upon which Jesus will elaborate in 14.2-3.[39] Once again, Peter does not understand what Jesus means and responds by asking Jesus to wash his feet, head and hands. In a manner similar to the overly literal 'disciples' in chapter 6, Peter fails to see the symbolism in the washing of his feet and focuses rather on the act itself. If the act of washing brings one into union with Jesus, Peter wants more than a foot-washing; he desires that his entire body be cleansed. The audience cannot doubt Peter's sincerity, but is beginning to question his spiritual insight.

Peter in John 13.16-38

After the foot-washing is complete, Jesus begins to be troubled in spirit and informs the Twelve that one among them – the one who was previously called a 'devil' – will betray him (13.18-22). Upon hearing this statement the disciples are at a loss (ἀπορέω) and begin speculating as to who the betrayer might be. In v. 23 the audience meets the 'disciple whom Jesus loved' for the first time.[40] From this point forward, when the reader encounters Peter, the Beloved Disciple is usually present.[41] Here the Beloved Disciple is seated next to Jesus and leaning against his breast (ἐν τῷ κόλπῳ τοῦ Ἰησοῦ) – a description that recalls the words of the Prologue where Jesus is described as εἰς τὸν κόλπον τοῦ πατρὸς (1.18). This description sets up an implicit contrast between the Beloved Disciple, who is experiencing an intimate union with Jesus like the one Jesus displays with the Father, and Peter who descends

---

38   On this see Daniel B. Wallace, *Greek Grammar Beyond the Basics: An Exegetical Syntax of the New Testament* (Grand Rapids: Zondervan, 1997), p. 546.

39   See BDAG, s.v. μέρος.

40   It is possible, though not certain, that the narrator intends the unnamed disciple with Andrew (1.37-40) to be regarded by the reader as the Beloved Disciple.

41   The only time they are separated throughout the remainder of the Gospel is in chs 18–19. A critical contrast is set up between Peter (ch. 18), who denies Jesus, and the Beloved Disciple (ch. 19), the only member of the Twelve to draw near to Jesus' cross. They are together at the empty tomb and they are together in ch. 21. Some believe that the 'other disciple' in 18.15 should be understood as the Beloved Disciple.

into greater incomprehension. Filled with curiosity about the betrayer, Peter asks the Beloved Disciple to play the role of intermediary and find out the identity of the person about whom Jesus is speaking. The Beloved Disciple asks (v. 25) and Jesus answers (v. 26) but curiously the Beloved Disciple never reports the answer to Peter. The audience, however, is informed that Judas Iscariot is the betrayer, and by receiving the dipped morsel, Judas confirms the prophetic pronouncement uttered by Jesus when he quoted Ps. 41.10 (40.10 LXX). In accord with Jesus' command (v. 27), Judas departs immediately (v. 30).

On the heels of Judas's departure Jesus begins to explain his 'glorification'. He has spoken of his glory on a number of previous occasions in the narrative.[42] In this setting he speaks of his glorification in the context of his betrayal and death. The 'hour' for which the audience has been waiting has finally arrived.[43] Jesus tells the disciples that he will be going away and they will not be able to join him (13.33; cf. 7.33). Again Peter's ignorance is front and centre when he asks Jesus, 'where are you going?' (v. 36a). The Prologue has revealed that Jesus is from the Father (1.1-2) and the audience is now learning that Jesus will return to the Father through his crucifixion. Peter is unaware of Jesus' heavenly origins and therefore fails to appreciate what it means for Jesus to return, even if through the violent means of the cross.

Jesus refuses to answer and reinforces what he has earlier said in v. 33 – the disciples cannot come to where he is going. His hour has come and his glorification entails a departure to the Father who sent him. Because Peter does not understand this truth, he ignorantly protests that he is willing to lay down his life for Jesus. Peter's insistence that he will die with Jesus is met with a sarcastic question (τὴν ψυχήν σου ὑπὲρ ἐμοῦ θήσεις;) and an authoritative contradiction (ἀμὴν ἀμὴν λέγω σοι οὐ μὴ ἀλέκτωρ φωνήσῃ ἕως οὗ ἀρνήσῃ με τρίς, v. 38). The audience is arrested by the prediction of Peter's denials. While Peter may fall short of fully comprehending the truth of Jesus' origins and identity, he has been a positive and sympathetic character up to this point in the story. Nevertheless, his numerous misunderstandings have put him on an increasingly negative trajectory that will not be reversed until chapter 21.

d. John 18

Exegetical Summary

At the conclusion of the Farewell Discourse, Jesus and the disciples have departed across the Kidron Valley (18.1). In an unnamed garden the events of Jesus' final night and day begin to unfold. Judas Iscariot, earlier dispatched

---

42   The theme was introduced in the Prologue in 1.14. The audience sees Jesus 'reveal his glory' in 2.11. Then, in 8.50, 54; 11.4, 40; 14.13; 16.14; 17.4, 5, 10, 22, 24, Jesus speaks of the glory he and the Father share that will ultimately be revealed in his betrayal, crucifixion and resurrection.

43   Jesus has previously spoken about his 'hour' in 2.4; 4.21, 23; 5.25, 28; 7.30; 8.20; 12.23, 27.

to complete his commission 'quickly' (13.27), leads Roman soldiers and a detachment from the chief priests and Pharisees to arrest Jesus in the garden. After a brief conversation in which Jesus self-identifies twice as the 'I am' (cf. vv. 5, 6, 8), he is taken to the Jewish authorities. While Jesus is inside facing the Jewish leaders, Peter is outside denying that he knows Jesus. The predictions of betrayal from chapter 13 are realized.

Peter in John 18.1-14

Jesus and the disciples have now ventured out into a garden where the earlier prediction of betrayal by one of Jesus' closest friends is now coming to pass. Judas appears accompanied by an unlikely pairing of groups. With him are a Roman cohort[44] and a delegation of temple officers sent from the chief priests and Pharisees. In v. 5, the narrator indicates that Judas is 'with them' (μετ' αὐτῶν). Such a description indicates where Judas's loyalties now sit. Opposition to Jesus makes for strange bedfellows as he is face to face with one of his own (Judas), the Jewish leaders (with whom he has been at odds throughout the entire narrative), and a new group (representatives of the Roman government).

Peter and the other disciples are granted release from the imminent police action of the mob though Peter's actions in v. 10 reveal once again a fundamental misunderstanding of Jesus' mission. If Jesus is going to return to the Father, he must be arrested by the delegation of police and soldiers. This is the way to the cross, which for the Johannine Jesus is the way back to the Father. Instead of departing, however, Peter pulls his sword and strikes Malchus, the servant of the high priest, cutting off his right ear. Jesus rebukes Peter for his impetuous action by commanding him to put his sword away, and by pointing out that he must fulfil the will of the Father (v. 11). Jesus' question[45] to Peter is the climactic moment in this scene and, as in previous scenes, there is no response from Peter and no explanation by the narrator. The setting shifts without a word about Peter's misunderstanding. The audience needs no explanation; the narrator intends this silence as an implicit criticism of Peter's inability to see the divinely ordained destiny of Jesus.

Exegetical Summary

As the mob leaves the garden, Jesus is bound, taken into custody, and brought before the Jewish leadership. While Jesus is inside being questioned by Annas, Peter is outside being questioned by those who are standing around and warming themselves. A critical contrast develops between the actions of Jesus and Peter. Jesus speaks boldly before those who have authority to condemn him, while Peter cowers in the presence of a little girl and a slave (18.17, 26). Jesus confesses the truth, while Peter denies it, consequently disavowing

---

44   A Roman cohort was a military unit with a capacity of 600 soldiers.

45   In v. 11 Jesus says: τὸ ποτήριον ὃ δέδωκεν μοι ὁ πατὴρ οὐ μὴ πίω αὐτο. When οὐ μή is combined with the subjunctive to form a question, the resulting clause has the force of an affirmation. On this, see BDF, s.v. 365.

Jesus. Even the prior confession of Jesus (ἐγώ εἰμι, vv. 5b, 6b, 8a) stands in contrast to Peter's denials (οὐκ εἰμι, vv. 17, 25).

Peter in John 18.15-27

While Jesus is inside being questioned by Annas, Simon Peter and 'another disciple' (ἄλλος μαθητής) are following at a distance. The other disciple is acquainted with the high priest and is able to gain access to the courtyard (v. 15). Eventually Peter (v. 16) gains access to the inside when the other disciple speaks to a slave girl who watches the door and Peter is allowed to enter. The introduction of this slave girl provides Peter with his first opportunity to confess or deny Jesus. As he enters the courtyard, the slave girl inquires of him, μὴ καὶ σὺ ἐκ τῶν μαθητῶν εἶ τοῦ ἀνθρώπου τούτου; Her question expects a negative answer and that is exactly what Peter provides. By replying οὐκ εἰμί (v. 17b), Peter not only denies Jesus but also utters words that stand out against the threefold appearance of ἐγώ εἰμι in vv. 5-8.

This scene ends with a side comment from the narrator. A group of characters, including slaves and guards, are warming themselves by the fire in the courtyard of the high priest (v. 18a). The narrator comments that Peter is μετ' αὐτῶν (v. 18b), a phrase that recalls the presence of Judas among the members of the arresting party ('Ιούδας ὁ παραδιδοὺς αὐτὸν μετ' αὐτῶν, v. 5). The connection between the betrayals of Judas and Peter that was so vividly drawn in chapter 13 is re-emphasized in this scene. The irony here is that, while Jesus is inside facing the judgement by the Jewish leaders, Peter is outside in subtle, if unintentional, collusion with those who oppose Jesus. Even when Peter is on the inside (in the courtyard with the other disciple), he remains an outsider because he is 'with them'.

The setting briefly flashes back to Jesus' interview before Annas (vv. 19-24) before returning to Peter who is still 'with them'. When being questioned, Jesus responds to Annas, 'Ask those who have heard me' (v. 21). Ironically, this could be accomplished by going out and questioning Peter! Meanwhile, an unidentified group within the courtyard asks Peter for a second time whether he is one of Jesus' disciples. As with his first denial, the question posed to Peter expects a negative answer, which he is wont to provide: οὐκ εἰμί (v. 25). Without a break in the action Peter is questioned for a third time about his relationship to Jesus. This time a relative of Malchus (18.10) poses the question with the expectation of an affirmative answer: οὐκ ἐγώ σε εἶδον ἐν τῷ κήπῳ μετ' αὐτοῦ; (v. 26). The last words of the question recall Peter's presence with those in the courtyard and again draw the intended contrast. Will Peter confess to having been μετ' αὐτοῦ or will he deny it and remain μετ' αὐτῶν? Having heard Jesus' prediction in chapter 13, the audience is not surprised that Peter denies knowing Jesus for a third time. After the third denial the cock crows immediately. In denying Jesus, Peter has failed to honour the love commandment and has become a betrayer on the level of Judas Iscariot.

e. John 20

Exegetical Summary

The last time the reader saw Peter was on the occasion of his third denial (18.26-27) and his final words in the text were words of disavowal (οὐκ εἰμί, 18.25). Since that point there has been no mention of Peter and no attempt to absolve him of the responsibility of denying Jesus three times. Nevertheless, Peter retains the important status he has achieved throughout the Gospel. This much is clear in the depiction of Mary's discovery of the empty tomb. Peter becomes the first recipient of the news (v. 2) and, despite his recent indiscretions, he remains chief among the small group of Jesus-followers.

Peter in John 20.1-10

It is now early on the first day of the week. The narrator makes sure to point out that these events take place σκοτίας ἔτι οὔσης ('while it was still dark', v. 1a). The audience recognizes the theological motif of 'darkness' and its association with unbelief throughout the Gospel.[46] Again, the audience is led back to the words of the Prologue: 'The light shines in the darkness but the darkness has not overcome it' (1.5). The light of the world has seemingly been extinguished by the proceedings of the previous few days, but the events at the empty tomb will confirm that the light has triumphed over darkness.

Mary Magdalene, whom the reader has only just met at the foot of the cross in 19.25, is the first to venture to the tomb of Jesus.[47] Upon arriving she notices that the stone has been rolled away from the entrance. The terse description provided by the narrator (βλέπει τὸν λίθον ἠρμένον ἐκ τοῦ μνημείου), makes it appear that Mary's immediate response is not to investigate the tomb but rather to run directly to the disciples. She remains, for the moment, ἐν σκοτίᾳ. Mary finds Simon Peter and the Beloved Disciple and reports that the tomb is empty (v. 2). Her report leads to immediate action on the part of the two disciples.

In v. 3 the two disciples depart *toward* the tomb (ἐξῆλθεν οὖν . . . καὶ ἤρχοντο εἰς τὸ μνημεῖον), and v. 4 reports that as they make their way to the tomb they are running together (ἔτρεχον δὲ οἱ δύο ὁμοῦ). The picture of the two disciples in vv. 3-4 contrasts with the description of Mary Magdalene who in v. 2 ran away from the tomb (τρέχει οὖν καὶ ἔρχεται πρὸς Σίμωνα). As the two disciples are running, the Beloved Disciple passes Peter and arrives first.[48] The audience already knows of the Beloved Disciple's position as the disciple *par excellence* in the Fourth Gospel (cf. 13.23-26; 19.25-27).

---

46   Cf., e.g., 1.5; 3.2; 6.17; 8.12; 9.4; 11.10; 12.35, 46; 13.30; 19.39.

47   Mary appears in the passion and resurrection narratives of all three Synoptics (Mark 15.40, 47; 16.1; Matt. 27.56, 61; 28.1; Luke 24.10). She also appears earlier in Luke's Gospel (8.2), where it is reported that Jesus cast seven demons out of her. Mary Magdalene is not a prominent figure in the Fourth Gospel. However, in light of her appearance in the Synoptic resurrection traditions, it is unlikely that she was unknown to the original readership of John.

48   Some commentators have seen this as a race to the tomb; cf., e.g., Walter Bauer, *Das Johannesevangelium erklärt* (HKNT 6; Tübingen: J.C.B. Mohr, 1933), p. 229.

Throughout the Gospel the reader has also seen Peter in a position of leadership over the disciples – though his example has not always been exemplary. In this instance, however, both disciples run away from the situation of darkness and 'unfaith' evident in Mary's words and depart toward the tomb, the place of faith associated with God's intervention in the story. The Beloved Disciple is the first of Jesus' disciples to witness the linen cloths lying inside the empty tomb. He observes the tomb but cautiously stops short of entering (v. 5); by contrast Peter reaches the tomb second and immediately enters (v. 6).

The description of what Peter sees in the tomb is much more detailed than what the Beloved Disciple witnesses. The latter simply sees κείμενα τὰ ὀθόνια ('the strips of linen cloth there', v. 5). Peter, on the other hand, sees 'the strips of linen cloth there' (v. 6b), 'the towel which had been upon his head' (v. 7a), and notices that 'it was not with the strips of linen cloth but rolled up in a place by itself' (v. 7b). Despite this information, the narrator does not comment on Peter's response to what he has witnessed, though the audience is explicitly told that the Beloved Disciple εἶδεν καὶ ἐπίστευσεν ('he saw and believed', v. 8). It is hard to miss the contrasts created by this presentation of the two disciples. While both disciples move toward genuine Johannine faith, the narrator continues to elevate the Beloved Disciple. Both see the empty tomb (vv. 6-8). Both fail to understand the scripture indicating that Jesus must rise from the dead (v. 9). But only the Beloved Disciple is said to believe.

While both disciples are moving in the direction of faith, the narrator persists in providing a picture of the Beloved Disciple as the disciple *par excellence*. Peter is shown moving from darkness toward light and from unfaith toward faith, but he will not fully learn what the audience knows until he comes face to face with the risen Jesus.

In his previous two appearances, Peter had failed to understand Jesus' symbolic actions (the foot-washing, 13.1-20), explicit teaching about his departure (13.24-38), non-resistance to his departure (18.10-11), or the importance of laying down one's life as implied by the love command (18.15-18, 25-27; cf. 13.34-35). Nevertheless, when he, along with the Beloved Disciple, hears the report of the empty tomb he responds by moving toward the location of God's entrance into the story (20.3-10). In this unit Peter regains some of his lustre of early appearances and is on his way toward becoming the 'Rock' alluded to in 1.42. He shows a level of trust and spiritual comprehension, but he has not yet been fully restored in the eyes of the implied audience.

IV. Conclusion

Throughout this essay I have argued that the Prologue provides a grid through which to read the entire narrative, especially misunderstanding characters. An exegetical consideration of Simon Peter helps validate the theory that character misunderstanding is part of the narrator's rhetorical strategy and is related both to the Prologue's description of Jesus and to the Gospel's overall Christological presentation. We see that Peter's misunderstandings reveal his ignorance about concepts to which the implied audience has already been exposed in John 1.1-18. Throughout the story, the audience must continually return to the information revealed in the Prologue in order to evaluate character responses to Jesus along with other elements of the narrative. Uncomprehending characters such as Peter advance the plot by causing the audience to look back at what has been revealed, which in turn points forward to the cumulative effect of the story to that point. In each instance of incomprehension the audience is reminded of the information already given about Jesus and also of how each character in the story has received him thus far. This constant back-and-forth movement helps contribute to the narrator's desired effect by keeping the audience aware of what has transpired and building anticipation for what will take place as the story moves toward its climax. In this way, John's uncomprehending characters advance the action of the story while emphasizing the Gospel's Christology.

John's uncomprehending characters also help clarify the presentation of several interwoven theological themes in the Gospel. The identity of Jesus is laid out in the Prologue and a proper or improper understanding of Jesus' identity has implications for the audience's view of belief, Christology, and the Johannine theology of the cross. These related themes come to the forefront of the narrative every time an uncomprehending character fails to understand Jesus. The implied audience (which already knows the story of Jesus but is being exposed to the Johannine version for the first time) understands that Jesus is from above and that he is the revealer of the Father who will eventually die on a Roman cross. An understanding of Jesus' identity informs the Gospel's Christological presentation. An understanding of John's Christology clarifies Jesus' mission toward the cross, which in turn clarifies the nature of authentic Johannine belief. Whether explicit or implicit, these themes are present in the reader's every encounter with an uncomprehending character. A synchronic approach to the narrative provides the audience with the knowledge that Jesus is the Christ, the Son of God, and the revealer of the Father who has come from above, to be glorified on the cross and at the tomb. For one to believe in Jesus, an understanding of these truths must be present. By using the Prologue in concert with misunderstanding characters the narrator illustrates improper belief in Jesus and beckons the audience to respond in belief (cf. 20.31) from a perspective informed not by sight, but by a knowledge of Jesus' origins and identity.

PART TWO

JOHANNINE CHARACTER STUDIES

Chapter 8

THE FOURTH GOSPEL'S CHARACTERIZATION OF GOD: A RHETORICAL PERSPECTIVE

Stan Harstine

I. Introduction

A major challenge to scholarship today is the diverse points of view brought to the Fourth Gospel by scholars from differing schools of thought. Theologians, historical critics, source critics, narrative critics and varying readers too numerous to name bring their backgrounds and tools to the text. These diverse elements of Johannine scholarship have highlighted various difficulties within the Gospel that make a trip through the Gospel arduous at best, hazardous at worst. The focused study of the character of God in this Gospel encounters these obstacles at every turn and even on the straightaways. Consequently, the best one can hope for is to reach conclusions that represent the endeavour without having totally diverted from the course.

Two obstacles should be noted that greatly shape this attempt. The primary obstacle pertains to the unique relationship between Jesus and God in this Gospel. While God is portrayed throughout the Bible as a deity who defies complete comprehension, in the Fourth Gospel Jesus is portrayed as both *Logos* and God. It is almost enough to bring the whole pursuit to a halt. R. A. Culpepper noted three decades ago, 'It might be better, therefore, to say that God is characterized by Jesus and that having understood the Gospel's characterization of Jesus one has grasped its characterization of God.'[1]

Any attempt to discuss God as a unique character must select and define parameters that will make focusing solely on God obtainable. The first parameter must delineate between Jesus and God. Those passages where Jesus is equated with God or, in the specific language of this Gospel, the Son with the Father, must be approached with caution.[2] The second parameter concerns this specific Son and Father language in the Gospel. Any study of the character God must include language of Father whenever it refers to God.[3]

---

1   R. Alan Culpepper, *Anatomy of the Fourth Gospel: A Study in Literary Design* (Philadelphia: Fortress, 1983), p. 113. Culpepper concludes that thought with the note that the Father 'requires independent consideration'.

2   See passages like John 1.1, 18; 10.30, 38; 14.10-11; 16.32; and 20.28.

3   See John 6.27, 8.42, 54, where God and Father are used in parallel to one another. See

The second obstacle entails the study of characterization itself. Recognizing various approaches to the study of characterization and how other authors have focused on the character God,[4] this essay will examine characterization with an emphasis on its rhetorical value.[5] All narrative includes some element of rhetoric. 'Narrative itself can be fruitfully understood as a rhetorical act, somebody telling somebody else on some occasion and for some purpose(s) that something happened.'[6] The standard categories of plot (something happened) and point of view (somebody telling) are dependent upon the literary work's characters for movement and change. The author of a text can even use character narrators to communicate to the audience.[7] The recognition of narrative's rhetorical role provides an opportunity to study not merely 'characterization' but also the rhetorical value of characterization to the text. This realization shifts the main question for this study from merely 'How is God characterized?' to 'What rhetorical role does the character God provide?' However, due to the interrelatedness of these two questions the first must be clarified before the second can be explored.

II. Theory of Characterization

Modern literary theory presents various approaches to the study of characterization. Character is no longer understood in simple terms of a 'flat' or 'round' description of a named or unnamed human subject in a text.[8] This study will utilize three components of character – mimetic, thematic and synthetic – to help identify the rhetorical value of the character God.[9] These components relate to one another differently in various narratives and their relationship is defined by the progression of each narrative.[10] Each component

also Marianne Meye Thompson, '"God's Voice You Have Never Heard, God's Form You Have Never Seen": The Characterization of God in the Gospel of John', *Semeia* 63 (1993), pp. 177–204; Paul W. Meyer, '"The Father": The Presentation of God in the Fourth Gospel', in R. Alan Culpepper and C. Clifton Black (eds), *Exploring the Gospel of John* (Louisville: Westminster John Knox, 1996), pp. 255–73; and D. François Tolmie, 'The Characterization of God in the Fourth Gospel', *JSNT* 68 (1997), pp. 57–75.

4   Thompson, 'Voice', pp. 178–85, and Tolmie, 'Characterization', pp. 58–61.

5   James Phelan, *Reading People, Reading Plots: Character, Progression, and the Interpretation of Narrative* (Chicago: University of Chicago Press, 1989), pp. 7–8; idem, *Narrative as Rhetoric: Technique, Audiences, Ethics, Ideology* (Columbus, OH: Ohio State University Press, 1996).

6   James Phelan, *Living to Tell about It: A Rhetoric and Ethics of Character Narration* (Ithaca, NY: Cornell University Press, 2005), p. 18.

7   Ibid., p. 1.

8   These categories were first set forth by E. M. Forster in his important work, *Aspects of the Novel* (New York: Harcourt, Brace and Company, 1927).

9   James Phelan utilizes these three elements in his works cited above to analyse characterization in literature.

10   James Phelan, 'Character and Judgment in Narrative and in Lyric: Toward an

includes both dimensions and functions.[11] A dimension consists of the attributes of a character that exist in a neutral environment, that is, apart from the text. A function is seen in how the attribute is relevant in and throughout the text.[12] For example, the mimetic dimensions of God in the Fourth Gospel can be listed in a set of traits while the mimetic functions of God can only be discussed relative to the text of the Fourth Gospel. Our pursuit of the rhetorical role of God as a character will examine each of these components and their relationships throughout the narrative's progression. Yet, it is important to recognize that the Fourth Gospel is a text written by an author from the world of the first century. Narrative conventions then and now are not identical; some modern expectations of character will not be found in the text of the Fourth Gospel.[13]

III. Character Dimensions

The mimetic dimension of characterization represents traits normally associated with a real person.[14] The use of mimesis by an author invites the audience to identify with the character in familiar, human terms. One of the standard entry points for understanding a character is to evaluate the actions and descriptions associated with that character in the text.[15] These traits are readily available to the reader and help define the character throughout the progression of the text.

The prominent portrait of God/Father in the Fourth Gospel is one who sends.[16] The sending role of God/Father is part of the Gospel from the Prologue to the resurrection of Jesus. In chapters 1–3, God is the one who sends, while in chapters 5–14, Father is the sender. This simple observation begs the question, 'Is there a rhetorical reason for the specific language use in these two sections?' However, that discussion will need to wait until later. A second portrayal of God/Father is one who loves.[17] Only once is God

---

Understanding of the Audience's Engagement in *The Waves*', *Style* 24 (Fall 1990), pp. 408–21 (409).

11   Phelan, *Reading*, pp. 8–10.

12   Ibid., p. 9.

13   See the work of Robert Scholes and Robert Kellogg (*The Nature of Narrative* [London: Oxford University Press, 1966]), who describe the development of characterization in narratives from Homer to the present.

14   Phelan, *Reading*, p. 2. See also W. J. Harvey, *Character and the Novel* (Ithaca, NY: Cornell University Press, 1965).

15   See Shlomith Rimmon-Kenan, *Narrative Fiction: Contemporary Poetics* (New York: Methuen & Co., 1983), pp. 59–70.

16   John 1.6; 3.16-17, 33-34; 5.36-37; 6.57; 8.16-18; 10.36; 12.49; 14.24, 26; 17.3; 20.11. This analysis is not new; see Culpepper, *Anatomy*, p. 113; Tolmie, 'Characterization', p. 68; and, as Thompson ('Voice', pp. 189–90) notes, the activity of God's sending is narrated by Jesus.

17   John 3.16, 35; 5.20; 10.17; 14.21; 15.9; 16.27.

described in relation to love, 3.16; elsewhere it is Father who loves, either the Son or those who love the Son. Third, God/Father is described as one who gives, specifically to Jesus.[18] Finally, God is portrayed as one who speaks, commands, or teaches.[19]

These mimetic dimensions – one who sends, loves, gives and speaks – are noted elsewhere by others and self-apparent to many readers of this Gospel.[20] These portraits describe God as a character in the narrative through association with human traits.[21] Each of these traits occurs in several narrative sections of the text, indicating their constancy throughout the narrative progression. However, the primary focus for this study is the second question, 'What rhetorical role does the character God/Father provide?' This query must include the full range of character components and not limit itself to mimetic dimensions.

The thematic dimensions are those elements that provide significance to a character in the narrative. This significance is not restricted to the narrative itself; it can also be derived by transplanting the thematic element from its context and asking why the actual reader should be concerned about this particular character.[22] Discussions on theology in the Fourth Gospel are one way that thematic elements for the character God are commonly identified. One problem inherent in the pursuit of thematic elements has already been discussed: the Gospel's predilection to associate Jesus and God as one. Thus any *theology* is essentially a *Christology* when talking about the Fourth Gospel.[23]

A second difficulty in the pursuit of thematic dimensions is the 'distinction between characters as individuals [the mimetic] and characters as representative entities [the thematic]'.[24] For instance, the blindness of the man in John 9 can be understood to demonstrate a thematic function of spiritual darkness, so that his movement from blindness to sight counters the Pharisees who see, yet are blind.[25] The blind man becomes a representative for the many who 'don't see but believe'.[26] The query for this study is: 'Does (can) a monotheistic view of God permit God to represent something other than the one God?'

---

18   John 3.35; 5.36; 10.29; 11.22; 13.3.

19   John 8.28; 9.29; 12.50; 14.31.

20   Culpepper, *Anatomy*, pp. 112–15; Thompson, 'Voice', pp. 189–94; and Tolmie, 'Characterization', pp. 61–75. This set of four characteristics is not exhaustive. There are other traits that occur once or twice and function within the rhetoric of their passage: God is spirit (4.24), the Father desires worshippers (4.23), the Father draws people to the Son (6.44), and the Father sanctifies (10.36).

21   The description of a deity through anthropomorphic expressions is common in the ancient world and not uncommon even in the modern world, as indicated in the movie realm with, for example, *Oh, God!* in 1977, and *Bruce Almighty* in 2003.

22   Phelan, *Reading*, pp. 2–3.

23   Meyer, 'Father', pp. 255–7.

24   Phelan, *Reading*, p. 13.

25   Culpepper, *Anatomy*, p. 140.

26   John 20.29.

In the context of this essay, the question should be clarified: 'Within a literary work like the Fourth Gospel, can God/Father as a character represent something in a thematic sense that is beyond the mimetic representation?' While it is uncomplicated to regard God/Father as representing a deity figure from certain religious perspectives, in the literary world this character can present thematic dimensions and have thematic functions within the text. However, in contrast to the mimetic representation that is primarily informed by the actions of the character, the thematic element is informed by the attributes of the character as described by others. Several thematic dimensions are God as authority related to sovereignty,[27] God as creative artist,[28] and God as goal or purpose for living.[29]

The synthetic dimension is the artificial component of a character in a narrative. It is the recognition that, although the character may represent a real person, the character described in the text is not a real person, merely a representation of the person.[30] A character described in a narrative is unique to that narrative. While the character may appear in other narratives, unique traits may be assigned by *that* narrative which are not present elsewhere, traits necessary for the progression of that particular narrative.

In order to discuss the synthetic dimension it is important to recognize and define the audience for the text. There are essentially two audience types that participate in a text: those outside the text and those within the text. Peter J. Rabinowitz identifies the first as including either the actual or the authorial audience and the latter as either the narrative or the ideal narrative audience.[31] For the two narrative audiences, who by definition participate fully in the text, no synthetic component exists to the character God. Everything in the text is accepted or would be accepted whether it is 'real' or not. The actual audience consists of anyone who might read the text at any point in time and from any cultural background. Such an audience is too complex to discuss possible synthetic dimensions in this short project. That leaves the task of describing the synthetic dimensions for the authorial audience, the hypothetical audience of the text for whom the author designs the work.[32]

The authorial audience of the Fourth Gospel can be described as familiar with Greek writings of Second Temple Judaism, especially Genesis, and with the oral tradition of the Jesus community.[33] Consequently the introduction

---

27   E.g., the kingdom of God (3.5), the Father has given everything to the Son (3.35), God set his seal (6.27), authority is given from above (19.11).

28   E.g., all things came into being (1.3), the Father shows the Son what he is doing (5.20).

29   Work for that which gives eternal life (6.27), eternal life is knowing God (17.3).

30   Phelan, *Reading*, pp. 1–2.

31   Peter J. Rabinowitz, 'Truth in Fiction: A Reexamination of Audiences', *Critical Inquiry* 4 (1977), pp. 121–41.

32   Norman R. Petersen, 'The Reader in the Gospel', *Neot* 18 (1984), pp. 38–51; and Peter J. Rabinowitz and Michael W. Smith, *Authorizing Readers: Resistance and Respect in the Teaching of Literature* (Language and Literacy Series, New York: Teachers College Press, 1998).

33   Richard Bauckham (ed.), *The Gospel for All Christians: Rethinking the Gospel Audiences* (Grand Rapids: Eerdmans, 1998); Charles H. Talbert, *Reading John* (Reading the New

of 'God' in the second phrase of this Gospel, John 1.1b, would not create any synthetic or artificial dimensions, since the authorial audience would recognize God as a real aspect of their culture and literature and bring such prior knowledge into their understanding of the text. Only in John 12.28 when a voice comes from heaven does the character God provide any event the authorial audience might consider 'artificial'. However, the various references in the LXX to a voice from heaven would limit the synthetic nature of such an event.[34] Subsequently, the synthetic dimension for the authorial audience is minimized.

IV. Mimetic Functions

An investigation of the mimetic and thematic functions of the character in the text is required because it is precisely in these functions that the rhetorical argument, in opposition to the structuralist, can be found. The author introduces a character and, by so doing, introduces the potential for that character to participate significantly within the text's rhetoric. Whether that potential is achieved is determined by the development and interaction of that character throughout the text.[35] However, the rhetorical role of the character is not limited to information gleaned from the text; some of the rhetorical value is inherent in the character's initial description. When the audience of the Fourth Gospel, authorial, actual, or implied, is confronted with the three letters forming the word 'God' in English, or four letters of θεός in Greek, the audience has a preconceived notion of the signified referent for the arrangement of those specific symbols. Thus, prior to any dimensions introduced by the text the reader has an informed view of that representation. The text then affirms or alters that informed view throughout the text. For example, John 1.1: 'In the beginning the Word was, and the Word was with God, indeed the Word was God.' Based on the words *in the beginning* the reader will determine who/what *the Word was*, without any prompting by the text and its later identification of the Word and God.

God's entrance into the Gospel narrative as a sending agent comes in 1.6 where God sends John as a testimony to the light. The sending motif would not be perceived as an unusual activity for God since it is a motif consistent with LXX descriptions.[36] This motif is replicated in 3.17 where God sends the Son, in 3.34 where the one sent speaks the words of God, and in 17.3 where eternal

Testament; New York: Crossroad, 1992), pp. 61–5; Martin M. Culy, *Echoes of Friendship in the Gospel of John* (NTM, 30; Sheffield: Sheffield Phoenix Press, 2010) especially pp. 178–88; and Stan Harstine, *Moses as a Character in the Fourth Gospel* (JSNTSup, 229; London: Sheffield Academic Press, 2002), pp. 28–37.

34   For examples of voices from heaven see Gen. 21.17; Exod. 20.1-18; Deut. 4.36; 2 Sam. 22.14; 1 Kgs 19.11-14; and Dan. 4.31.

35   Phelan, *Reading*, p. 10.

36   2 Chron. 32.21; Zech. 6.15; Bar. 1.21.

life is described as recognizing the one true God and the one whom he sent, Jesus Christ. These four appearances coalesce into a mimetic function for God as sender: to bring about life rather than judgement. The character God serves a mimetic function in the text as the source of life, a function established for the audience in 1.1-4. However, between chapters 3 and 17, it is not God who sends, but Father.[37]

When Father is first reported as sending, 5.36-37, the context reminds the audience, by amplifying the reference to John's testimony (5.32-36), that God sent John. The parallel between God and Father as sender is established in the mind of the audience. Jesus reports that Father sent him to provide life in 6.57, while life, testimony and judgement unite in 8.12-18 to highlight the veracity of Jesus. Father sent Jesus to speak words of life rather than to judge in 12.49-50, where the words he speaks are described as eternal life. In 14.23-24 Father sent Jesus and Jesus speaks the words of Father. Finally, Father will send a *Paraclete* to help them recall these same words (14.26). God's mimetic function, source of Life noted above, is doubly reinforced when the sending attribute associated with 'God' is carried by the character 'Father' as well.

The second mimetic trait of God/Father, one who loves, is likewise developed throughout the text. Introduced in 3.16-17, God loves the world and this love is expressed through sending the Son. Thereafter in the text Father is the one who loves. The object of Father's love is the Son[38] and those who love the Son.[39] A close relationship between 'Love' and 'Sending' is thus identified within the text. Having observed earlier that sending is a critical component to the text, we observe also that love is a factor directly related to sending, especially in its first appearance, 3.16, as well as in 17.23 where 'the world' is to know the love of Father. The relationships described in the text between Father, Son, and those who love the Son, are characterized by this love, particularly in chapters 13-17, where ἀγάπη or ἀγαπάω appear prominently in the Fourth Gospel.[40] The Greek term φιλέω is used of Father only twice: where the objects of love are the Son, 5.20, and those who have loved and have believed that Jesus came from Father, 16.27. In this fashion 'love' of God, expressed first by God in sending, becomes the appropriate response to the one sent, Jesus, and to the sender, Father. Not only is love a new commandment in the text (13.34), it is the one response that demonstrates the acceptance of both the Son and Father. Love functions mimetically as the characteristic of agreement in the text; one who agrees with Jesus in the text loves, one who does not agree does not love.

---

37   John 5.36-37; 6.57; 8.16-18; 10.36; 12.49; 14.24, 26. Although it is common to use the phrase 'the Father', I simply use 'Father' as a proper noun to accentuate the character rather than the relationship.

38   John 3.35; 5.20; 10.17; 15.9.

39   John 14.21, 23; 16.27.

40   The terms ἀγάπη / ἀγαπάω appear 44 times in the entire text, 31 of which are found in chs 13–17.

The third trait, God/Father as one who gives, is more diverse in scope regarding the object given.[41] As with the first two traits examined, this trait is also introduced in John 3.16, where God gave the only son, τὸν υἱὸν τὸν μονογενῆ. God is also characterized as the one who gives when Martha affirms God will give Jesus whatever he requests from God (11.22). The other references pertain to those things Father gave, gives, or will give. These can be grouped into three categories. First, Father gives everything: everything and all judgement to Jesus, and whatever is asked in Jesus' name.[42] Second, Father gives life: life to Jesus, works of eternal life to Jesus, the true bread that is life, and the commandment that is eternal life.[43] Finally, Father gives to Jesus all those who come to him.[44]

The characteristic trait, one who gives, functions mimetically in the text to identify the character God/Father as source for everything, not merely for the activities of Jesus as the only son, but also as the source for those who will believe and for life itself. The text develops this trait so that God/Father is understood as the source of all that is, in what may be a variation on the same mimetic function for God as one who sends. As in the discussion on God as one who sends, the mimetic dimension of God as one who gives is also established for the authorial audience initially in 1.1-4.

The final trait under consideration, God as one who speaks, commands, or teaches, is more difficult to analyse. While there are specific references to God/Father speaking, many of them are from a third-person point of view, reporting what God/Father said. In every instance save one Jesus is the object of God's verbal activity; on that one occasion the crowd affirms that God did indeed speak with Moses (9.29). Jesus reports to his listeners on four occasions that what he speaks originated with God/Father.[45] In the earliest appearing incident in the text, the crowd is astonished at Jesus' teaching so he clarifies for them that his teaching is from God.[46] In the one instance where it is implied that God is actually speaking, the text narrates a voice from heaven reporting to glorify Father's name in response to Jesus' prayer/request (12.28).

This trait, one who speaks, is critical to the overall purpose of the text: to have the authorial audience accept the words that Jesus, the *Logos*, speaks.[47] This authorial audience, familiar with Greek writings of Second Temple Judaism and the oral tradition of the Jesus community, is accustomed to the concept of God speaking. In this text God/Father is portrayed as communicating to Jesus the Son who proceeds to communicate with the other human characters. God

---

41   John 3.16, 35; 5.22, 26, 36; 6.32; 10.29; 11.22; 12.49; 13.3; 14.16; 15.16; 16.23; 17.11, 24; 18.11.

42   Everything (3.35 and 13.3), all judgment (5.22), and whatever is asked (15.16 and 16.23).

43   Life (5.26), works of life (5.36), true bread (6.32), and commandment (12.49).

44   John 6.37, 65; 10.29; and 17.24. Two other instances where Father gives objects do not fit into these broader categories: the *Paraclete* and the cup Jesus must drink, 14.16 and 18.11.

45   John 8.28, 40; 12.50; 14.31.

46   John 7.17; this is the same claim that Nicodemus makes toward Jesus in 3.1-2.

47   John 4.41; 5.24, 47; 6.63, 68; 8.31, 37, 47, 51; 12.48; 14.10, 23-24; 17.8.

speaks the Word of God to the *Logos* incarnate – Jesus, God in the beginning – so that humanity might hear it. God/Father is thus presented as originating the words of Jesus that are received by those who love the Son. When the authorial audience recognizes this characteristic of God the text itself springs to life as the source of Life.

In summary, the mimetic functions of the character God represent several different messages from the text itself. The text communicates a message of life while the character God/Father is presented as the source of this life in both the first and third traits, as one who sends and one who gives. The purpose of the text, recorded in 20.31, is to have life in the name of the Son of God through the act of believing. Both presentations of the character, first as God and second as Father, are essential for the text to fulfil its purpose of providing life. The second and fourth traits, one who loves and one who speaks, represent acceptance of the messenger and of the text's message. Love is the response anticipated in the authorial audience and represents agreement with the text. The acceptance of Jesus as speaking that which originated from God/Father is critical to Life, of which God is the source.

V. Thematic Functions

Continuing the investigation to include the thematic functions of the character further accentuates the rhetorical argument present in the text. Thematic dimensions for the character God/Father noted earlier are: authority related to sovereignty, God as creative artist, and God as goal or purpose for living.

While there are other possible thematic dimensions, how does God/Father function in the thematic sense with regard to these three? For the narrative audiences and the authorial audience the concept of authority is a familiar theme. However, many actual readers of the Fourth Gospel in the modern world may not easily recognize this representative element, since ancient and modern social structures can vary greatly.[48] The Fourth Gospel text has several confrontation scenes where the controversy revolves around the issue of who has authority.[49] The question of authority is crucial to the trial scene with Pilate and the characterization of Pilate, indeed it is the issue: will Pilate accept Jesus' authority as king?[50] The focus of this Gospel is on the authority of God rather than on that of Jesus, who is portrayed as having received his authority from God/Father.[51]

---

48   Several fine works have focused on relating authority structures of the ancient world to the Fourth Gospel's approach. See Warren Carter, *John and Empire: Initial Explorations* (London and New York: T&T Clark, 2008), and Tom Thatcher, *Greater than Caesar: Christology and Empire in the Fourth Gospel* (Minneapolis: Fortress, 2009).

49   Nicodemus in ch. 3; healing on the Sabbath in chs 5 and 9; and dispute over Jesus' words in ch. 10.

50   Culpepper, *Anatomy*, pp. 142–3.

51   John 5.17-27; 7.16-17; 10.18; and 17.2.

In a similar fashion the creative artistry of God is easily recognizable except by some modern, actual audiences. The creative motif is prevalent in the Fourth Gospel, from the Prologue to the resurrection.[52] This thematic function is closely related to the mimetic function mentioned above, God as the source for everything. Both of these thematic dimensions are closely related to the mimetic presentation, not surprising given the highly mimetic world of literature from this period.

The third thematic dimension identified, God as goal or purpose for living is the thematic function that best approximates to the text's stated purpose in 20.31. Life is a major theme in the Gospel, and experiencing or receiving this life is a substantial, motivational element for the Fourth Evangelist. At the conclusion of the conflict scene in John 6, Peter explains his purpose for continuing to follow Jesus: 'You have the words of eternal life.' Later, Jesus deflects the origin of this life from himself and his words to God/Father who gives him the words to speak.[53] Jesus presents himself as both the means to life and life itself in 14.6, yet eternal life is ultimately defined as knowing the only true God.[54] Thus, although the stated purpose of this Gospel is belief in Jesus as the Christ,[55] the goal of such belief is knowing God/Father.

In summary, the thematic functions of God/Father as a character in the Fourth Gospel reinforce God as authority, creative artist and goal. The first two are similar to the mimetic functions of God as sender and source. The third undergirds the text and its stated purpose while also reinforcing God/ Father as one who speaks. The thematic functions for the character God/Father provide a subtle reinforcement that the text is not entirely about Jesus, but indeed is ultimately about the one who sent Jesus.

VI. Rhetorical Functioning

> Rhetorical reading acknowledges that individual readers will find some authorial audiences easier to enter than others, and it stops short of ever declaring any one reading as definitive and fixed for all time. But it assumes that one significant value of reading narrative is the opportunity it offers to encounter other minds—that of the author who has constructed the narrative and those of other readers also interested in shared readings.[56]

The Fourth Gospel is not simply an account of 'the life and times' of one first-century Jewish male who travelled around Galilee, Samaria and Judaea.

---

52   J. A. du Rand, 'The Creation Motif in the Fourth Gospel: Perspectives on its Narratological Function within a Judaistic Background', in G. van Belle, J. G. van der Watt and P. J. Maritz (eds), *Theology and Christology in the Fourth Gospel* (Leuven: Peeters, 2005), pp. 21–46. See John 1.1-4; 2.7-9; 5.17; 6.18-19; 8.12; and 20.22.

53   John 12.49-50.

54   John 17.3.

55   John 3.15, 16, 36; 5.24; 6.40; and 11.25.

56   Phelan, *Living to Tell about It*, p. 19.

Indeed, it is a narrative that attempts to persuade its audience that Jesus is the Christ, the Son of God. Each character in the narrative is part of the author's selected account of the signs/proofs that are 'written in this book'.[57] The character God/Father has a role to play in the rhetoric of the narrative. Having explored the mimetic, thematic and synthetic dimensions and functions, it is now feasible to propose some conclusions regarding the rhetorical function of this one character in the narrative.

What rhetorical function does the character God/Father perform in the text of the Fourth Gospel? The first portrait of God/Father as an acting subject in the text is during the monologue following Jesus' encounter with Nicodemus (3.13-21). The question of whose voice we hear, Jesus' or the narrator's, is muted when we ask instead about the characterization of God/Father in the text. Within this pericope Jesus has been affirmed a reliable teacher by Nicodemus and the monologue reflects the teaching of Jesus. God is portrayed as loving the world, giving the Son, and sending the Son for the purpose of granting life to those who believe. The text has already acknowledged Jesus as the Son of God through the confessional words of Nathanael in 1.49. The characterization of God/Father authenticates Jesus' teaching and associates Jesus with the God of Abraham, Isaac and Jacob. Rhetorically the text has established the veracity and lineage of Jesus and established the motif of (dis)belief as central to the Fourth Gospel.

A second rhetorical element of the Fourth Gospel is to reinforce or perhaps modify the audience's understanding of God. None of the mimetic dimensions, one who sends, loves, gives, or speaks, is particularly unique to the God of Abraham, Isaac and Jacob as portrayed in the LXX. God had sent prophets,[58] spoken,[59] and been portrayed as loving[60] and as giving.[61] But this had been in a relationship of covenant between deity and nation.[62] These attributes associated with God as sovereign deity were nothing new; but associated with Father? That is a radical concept. As a reader progresses through the text of the Fourth Gospel, the first three attributes are ascribed to God before they are associated with Father.[63] The fourth trait, the idea of God communicating, has various terms that can convey the idea. However, John 1.1 sets the stage for this God who communicates, a communication that draws the authorial audience back to Genesis 1.3 where God's announcement brings light into existence. In the earlier summary of the actions associated with God in chapters 1–3 and with Father in chapters 5–14, the question was posed, 'Is there a rhetorical reason

57   John 20.30-31.
58   Gen. 45.5; Exod. 3.13; Deut. 9.23; Judg. 6.8; 2 Sam. 12.1; 2 Chron. 24.19; 36.15; Jer. 7.25; 35.15; Zech. 6.15.
59   Gen. 8.15; 17.3; Exod. 3.12; 7.1; Deut. 1.6; 2 Sam. 12.7; 1 Kgs 12.22; Isa. 40.1; Jer. 30.2; Joel 2.12; Amos 3.11.
60   Deut. 23.5; 1 Kgs 10.9; Neh. 13.26; Hos. 3.1; Zech. 10.6.
61   Gen. 1.29; 15.7, Exod. 13.11; Lev. 20.24; Deut. 2.29; 28.11; Josh. 1.11; 1 Sam. 1.17; Ezra 1.2; Ps. 84.11; Isa. 42.5; Amos 9.15.
62   Exod. 19.3-6 and Ezek. 37.24-26.
63   Loves, gives, sends (John 3.16-17), and teaches (7.17).

for the specific language use in these two sections?' An answer might now be proffered based on the closer examination of the mimetic functions: the transferral of these traits to Father is the rhetorical event.

The literary portrait of Father regarding these traits in ancient texts is mixed. The LXX contains no instances of 'Father' sending anyone, not to mention a son,[64] while non-Christian texts in the Greek corpus have very few references.[65] From the perspective of audience conventions, the authorial audience familiar with Jesus-related oral tradition, more specifically Johannine oral tradition, would have followed this transferral relatively easily. However, for readers familiar with Second Temple writings but unfamiliar with the oral tradition streams, the portrait of a father sending his son would not have been a familiar literary convention.

The second trait, Father who loves (ἀγαπάω), while rare, is not entirely absent from the LXX.[66] In the non-Christian texts, it is similarly rare.[67] This is not the case, however, in classical texts with φιλέω. Socrates utilizes the example of a father's love for the son in his dialogue with Lysis concerning happiness and the benefit of intelligence.[68] A father's love for the son is the exemplar for a discussion among non-equals in the *Magna Moralia* attributed to Aristotle.[69] What is unusual is the concept of deity loving humans. The exposition on friendship in the *Magna Moralia* defines what kind of friendship is to be discussed:

> For friendship here we say exists where there is being loved back, but friendship with the god neither allows of being loved back nor, on the whole, of loving. For it would be odd if someone were to say he was friends with Zeus. Neither indeed can one be loved back by lifeless things, though there can of course be love of lifeless things, as of wine or something else of the sort. That then is why we are not investigating friendship with the god, nor with lifeless things, but with living things and with those where there is loving back.[70]

Within Hellenistic philosophy, at least, the concept of loving or being loved, φιλέω, by a god was unusual.[71]

---

64   There are instances when a father sends a son, but the father is a named character in the text: Gen. 21.14 (Abraham sending Hagar and Ishmael), Gen. 27.45 and 28.5 (Rebekah and Isaac sending Jacob away), Gen. 37.13 (Jacob sending Joseph to his brothers), Gen. 46.28 (Israel sending Judah ahead), and 1 Sam. 16.11 (Jesse sending for David).

65   Plutarch, *Demetr.* 8.7.2 recounts that Demetrius was 'sent by his father' to free Athens, ὅτι πέμψειεν αὐτὸν ὁ πατὴρ ἀγαθῇ τύχῃ, τοὺς Ἀθηναίους ἐλευθερώσοντα.

66   It appears twice in the Joseph narrative in reference to Jacob loving Joseph (Gen. 37.4; 44.20), once with ἀγαπάω and once with φιλέω. One other occurrence with φιλέω is found in Gen. 27.14, in reference to the food Jacob preferred.

67   Dio Cassius 41.57.4.4, Plutarch, *Art.* 23.7.1, Josephus, *AJ* 12.195.1, and Homer, *Od.* 16.17.

68   Plato, *Ly.* 207.d-210.e.

69   Aristotle, *MM* 1211b.8.

70   Aristotle, *MM* 1208b.28-35.

71   On the conceptual field of friendship in the ancient world see Culy, *Echoes of Friendship*, pp. 34–86.

There are references to Zeus loving (again using φιλέω) certain beings in the Hellenistic literature. Most prominent is a passage from the *Iliad*, 'Proud is the heart of kings, fostered of heaven; for their honour is from Zeus, and Zeus, god of counsel, loveth them', quoted by several other ancient writers as well.[72] Later in the *Iliad*, the two spearmen, Aias and Hector, are declared by the heralds as 'loved of Zeus',[73] while in book 10, Nestor proclaims of Odysseus and Diomedes,

> Come tell me now, Odysseus, greatly to be praised, great glory of the Achaeans, how ye twain took these horses . . . Nay, methinks some god hath met you and given you them; for both of you twain doth Zeus the cloud-gatherer love and the daughter of Zeus that beareth the aegis, even flashing-eyed Athene.[74]

While such references to Zeus' love for other gods, kings and heroes is part of the literary lore, it is not for everyone but appears limited to an exclusive club.[75] It would seem that the Johannine presentation of God/Father discloses a new side to the deity–human relationship.[76]

This study has appropriated technical elements of characterization in order to describe the role and rhetoric of God/Father within the Fourth Gospel. Examining where God/Father is described in the third person as acting within the text has permitted a proposal regarding the rhetorical function of the character God/Father.[77] However, there remains a further rhetorical element in the text, when God/Father is engaged as a dialogue partner in the second person, specifically in John 17. What does a focused examination of this

---

72   τιμὴ δ' ἐκ Διός ἐστι· φιλεῖ δέ ἐμητίετα Ζεύς. Homer, *Il.* 2.197. Trans. by A. T. Murray (Cambridge, MA: Harvard University Press, 1924). *Perseus Digital Library Project*, ed. Gregory R. Crane, Tufts University, June 2011, http://www.perseus.tufts.edu. This same passage is quoted in Dionysius Halicarnassensis, *Rh.* 9.8.18, Aristonicus, *De signis Iliadis*, Scholion 5.h193-7,*Vitae Homeri, de Homero* 2, line 2243, and in Joannes Stobaeus, *Anthologium*, 4.6.2.3. Retrieved from *Thesaurus Linguae Graecae*, The Regents of the University of California, June 2011.

73   Homer, *Il.* 7.280.

74   Homer, *Il.* 10.544-53. Trans. by A. T. Murray (Cambridge, MA: Harvard University Press, 1924). *Perseus Digital Library Project*, ed. Gregory R. Crane, Tufts University, June 2011, http://www.perseus.tufts.edu.

75   See also, Homer, *Od.* 15.245 regarding Amphiaraus, quoted by Plato, *Spuria* 368.a.2, Aristonicus, *De Signis Odysseae*, Scholion 1.246, *Vitae Homeri, De Homero* 2, line 1720, and Eustathius, *Commentarii ad Homeri Odysseam* 2.97.28.

76   Klaus Scholtissek notes, 'Der Gott des JohEv offenbart sich als ein Vater, der in seinem Sohn Mit-Liebende such', in his essay, '"Ich und der Vater, wir sind eins" (Joh 10,30) Zum Theologischen Potential und zur Hermeneutischen Kompetenz der Johanneischen Christologie', in G. van Belle, J. G. van der Watt and P. J. Maritz (eds), *Theology and Christology in the Fourth Gospel* (Leuven: University Press, 2005), pp. 315–45 (339).

77   The third and fourth traits of God/Father, while essential to the thematic functions of the text, are not sufficiently rare in Greek literature to warrant consideration as an unusual audience convention or consequently part of the rhetorical function of the characterization. For instance see Plutarch, *Moralia: De vitando aere alieno* 831.D.3, Demosthenes, 85.6, Philo Judaeus, *Rer. Div. Her.* 205.2, and Xenophon, *HG* 1.5.3.4.

conversation by Jesus reveal about the character God/Father in the Fourth Gospel?

VII. John 17 as Example

Jesus' prayer in John 17 is the longest recorded dialogue, albeit one-sided, with God in the Fourth Gospel. As Jesus spoke with his eyes to heaven, he made statements about God/Father that have mimetic dimensions and functions similar to those found elsewhere in the text of the Fourth Gospel. Pertinent to this study is the recognition that each of the four traits identified above are present in this segment of the text. The characterization of God/Father in John 1–16 in the third person is fully consistent with the portrait provided in the second person in John 17. The portrayal of God/Father as one who sends is identified six times in this chapter.[78] On two occasions the text unites 'belief' with the idea that Father sent Jesus, a combination of ideas repeated three times earlier in the text.[79] On the other four occasions the critical element is 'knowing' that Father sent Jesus. This combination of ideas does not appear outside the prayer of Jesus.[80]

The second mimetic trait identified, one who loves, does not appear until the very end of the passage.[81] In each instance the object of God/Father's love is Jesus, the Son. However, this love is not limited to the singular relationship of Father and Son, but is to incorporate those who know that Father sent Jesus. The third trait, one who gives, is present nine times.[82] Among the things Father gives are authority,[83] eternal life,[84] work,[85] everything,[86] people,[87] His name,[88] and glory.[89] Finally, God/Father as one who speaks/commands/teaches is present, appearing in verses 6, 8, 14 and 17, in the form of the word(s) from God.

The mimetic functions associated with God/Father are also present. The essential function of God as sender, source of Life, is the earliest declaration by Jesus in this prayer and could be interpreted as the primary purpose for his

---

78   John 17.3, 8, 18, 21, 23, 25.

79   John 5.38; 6.29; and 11.42.

80   In John 7.28-29 Jesus affirms that they do not know 'Him' while he himself does know 'Him' because 'He' sent him. While related in terminology, this passage does not repeat the idea of John 17 that 'they' know that God sent Jesus.

81   John 17.23, 24, 26.

82   John 17.2, 4, 6, 7, 9, 11, 12, 22 and 24. It is present two more times but those will be covered in the discussion below of the fourth trait.

83   John 17.2; cf. also 1.12 and 5.27.

84   John 17.2; cf. also 4.14; 5.26; 6.27, 33, 51; and 10.28.

85   John 17.4; cf. also 5.26.

86   John 17.7; cf. also 3.35; 6.37, 39; and 13.3.

87   John 17.6, 9, 24; cf. also 6.65; and 10.29.

88   John 17.11, 12.

89   John 17.1, 5, 22, 24.

having been sent.[90] Since there is a close relationship between the two traits, one who sends and one who loves, it is no surprise that Jesus' last declaration in this prayer is that Father's love might be in those who know that God/ Father sent Jesus.[91] Although the trait, one who gives, is diverse in scope, in this situation the mimetic function specifically portrays God as the source of all that Jesus has done, rather than as the source of all that is. In this instance, the text is looking backwards and reviewing what has been portrayed while emphasizing the source element of God/Father's character. The functions of the second and third traits relate closely to the first, although with different emphases.

The fourth trait, God/Father speaks, builds upon its earlier function. The first occurrence relates the concept of keeping the word originating from God and being given by God to Jesus.[92] The second reference identifies a close relationship between those who believe God sent Jesus and receiving the words God gave Jesus.[93] The third appearance in 17.14 acts as an *inclusio* with 17.8, building on the concept of Jesus giving God's word to those God has given Jesus. Finally, the Word of God/Father is identified as truth,[94] setting the stage for a better understanding of the question by Pilate in 18.38. The mimetic function of this character trait relates the acceptance of the Word of God/Father spoken and the results of such acceptance, both negative and positive.

VIII. Conclusions

This study has sought to answer the question, 'What rhetorical effect does the character God/Father provide in the Fourth Gospel?' The stated rhetorical purpose of the text, 'But these signs have been written (in this book) so that you may believe that Jesus is the Christ, God's Son, and in believing may have life in his name' (John 20.31), centres on recognition and acceptance of the identity of Jesus as Christ, even as Son of God, and on the life that accompanies said recognition. The character God/Father reinforces this stated purpose of the text.[95]

The mimetic dimensions associated with God/Father in the Fourth Gospel, 'one who loves' and 'one who speaks', highlight the acceptance of the Son, through responses of love for the Son and recognition of the Son's words as

---

90   John 17.2-3.
91   John 17.26.
92   John 17.6. See also 8.51-52; 14.23-24; 15.20 for keeping Jesus' or God's word.
93   John 17.8.
94   Repeated twice in 17.17 and 19.
95   As Tolmie ('Characterization', p. 66) indicates, 'This extensive characterization of God is aimed primarily at characterizing Jesus, since nearly all of the traits associated with God are extended to Jesus, implying that he possesses similar traits. This strategy is used by the implied author to convince the implied reader that Jesus is indeed to be viewed as equal to God.'

Father's. The sending and giving motifs are critical for understanding that God, as source of all that is, sends Jesus the Son in order to provide life. The mimetic functions reveal the direct relationship between this character and the rhetorical purpose of the text. Thus the character God/Father works to authenticate Jesus as Christ within the tradition of Abraham, Isaac and Jacob. But perhaps equally important is the re-characterization of the God of Abraham, Isaac and Jacob to include the relational perspective of Father. This relational perspective is not unique to the Johannine tradition, but is accentuated within the Fourth Gospel as the text moves to define the relational element of Jesus as Son to God/Father.

The thematic dimensions of the character provide an initial focus on the authority of God manifest in his creative expression and the goal of life. The thematic functions centre on the authority of God as beginning and end: the one who sends and to whom the text points. The only words this character speaks, 'I have glorified [my name] and I will glorify [my name] again', reveal this activity from past to future.[96] Not only is God/Father the source of all that is, but knowing God/Father is the desired endgame for the text.[97]

This author anticipates that these conclusions are not the final word on the characterization of God by any means. Each reading of a text informs and shapes the next reading. The act of rereading amplifies the rhetorical impact of a character. This attempt hopes to encourage readers of this chapter not only to encounter the mind of this author, but also to engage in the reading process and encounter the minds of other readers of the Fourth Gospel.

---

96   John 12.28.

97   As Klaus Scholtissek ('Ich und der Vater', p. 337) summarizes, 'Weil Jesus aus seiner singulären Einheit mit dem Vater lebt, offenbart sich im Leben und Wirken Jesu der Vater selbst.'

Chapter 9

JOHN THE BAPTIST: WITNESS AND EMBODIMENT OF THE PROLOGUE IN THE GOSPEL OF JOHN

Sherri Brown

I. Introduction

In the introduction to his work on the passion narrative in the Gospel of John, Charles Giblin claims that

> as every Irishman knows, the meaning of a story lies largely in the way it is told. For each storyteller wants himself to be understood appreciatively through his own way of telling the tale, whether that tale is not as yet known or, and indeed preferably, if it already is. That is how the storyteller functions as a teacher.[1]

Giblin's assertion is certainly pertinent to the characters and characterization in the Gospel of John. This evangelist is the consummate storyteller, and his distinctive style has captivated readers and writers since he first composed his version of the good news of Jesus Christ. This attraction to the Fourth Gospel, however, has not mitigated the difficulty in getting at just what is happening as these characters act and interact across the narrative. The present study therefore builds upon recent work on storytelling techniques in the Fourth Gospel to examine the role of John the Baptist through a narrative lens that focuses on his key appearances through the Gospel's first three chapters, including 1.1-18 (esp. vv. 6-8, 15); 1.19-37; and 3.22-42.[2] Examining the Baptist's role through the prism of dialogue will shed light upon the evangelist's intention for these complex interactions on both the narrative level and the discourse or, using Giblin's term, the 'teaching' level of the Fourth Gospel. Focus thus rests upon the dialogical nature of the revelatory process and incorporates scholarship that suggests a relationship between the Fourth Gospel and ancient drama, rendering a speech-as-action structural model.[3]

---

1   Charles Giblin, 'Confrontations in John 18, 1-27', *Bib* 65 (1984), pp. 210–31 (215).

2   As is often noted, John is not called 'the Baptist' in the Fourth Gospel. This title, however, distinguishes him from the Gospel's traditional author.

3   E.g., Jo-Ann A. Brant, *Dialogue and Drama: Elements of Greek Tragedy in the Fourth Gospel* (Peabody, MA: Hendrickson, 2004). Her work on index in dialogue is helpful here. In the three-part typology of artificial language (icon, index, symbol), dramatic texts rely heavily upon index: any sign that refers to objects denoted by being affected by those objects. *Deixis* is

The bridge from the Prologue to this action of the body of the Gospel is manifested in John, the human witness sent from God (1.6-8, 15). His character becomes the embodiment of the Prologue as he gives valuable information about Jesus and the story to come, now in the form of dialogues with other human characters (1.19-37; 3.22-36).

Much like the chorus in ancient Greek dramas, the Prologue gives readers a synthesis of events to come. It tells readers the *who* and the *what* of the events at hand, but leaves open the *how*. The story itself is necessary to understand how it all plays out. John the Baptist is presented in the Prologue as 'sent from God' (v. 6) and crosses into the body of the narrative as the one true witness whom the reader can trust to give accurate information about Jesus. As John's role draws to a close in chapter 3, he continues to defy human expectations precisely because his role lies outside human bounds, so that his very decline in the face of Jesus' increase means that his duty is complete and his role fulfilled. Herein lies the Baptist's particular characterization and catechetical role in the Gospel of John as the witness to perfect faith in relationship with both God and the Lamb of God who takes away the sin of the world.

II. Beginnings: The Prologue to the Body of the Gospel (1.1-18)

As a first page, the Prologue is fundamental to the narrative structure of the Gospel.[4] Its positioning must be understood as part of the evangelist's strategy, the threshold for the narrative to come.[5] Readers come to the body of the Gospel with the information in the Prologue – information only the narrator and readers have. Although readers may not fully understand the enigmatic ideas of the Prologue, these are precisely what create the tension that begs the question of the 'how' of God's action in the world. The subsequent narrative 'shows' what the Prologue 'tells'.[6] The Fourth Evangelist's use of the poetic Prologue as a foundation for

---

language used to point to subjectivity, temporality, spatiality and modality, particularly personal and demonstrative pronouns and adverbs such as 'here' and 'now'. Employing this language, including indices of movement, setting and conflict, attracts attention and identifies contextual elements (pp. 77–8).

4   Francis J. Moloney, *Belief in the Word: Reading John 1–4* (Minneapolis: Fortress, 1993), p. 23.

5   See the literary analysis in Frank Kermode, 'St John as Poet', *JSNT* 28 (1986), pp. 3–16. For the Prologue's unity with the rest of the Gospel, see C. K. Barrett, *The Gospel According to St John: An Introduction with Commentary and Notes on the Greek Text* (Philadelphia: Westminster, 2nd edn, 1978), pp. 125–6. Elsewhere he concludes, 'The Prologue is not a jig-saw puzzle but one piece of solid theological writing'; *The Prologue of St John's Gospel* (London: Athlone Press, 1971), p. 27.

6   'Showing' and 'telling' are the two means by which narratives reveal character; Wayne Booth, *The Rhetoric of Fiction* (Chicago: University of Chicago Press, 2nd edn, 1983), pp. 3–9. Tom Thatcher elaborates: '"Telling" occurs when the narrator makes direct evaluative statements or gives information not normally available in the readers' experience. "Showing" occurs when the narrator offers selective information about the actions of the characters and allows readers to draw conclusions from them. By combining "telling" and "showing" the author enables readers to develop "both intrinsic and contextual knowledge" of the characters'; 'Jesus, Judas, and Peter:

his Gospel that suddenly and definitively breaks into prose narrative can also be understood as a reflection of his theological perspective. The incarnation of the Word suddenly and definitively turns the custom and 'truth' of the world on its ear.

The structure of these 18 verses is elusive. For the purposes of this study, however, the work of Alan Culpepper proves most insightful.[7] Recognizing the complexity of these verses, Culpepper acknowledges that more than one structuring technique may well be in play and is open to the fluidity of the evangelist's style. Nonetheless, he is convinced that the underlying framework of the Johannine Prologue is the chiasm. Therefore, he builds upon the work of his predecessors to determine the Prologue's flow and pivot.[8] He concludes that the evangelist's extended chiasm has seven corresponding elements that turn on v. 12b.[9] The crux of the Prologue, and thus the focus of the narrative the Prologue introduces, is the mission of the Word of God who gives those who receive him 'power to become children of God'. A detailed analysis of the Prologue is beyond the scope of this study, therefore the focus in what follows is the Baptist material of vv. 6-8 and 15.

Werner Kelber remarks that, 'Both in life and in literature beginnings are consequential, but risky undertakings' that often create the central predicament of the coming story.[10] Further, beginnings are the manner by which the evangelists present keys to understanding all that follows.[11] This role of the Prologue coupled with Culpepper's structure serve as the guide to examine the key the Fourth Evangelist provides to open the passageway into his Gospel.

a. In the Beginning was the Word (vv. 1-11)

The first words of the Gospel, ἐν ἀρχῇ, are identical to the opening words of Genesis in the LXX. They serve to bring readers to 'the beginning', not only of

Character by Contrast in the Fourth Gospel', *BSac* 153 (1996), pp. 435–48 (435). See also William J. Harvey, *Character and the Novel* (Ithaca, NY: Cornell University Press, 1965), p. 32.

7   R. Alan Culpepper, 'The Pivot of John's Prologue', *NTS* 27 (1980), pp. 1–31. D. A. Carson concurs that this is the most persuasive structure presented to date; *The Gospel According to John* (Grand Rapids: Eerdmans, 1991), p. 13. For other recent scholarship, see Mary Coloe, 'The Structure of the Johannine Prologue and Genesis 1', *AusBR* 45 (1997), pp. 40–55; Charles Giblin, 'Two Complementary Literary Structures in John 1:1-18', *JBL* 104 (1985), pp. 87–103; Jean Irigoin, 'La composition rythmique du prologue de Jean (I, 1-18)', *RB* 98 (1991), pp. 5–50.

8   Quoting Willem van Unnik, Culpepper fears the upshot of his study will be 'the new things he said were not true and the true things he said were not new' ('The Purpose of St John's Gospel', *StudEv* 1 [1959], pp. 382–411 [383]). Culpepper nonetheless determines to refine recent scholarship ('Pivot', p. 1).

9   Culpepper, 'Pivot', p. 8. His analysis is based upon (1) language; (2) conceptual parallels; and (3) content (pp. 9–17). The chiasm is diagrammed as: **A:** vv. 1-2; **B:** vv. 3a; **C:** vv. 3b-5; **D:** vv. 6-8; **E:** vv. 9-10; **F:** v. 11; **G:** v. 12a; **H:** v. 12b; **G':** v. 12c; **F':** v. 13; **E':** v. 14; **D':** v. 15; **C':** v. 16; **B':** v. 17; **A':** v. 18 (p. 16). The Baptist material is marked **D** and **D'**.

10   'Transcendental and earthly beginnings, this double gesture of centering and decentering . . . creates the central predicament for the subsequent narrative'; Werner Kelber, 'The Birth of a Beginning: John 1:1-18', *Semeia* 52 (1990), pp. 121–44 (121).

11   Morna Hooker, *Beginnings: Keys That Open the Gospels* (Harrisburg, PA: Trinity Press International, 1997), p. xiii. For the Prologue as the key to this Gospel, see pp. 64–83.

this narrative but also of their sacred narrative of history, when God literally spoke creation into existence (Gen. 1).[12] By resonating this shared story of God's action in history, the evangelist grounds his story to come in the realm of the sacred scripture of Israel. This literary intention is furthered with the fullness of the initial clause: 'In the beginning was the Word' (λόγος). The use of *logos* terminology here allows for rich and varied symbolism, evoking God's revelation in Torah as well as the broader voice of the sages through the cultural milieu.[13] On the narrative level, it allows for a fundamental identification of the *Logos* with the creative activity of God. The 'word' introduced here corresponds with God's word of creation in the beginning.[14] Verse 2 parallels and affirms the claims of v. 1. The chiasm pushes forward as the nature and role of the *Logos* is presented as the vehicle for creation (v. 3) who is the giver of life (v. 4) and stands fast in the darkness lighting the way for humankind (vv. 4-5). This presentation affirms what 'came to be' (ἐγένετο) through the *Logos* that always existed (ἦν, v. 1). The final words of v. 5 further hint at the conflict to come between the Word of light and the darkness that exists among the people who are the caretakers of God's creation (Gen. 1.26-30). This leads to the introduction of John, the one who comes to give testimony to the light and who becomes the driving force to the Prologue's crux.

The next segment introduces the first human being (ἄνθρωπος) into the story, a man named John (vv. 6-8).[15] He is described as having come to be (ἐγένετο) like the rest of creation, in distinction to the eternally existing *Logos*. Simultaneously, however, the evangelist describes this man as 'sent from God', the only fully human character in the narrative identified as such. John, then, is special: he is sent into the world from God with a mission. Readers are alerted that this man is to be trusted. His mission is to testify (vv. 7-8). John bears witness (μαρτυρήσῃ) to the light of the eternal *Logos*. As he is the witness sent from God, everything John says

12   For the Prologue as a targumic exposition of Gen. 1.1-5, see Peder Borgen, 'Observations on the Targumic Character of the Prologue of John', *NTS* 16 (1970), pp. 288–95; idem, 'Logos was the True Light: Contributions to the Interpretation of the Prologue of John', *NovT* 14 (1972), pp. 115–30. Similarly, see Daniel Boyarin, 'The Gospel of the Memra: Jewish Binitarianism and the Prologue to John', *HTR* 94 (2001), pp. 243–84 (267).

13   *Logos* terminology has roots in the Jewish wisdom tradition as well as the Hellenistic philosophical tradition; Thomas Tobin, 'The Prologue of John and Hellenistic Jewish Speculation', *CBQ* 52 (1990), pp. 252–69. Derek Tovey suggests the *Logos* functions as a 'character-substitute' that prompts readers to wonder about the identity of this mysterious figure. The audience thus becomes determinative of the formative background of the *Logos* concept; 'Narrative Strategies in the Prologue and the Metaphor of ὁ λόγος in John's Gospel', *Pac* 15 (2002), pp. 138–53 (141).

14   Boyarin, 'Gospel of the Memra', pp. 255–9; Martin McNamara, 'Logos of the Fourth Gospel and Memra of the Palestinian Targum: Ex 12:42', *ExpTim* 79 (1968), pp. 115–17.

15   These verses, with their counterpart in v. 15, interject striking prose into the fluid hymn-like poetry of the rest of the Prologue, leading to the argument that they are interpolations to the *Vorlage* of the Prologue. John A. T. Robinson, for example, refers to these verses as 'rude interruptions'; 'The Relation of the Prologue to the Gospel of John', *NTS* 9 (1963), pp. 120–9. For the accepted argument that these verses are an integral connection to the body of the narrative to follow, see Morna Hooker, 'John the Baptist and the Johannine Prologue', *NTS* 16 (1970), pp. 354–8. Culpepper concurs and argues that the double articulation of John and his role is further evidence of the chiastic presentation of the Prologue ('Pivot', pp. 12–13).

about Jesus is true. Through the introduction of John and his role, the evangelist also introduces the concept of 'belief' in the Word. John the human witness is carefully distinguished from the light, but his purpose is crucial to point to the light and thus facilitate the process of belief (ἵνα πάντες πιστεύσωσιν δι' αὐτοῦ, v. 7).

Focus then returns to the light in vv. 9-10, flowing from the final words that introduce John. The light is further characterized by way of truth: τὸ φῶς τὸ ἀληθινόν (v. 9). The true light whose reign reaches everyone was coming into the world. The incarnation foreshadowed here comes to pass in the counterpart to these verses, v. 14. The imminent conflict of the Gospel story is also reaffirmed, this time in terms of knowledge (v. 10; see v. 8). The *Logos*, instrumental giver of life and light in intimate relationship with God, comes into what is his own and is not received by his own people (v. 11). Giving, receiving and rejecting in relationship thus become the operative interactivity of the incarnation of the Word.

b. The Children of God: The Chiastic Centre of the Prologue (v. 12)

Readers now arrive at the pivot of the Prologue (v. 12b) and the hinges upon which the pivot turns (vv. 12a and 12c).[16] The force of the entire Prologue is poised on the fulcrum of the mission of the Word 'to give them power to become children of God'.[17] The evangelist's syntax allows the central assertion of the Word's giving action to be framed by the introduction (v. 12a) and description (v. 12c) of the potential recipients of the gift of the Word. These verses are thus corresponding phrases that hinge the core assertion of v. 12b, the crux of the Prologue's message.[18] This crux also determines the rest of the corresponding elements that balance the Prologue.[19] The claim is that those who receive the Word are given the power to become children of God, and one receives him in order to achieve this childhood by believing in his name (v. 12c).

c. Gift upon Gift: The Word Became Flesh and Dwelt among Us (vv. 13-18)

The remainder of the Prologue thus sheds light on what it means to become 'children of God' and how this could be the *telos* of John's Gospel. Verse 13 stands in apposition to v. 12 and also corresponds antithetically to v. 11. Verse 12c describes the role of 'receivers' in this relationship, while v. 13 describes the

---

16   Culpepper, 'Pivot', pp. 15–17.

17   Ernst Käsemann also identifies this climax: 'Verse 12 specifies the gift which is his to bestow and the goal of his redeeming effectiveness'; 'The Structure and Purpose of the Prologue to John's Gospel', in *New Testament Questions of Today* (London: SCM, 1969), pp. 151–2.

18   For correlation of these phrases (not identified as a chiasm), see Raymond E. Brown, *The Gospel According to John* (AB, 29; New York: Doubleday, 1966), p. 10.

19   The correspondence of receiving the Word to becoming children of God also suggests 'while Israel, which had been given the Torah, nevertheless rejected the Logos, some others, not necessarily Israel by virtue of flesh-and-blood parentage, became children of God' by receiving the *Logos* (Boyarin, 'Gospel of the Memra', p. 278). See also C. H. Dodd, *The Interpretation of the Fourth Gospel* (Cambridge, UK: Cambridge University Press, 1960), p. 271.

role of God and the 'how' of becoming God's children. Spiritual birth comes from above.[20] Because of the Word's coming into the world and the rejection by his own, the privilege of becoming the covenant people of God likewise changes forever.[21] Concluding this initial characterization of the children of God, the evangelist returns to what God did to make this possible. Corresponding to the proclamation in vv. 9-10, v. 14 announces how the true light came into the world, who the *Logos* becomes, and what is given in the process: 'And the Word became flesh'. With regard to the Prologue's flow, these words announce an event long coming, made possible by the plan of God to re-envision the covenant people as children of spiritual, not human, birth. Just as God's action in the covenantal giving of Torah changed the nature of God's relationship with creation, the incarnation of the Word, while very much in accord with that history, once again decisively alters the manner by which creation relates to God.

The enfleshed *Logos* made his dwelling 'among us'. The narrator begins to speak inclusively from the perspective of the children of God.[22] The visible and powerful manifestation of the glory of God dwelling in creation also harks back to the revelation of the glory of God to Moses on Mount Sinai (Exod. 34.15-16).[23] The glory of the incarnate Word is then described in the context of a father's uniquely begotten son who is πλήρης χάριτος καὶ ἀληθείας.[24] In keeping with the evocation of the OT concept of God's covenant love, a translation that takes seriously this careful diction and allows for the continuing articulation of the mission of the Word renders χάριτος with its more widely held denotation of 'an unexpected favour, a kindness' and reads the καί as epexegetical, thus allowing the second term, ἀληθείας, to explain the first. The phrase is thus 'full of a gift which is truth'.[25] The Word, giver of light and life, now incarnate, is filled with a new gift: truth. The giving and receiving of this gift of truth is intimately connected to the power to become children of God (v. 12b) and thus to the crux of the mission of the incarnate Word.[26]

This incarnate Word is then firmly grounded in history as the narrator returns in v. 15 to John, the human witness sent by God (vv. 6-8). In this role, John provides

20   Carson, *John*, p. 126; Brown, *John*, Vol. 1, p. 11; Kermode, 'St John as Poet', p. 10.

21   John Pryor, 'Covenant and Community in John's Gospel', *RTR* 47 (1988), pp. 44–51 (48). Heritage and ethnic identity have become irrelevant to birth from God.

22   This inclusive narration also draws the reader into the potentiality of becoming part of that group; Clayton R. Bowen, 'Notes on the Fourth Gospel', *JBL* 43 (1924), pp. 22–7 (22).

23   Brown, *John*, Vol. 1, p. 34. Morna Hooker reads all of John 1.14-18 as midrash on Exod. 33–34; 'Johannine Prologue and the Messianic Secret', *NTS* 21 (1974), pp. 40–58 (53–6).

24   Raymond Brown argues OT covenant love is evoked here (Exod. 34.6; *John*, Vol. 1, pp. 14, 35). See also Andrew Lincoln, *The Gospel According to Saint John* (BNTC 4; London: Continuum and Peabody, MA: Hendrickson, 2005), p. 105.

25   Francis J. Moloney, *The Gospel of John* (SP, 4; Collegeville, MN: Liturgical, 1998), p. 45; LSJ, s.v. χάρις; BDF §442.9, 16.

26   Andrew Osborn asserts that the NT use of the word means more than truth in utterance: 'It refers to that truth in character which not only leads to truth in speech, but manifests integrity in action, together with a firm belief in that which is real and true as opposed to vanity and hypocrisy'; 'The Word Became Flesh: An Exposition of John 1:1-18', *Int* 3 (1949), pp. 42–9 (46). In OT terms, this also encompasses the relationship with God in covenantal obedience.

the first direct speech about the Word and the first direct speech of the Gospel. To assert both the correspondence of this verse to vv. 6-8 as well as the trustworthy nature of John's message, the evangelist places in John's mouth the narrator's major verbs about him thus far and has him repeat them, thereby confirming in direct speech what the narrator claimed for him.[27] Thus, John is the readers' accurate witness, but not the true light. This role of direct speech in Hebrew narrative is not uncommon: 'Phrases or whole sentences first stated by the narrator do not reveal their full significance until they are repeated, whether faithfully or with distortions, in direct speech by one or more of the characters.'[28] The technique here affirms the integrity of this human witness. John testifies that the Word is 'the one who comes' after him temporally, but ranks before him. He further explains that this is so 'because he was before me'. With this historical grounding and temporal designation in place, as well as the corresponding element to John's initial witness (vv. 6-8), the Prologue surges forward with the mission of the Word.

The narrator continues to speak in the collective voice of the children of God as he details the process of God's action in creation in terms of their reception of God's gifts (v. 16). What God has done through the enfleshed Word is give a gift upon a gift: χάριν ἀντὶ χάριτος.[29] These gifts are illuminated in v. 17: 'For the law (ὁ νόμος) was given (ἐδόθη) through Moses; the gift which is truth (ἡ χάρις καὶ ἡ ἀλήθεια) came to be through Jesus Christ.' The law was a gift from God, and the reference to Moses ensures that the covenantal gift of Torah resonates through this proclamation. The gift which is truth came to be (ἐγένετο), harking back to v. 14 (ὁ λόγος σὰρξ ἐγένετο). This gift of truth is likewise a gift of God that acts in history in covenant with creation. The giving of the gift of the law was God's revelatory covenantal activity at Sinai. The incarnation of the Word that is full of the gift which is truth is God's revelatory covenantal activity in and through Jesus. The final verse of the Prologue returns to the beginning while elucidating the relationship of Jesus as 'only son' who is turned toward the Father, now in history

27 Jeffrey Staley, 'The Structure of John's Prologue: Its Implications for the Gospel's Narrative Structure', *CBQ* 48 (1986), pp. 241–63 (252).

28 Robert Alter, *The Art of Biblical Narrative* (New York: Basic Books, 1981), p. 182. Jo-Ann A. Brant (*Dialogue and Drama*, pp. 77–8) would refer to this as *Redundant Narration*, a technique whereby the narrator uses language that refers to objects, time and place that is then also used by the characters in dialogue (usually verbatim). This technique confirms the veracity or integrity of those characters.

29 I continue to follow Moloney for the rendering of χάρις; *John*, p. 46. Typically the preposition ἀντί is translated *upon* to render the idea of a superabundance of grace, though this translation is questionable. For more detail, see Ruth B. Edwards, '*Charin anti charitos* (John 1.16): Grace and Law in the Johannine Prologue', *JSNT* 32 (1988), pp. 3–15. I retain the English 'upon' to include the full range of meaning – since ἀντί could denote 'instead of', 'for', or 'on behalf of' in addition to the stricter 'instead of' (BDAG, s.v. ἀντί) – and to avoid reference to replacement or supersessionism, a tragic misreading of the Fourth Gospel. As Boyarin asserts, 'Jesus comes to fulfil the mission of Moses, not to displace it' ('Gospel of the *Memra*', p. 280). See the evidence in John Suggit, 'John XVII. 17, Ο ΛΟΓΟΣ Ο ΣΟΣ ΑΛΗΘΕΙΑ ΕΣΤΙΝ', *JTS* 35 (1984), pp. 104–17.

(v. 18; see vv. 1-2).[30] He is the one who makes God known (ἐξηγήσατο), and in this way gives humankind the ability to become children of God. This is indeed a new covenantal move in history, but the gift of truth in no way supersedes the gift of the law, for this is the Word made flesh. The remainder of the Gospel will narrate the 'how' of the covenantal claim that the Prologue introduces. In essence, the new covenant gives the power to become children of God which comes to pass in the receiving of the gift that is truth as revealed by the Word incarnate, Jesus Christ the only son who is in perfect relationship with God the Father.

III. John the Baptist: The Prologue Embodied in the Gospel Action (1.19-42)

The function of the Prologue in the Gospel of John, as in Greek literature in general, is to give a synthesis of the story to come, to communicate to readers at the onset just who the protagonist is and what he has done. The revelatory impetus of this story is thus the in-breaking of God into human history through Jesus Christ. Misunderstanding occurring throughout the dialogues of the story to come is rooted in this in-breaking and occurs because the characters have not read the Prologue. Only the storyteller and the audience know the Prologue. This literary technique draws readers into the narrative world of the evangelist as insiders and gives them everything they need to know to make right decisions about Jesus along the way. John the Baptist, introduced by the narrator so effectively in 1.6-8 and 15 as the human witness sent from God, opens the narrative as the first character in the story with dialogical force. Since the narrator placed the readers' didactic trust in this man named John, this character, upon launching the story, thus becomes the Prologue embodied. He is the one character who always witnesses accurately to the Word made flesh.[31] His first dialogue at 1.19-28, followed by the monologue of 1.29-34, together with his final initial witness in 1.35-42, provide readers with the grounds from which to form decisions about the characters in the narrative, and about their own belief in the Word.

a. Testimony Declared (1.19-28)

All of 1.19-42 occurs over the course of three consecutive days (1.29, 35) during which John testifies, just as the Prologue articulates he was sent to do. The detail of John's witness over this three-day progression parallels the pattern set forth in vv. 6-8. On day one John declares he is not the light (vv. 19-28), on day two he witnesses positively to the light (vv. 29-34), and on day three people begin to believe through him (vv. 35-42).[32] On the first day John is approached by a

---

30   Francis J. Moloney, 'John 1:18 "in the Bosom of" or "Turned Towards" the Father?', *AusBR* 31 (1983), pp. 63–71.

31   Cornelis Bennema, 'The Character of John in the Fourth Gospel', *JETS* 52 (2009), pp. 271–84 (272–4).

32   C. H. Dodd, *Historical Tradition in the Fourth Gospel* (London: Cambridge University Press, 1976), p. 248; Brown, *John*, Vol. 1, p. 45; Dirk G. van der Merwe, 'The Historical and

delegation and finds himself in dialogue over his identity. His task at this point is primarily to assert their misconceptions about who he is and what he is doing; thus his initial testimony is largely negative.

The opening of this scene connects the action of the day at hand with information provided in the Prologue: 'And this is the testimony (καὶ αὕτη ἐστὶν ἡ μαρτυρία) given by John' (v. 19). Both the demonstrative pronoun and the subject noun are indices that point back to John's mission as stated in the Prologue and focus readers' attention to the beginning of the action proper. John is first interrogated by a delegation 'sent . . . from Jerusalem' (ἀπέστειλαν . . . ἐξ Ἰεροσολύμων). The one who is sent from God (ἀπεσταλμένος παρὰ θεοῦ, v. 6) is confronted by 'the Jews' sent by others of this world. They are identified as 'priests and Levites', which alerts readers that they will be interested in John's activity as it pertains to ritual purity. They approach him with the question that will mark these first days and, indeed, the first part of the body of the Gospel: 'Who are you?'[33] Again, their use of a deictic pronoun in direct speech, this time the personal pronoun σύ, emphasizes and focuses attention on the person of John and the identity and self-identification in question.

The beginning of John's testimony is a response that characterizes what he is not. 'He confessed, and did not deny, but confessed, "I am not the Christ"' (v. 20). The pleonastic introductory formula of his initial response correlates the content of the testimony (ἡ μαρτυρία, v. 19) with the act of confessing (ὡμολό γησεν [twice], v. 20). When confronted with official interrogation, the witness can choose to confess or deny his identity and self-understanding, and John chooses to confess.[34] In response to their general question, 'Who are you?' John chooses to turn the dialogue to the question of Christology.[35] He asserts, 'I am not the Christ' (ἐγὼ οὐκ εἰμὶ ὁ χριστός). Using his own deictic pronoun ἐγώ, John points negatively to his own agency in a manner that will correspond to the positive claim that Jesus will make time and again over the course of the Gospel.[36]

Theological Significance of John the Baptist as He is Portrayed in John 1', *Neot* 33 (1999), pp. 267–92 (273, n. 18); opposing Jeffrey Staley who sees ironic tension between John's portrayal in the Prologue and 1.19-28; *The Print's First Kiss: A Rhetorical Investigation of the Implied Reader in the Fourth Gospel* (SBLDS, 82; Atlanta: Scholars, 1988), pp. 76–7.

33 The delegation asks John this at 1.19 and 1.22. This identity question is put in various ways to Jesus and to others about Jesus throughout his ministry (5.12, 8.25, 9.13-41 and 12.34).

34 Moloney (*John*, p. 58) correlates John's act of confessing with the Johannine community's situation where 'uncompromising confession of Jesus as the Messiah was leading to exclusion from the synagogue'. The verb ὁμολογέω also appears at 9.22 and 12.42 where synagogue exclusion is at stake.

35 Although, historically, questions of the Baptist's messianic claims could have circulated and spurred this delegation (Barrett, *St John*, p. 172), the rhetorical force of John turning the dialogue to the question of Christology affirms the Baptist's role as the witness sent from God.

36 ἐγώ εἰμι . . . (4.26; 6.20, 35, 41, 48, 51; 8.12, 24, 28, 58; 10.7, 9, 11, 14; 11.25; 13.19; 14.6; 15.1, 5; 18.5, 8; Barrett, *St John*, p. 172). For the negative Christological nature of this assertion and its effect on later positive claims by Jesus, see Edwin Freed, 'Ego Eimi in John 1:20 and 4:25', *CBQ* 41 (1979), pp. 288–91.

The delegation continues with its quest for identification, 'What then?' (v. 21). Even as they take the lead in suggesting possible titular claims, dialogically they continue to point emphatically to the subjectivity of John's role with the personal pronoun: 'Are you Elijah? . . . Are you the prophet?' (σὺ Ἡλίας εἶ; . . . ὁ προφήτης εἶ σύ;). With his unambiguous Christological refutation of v. 20, John's succeeding denials progress more concisely, cutting short any designs his interlocutors may have for information or even the dialogical upper hand: 'And he said, "I am not" . . . And he answered, "No."'[37] With the transitional conjunction οὖν of v. 22 ('so . . .'), one can almost feel the frustration of the interrogators as they find themselves where they began: 'Who are you?'[38] They must have an answer 'for those who sent us', but they concede all identification power, and thus the dialogical lead, to John: 'What do you say about yourself?'

Only then does John testify positively regarding who he is by accepting the role of the Isaian voice (v. 23; see Isa. 40.3).[39] The canonical Gospels agree in giving John the Baptist this Isaian voice (Mk 1.3 // Matt. 3.3 // Lk. 3.4), but unlike the Synoptic evangelists who narrate this identification, the Fourth Evangelist allows John the witnessing agency to give voice to his own self-identification. The Baptist 'says' (ἔφη) that he is the 'voice' (φωνή) 'crying out in the wilderness' in order to prepare the people to 'make straight the way of the Lord'.[40] He allies his own voice with that in the book of the prophet Isaiah and finally positively asserts his testimonial role. Isaiah refers to the role of the angels, who level hills and fill valleys to prepare the way in the wilderness for the children of Israel to return to Judah from the Babylonian captivity. By contrast, 'John the Baptist is to prepare a road, not for God's people to return to the promised land, but for God to come to His people'.[41] However, these two contexts are not mutually exclusive. As the human link between the Prologue and the Gospel narrative, John also prepares a way for the new children of Israel to receive the Word and come to the promised gift of truth, thereby becoming children of God.

---

37   For Jewish expectations of the eschatological figures of the Messiah, Elijah, the prophet (like Moses), see Brown, *John*, Vol. 1, pp. 46–50. Regardless of his conception in the larger Gospel tradition, the Baptist here gives no indication of himself in the role of Elijah; John A. T. Robinson, 'Elijah, John and Jesus, and Essay in Detection', *NTS* 4 (1957–58), pp. 263–81. This could result from the Evangelist's desire that the Christ should not be interpreted as dependent upon the Baptist; Marinus de Jonge, 'John the Baptist and Elijah in the Fourth Gospel', in Robert Fortna and Beverly Gaventa (eds), *The Conversation Continues: Studies in Paul and John in Honor of J. Louis Martyn* (Nashville: Abingdon, 1990), pp. 299–309.

38   Daniel B. Wallace (*Greek Grammar*, p. 674) notes that the 'transitional force of οὖν' sometimes approaches 'inferential force, as here' (2.18, 20; 3.25; 4.33, 46; 5.19; 6.60, 67; 7.25, 40; 8.13, 57; 9.10, 16).

39   For detail, see Martinus J. J. Menken, 'The Quotation from Isa 40:3 in John 1:23', *Bib* 66 (1985), pp. 190–205.

40   For contrast of the voice (φωνή) of John and the word (λόγος) of Jesus, see Oscar Cullmann, *Christology of the New Testament* (trans. Shirley Guthrie and Charles A. M. Hall; Philadelphia: Westminster Press, 1959), p. 260.

41   Brown, *John*, Vol. 1, p. 50.

The dialogue of this first day is followed by an interlude in which the narrator states that 'some Pharisees were also sent' (v. 24).[42] This evangelist uses the pluperfect to take the reader 'behind the scenes'.[43] This back-grounding technique allies readers with the narrator who continues to share information that will aid their understanding and decision making. Narratively, the full range of the opposition to the good news is laid out on this first day. This delegation initiates a further dialogical exchange in v. 25. Repeating the Baptist's three-part denial of vv. 20-21, they ask him why, then, he is baptizing. This first reference to baptism indicates indirectly what prompted the delegation in the first place. John's practice of baptizing must have brought him to the attention of the Jerusalem authorities and has now given him the opportunity to fulfil his particular testimonial role in this Gospel narrative. The interrogators inquire why, if John does not claim any recognizable eschatological identity of the messianic era, he is performing an act of purification like baptism.[44] The question thus serves to keep the Christological issue before readers.[45]

John's response affirms his baptizing role, even as he continues to witness to the one who is coming after him (vv. 26-27). Again with the deictic use of the pronoun ἐγώ, the Baptist points first to what he does do (baptize), then to what he is not. The task of untying 'the strap of the sandal' was given to the lowest in the hierarchy of a master's slaves and John disclaims his worthiness even to perform that task.[46] The strength of this image is magnified by John's claim that the one who is coming is already standing among them, and they do not know him. John's apocalyptic allusion to the hidden one to come emphasizes what the interrogators 'do not know', and the Messiah they will be hard pressed to recognize and receive in the narrative to come.

The narrator concludes the first day by geographically situating these events in 'Bethany across the Jordan' (v. 28). Closing an episode with this sort of index of setting is common in this Gospel (see 2.12; 4.54; 6.59; 8.20; 9.54) as the evangelist draws readers into the place inhabited by the characters and points them to space beyond the current sphere of activity. The final phrase of the scene confirms that John's witness was marked by his ongoing baptizing activity.[47]

b. Testimony Fulfilled (1.29-34, 35-42)

The Baptist's embodiment of the Prologue continues in terms of fulfilment the very next day (v. 29) as he points verbally to the promised coming one (ἐρχόμενος, vv. 15, 27) when he sees Jesus coming toward him (ἐρχόμενον πρὸς αὐτόν). The first day's testimonial dialogue becomes a monologue on this second day of promise fulfilment. John's interlocutors have faded from the scene and John bears

---

42   Wallace, *Greek Grammar*, p. 585.
43   A. T. Robertson, *A Grammar of the Greek New Testament in the Light of Historical Research* (New York: Hodder & Stoughton, 4th edn, 1923), pp. 904–5.
44   Brown, *John*, Vol. 1, p. 51.
45   Moloney, *John*, pp. 51–3.
46   Ibid., p. 58.
47   Wallace, *Greek Grammar*, p. 648; Barrett, *St John*, pp. 10, 175.

witness to any and all who would hear. He begins his testimony with the deictic interjection ἴδε, which verbally points to Jesus, 'here!' He then gives Jesus the title, 'Lamb of God', and mission, 'who takes away the sin of the world', that link the human being Jesus who has finally come onto the scene of the Gospel drama with the divine *Logos* of the Prologue. Jesus is the Lamb 'of God' who has come into 'the world' (see vv. 1-2, 9-10). John now also indicates a correlation between Jesus the Lamb's role in 'taking away sin' with Jesus the incarnate Word's mission of giving the gift of truth that empowers receivers to become children of God (see vv. 12, 14, 17). Questions about this title that is otherwise unknown in the Gospel narratives abound.[48] In the context of the Fourth Gospel, however, John's pointing to Jesus as the Lamb of God becomes particularly poignant, as both characters in the story and readers of the story experience the passion. Jesus is condemned at the moment the paschal lambs are being sacrificed (19.14) and he is led to the slaughter like the suffering servant of Isa. 53.7. Therefore, much of the story to come is indicated in this first sight of Jesus by the Baptist and the witness that encounter evokes.[49]

John the Baptist grounds this testimony of fulfilment by referring to and repeating verbatim his witness from the Prologue ('This is the one of whom I said . . .', v. 30; see v. 15). Again, John is the one entirely human character who bridges the omniscient narration of the Prologue into the discrete narrative of the body of the Gospel. Both the demonstrative pronoun that points to Jesus (οὗτος; 'this one') and the personal pronoun that points back to himself (ἐγώ; 'I') provide deixis that strengthens these verbal connections. The one sent by God to witness comes to embody that Prologue as he continues to give information that transcends the space, time and culture of the story world and keeps readers apprised of God's action in history.

John's testimony continues on this second day through vv. 31-34. The issue of human knowledge that he first mentioned on day one (v. 26) comes up again as John now affirms the limits of his own powers of perception (vv. 31, 33). He acknowledges that his entire ministry of baptism is so that through the movement of the Spirit (in the form of a dove, v. 32) he might hear the word of the one who sent him and recognize Jesus as the coming one who will baptize with the Holy Spirit (v. 33). By not recounting a baptism, the evangelist maintains focus on John's role as witness and Jesus' burgeoning role as mediator of God's covenant through the Spirit. John is then able to testify to God's revelation in Jesus (v. 31). With these statements affirming his own role and alluding to the role of Jesus in God's plan, John can also conclude this second day's witness with the strong statement that he understands he is fulfilling the mission God sent him to complete even as his testimonial promise of the first day is fulfilled in the coming of Jesus: 'And I myself have seen and have testified that this is the Son of God' (v. 34). Speaking again in the perfect tense, the Baptist brings focus to the completion of

---

48   For an insightful overview of the scholarship and his own conclusions, see Christopher W. Skinner, 'Another Look at "the Lamb of God"', *BSac* 161 (2004), pp. 89–104.

49   Raymond Brown, 'Three Quotations from John the Baptist in the Gospel of John', *CBQ* 22 (1960), pp. 292–8 (292).

this portion of his duty. Jesus is the Son of God who has broken into the world and who will transcend all human expectations for his mission. Therefore, this 'second day of preparation for the gift of the *doxa* further informs the reader of the story, but not the other characters *in the story*, of *who* Jesus is and *what* he does. The question of *how* all this takes place becomes more urgent.'[50]

Day three of the Fourth Gospel begins with John again, this time standing in the company of two of his disciples (v. 35). His introductory testimony declared and fulfilled, John now bridges the narrative into the ministry of Jesus as he verbally points his disciples to Jesus who is passing by (λέγει· ἴδε; 'he says, "look"'). He links this day's testimony to his previous witness by using his title of choice for Jesus and his mission: 'the Lamb of God' (v. 36). This designation from their first teacher becomes a direction for these two disciples as they turn and follow Jesus (v. 37).[51] John, his mission complete, now fades from the scene as readers turn with the disciples along the path of John's verbal index finger and follow on the journey of these disciples as they begin to participate in the mission of Jesus.

For his part, Jesus takes up the mantle of control of the dialogue, which he will guide and maintain for the rest of the Gospel, and initiates conversation with his new followers (v. 38). His first direct speech of the Gospel will mark his questioning discourse to all who would listen and follow him for the rest of his ministry and beyond. The first chapter of the Gospel of John comes to a close as the gathering of these first disciples is completed. John has witnessed to Jesus as the Lamb of God and Son of God (vv. 29, 34, 36). Discipleship in the Fourth Gospel has been illustrated as being and abiding with Jesus (v. 38). Both the disciples and readers are ripe for the revelation of God in Jesus, the Son of Man. Kelly and Moloney offer the observation that provides a fitting coda to these opening days of the Gospel journey:

> In the remainder of the Gospel's first chapter, all the actors in the unfolding drama are present: John the Baptist (1:19-37), the God who has sent the Baptist and spoken to him (1:33), the Holy Spirit (1:32-33), Moses and the prophets (1:45), the disciples (1:35-51), 'the Jews' (1:19) – and, of course, the evangelist himself. In a quite literal sense, John the Baptist sets the stage on which the drama will be enacted, and the experience of God will occur.[52]

IV. The Prologue Embodied Reprise: The Faith of John the Baptist (3.22-36)

The fullness of the first portion of Jesus' public ministry provides Johannine teaching on the nature of authentic faith (2.1–4.54). The two signs at Cana in Galilee

---

50 Moloney, *John*, pp. 53–4. Italics in the original.

51 Cornelis Bennema highlights John's simultaneous characterization as witness, herald and teacher in these first days; 'Character of John', pp. 277–9.

52 Andrew Kelly and Francis J. Moloney, *Experiencing God in the Gospel of John* (New York: Paulist, 2003), pp. 61–2.

that form the beginning and ending of this instruction are the literary frames of this journey of faith.[53] The physical movement between these two events mirrors the theological journey whereby Jesus brings the Word to the universal community of potential receivers and believers. The Cana to Cana narrative (2.1–4.54) thus offers instruction on the universal possibility of a journey of faith. As is commonly noticed, 'belief' as a noun (πίστις) does not occur in the Fourth Gospel, but forms of the verb 'to believe' (πιστεύω) occur often (98 times). Thus, faith in the Gospel of John is always an action and rightly described in terms of a process, or better, a journey. Faith is dynamic and communicative, and whenever Jesus' dialogue partners think they 'have' it, Jesus verbally challenges them to go further. The revelation of God in Jesus must always be anchored in the historical event of the cross and the glorification that can only be revealed upon belief in that word of Jesus. It is in this context that readers encounter the embodiment of the Prologue one last time through the faithful, active witness of John the Baptist in 3.22-36.

At the conclusion of his time at the wedding feast in Cana, Jesus and his entourage went down to Capernaum and remained there a few days (2.12). When the feast of the Passover drew near, he went up to Jerusalem where his demonstration against commerce in the temple area brought him into his first confrontational dialogue with 'the Jews' there (2.13-22). Although 'the Jews' reject the word of Jesus about the temple (v. 20), the dialogue has the positive effect on the disciples of remaining with them, such that 'after he was raised from the dead, they believed (ἐπίστευσαν) the scripture and the word (τῷ λόγῳ) that Jesus had spoken' (v. 22). The narrator's comment about the knowledge and faith of Jesus (vv. 23-25) leads into an extended dialogue instigated by Nicodemus, 'a leader of the Jews' (3.1-21). This questioning provides Jesus with the opportunity for discourse about God's love and plan for the world and the role of the Son of Man in that plan (3.11-16). The scene ends with Jesus' final words hanging in the air: 'But the one who does the truth comes to the light, so that one's deeds might be shown as laboured in God' (3.21).

After these things (μετὰ ταῦτα) Jesus and his disciples move from Jerusalem to the Judaean countryside. Key characters are gathered into a temporal and spatial setting that provides the impetus and motivation for the dialogue that follows (vv. 22-24). John, Jesus and his disciples are all participating in baptizing ministries where both people and water are abundant (vv. 22-23). The narrator then reveals that 'John had not yet been thrown into prison' (v. 24). Through this last index of setting, the narrator points beyond the space inhabited by the characters in the narrative, indeed beyond what he will ever narrate. Yet with this one aside, he provides both historical and temporal grounding for the event at hand and alludes to the entirety of the rest of the Baptist's story. By assuming that readers are intimately familiar with the end of the Baptist's story, the narrator exchanges a knowing nod with his readers and punctuates this final scene of the martyr *par excellence*.

---

53   For how minor characters develop the journey of belief, see John M. Howard, 'The Significance of Minor Characters in the Gospel of John', *BSac* 163 (2006), pp. 63–78.

A debate arises between the disciples of John and 'a Jew' regarding purification (v. 25).[54] Although no details of this controversy are provided, it spurs John's disciples to come to him with concern over the increasingly successful ministry of Jesus.[55] The conflict creates a narrative tension that intensifies attention both on the question itself and on the Baptist's response. John's disciples address him as 'Rabbi' and inform him that 'the one who was with you across the Jordan, to whom you witnessed (σὺ μεμαρτύρηκας), look (ἴδε), this one (οὗτος) is baptizing and all are going to him' (v. 26). The deictic use of the personal and demonstrative pronouns coupled with the interjection ἴδε emphasizes the contrasting subjects of John and Jesus, while illustrating the disciples' anxiety over the situation. The hyperbolic 'all' confirms that the Baptist's ministry is declining noticeably. John, however, continues his persistent defiance of human norms by responding counter-culturally and offering his final witness to Jesus. According to John, Jesus' increasing renown does not diminish his role, rather it affirms his merit.[56]

The pleonastic construction 'John answered and said' highlights the solemn definitiveness of the Baptist's response.[57] He begins by speaking not of Jesus directly but of the sovereignty of God. A human being is able to receive only what is given from heaven (v. 27). As presented in the Prologue, John highlights the gift-giving prerogative of God and the receiving power of humankind (1.12, 16-17). Resonating his first witness to the Jewish delegation, John repeats, 'I am not the Messiah' (οὐκ εἰμὶ ἐγὼ ὁ Χριστός, v. 20). He goes on to affirm, 'Rather, I was sent before that one.' The one proclaimed in the Prologue to be sent to witness to the light continues to testify to his role. By using the demonstrative pronoun ἐκεῖνος, John points not just to 'the Messiah' (the grammatical referent of the pronoun), but also to the one he verbally pointed to those first days (1.29, 35-36) thereby linking the expected Messiah with the one whose ministry is now in question (Jesus, v. 22).

John then turns to the imagery of marriage and applies the role of the friend of the groom (ὁ φίλος τοῦ νυμφίου) as a metaphor for his role in the events at hand

---

54   The only serious textual difficulty of this scene is found in v. 25. A tradition has arisen in scholarship that the original reading was 'Jesus', such that the controversy arose between John's disciples and Jesus. For a recent advancement of this position, see John Pryor, 'John the Baptist and Jesus: Tradition and Text in John 3.25', *JSNT* 66 (1997), pp. 15–26. The present study, however, accepts the singular 'a Jew', thereby connecting this off-stage interlocutor with the region of Judaea where both parties are located, without directly connecting him with 'the Jews' of Jerusalem who serve as the primary interrogators of John and opponents of Jesus (Rudolf Schnackenburg, *The Gospel According to St. John*, Vol. 1 [trans. Kevin Smyth; HTCNT, 3 vols; London: Burns & Oates, 1968–82], pp. 413–14).

55   For connections of 'purification' with the ensuing question of baptism, see Brown, *John*, Vol. 1, pp. 151–2 and Moloney, *John*, p. 109. The real issue is the debate that has arisen more so than its content. The term should thus be translated strongly as 'controversy' or 'conflict' as the issue for John's disciples is envy; Jerome Neyrey and Richard Rohrbaugh, 'He Must Increase, I Must Decrease (John 3:30): A Cultural and Social Interpretation', *CBQ* 63 (2001), pp. 464–83. On the simultaneous characterization of John as witness, baptizer and best man in this scene, see Bennema, 'Characterization of John', pp. 274–7, 279–81.

56   Neyrey and Rohrbaugh, 'He Must Increase', pp. 464–83.

57   Moloney, *John*, p. 109. This semiticism is often used by the Fourth Evangelist.

(v. 29). As the friend, or best man, he rejoices at the success of groom.[58] He is not the voice of the groom (v. 29). He is the voice of one crying in the wilderness (1.23) who witnesses to the coming one, whom he now characterizes with the messianic image of the bridegroom. Therefore as the friend 'who stands and listens for him', rather than being envious, or in any way concerned, he 'rejoices greatly' (χαρᾷ χαίρει) on account of that voice. John can then proclaim that this joy 'is fulfilled'. Just as there is no competition for the bride between the groom and the best man, there is no competition between John the Baptist and Jesus. The deictic language that John uses points to the emphatic finality of his current witness, now referring directly to Jesus: 'It is necessary for that one (ἐκεῖνον) to increase, but me (ἐμὲ) to decrease'. Contrary to first-century Palestinian religious or cultural expectations of one whose ministry has achieved as John's has, he willingly yields to Jesus' expanding ministry. John explodes convention precisely because his role lies outside human bounds, so that his very decline in the face of Jesus' increase means that his duty is complete and his role is fulfilled.

The final words of this scene, and the final verses of this first journey through Jewish territory, expand upon the role and experience of the one who comes from above (3.31-36; see the geographical shift in 4.1-4). The present study understands vv. 31-36 as a final discourse by the narrator to summarize and conclude this first leg of the journey from Cana to Cana.[59] The initial verses affirm why Jesus must increase, and also reject the concern of John's disciples, who can be included among those who belong 'to the earth' and speak about 'earthly things' (vv. 31-32). These condemning words also apply to 'the Jews' who rejected Jesus (2.18-22) as well as to Nicodemus who has not yet let go of earthly categories and concerns (3.1-21). The narrator then reiterates key positive actions introduced in the Prologue and manifested in the narrative thus far: witnessing (μαρτυρία, v. 33), giving (δίδωμι, v. 34) and receiving (λαμβάνω, v. 33). The trustworthiness of the one sent from God is affirmed (v. 34), and whoever receives his witness seals that God is true (v. 33). Further, the love of God the Father for the Son introduced in the Prologue is echoed (v. 35). Because of this familial relationship, the Father has given all things to the Son. The words and actions of Jesus in the story thus far, and in the fullness of the Gospel to come, flow from this relationship.

The narrator closes this summary by providing the choice this gift of God puts before the world (v. 36). The one who believes in the Son (ὁ πιστεύων) decides for eternal life, while the alternative to believing is characterized not as disbelief but

---

58   For detail, see Mary Coloe, *Dwelling in the Household of God: Johannine Ecclesiology and Spirituality* (Collegeville, MN: Liturgical, 2007), pp. 25–37. John uses a common social custom to illustrate that he is stepping outside such cultural norms of competition in his refusal to be envious of Jesus' ministry; Neyrey and Rohrbaugh, 'He Must Increase', pp. 464–83.

59   Those who read vv. 31-36 as a continuation of the Baptist's speech include Barrett, *St John*, pp. 224–5; Jeffrey Wilson, 'The Integrity of John 3:22-36', *JSNT* 10 (1981), pp. 34–41. Those who assert that these are Jesus' words include Brown, *John*, Vol. 1, pp. 159–60; Dodd, *Interpretation*, p. 309; Rudolf Schnackenburg, 'Die situationsgelösten Redestücke in John 3', *ZNW* 49 (1958), pp. 88–99. Those who understand these verses as a final reflection of the narrator include Marie-Josef Lagrange, *Évangile selon Saint Jean* (EBib; Paris: Gabalda, 1936), p. 96; Carson, *John*, pp. 212–14; Moloney, *John*, pp. 104–13.

as disobedience. The one who disobeys (ὁ ἀπειθῶν) chooses not life but abides in the wrath of God. 'Abiding' is intrinsic covenantal language in the Johannine literature.[60] Likewise, the 'wrath of God' describes God's reaction to Israel's covenantal disobedience (e.g., Exod. 32.10-12; Isa. 9.19; Jer. 44.6; Ezek. 38.19; Hos. 13.11; Mic. 5.15; Zech. 7.12). Just as Israel's covenant obligations to God were based on obedience, the Fourth Evangelist uses the activity of disobeying to narrate the action of all who do not believe the Son and therefore do not receive the gift of God. The gift of truth, from the God who is true (v. 33), confers life (v. 36; see 1.4). This is the covenantal activity of the Son that is increasing in 3.22-36, even as John the Baptist's witness completes and, his role fulfilled, he must decrease.

V. The Dialectic of Fulfilment: The Witness of John the Baptist in the Gospel of John

Following the Prologue, the movement of the beginning of the body of John's Gospel is delineated by the temporal markers that push the story forward through a flurry of activity across the span of a first week (1.29, 35, 43; 2.1).[61] This temporal structuring is often seen as the week of a new creation.[62] But creation is not the only primary motif in this narrative. Revelation is as well. If the cue is taken rather from Exodus 19, where the glory of God is revealed 'on the third day', then the first four days plus the three-day narrative gap is a direct reference to the revelation on Sinai that results in God's covenant with Israel.[63] The first three days show the Baptist living out everything claimed about him in the Prologue, and he is – aside from the Beloved Disciple – the only one in the Gospel who always gets it right about Jesus. John the Baptist is the Prologue embodied, and he thus accurately portrays his own role (on day one), points to Jesus as the Lamb of God and the Son of God (on day two), and directs the first disciples to Jesus (on day three). As days three and four progress, the gathering disciples heap titles onto Jesus, but these all remain in the religious and political categories within which the disciples are comfortable. Jesus constantly shatters comfortable categories. Thus, at the end of day four Jesus prepares both his new disciples and the Gospel readers for the revelatory process to come in terms of his own role as the Son of Man (1.51).

---

60   Edward Malatesta, *Interiority and Covenant: A Study of* εἶναι ἐν *and* μένειν ἐν *in the First Letter of Saint John* (AnBib, 69; Rome: Pontificio Istituto Biblico, 1978).

61   Harold Saxby, 'The Time-Scheme in the Gospel of John', *ExpTim* 104 (1992), pp. 9–13.

62   Marie-Emile Boismard is the most famous advocate of this position; *Du Baptême à Cana (Jean 1,19-2,11)* (LeDiv, 18; Paris: Cerf, 1956) esp. pp. 14–15; idem, *Evangile de Jean: Etudes et Problemes* (RechBib, 3; Bruges: Desclée de Brouwer, 1958).

63   Moloney, *John*, pp. 50–63. The rabbinic work *Mekilta on Exodus* provides instructions on how to spend four days prior to the three days of preparation for the celebration of Pentecost, the commemoration of the revelatory gift of the law on Sinai. See Jacob Lauterbach (ed.), *Mekilta de Rabbi Ishmael* (3 vols; Philadelphia: Jewish Publication Society of America, 1961); Jacques Potin, *La Fête juive de la Pentecôte* (LeDiv, 65; Paris: Cerf, 1971).

Raymond E. Brown suggests that the Fourth Gospel is 'a gospel of encounters'. Characters 'one after another' make 'their entrance onto the Johannine stage to encounter Jesus, the light come into the world' and in so doing they judge themselves 'by whether or not they continue to come to the light or turn away and prefer darkness'.[64] In the encounters that stem from these opening days, Jesus interacts in dialogue with several different types of characters as he first initiates then strives to fulfil his mission in the world. The nature of his mission as introduced in the Prologue and witnessed by John the Baptist is to give the covenantal gift of truth in the glory of God. This mission puts Jesus in tension with the prevailing authorities, both political and religious, of his own contemporary cultural milieu. This is not to say that the mission and identity of Jesus are in conflict with Israel's scripture or its story of covenantal relationship with God. Rather, the good news of the Christ event is that the biblical narrative is brought to its fulfilment in Jesus, and all those who believe in the word of Jesus, who receive the gift of truth, are given the power to become children of God. The dialectic sparked by the word of Jesus creates dramatic dialogical interactions that actively move his story to its fulfilment on the cross. The evangelist also provides a guide for readers as they, too, journey toward the cross and beyond. Encountering Jesus is faithfully modelled by John the Baptist, the witness sent by God who then comes to embody the message of the Prologue for the reader. He makes straight the way of the Lord and points disciples and readers to the one who creates a new covenantal community of God's children who receive the Word.

64   Raymond Brown, 'The Resurrection in John 20: A Series of Diverse Reactions', *Worship* 64 (1990), pp. 194–206.

Chapter 10

THEOLOGICAL COMPLEXITY AND THE CHARACTERIZATION OF NICODEMUS IN JOHN'S GOSPEL

Craig R. Koester

I. Introduction

Characterization is 'the art and techniques by which an author fashions a convincing portrait of a person within a more or less unified piece of writing'.[1] The portrait emerges through what the narrator says about a person, through the person's own words and actions, and through the way that others in the story respond to the person. A major feature of characterization in the Fourth Gospel is the depiction of a person's relationship to Jesus. The way the writer carries out this task fits the overall purpose of the Gospel itself. The writer tells of people in the story encountering Jesus in order that the readers themselves may 'believe that Jesus is the Christ, the Son of God', and that through believing they might 'have life in his name' (20.31).

The Gospel's apparently simple statement of purpose, however, masks the theological complexity of the writer and the implications for our understanding of characterization. One might expect the Gospel to offer a clear set of alternatives, encouraging readers to emulate the people who respond positively to Jesus and to repudiate those who respond negatively. But, in practice, the alternatives are not so clear-cut. Nicodemus is perhaps the most notable example of a character who confounds easy categorization, so that interpreters sometimes consider him a positive figure and sometimes a negative one. More importantly, the Gospel's theological perspective assumes that faith is engendered through the activity of God, who sends the Son into the world. Accordingly, character portrayal deals not only with the way that people respond to each other but also with the way that God interacts with human beings.

---

1   R. Alan Culpepper, *Anatomy of the Fourth Gospel: A Study in Literary Design* (Philadelphia: Fortress, 1983), p. 105.

II. Dualism and the Problem of Ambiguity

Studies of Nicodemus often point out that the Gospel works with a dualistic worldview, which is prominent in Nicodemus's initial encounter with Jesus (3.1-21). The passage refers to God and the world, to the heavenly realm above and the earthly realm below. It contrasts Spirit with flesh, light with darkness, belief with unbelief, and life with perishing.[2] The sharp dichotomies seem to invite readers to place Nicodemus in one category or the other, and yet doing so is not simple because the Gospel provides 'mixed signals' about Nicodemus's character.[3]

Nicodemus comes to Jesus and calls him a teacher who has come from God, which seems positive, and yet he arrives during the night and fails to comprehend what Jesus tells him about new birth, which seems negative (3.1-10). Later the Jewish authorities want to arrest Jesus, and Nicodemus points out the need to give someone a hearing before passing judgement, which again seems positive; and yet he stops without making a statement of faith, which can be seen as negative (7.50-51). At the end of the Gospel Nicodemus entombs the body of Jesus with a hundred pounds of spice, which seems to be a gesture of honour, and yet readers are reminded that he first came to Jesus by night; and Nicodemus is assisted at the burial with someone who kept his faith in Jesus a secret (19.38-42). So what are readers to make of that?

Literary studies sometimes work with the idea that characters are 'particular sorts of choosers', and given 'the pervasive dualism of the Fourth Gospel the choice is either/or. All situations are reduced to two clear-cut alternatives, and all the characters must eventually make their choice. So must the reader.'[4] Given the dualism, it is surprising that the assessments of Nicodemus vary so widely.

Some see Nicodemus moving in a positive direction from his initial confusion at Jesus' words (3.1-10), to his tentative defence of Jesus (7.50-51), to his final act of claiming Jesus' body for burial, which is understood to convey faith (19.38-42).[5] Others read the evidence negatively, noting that he is initially depicted as an unbeliever (3.11-12), speaks only of what the law requires and makes no claims about Jesus (7.50-51), and finally demonstrates his lack of understanding by piling the spices used for the dead on a Jesus who is the resurrection and the life (19.38-42). If he has any faith he keeps it

---

2   Culpepper, *Anatomy of the Fourth Gospel*, p. 104; Gabi Renz, 'Nicodemus: An Ambiguous Disciple? A Narrative Sensitive Investigation', in John Lierman (ed.), *Challenging Perspectives on the Gospel of John* (WUNT, II/219; Tübingen: Mohr Siebeck, 2006), pp. 255–83 (255).

3   Jouette M. Bassler, 'Mixed Signals: Nicodemus in the Fourth Gospel', *JBL* 108 (1989), pp. 635–46.

4   Culpepper, *Anatomy of the Fourth Gospel*, p. 104; Renz, 'Nicodemus', p. 285.

5   Raymond E. Brown, *The Gospel According to John* (AB, 29A; New York: Doubleday, 1970), pp. 959–60; Francis J. Moloney, *Glory not Dishonor: Reading John 13–21* (Minneapolis: Fortress, 1998) 149; J. N. Suggit, 'Nicodemus – The True Jew', *Neot* 14 (1981), pp. 90–110.

hidden, so that he remains among the Jewish authorities who are condemned for clinging to the honour they receive from other human beings instead of seeking the glory that comes from God (12.42).[6]

Still others stress the ambiguities in the portrayal of Nicodemus. They suggest that he hovers between the light of faith and the darkness of unbelief, attracted to Jesus and yet unable to commit himself. Given the assumption of a dualistic worldview, this ambiguity will also lead to a negative assessment: to be 'anything less than fully committed to the Johannine Jesus' is 'to retain the damning and dangerous connections with darkness, the "Jews", and "the world"'. Nicodemus 'moves through the narrative with a foot in each world, and in this Gospel that is just not good enough'.[7]

Literary studies have been supplemented by attempts to relate John's dualistic outlook and portrayal of Nicodemus to a reconstruction of the social context in which the Gospel was composed. Some note that the conversation between Jesus and Nicodemus, which is set during Jesus' ministry early in the first century, seems to reflect the Christian community's conflict with the synagogue later in the first century. The Johannine Jesus speaks as if he has already ascended to heaven, so that his words reflect a post-Easter perspective (3.13). He seems to speak for the Johannine Christians when he says, '*We* speak of what *we* know and bear witness to what *we* have seen' (3.11a; cf. 1.14). By addressing Nicodemus in the plural he censures the uncomprehending Jewish community when he says, '*you people* do not receive our testimony' (3.11b).

For some, this characterization of Nicodemus is an appeal for outsiders to become insiders. To 'be born from above requires a decision to believe in the one sent from God' and 'adherence to the *community* of such believers', publicly signified by baptism.[8] For others, the implication is just the reverse: it reinforces the community's boundaries. The confusing conversation about new birth is construed as 'anti-language', which is meaningful to insiders but opaque to outsiders. From this perspective the social function of the language is to maintain the distinctive identity of the Johannine Christians over against the Jewish community and competing Christian groups.[9] Some add that

---

6   Marinus de Jonge, *Jesus, Stranger from Heaven and Son of God: Jesus Christ and the Christians in Johannine Perspective* (Missoula, MT: Scholars, 1977), pp. 29–47; Culpepper, *Anatomy of the Fourth Gospel*, p. 136; Dennis D. Sylva, 'Nicodemus and his Spices', *NTS* 34 (1988), pp. 148–51; Jerome H. Neyrey, *The Gospel of John* (NCBC; Cambridge, UK: Cambridge University Press, 2007), pp. 77, 314–15.

7   Bassler, 'Mixed Signals', p. 646; cf. Colleen M. Conway, *Men and Women in the Fourth Gospel: Gender and Johannine Characterization* (SBLDS, 167; Atlanta: Society of Biblical Literature, 1999), pp. 85–103; S. A. Hunt, 'Nicodemus, Lazarus, and the Fear of "the Jews" in the Fourth Gospel', in G. van Belle, M. Labahn and P. Maritz (eds), *Repetitions and Variations in the Fourth Gospel: Style, Text, Interpretation* (BETL, 223; Leuven: Peeters, 2009), pp. 199–212.

8   David Rensberger, *Johannine Faith and Liberating Community* (Philadelphia: Westminster, 1989), p. 58.

9   Richard L. Rohrbaugh, 'What's the Matter with Nicodemus? A Social-Science Perspective on John 3:1-21', in Holly E. Hearon (ed.), *Distant Voices Drawing Near: Essays in*

ascribing a few positive traits to Nicodemus could have helped to maintain the basic dichotomy between insiders and outsiders by accounting for the fact that not all members of the Jewish community were antagonistic toward Jesus, and yet showing that such people were still outsiders to the Christian community.[10]

There are, however, important reasons to think that the Gospel's approach to character portrayal is less dualistic. From a literary perspective, the characters who play positive roles in the story may exhibit significant shortcomings in both faith and understanding. For example, the Samaritan woman fails to comprehend what Jesus means by 'living water' (4.7-15). She makes an evasive remark about having no husband (4.17), and when Jesus tells her that he is the Messiah, she stops short of saying she believes it (4.25-26). She invites her townspeople to 'Come and see a man who told me everything I have ever done', while adding a question that technically expects a negative answer, 'He cannot be the Christ, can he?' (4.29). Her role is certainly positive in that she is the catalyst for bringing others to meet Jesus, even though her final comments stop short of a clear statement of belief.

The same mixed picture is true of the disciples. They readily identify Jesus as the Messiah, the Son of God, and the King of Israel (1.41, 49) and invite others to 'Come and see' Jesus (1.46). When Jesus turns water into wine they believe (2.11). Yet in Samaria they are as baffled about the nature of Jesus' 'food' as the woman is about his 'living water' (4.31-38). When they go to town they merely return with lunch, whereas the woman brings the town to meet Jesus. The insiders may be called 'disciples' but the woman who is an outsider actually does the work of a disciple by inviting others to 'Come and see' (4.29).

One might look for a more straightforward paradigm in the story of the man born blind, who is healed at the beginning of the episode and worships Jesus at the end (9.7, 38). His final statement of faith makes him a very positive figure. But it is interesting to ask where he can actually be called a believer. Is it at the beginning, when he silently goes to the pool as directed by Jesus (9.7)? Or when he acknowledges that 'the man called Jesus' put mud on his eyes and told him to wash (9.11)? In the middle of the story he calls Jesus 'a prophet' (9.17) and someone 'from God' (9.33), but he does not call Jesus the Messiah and in the final scene has to ask who the Son of Man is (9.36). So are readers to think he is a believer only at the end, when he says, 'I believe' (9.38), or has faith emerged along the way?

The Gospel sometimes makes sharp contrasts between belief and unbelief, yet its characters often resist easy categorization. If dualistic statements create clear categories like light and darkness, the Gospel's approach to character portrayal recognizes that life is more complex. Readers cannot use the dualistic categories to define a character's response to Jesus without also asking how a character's response to Jesus might redefine the categories.

Honor of Antoinette Clark Wire (Collegeville, MN: Liturgical, 2004), pp. 145–58.

10   Raimo Hakola, 'The Burden of Ambiguity: Nicodemus and the Social Identity of the Johannine Christians', *NTS* 55 (2009), pp. 438–55.

These literary observations about the complexity in John's approach to characterization can be correlated with a more multidimensional reconstruction of the Gospel's social context. It seems likely that conflicts between the followers of Jesus and non-Christian Jews contributed to the present shape of the Gospel, which gives prominent attention to Jewish objections for the claims made about Jesus. At the same time, it recognizes that Jesus' followers were initially drawn from the Jewish community – like Nathanael the 'Israelite' (1.47) – and it shows that within the Jewish community responses to Jesus were mixed. Significantly, the Gospel assumes that scripture and Jewish tradition, rightly understood, bear witness to Jesus.[11]

The Gospel recognizes the tensions between the believing community and 'the world' outside it (15.18-25), and yet it emphasizes that the disciples who have been called out of the world are again sent into it (17.18; 20.21). Scenes in which Jesus is active in Samaria and the Greeks come to see him extend hope that some from 'the world' will become part of the Christian community (4.42; 12.19-20). The Gospel distinguishes belief from unbelief and the community from the world, while recognizing that the situation is dynamic rather than static. The multidimensional portrayal of Nicodemus fits well within a situation where the community's boundaries must remain permeable.[12]

III. Nicodemus as an Individual, Group Representative, and Member of the Human World (3.1-21)

The Fourth Gospel portrays Nicodemus as a figure whose identity has several dimensions. In his initial encounter with Jesus these dimensions unfold in concentric circles. At first readers see an individual Pharisee, who comes to Jesus by night and is addressed in the second person singular (3.1-10). In the middle of the episode the horizon expands as the language shifts into the first and second person plural, so that readers have the impression that Jesus speaks for one group ('we') and addresses Nicodemus as the representative of another group ('you' plural, 3.11-12). Then, in the last part of the passage, the language moves into the third person, so that readers can see how the encounter between Jesus and Nicodemus discloses the character of God's relationship to the world (3.13-21). The pattern is not unique to this passage. In the next chapter the Samaritan woman is introduced as an individual (4.7-9), who later is the spokesperson for her community ('we' and 'you' plural, 4.20-21), and the Samaritans in turn announce Jesus' significance for 'the world' (4.42).[13]

---

11   On the variety of perspectives on 'the Jews' see Lars Kierspel, *The Jews and the World in the Fourth Gospel: Parallelism, Function, and Context* (WUNT, II/220; Tübingen: Mohr Siebeck, 2006).

12   On this approach to the context see Craig R. Koester, *Symbolism in the Fourth Gospel: Meaning, Mystery, Community* (Minneapolis: Fortress, 2nd edn, 2003), pp. 18–24, 247–64.

13   See also the way Jesus addresses Nathanael (1.50-51) and the royal official (4.48) in the plural to suggest that what is true of them as individuals is also true of others.

As an individual, Nicodemus is 'a man' (ἄνθρωπος), a Pharisee, and 'an authority' (ἄρχων) among the Jews (3.1). When Nicodemus speaks of the impossibility of 'a man' being born 'when he is old', he seems to characterize himself as someone well along in years (3.4), which would be fitting for someone called 'the teacher of Israel' (3.10). Although groups of Pharisees, Jews and authorities are mentioned elsewhere in the Gospel, Nicodemus is one of the rare Jewish leaders to be identified by name. The only other Jewish leaders who are named are the high priests Annas (18.13, 24) and Caiaphas (11.49; 18.13, 14, 24, 28). Whereas Jews and Pharisees commonly speak as a group, Nicodemus stands out as a figure with his own identity, and at times he will speak and act in ways that distinguish him from his peers.

In the initial encounter readers are told that 'this one' (οὗτος) came to Jesus by night. The singular suggests that Nicodemus is alone. No one else is said to be present and Jesus speaks to Nicodemus in the second person singular, 'Truly, truly I say to you (σοί)' (3.3, 5). The fact that Nicodemus comes at night (3.2) is sometimes thought to emphasize his role as an individual who comes at night because he does not share the views of other Pharisees and does not want to be seen by them.[14] In one sense this could be positive, since it would mean that Nicodemus is separating himself from the others by coming to Jesus, but in another sense it is negative, since those who keep their faith a secret are censured later in the Gospel (12.42-43). The tensions are heightened because it is not clear whether Nicodemus is coming out of the darkness to Jesus, who is the light, or whether Nicodemus remains cloaked in darkness even as he comes. The implications need to be worked out as the story progresses.

The next dimension concerns Nicodemus's representative role, which is signalled by his initial words to Jesus, 'Rabbi, *we* know that you are a teacher who has come from God' (3.2). Jesus picks up this dimension in the middle of the conversation when he uses the plural to tell Nicodemus, '*you people* do not receive our testimony. If I told *you people* about earthly things and *you people* do not believe, how will *you people* believe if I tell *you people* about heavenly things?' (3.11-12). The implication is that Nicodemus's incredulity is typical of the group to which he belongs. What complicates interpretation is that the context identifies Nicodemus with two different groups.

First, he is a Pharisee and an authority among the Jews (3.1). Although Pharisees are technically a subgroup within the Jewish community, the Gospel often treats Pharisees and Jews as one category. Earlier in the Gospel the Pharisees and Jews of Jerusalem together sent delegates to ask John the Baptist about his identity and reason for baptizing (1.19, 24). Accordingly, readers might assume that Nicodemus represents these groups when he goes to Jesus. Moreover, when Jesus drove the merchants and moneychangers out of the temple, 'the Jews' demanded to know, 'What sign can you show us

---

14   Andrew T. Lincoln, *The Gospel According to Saint John* (BNTC, 4; London: Continuum and Peabody, MA: Hendrickson, 2005), p. 149.

for doing these things?' (2.18). Jesus told them, 'Destroy this temple and in three days I will raise it', but they failed to comprehend that he referred to the temple of his body (2.19-22). Nicodemus seems to share the outlook of this group since he too has an interest in signs and yet fails to comprehend what Jesus means by new birth (3.2, 4).

Yet Nicodemus also has connections with a second group in Jerusalem, which consists of people of unreliable faith. After the cleansing of the temple, the Gospel says that during the Passover festival 'many' (πολλοί) believed in his name when they saw the signs that he did (2.23). Their positive response seems to differentiate them from the more sceptical Jews in the temple and to align them with the disciples, who believed when they saw the sign Jesus performed at Cana (2.11). Nicodemus seems to speak for this group when he says, 'Rabbi, we know that you are a teacher come from God, for no one can do these signs that you are doing unless God is with him' (3.2). The problem is that the Gospel is clearly critical of those whose faith relies on signs. The writer makes a play on the word 'believe' (πιστεύω) by saying that they 'believed' in Jesus' name because of the signs, but Jesus did not 'believe' in them (2.24). Their faith – however sincere – was untrustworthy.

The complex characterization of Nicodemus has a levelling effect. He has traits of two groups that on one level seem different: the Jews and Pharisees are presumably more negative toward Jesus, while those who believe because of the signs are more positive. But on another level both groups are alike in that neither seems able to understand Jesus' identity and mission. Accordingly, the nocturnal setting of Nicodemus's conversation with Jesus seems appropriate. Both sceptics and misguided believers are 'in the dark' when it comes to discerning the nature of God's kingdom and the work of the Spirit that brings new life.

The horizon continues to expand as the Gospel shows how the conversation between Jesus and Nicodemus not only characterizes the encounter between different groups, but depicts God's relationship to humanity. When speaking about the unreliable believers in Jerusalem the Gospel says, 'Jesus did not entrust himself to them, because he knew all people and had no need for anyone to testify concerning man (τοῦ ἀνθρώπου), for he himself knew what was in man (τῷ ἀνθρώπῳ). Now there was a man (ἄνθρωπος)', a Pharisee named Nicodemus (2.24–3.1). What is true for him as an individual and for the groups he represents also typifies the condition of humankind generally.[15]

Jesus' opening comments to Nicodemus deal with a *human* problem: the need to be born or begotten anew (3.3, 7). By using images of procreation, Jesus speaks in terms applicable to people of all sorts. The barrier to the kingdom of which Jesus speaks is not limited to the perspective of the Pharisees or those preoccupied with the signs. The problem concerns the limitations of 'the flesh' (σάρξ) that all human beings share (3.8). In John's Gospel the flesh is not

---

15   Francis J. Moloney, *Belief in the Word: Reading John 1–4* (Minneapolis: Fortress, 1993), p. 106; J. Ramsey Michaels, *The Gospel of John* (NICNT; Grand Rapids: Eerdmans, 2010), pp. 175–6.

inherently evil – after all, the Word of God becomes 'flesh' (1.14; cf. 6.51-56). Rather, flesh is limited and mortal; it cannot generate the eternal life that God provides (3.15, 16). The incapacity to generate eternal life characterizes the human condition.

In the final part of the episode, Jesus' encounter with Nicodemus becomes a microcosm of God's encounter with 'the world' (ὁ κόσμος). In John's Gospel 'the world' was created by God (1.10) and has become alienated from God, as shown by its negative reactions to Jesus and his followers (7.7; 15.18-19). The images of darkness in 3.19-20 reflect the world's alienation from its Creator, and yet this same passage also refers to the love God has for the world, moving him to send the Son into the world to give it life (3.13-17). The Jewish leader who came 'by night' is emblematic of the world of darkness into which the light of divine love and truth has come in Jesus (3.2, 19). If Nicodemus was an individual 'man' (3.1) and Jesus knew what was in 'man' (2.25), the final section deals with how the light affects 'men' (οἱ ἄνθρωποι), that is, the human beings who comprise the world that God loves.

All three dimensions of Nicodemus's identity need to be taken together. He is an individual but not only an individual. He can also represent a group while exhibiting traits that go beyond that group. Finally, he can exhibit traits of humankind and 'the world' as a whole, and yet he does not cease being an individual, so during the narrative readers will find him speaking and acting in ways that differentiate him from others.[16] By portraying Nicodemus with these concentric circles of identity the writer invites readers to see that what is true for him may be true for others, and true for the readers themselves.

IV. Jesus Discloses the Character of Nicodemus (3.1-21)

Nicodemus's initial encounter with Jesus is challenging to interpret because it brings post-resurrection perspectives into a pre-passion conversation. Whether speaking of the work of the Spirit, which would be infused into the Christian community after Jesus' resurrection (3.5-8; cf. 7.37-39; 16.7; 20.22), or the way Jesus would be 'lifted up' through crucifixion (3.14-15; 12.32-33), the episode points to forms of divine action that would be meaningful to readers of later times but unintelligible in a conversation before that time – like the one involving Nicodemus. What the portrayal of Nicodemus will show is that the Son of Man 'must' (δεῖ) be lifted up (3.14), because apart from God's action people cannot 'see' the kingdom of God (3.3) or believe and have life (3.15).

The conversation begins with Nicodemus's claim to have knowledge of God. He says, 'Rabbi, we know that you are a teacher who has come from God, for no one can (οὐδεὶς δύναται) do these signs that you do unless (ἐὰν μή) God is with him' (3.2). Jesus' response inverts Nicodemus's comment

---

16   Koester, *Symbolism in the Fourth Gospel*, pp. 33–47; Conway, *Men and Women*, p. 47.

and redefines the issue. Where Nicodemus focuses on what Jesus *can do* in relation to God, Jesus focuses on what people *cannot do* apart from God. Where Nicodemus has seen signs, Jesus speaks of seeing God's kingdom, which is of another order. Jesus says, 'Truly, truly I say to you, unless (ἐὰν μή) someone is born anew he cannot (οὐ δύναται) see the kingdom of God' (3.3). The conversation exposes Nicodemus's limitations on two levels. First, it shows that his claim to 'know' is incorrect, since he proves to be incapable of understanding what Jesus is saying. Second, it points to a deeper inability to see or enter the kingdom, which is something Nicodemus shares with all human beings.

Jesus' statement identifies seeing God's kingdom as the goal, a person's incapacity as the problem, and new birth as the means for overcoming the problem. Introducing the kingdom as the goal is surprising since Nicodemus said nothing about it in his opening remark, and it was at most a subtheme in the previous chapters. The delegation from the Pharisees apparently wanted to know whether John the Baptist was the Messiah, a royal figure (1.20, 25), and the first disciples called Jesus the Messiah and King of Israel (1.41, 49), whose act of turning water into wine had messianic overtones.[17]

The principal function of the kingdom theme is to foreshadow the passion narrative. Such foreshadowing fits the pattern of previous chapters where John the Baptist introduced Jesus as the sacrificial Lamb of God (1.29), Jesus responded to his mother's concern about wine with a cryptic reference to the coming 'hour' of his passion (2.4), and he told the Jews in Jerusalem about the destruction and raising up of the 'temple' of his body (2.19). The kingdom (βασιλεία) that is briefly mentioned in the dialogue with Nicodemus later reappears when Jesus tells Pilate that his kingdom is not from this world (18.36), in a context where Jesus' identity as the King (βασιλεύς) of the Jews is the focus of debate (18.33, 37, 39; 19.3, 12, 14, 15). That title is inscribed above his cross in three languages (19.19-22). In John's Gospel, people cannot truly 'see' God's kingdom until the passion narrative discloses the character of Jesus' kingship (6.15; 12.13-16, 34-36).

Nicodemus passes over the significance of the kingdom without comment, focusing instead on the question of access to it. He is drawn to the cryptic expression Jesus used: γεννηθῇ ἄνωθεν. This expression has multiple layers of ambiguity. First, the word γεννηθῇ can be used for either parent. It can mean being 'born' from the mother or 'begotten' by the father. Second, the word ἄνωθεν can have either the temporal sense of 'again' or the spatial sense of 'from above'. Third, when used in an ordinary way, begetting and giving birth lead to life in a physical sense, yet the language can also be used in a transferred sense for something spiritual.

Jesus' ambiguous words prove revelatory for they draw out a response from Nicodemus and disclose the limits of his understanding. Nicodemus

17   Brown, *The Gospel According to John*, Vol. 1, p. 105; Koester, *Symbolism in the Fourth Gospel*, pp. 82–6.

takes γεννηθῇ as birth from the mother, ἄνωθεν as 'again' or 'a second time', and construes the whole expression in a physical sense, which leads to the ridiculous picture of a grown man trying to crawl back into his mother's womb in order to start the birth process all over again (3.4). As Nicodemus spells out the incongruity, he knows that his interpretation is absurd. He says that a man 'cannot enter into his mother's womb a second time and be born, can he?' The expected answer is 'No, of course not.'

Nicodemus can see that his interpretation does not work, but he cannot discern an alternative. He is not able to 'see' what Jesus is talking about. Jesus responds by emphasizing the role of divine action in the process. He tells Nicodemus that unless one is 'born' – or perhaps 'begotten' – of water and the Spirit, one is not able to enter the kingdom of God (3.6). Human incapacity (οὐ δύναται) remains the problem, and if that barrier is to be overcome it will be through divine agency. Nicodemus heard ἄνωθεν only as 'a second time', but the term can also mean 'from above', which is the primary sense elsewhere in John's Gospel (3.31; 19.11; cf. 19.23).[18] And one way God acts 'from above' is by sending the Spirit.

Jesus continues to confound Nicodemus by using the term πνεῦμα in three different ways in rapid succession. He says that what is born or begotten through God's 'Spirit' is 'spirit', and this divine activity is as incomprehensible as the blowing of the spirit or 'wind' (3.6-8). When read in the context of the whole Gospel, the comments indicate that the Spirit is the means through which God engenders the new 'spirit' of faith within a person, but the interplay between the different dimensions of meaning leaves Nicodemus with the question: 'How can these things be?' (3.9). It is a revelatory moment and Jesus says to Nicodemus, 'Are you the teacher of Israel and yet you do not know these things?' (3.10). The question brings out the irony. The Jewish leader who began by telling Jesus, '*we know* that you are a teacher who has come from God', proves that he really *does not know* what Jesus is saying (3.2, 9).

The conversation characterizes Nicodemus as someone with a dilemma. He began by claiming to 'know' Jesus, but has now been exposed as one who does not understand. This is not primarily a problem of lack of information; it has to do with a more fundamental inability to comprehend the ways of God. Jesus says, 'If I have told *you people* earthly things and you do not believe, how will *you people* believe if I tell you heavenly things?' (3.12). Heavenly discourse will not overcome the problem. The issue is not that Nicodemus has made the wrong choice instead of the right choice. Rather, he has been shown that apart from the activity of God he really has no choice to make. Flesh cannot generate life and God's Spirit blows in ways he cannot comprehend or control.

Nicodemus's dilemma gives divine action a central place in characterization. Given what has been said thus far, Nicodemus has shown that he 'cannot' (οὐ

---

18   Both dimensions of ἄνωθεν may be operative here, but Nicodemus discerns only one of them. See Moloney, *Belief in the Word*, pp. 109–10; Gail R. O'Day, *The Gospel of John* (NIB; Vol. 9; Nashville: Abingdon, 1995), pp. 549–50.

δύναται) see or enter God's kingdom; he lacks the capacity to engender the new birth into life. The question is whether God will act, and if God does act, then how might readers discern it through the portrayal of Nicodemus? The passage points to actions of God that for the readers are past but in the flow of the narrative are yet to come. If Jesus 'must' (δεῖ) be lifted up in crucifixion for people to believe and have life (3.14-15), then readers must wait to see what effect the crucifixion might have on someone like Nicodemus.

Nicodemus's nocturnal encounter with Jesus concludes with comments about what it means for light to enter a benighted world. It provides a framework for interpreting the conversation between Nicodemus and Jesus that has just occurred, as well as subsequent appearances of Nicodemus in the narrative. On the one hand, the one who does evil will love darkness and 'not come' to the light in order that he might not be 'exposed' (ἐλεγχθῇ, 3.19-20). On the other hand, 'the one who does what is true comes to the light, in order that it might be revealed that his deeds have been done in God' (ἐν θεῷ, 3.21). Coming to the light discloses divine action, just as Jesus later brings light to the eyes of a blind man in order that 'the works of God might be revealed in him' (9.4).[19] God's activity is revealed through its effects in human beings. Thus far Nicodemus has 'come' to Jesus (3.2), which someone who hated the light would not do; and during the conversation his incomprehension was relentlessly 'exposed'. At the same time it cannot be said that he is fully enlightened or gives evidence of doing 'what is true'. Whether he will do so is a question that must be carried forward in the narrative.

V. Nicodemus Reveals the Character of the Other Pharisees (7.50-51)

Nicodemus's second appearance occurs during the Festival of Booths as people engage in sharp debates over Jesus' identity. Throughout this episode people speak as groups rather than as individuals (7.1–8.59). The Jews, Pharisees and crowd have various opinions about Jesus, with some more positive and others more negative. The only people who are named and speak as individuals are Jesus and Nicodemus. Jesus repeatedly exposes his opponents' hostility and pretensions to know the ways of God, and he warns them not to judge by appearances but with right judgement (7.24). Nicodemus has a similar role, for he asks a question that reveals how the Jewish authorities' claim to know the law actually masks their ignorance of what it requires.

The 'crowd' (ὁ ὄχλος) has mixed opinions about Jesus. Some think he is a good man (7.12). They interpret Jesus' signs positively and are said to believe in him (7.31). When Jesus speaks of the gift of living water, some conclude that he might be 'the prophet' like Moses or even the Messiah (7.40-41). Their views seem commendable, though prior to Nicodemus's last appearance

---

19   On ἐν θεῷ, as an indication of God's activity, see Michaels, *The Gospel of John*, pp. 209–10.

readers were told that Jesus did not trust those whose faith depended on signs (2.23-25). The others in the crowd have a negative perception. They charge that Jesus is deceiving people (7.12) and that he has a demon because he imagines that people want to kill him (7.20). They dismiss the idea that Jesus might be the Messiah because he does not fit their expectations (7.27, 41-42).

The Jewish leaders share the idea that Jesus is deceiving people (7.47). The animosity of those called 'the Jews' (οἱ Ἰουδαῖοι) has grown because Jesus healed on the Sabbath and called God his own Father, which they construed as a wrongful attempt to make himself equal to God (5.16-18). Their desire to kill Jesus makes others afraid to speak openly (7.1, 11, 13). Later, 'the Jews' wonder at how Jesus can have such learning, not recognizing that his teaching is from God (7.15), and they puzzle over what he means by 'going away', unable to see that he is going to God (7.35). 'The Jews' work together with the Pharisees and high priests, who want Jesus arrested (7.32, 45).

Before Nicodemus is reintroduced, a crack appears in what has seemed to be monolithic opposition to Jesus among the authorities. The Pharisees and chief priests send some officers (οἱ ὑπηρέται) to arrest Jesus (7.31-32). But after Jesus extends the promise of living water, evoking a mixed response from the crowd, the officers return without arresting him and say, 'Never has anyone spoken like this man!' (7.45-46). Their response indicates that listening to Jesus can have surprising effects. Where the Pharisees had called for Jesus' arrest, the words of Jesus moved the officers to disobey the Pharisees and refrain from the arrest. In response the Pharisees wonder if the officers have been deceived, and they argue that those who respond positively to Jesus show ignorance of the law (7.47-49).

At this point Nicodemus is reintroduced as the one who 'had gone to [Jesus] before' (7.50a). Although Nicodemus is said to be 'one of them' (7.50b), his words run counter to the views of the other Pharisees. He asks, 'Our law does not judge a man unless it first hears from him and comes to know what he is doing, does it?' The question expects a negative answer: 'No, our law does not work that way.' In a basic sense the question calls for following due process, so that people learn the facts of a case before they render judgement. Yet the idea that people should 'hear' Jesus also suggests listening and heeding what he says (10.3, 16, 27), and coming to 'know' what he is doing points to the need for understanding (6.69; 10.38; 13.7).[20] The way the officers changed course – at least for the moment – when they heard Jesus suggests that listening could bring positive results.

Interpreters have asked whether Nicodemus can be called a believer at this point, since certain comments in the text point in this direction. When the crowd says, 'None of the authorities (οἱ ἄρχοντες) know that this is really the Messiah, do they?' (7.26), their question expects a negative answer. They assume that none of the authorities believes, and yet they have also been

---

20   Severino Pancaro, 'The Metamorphosis of a Legal Principle in the Fourth Gospel: A Closer Look at Jn 7,51', *Bib* 53 (1972), pp. 340–61.

told not to judge by appearances but to judge with right judgement, which suggests that they could well be wrong (7.24). Later, the Pharisees tell the officials, 'None of the authorities or the Pharisees has believed in him, have they?' (7.47-48), and they too expect a negative answer. But since readers are to see that their judgements about the law and Jesus are incorrect, it seems likely that here again they are incorrect, and that Nicodemus is an 'authority' (3.1) who does believe. The other Pharisees apparently think he is moving in this direction and say, 'You are not from Galilee too, are you?' (7.52). From their perspective, Nicodemus is aligning himself all too closely with Jesus the Galilean (7.41).

Despite these positive signals, some interpreters point out that Nicodemus speaks of the law rather than making an open statement of faith. If the basic categories are a public verbal profession of belief and anything else, then Nicodemus falls short. Moreover, his words might point to the need to 'hear' and 'know' Jesus, but that does not mean he understood the deep theological implications of those words.[21] So, given the complexity, it is worth asking whether the usual categories are adequate for interpretation.

The previous episode concluded with a contrast between those who do evil and those who do what is true (3.19-21). Here Nicodemus exposes the truth about the other Pharisees on two levels. First, they claim that those who listen to Jesus are ignorant of the law, yet by disregarding due process in their condemnation of Jesus, they show their own ignorance of the law. Second, Nicodemus shows that the Pharisees, who have not first (πρῶτον) given Jesus a hearing, cannot claim to 'know' (γνῷ) what he is doing (7.51). When Nicodemus went to Jesus before (πρότερον, 7.50), Jesus showed him how little he could claim to 'know' (γινώσκεις, 3.10). In this episode Nicodemus is the one who exposes the lack of knowledge among his peers.[22] In the categories of his previous visit, Nicodemus 'does what is true' (3.21a). And if that is the case, then readers need to ask whether in him they can discern the work of God (3.21b).

VI. The Crucifixion Discloses the Character of Divine Action (19.38-42)

Nicodemus's final appearance comes after the crucifixion, which fits the arc of the narrative. Jesus' first words to Nicodemus concerned the need to 'see the kingdom of God' (3.3), which is developed in John's account of Jesus' trial. In the first encounter Jesus also said that it was necessary for the Son of Man to be 'lifted up', alluding to the crucifixion, which for Nicodemus was still in the future (3.14-15). These elements provide perspectives on Nicodemus's role in the aftermath of the crucifixion.

---

21   Renz, 'Nicodemus', pp. 269–70.
22   Francis J. Moloney, *Signs and Shadows: Reading John 5–12* (Minneapolis: Fortress, 1996), pp. 91–2.

At Jesus' trial Pilate asks whether he is the King of the Jews, and Jesus replies that his kingdom (βασιλεία) is not from this world (18.33, 36). When Pilate offers to release the King of the Jews, the Jewish leaders reject the idea (18.39-40) and Roman soldiers use the title King of the Jews to ridicule Jesus (19.3). The Jewish leaders argue that Jesus' claim to kingship sets him against the emperor, warranting death (19.12-15). The theme culminates in the sign above the cross, which reads 'Jesus of Nazareth, the King of the Jews' (19.19). Since the sign could suggest that Jesus really is the King of the Jews, the chief priests want the sign changed (19.21). Yet Pilate refuses, and the sign identifying Jesus as the King of the Jews remains (19.22). At each stage the opposition is defined by a rejection of the idea that Jesus is King of the Jews.

In John's account of Jesus' burial, 'the Jews' as a group want the legs of those crucified to be broken and the bodies taken away. Their concern is proper observance of Jewish law. They do not want the bodies to remain on the cross on the Sabbath, which would begin at sundown (19.31). The request is fitting from a group that has condemned Jesus for violating the Sabbath (5.9-18; 7.23; 9.16) and charged that he deserved death under Jewish law (19.7). Asking that the bodies be removed appeared to show careful attention to the statute which said that if a person was condemned to death and hung on a tree, the body was not to remain on the tree overnight but was to be buried that same day (Deut. 21.22-23).

The Gospel casts Nicodemus in a subversive role that extends the trajectory set by his previous appearance. In both scenes the majority of the Jewish leaders assume that adhering to Jewish law means condemning Jesus, and in both scenes Nicodemus subverts their perspective by invoking Jewish law or practice in favour of Jesus. Together with Joseph of Arimathea, he gives Jesus a decent burial, which in Jewish tradition is an act of respect that is pleasing to God, whether performed publicly or in secret.[23] They wrap the body in linen cloths with spices, 'according to the burial custom of the Jews' (John 19.40), and complete the burial on 'the day of preparation of the Jews' (19.42). If the crucified Jesus is the rightful King *of the Jews*, as the Gospel says he is, then it is fitting that Nicodemus and Joseph show how the practices *of the Jews* rightly give honour to Jesus.

The royal motifs in the passage fit this pattern of subversive characterization. For 'the Jews' in the passion narrative, adherence to Jewish tradition meant rejecting the kingly role of Jesus. Nicodemus, however, gives Jesus a Jewish burial that is fit for a king. He entombs Jesus with one hundred pounds of spices, a quantity so large that it goes beyond anything used in ordinary burials, but it would be suitable for the King of the Jews (19.39).[24] What the

23   Josephus, *Against Apion* 2.211; Tob. 1.16-20; 2.3-8; 4.3-4; 6.15; 8.12; 14.10-13; János Bolyki, 'Burial as an Ethical Task in the Book of Tobit, in the Bible and in the Greek Tragedies', in Géza G. Zeravits and József Zsengellér (eds), *The Book of Tobit: Text, Tradition, Theology* (Leiden: Brill, 2005), pp. 89–101.

24   Brown, *The Gospel According to John*, Vol. 2, pp. 959–60; Hartwig Thyen, *Das Johannesevengelium* (Handbuch zum Neuen Testament, 6; Tübingen: Mohr Siebeck, 2005), pp. 754–5.

others have denied, Nicodemus affirms through his actions. He 'does what is true' (3.21).

Interpreters sometimes argue that the spices are at best an unwitting testimony to Jesus' kingship, and that the burial underscores the limits of Nicodemus's understanding. Why smother the one who is the resurrection and the life with a hundred pounds of spices intended for the dead?[25] An obvious response is that the Gospel does not picture any of Jesus' disciples comprehending the resurrection at this point, so Nicodemus can hardly be faulted on that account. Moreover, the question of the kingdom, which was introduced in 3.3, reaches its narrative climax in the scenes of trial and crucifixion. To 'see the kingdom' in this Gospel, one must come to terms with its crucified king, and Nicodemus points readers in this direction.[26]

Nicodemus can be characterized as one who 'does what is true' in the way that Mary did earlier. Before the passion she used a single pound of myrrh to anoint Jesus' feet in an act of devotion that foreshadowed his burial, and Jesus deemed that appropriate, even though Mary did not comprehend the full import of the action (12.1-8). Now that the crucifixion is complete, Nicodemus uses one hundred times as much spice to conduct the burial itself. As the Gospel portrays the scene, Nicodemus does not speak, but neither did Mary. They speak through their actions.

The remaining details in the scene raise questions about how categories work in the Gospel's pattern of characterization. The Gospel reminds readers that Nicodemus had 'at first come to [Jesus] by night' (19.39) and that Joseph of Arimathea was a disciple who had been keeping his faith a secret out of fear of the Jews (19.38). Accordingly, some see both of them as now stepping into the light by publicly claiming the body of Jesus.[27] Others see both lingering in the shadows, refusing to make an open commitment, so that they fall under the negative judgement made earlier, when it was said that many of the Jewish authorities believed in Jesus, but 'because of the Pharisees they did not confess it, for fear that they would be put out of the synagogue; for they loved human glory more than the glory that comes from God' (12.42-43).[28]

Here again it is helpful to ask how well the categories work. Nicodemus first came to Jesus by night (3.2), whereas the burial takes place on 'the day of preparation' for the Sabbath (19.31, 42). Since the Sabbath would begin in the evening, readers are to picture Nicodemus acting while it is still day rather than after 'night comes when no one can work' (9.4; cf. 12.35-36). Given the prominence of the light-and-darkness imagery earlier, one would expect it to play a major role here, and in an understated way it does support a

25   De Jonge, *Jesus*, p. 34; Sylva, 'Nicodemus and his Spices'.

26   Raymond E. Brown, *The Death of the Messiah: From Gethsemane to the Grave* (ABRL; New York: Doubleday, 1994), Vol. 2, p. 1267.

27   Brown, *The Gospel According to John*, Vol. 2, p. 959; O'Day, *The Gospel of John*, pp. 835–6.

28   Culpepper, *Anatomy of the Fourth Gospel*, p. 136; Bassler, 'Mixed Signals', p. 646; Neyrey, *The Gospel of John*, pp. 314–15.

positive interpretation of the characters at the burial. Moreover, if 'fear of the Jews' characterized Joseph and perhaps Nicodemus, it also characterizes the disciples after the crucifixion (20.19). Finally, the actions of Nicodemus and Joseph do not fit the categories used for the secret believers in 12.42-43. The way they give Jesus a lavish burial is designed to give Jesus the glory, not to protect their own. They do 'what is true' (3.21).

The characterization of Nicodemus provides glimpses into the way God interacts with human beings and the central role the crucifixion plays in the process. The crucifixion was foreshadowed in Jesus' initial encounter with Nicodemus, when he said, 'And just as Moses lifted up the serpent in the wilderness, so must the Son of Man be lifted up, that everyone who believes in him might have eternal life' (3.14-15). The word 'lift up' (ὑψόω) shows that in being physically elevated on the cross Jesus is also exalted in glory (3.14), and this is the transition point between the disclosure of unbelief (3.13) and the prospect of faith (3.15).

The theme returns at the close of Jesus' public ministry when throngs of people come to him because of the signs, and yet prove incapable of understanding who Jesus is (12.18, 34). That same scene also indicts the authorities, who would not profess faith because they wanted to protect the glory they received from other people (12.42-43). Yet in the face of such pervasive unbelief Jesus also says that 'I, when I am lifted up from the earth, will draw all people to myself' (12.32). Given only the signs, people 'did not' and 'could not believe' (12.37, 39). Yet through his elevation on the cross, Jesus promises to 'draw' people to himself. Through the portrayal of Nicodemus and Joseph at the burial, the Gospel shows people being 'drawn' to the crucified Christ. They give readers a way of seeing what Jesus' death would accomplish.[29]

VII. Conclusion

Theological complexity is integral to the characterization of Nicodemus. As an individual, an authority among the Jews, and a representative of 'the world' he demonstrates the human incapacity to 'see' the kingdom of which Jesus speaks (3.3). His limitations demonstrate the need for divine action and show why 'the Son of Man must be lifted up' in order that people might believe and have life (3.14-15). The portrayal of Nicodemus does not offer a simple example of someone determining to cross the line from unbelief into true faith. Rather, he gives readers glimpses of how the work of God is done. Initially, Jesus is the one who reveals the truth by exposing Nicodemus's pretensions to knowledge (3.1-13), but Nicodemus later assumes that role when he exposes the pretensions of the other Jewish leaders (7.50-51). As he 'does what is

---

29   Brown, *The Death of the Messiah*, Vol. 2, p. 1268; O'Day, *The Gospel of John*, pp. 835–6.

true' he reveals the activity of God (3.21). His actions after the crucifixion bear witness to the truth of Jesus' kingship, which the other Jewish leaders have denied 19.38-42), He 'does what is true' and helps readers to 'see' the cruciform nature of God's kingdom (3.3, 21). The portrayal of Nicodemus discloses how the crucified King of the Jews 'draws' people to himself (12.32), anticipating the way the readers could be drawn to faith through the agency of the Spirit (3.5-8).

Chapter 11

THE WOMAN OF SAMARIA: HER CHARACTERIZATION, NARRATIVE, AND THEOLOGICAL SIGNIFICANCE

Mary L. Coloe

I. Introduction

How often does one pick up a novel and find a disclaimer: 'Characters in this book are purely fictional and bear no relation to people in real life. When historical characters are involved the author has created scenes and conversations for which there is no evidence in current documentation.' Such disclaimers remind the reader that they are dealing with a text of fiction. Even though it may be an 'historical' novel, and the author has done research into the history of the person and the times, the overall aim of the book is to present an author's perspective on the events and people recorded. There is no claim for biographical or historical accuracy.

The authors of the Gospels provide no such disclaimer, but readers would do well to realize that the Gospels are a particular type of literature, and the authors' aims are not to reproduce historical 'facts' as we moderns might expect. The aims of the Fourth Gospel are clearly stated: 'Now Jesus did many other signs in the presence of the disciples, which are not written in this book; but these are written that you may believe that Jesus is the Christ, the Son of God, and that believing you may have life in his name' (20.30-31).[1]

Having such an explicit goal the Gospel cannot be considered simply an artistic discourse but needs to be read as an 'ideological discourse that originated in a particular real-life context'.[2] The writer, a believer in Jesus as the Christ and Son of God, has a particular view of events that took place during the life of Jesus, a point of view that is clearer now, in the post-resurrection time, than it was during the disciples' experience.[3] In the post-resurrection

---

1   English translations of the NT are my own unless otherwise indicated. The manuscript traditions allow for both 'you may believe' and 'you may continue to believe'. See the discussion in Bruce M. Metzger (ed.), *A Textual Commentary on the Greek New Testament* (New York: United Bible Societies, 4th rev. edn, 1994), p. 219.

2   Petri Merenlahti and Raimo Hakola, 'Reconceiving Narrative Criticism', in David Rhoads and Kari Syreeni (eds), *Characterization in the Gospels: Reconceiving Narrative Criticism* (JSNTSup, 184; London: T&T Clark, 1999), pp. 13–47 (17).

3   John makes this retrospective faith and perception explicit: 'When therefore he was

time, the author now shapes and writes a text to convey the post-Easter faith and perception of the community. This text, while based on memory and even eyewitness testimony (19.35), is not restricted to conveying events from a pre-Easter, partial-faith perspective, but the writer is now free to write of those events retrospectively, from his post-Easter faith.[4] A narrative-critical approach to the text asks how a narrator uses 'setting, rhetoric, character and plot to persuade the reader to adopt his evaluative point of view'.[5]

In this essay on the Samaritan woman in John 4, I will make use of the insights of James Resseguie and those other narrative critics who ask questions about how a character serves the ideological 'point of view' of the writers. My interest is not simply about what type of character this woman is, but how her characterization works to contribute to the theological perspective of the Gospel. Shimon Bar-Efrat writes that it is the characters 'who transmit the significance and values of the narrative to the readers'.[6] Another writer, who also emphasizes the importance of considering characterization in relation to the ideological or theological purpose of the Gospel, is Petri Merenlahti, who writes:

> Rather than static elements of design picked by a master author to fill a distinct literary or rhetorical purpose, they [the characters] are constantly being reshaped by distinct ideological dynamics. This ideologically attuned nature of character presents a challenge for any theory or model of characterization for the Gospel narrative . . . analysis of ideology should be an integral part of the analysis of the formal features of narrative.[7]

My interest in the woman of Samaria is not primarily on her developing perception of Jesus' identity or her faith journey. This has been the focus of a number of studies. My interest is why she is introduced into the narrative at this point? Is it important that the character is a *woman*? Is it important that she is a *Samaritan*? How does she, as a character, contribute to the plot of the Gospel? How does she, as a character, relate to the ideological point of view of the evangelist?

raised from the dead, his disciples remembered that he had said this; and they believed the scripture and the word which Jesus had spoken' (2.22).

4   On reading the Gospel of John from a post-Easter perspective see the work of Franz Mussner, *Die johanneische Sehweise und die Frage nach dem historischen Jesus* (Quaestiones Disputatae, 28; Freiburg: Herder, 1965), and Christina Hoegen-Rohls, *Der nachösterliche Johannes: Die Abschiedsreden als hermeneutischer Schlüssel zum vierten Evangelium* (WUNT, II/84; Tübingen: J.C.B. Mohr [Paul Siebeck], 1996).

5   James L. Resseguie, *The Strange Gospel: Narrative Design and Point of View in John* (BIS, 56; Leiden: Brill, 2001), p. 2.

6   Shimon Bar-Efrat, *Narrative Art in the Bible* (JSOTSup, 70; Sheffield: Sheffield Academic Press, 1992), p. 47.

7   Petri Merenlahti, 'Characters in the Making: Individuality and Ideology in the Gospels', in Rhoads and Syreeni (eds), *Characterization in the Gospels*, pp. 49–72 (50).

II. The Narrative Context

Before Jesus arrives in Samaria, the Gospel has already set the scene for this encounter in two ways; first, by the portrayal of John the Baptizer, and second in what the Gospel has already claimed about Jesus' identity. The role and identity of both of these male characters are critical for assessing the role of the Samaritan woman.

a. John

In the Prologue John is described as 'one who came for testimony, to bear witness to the light' (1.7). John speaks of himself as a voice, 'crying in the wilderness' (1.23), then, immediately before Jesus' journey through Samaria, John describes himself as 'the friend of the bridegroom' (3.29). I have dealt with John's characterization as 'friend of the bridegroom' elsewhere and so here I will summarize the salient features.[8]

The friend of the bridegroom, or deputy, was the one who went with the father of the prospective groom to begin the negotiations about a future marriage. Because of the significance of this event for both families, and the possible loss of face if the negotiations are not successful,[9] both fathers, of the bride and the groom, make use of a deputy. The friend/deputy therefore has the important task of being the voice of the bridegroom and bearing witness to his qualities so that a betrothal may eventuate. His negotiations play a crucial part in the father of the bride granting consent. It is for this reason that there were ancient laws forbidding the woman's father, should he refuse the request of the intended bridegroom, to give his daughter to the bridegroom's friend.

> If a son-in-law [intended] has entered the house of his [intended] father-in-law and has performed the betrothal gift, and afterwards they have made him go out and have given his wife to his companion – they shall present to him the betrothal gift which he has brought and that wife may not marry his companion.[10]

The term companion in this passage refers to the formal role called today in Western cultures, 'the best man', or in the Fourth Gospel, the 'friend of the bridegroom' (3.29). It is the deputies who negotiate the amount of dowry, the down-payment at the time of betrothal, the amount to be received at the time of the wedding and the likely date of the wedding.[11] When all such contractual

---

8   See Mary L. Coloe, 'Witness and Friend: Symbolism associated with John the Baptiser', in Jörg Frey, Jan van der Watt and Ruben Zimmermann (eds), *Imagery in the Gospel of John: Terms, Forms, Themes and Theology of Figurative Language* (WUNT, 200; Tübingen: Mohr Siebeck, 2006), pp. 319–32; ibid., *Dwelling in the Household of God: Johannine Ecclesiology and Spirituality* (Collegeville, MN: Liturgical, 2007), esp. ch. 2.

9   On the potential honour and shame involved in marriage negotiations see Frank P. Satlow, *Jewish Marriage in Antiquity* (Princeton, NJ: Princeton University Press, 2001), p. 104.

10   Adrian van Selms, 'The Best Man and Bride: From Sumer to St. John', *JNES* 9 (1950), pp. 65–70.

11   Fred H. Wight, *Manners and Customs of Bible Lands* (Chicago: Moody, 1953), p. 127.

matters have been arranged, then the prospective fathers-in-law rejoin the discussion to seal this arrangement in some way. On the day of the wedding the friend/deputy may be the one to lead the bride from her father's house to the house of the groom's father, where she will wait until after the festivities.[12] The friend/deputy will then conduct the groom into the bridal chamber, where the couple may see each other for the first time. The friend/deputy will wait outside to hear the sounds of joy as the couple meet each other. The deputy may then be the one to bring out the bridal sheet the following morning to bear witness to the bride's virginity.[13]

In the Fourth Gospel, John acts as this deputy/friend with respect to Jesus. He identifies himself as 'a witness' and 'the voice' (1.15, 23); he is the one to direct disciples to Jesus, and the narrator indicates that this took place about the tenth hour (1.36-39), which is the traditional time for a wedding, in the late afternoon.[14] Following the gathering of the first disciples, Jesus then attends a wedding where the wine runs out (2.1-12). Miraculously, Jesus intervenes to produce high-quality wine. What is significant is the action of the chief steward, who goes to the *bridegroom* and congratulates him on saving the best wine until later (2.10). The words of the steward indicate that it was the role of the bridegroom to provide the wine for the wedding, but in this case the wine was provided by Jesus. In this subtle, symbolic way the evangelist points to an aspect of Jesus' identity and role: he is the bridegroom. Jesus' identity as the bridegroom will later be confirmed by John (3.29).

There are textual indicators that this wedding took place within the festival of *Shavuot* (Pentecost) – the festival that celebrates the making of the Covenant at Sinai.[15] In the Old Testament the covenant between God and Israel was frequently described using the image of betrothal and marriage (Jer. 31.32; Ezek. 16.8-14; Isa. 54.5; Hos. 2.7; Joel 1.8). Here, at Cana, Jesus is identified as the presence of the covenantal God, the bridegroom of Israel. Immediately after the wedding he takes his disciples, his mother, and his brothers and sisters into the temple (2.13) which he names as 'My Father's House' (2.15). According to social customs, the father's house is where the

---

12   M.-Émile Boismard, 'L'ami de l'Époux (Jo., 111, 29)', in A. Barucq, et al. (eds), *À la rencontre de Dieu: Mémorial Albert Gelin* (Bibliothèque de la Faculté catholique de théologie de Lyon, 8; Le Puy: Xavier Mappus, 1961), pp. 289–95 (292).

13   Joachim Jeremias, 'νύμφη, νυμφίος', *TDNT*, Vol. 4, pp. 1099–106 (1101).

14   H. Clay Trumbull, *Studies in Oriental Social Life* (Philadelphia: The Sunday School Times Co., 1894), pp. 39–44; Edmond Stapfer, *Palestine in the Time of Christ* (trans. A. H. Holmden; New York: Armstrong and Son, 1885), p. 163.

15   The repetition of the phrase 'the next day', the statement that the episode at Cana took place 'on the third day', and the disciples' recognizing Jesus' 'glory' are some of the indicators that recall the initial Sinai covenant described in Exodus 19. Here, the people of Israel are told to get ready for 'the third day', when God's glory will be revealed on Sinai. This event was celebrated in the Festival of Weeks, Pentecost. Francis Moloney first noted the link between Cana and Pentecost and I have developed this further. See Francis J. Moloney, *John* (SP, 4; Collegeville, MN: Liturgical, 1998), p. 50; Mary L. Coloe, 'The Johannine Pentecost: John 1.19–2.12', *AusBR* 55 (2007), pp. 41–56.

bridegroom and bride will establish their own household. The next episode
with Nicodemus speaks of birth, and rebirth (3.3-5). The deep structure of the
narrative has thus far appropriated the customs of a marriage from betrothal
(1.36-39), to wedding (2.1-12), to setting up a household in the Father's house
(2.13), to birth (3.3, 5). This process is then concluded in the words of John,
who explicitly identifies himself as the friend of the bridegroom (3.29). John
introduces and concludes this narrative sequence, which has so far focused
on Jewish characters. In chapter 4, the narrator moves beyond the world of
Orthodox Judaism into the world of Samaria.

b. Jesus the Bridegroom and Temple

When Jesus enters Samaria he sits upon a well that is clearly associated with
Jacob. It is called Jacob's well (4.6). The village of Sychar is near the field
Jacob gave to Joseph (4.5). According to the Samaritan woman, Jacob is the
one who gave the well to the people (4.12). The narrator indicates the time –
'about the sixth hour' (4.6). Then a woman of Samaria approaches (4.7). The
scene is set. The characters are now present. What modern readers frequently
miss are the many resonances of this description with other Old Testament
well-meetings, which always lead to betrothal and marriage.[16] Abraham's
servant met Rebecca, the future wife of Isaac, at a well (Gen. 24.10-33);
Moses met his wife at a well (Exod. 2.15-22), and, most importantly for this
episode, Jacob met Rachel at a well, in the middle of the day (Gen. 29.1-14),
the same time indicated in the Johannine narrative. The many references to
Jacob, and the apparently inconsequential piece of information about the time
of the meeting between Jesus and the woman,[17] are all clues provided by the
narrator to alert the reader to the deeper symbolism and portent of this episode.

A second important aspect of the narrative so far is the use of tabernacle
and temple symbolism to point to the identity of Jesus. In John 1.14, the reader
hears first-hand testimony of the Word taking flesh and dwelling among us.
The Greek text uses the verb σκηνόω, which could more literally be translated
as 'pitched his tent' or 'tabernacled' among us, since the noun form, σκηνή,
is the word used in the OT to speak of the Tent associated with the Ark of the
Covenant, and that, in later traditions, is called the tabernacle.[18]

---

16   Robert Alter calls such meetings between a man and woman at a well a 'biblical type-
scene'. See his discussion on the characteristics of such scenes in Robert Alter, *The Art of Biblical
Narrative* (New York: Basic Books, 1981), pp. 51–2.

17   Juan Leal offers four criteria that can indicate when the narrative has a symbolic as
well as a literal meaning; (i) inconsequential details that seem to play no part in the narrative,
(ii) a discourse set within the narrative of an event such that they are mutually illuminating, (iii)
when the evangelist accentuates the importance of a person who has no significant role in context,
and (iv) when later liturgical and Christian expressions are used. See Juan Leal, 'El simbolismo
histórico del iv Evangelio', *EstBib* 19 (1960), pp. 329–48 (344–6).

18   Wilhelm Michaelis, 'σκηνή', *TDNT*, Vol. 7, pp. 368–94 (369–71). On the Ark, Tent of
Meeting and Tabernacle traditions see Mary L. Coloe, *God Dwells with Us: Temple Symbolism
in the Fourth Gospel* (Collegeville, MN: Liturgical, 2001), esp. ch. 3; Craig R. Koester, *The
Dwelling of God: The Tabernacle in the Old Testament, Intertestamental Jewish Literature, and*

Then in John 2 the narrator identifies Jesus as the temple: 'He spoke of the temple of his body' (2.21). Jesus is now the place in history where God dwells. The identification of Jesus as the temple of God's presence sheds light on the initial discussion between the Samaritan woman and Jesus.

In the first part of this episode Jesus and the woman enter into a dialogue about water. While the woman speaks of natural water, Jesus begins to speak of living water.[19] This image only makes sense in the light of Jewish traditions that associate the temple with the source of all the waters of creation. According to these traditions, the temple rests upon the fissure above the great abyss which is the source of the creative waters in Genesis 2.8.[20] After the great flood, the rock of Noah's altar sealed up the waters of the abyss, making this altar the foundation stone of a new creation. Jewish traditions link the altar of Noah with the foundation stone in the Holy of Holies that once supported the Ark of the Covenant.[21] According to this mythology the temple lies upon the wellspring of the earth, the centre and source of creation:[22] 'The waters under the earth were all gathered beneath the temple, they believed, and it was necessary to ensure that sufficient was released to ensure fertility, flood.'[23]

In verse 6, the evangelist uses the preposition ἐπί and most texts translate this word as 'beside', and so place Jesus on the ground beside the well. Possibly translators have in mind an image of above-ground wells, walled around with bricks and having a windlass to lower and raise a bucket. But this is both an incorrect image of a typical Middle-Eastern well, and a poor translation of the preposition ἐπί which, with the dative, usually means 'on' or 'upon'.[24] In the Middle East, wells were simply holes in the ground with a cover such as a large rock to protect them. This type of well is described in the meeting of Jacob and Rachel, where Jacob rolls the stone from the mouth of the well (Gen. 29.10). In John 4, the evangelist depicts Jesus sitting *on* (ἐπί) the well, presumably on the rock slab that lies across the well opening.[25] Just as the temple, in Jewish mythology, rests on the foundation stone above the waters of the great abyss, now Jesus, the new temple, rests upon the rock over the waters

---

the New Testament (CBQMS, 22; Washington, DC: Catholic Biblical Association of America, 1989).

19   For further discussion on the symbolism of 'living waters' and the possible reference to the Spirit or revelation see Coloe, *God Dwells with Us*, pp. 93–6. Here I argue that the strongest OT allusion is to Ezekiel 47 and the description of the life-giving waters flowing from the Temple.

20   Frédéric Manns, *Le symbole eau-esprit dans le judaïsme ancien* (SBFA, 19; Jerusalem: Franciscan Printing Press, 1983), p. 285.

21   Frédéric Manns, *L'Evangile de Jean à la lumière du judaïsme* (SBFA, 33; Jerusalem: Franciscan Printing Press, 1991), p. 135.

22   In Ezekiel, Jerusalem is called the Earth's navel, reflecting this mythological image (Ezek. 5.5; 38.12).

23   Margaret Barker, *The Gate of Heaven: The History and Symbolism of the Temple in Jerusalem* (London: SPCK, 1991), p. 18.

24   Wilhelm Köhler, 'ἐπί', *EDNT*, Vol. 2, pp. 21–3.

25   Brown notes that Jesus was sitting 'literally on the well'; see Raymond E. Brown, *The Gospel According to John* (AB, 29; New York: Doubleday, 1966), p. 169.

of Jacob's well. It is because Jesus is now the living Temple of God's presence that he is able to provide a type of living water that can well up to *eternity life*.

III. The Woman of Samaria

a. Water and Wells

In the opening dialogue, there is a significant shift in the woman's perception of Jesus, indicating a growing receptivity and openness to his words. She begins the meeting with some hostility, responding to Jesus' request for water by pointing to the long and traditional animosity between Jews and Samaritans and the further breaking of conventions of a man speaking to a woman who is not his wife: 'How is it that you, a Judaean (Ἰουδαῖος) ask a drink of me, a woman of Samaria?' (4.9).[26] In terms of the theology that will develop in this scene, her self-designation as 'a woman of Samaria' is critical, as is her description of Jesus as a 'Judaean'. These two designations, Samaria and Judaea, recall that time in Israel's history when the one Kingdom of David and Solomon was divided into two: the Northern Kingdom (Israel), with its capital in Samaria, and the Southern Kingdom (Judah) with its capital in Jerusalem. Within the land of Palestine, the usual self-designation of a person in the southern region uses the term Ἰσραήλ, translating the frequent Hebrew appellation 'children of Israel'.[27] So Nicodemus is called a teacher of Israel (3.10) and Jesus calls Nathanael an Israelite (1.47). But the Samaritans considered themselves to be the descendants of two Northern tribes who survived the Assyrian conquest and deportation in 722 BCE and thus believed themselves to be true Israelites.[28]

In calling Jesus a Ἰουδαῖος the woman is speaking from within a Samaritan context, describing Jesus as a Judaean who is outside the true (i.e. Samaritan) Israel. Here at the well of Jacob, who was renamed Israel (Gen. 32.28; 35.10), the initial hostility of the woman plays out the tragic division of David's Kingdom, which ultimately led to the destruction of the Northern Kingdom (Israel), the deportation of many of its inhabitants, the resettling of foreigners and the subsequent hostility between the two regions of Samaria and Judaea.

---

26   How to translate the term Ἰουδαῖος is a vexed question in Johannine scholarship. At times it appears to be neutral, simply a description of those following the religious customs and laws of Moses (e.g. 2.6; 5.1; 6.4); while most times it is used negatively to portray those characters in the text who stand against Jesus and his claims (e.g. 2.20; 5.16; 7.1). In some cases it could simply designate those people from the geographical region of Judaea (e.g., 11.19, 31, 36). At this point in 4.9 I believe the term has this geographical sense to make the contrast between a Judaean man and a Samaritan woman; it is also the only time in the Gospel that Jesus is called a Ἰουδαῖος. See also the discussion in Malcolm Lowe, 'Who were the IOUDAIOI?', *NovT* 18 (1976), pp. 101–30 (102–3). Many of the positive senses of the term could in fact have this same geographical sense, even when this is associated with believing Ἰουδαῖοι (e.g. 11.45; 12.9, 11), since these episodes occur in the vicinity of Jerusalem.

27   Walter Gutbrod, 'Ἰουδαῖος, Ἰσραήλ, Ἑβραῖος in Greek Hellenistic Literature', *TDNT*, Vol. 3, pp. 369–91 (385).

28   Robert T. Anderson, 'Samaritans', *ABD*, Vol. 7, pp. 940–7 (941).

The next time she speaks she uses a more polite form of address: 'Sir (κύριε)' (4.11). While still ignorant of his identity and perplexed by his statement about being able to offer her living water, the woman does not disengage from the conversation. In John 2, the Jewish authorities in the temple scoffed at Jesus' claim to rebuild the temple in three days by throwing his own words back at him (2.20).[29] They completely reject his claim. Nicodemus, in his encounter with Jesus, cannot move beyond what he knows and says to Jesus, 'this is not possible' (μὴ δύναται, 3.4), then concludes the discussion with a rhetorical final statement, 'How is this possible?' (3.9). By contrast, the woman responds to Jesus' strange words about 'living water' with a question that enables further dialogue. Rightly, she points out that Jesus has no bucket and that the well is deep, so she asks from where he can get this water (4.11). At this point she begins to compare Jesus with the eponymous father of the Northern Kingdom, Jacob/Israel: 'Are you greater than our father Jacob?' (4.12).

To follow the implications of the woman's question – Are you greater than our father Jacob? – it is necessary to know the Targumic traditions surrounding Jacob.[30] In the Genesis account, Jacob simply lifts the stone, and waters the flock. 'Now when Jacob saw Rachel the daughter of Laban his mother's brother, and the sheep of Laban his mother's brother, Jacob went up and rolled the stone from the well's mouth, and watered the flock of Laban his mother's brother' (Gen. 29.10).[31]

When this narrative was translated into Aramaic for use in the synagogues, the Targumist did not simply make a translation of the text but rendered it: 'When our father Jacob raised the stone from above the mouth of the well, the well overflowed and came up to its mouth, and was overflowing for twenty years – all the days that he dwelt in Haran' (*Tg. Neof.* Gen. 29.10).

The Targums elaborated on Jacob's action so that when Jacob lifts the stone, water gushes up to the mouth of the well and then overflows for 20 years. Through this miracle Jacob does not need a bucket; not only at this meeting but for the whole time he dwelt in Haran. The Targumic tradition lies behind the woman's question about Jesus' lack of a bucket, and the possibility that he might be able to do something even greater than Jacob. This woman of Samaria knows her people's history and scriptures.

In response to her question 'Are you greater than our father Jacob?' Jesus speaks of water welling up not just for 20 years but for eternity life (ζωὴν αἰώνιον).[32]

---

29   Francis J. Moloney, 'From Cana to Cana (Jn. 2.1–4.54) and the Fourth Evangelist's Concept of Correct (and Incorrect) Faith', *Sal* 40 (1978), pp. 817–43 (831).

30   The Targums were Aramaic translations of the Hebrew Scripture for use in the synagogues within Palestine. While their dating is problematic since some parts of the text appear to be influenced by the New Testament and are therefore later than the first century, the texts do reflect a liturgical origin, making it possible that these texts pre-date the Gospel. See the discussion in Geza Vermes, *Jesus and the World of Judaism* (London: SCM, 1983), pp. 74–88, especially his conclusion on p. 85.

31   English translations of the OT are taken from the Revised Standard Version.

32   Most editions translate ζωὴν αἰώνιον as eternal life. This seems to emphasize the temporal sense of life continuing forever. I prefer to translate ζωὴν αἰώνιον as eternity life to

He is far superior to Jacob. The woman now undergoes a complete change of attitude as she asks for this water. 'Sir, give me this water that I may not thirst, nor come here to draw' (4.15). The roles have now reversed. The dialogue began with Jesus asking her for water; now she asks for the water that he can give.

b. Husbands

The reader who is unaware of the deeper narrative structure, the clues provided by the narrator in the previous chapters and the setting of this scene at Jacob's well, may be caught by surprise with the shift of focus from water to husbands. But knowing Jesus' identity as the covenantal husband of Israel and the biblical typology of the well as a meeting place for a betrothal, we can understand the statement by Jesus, 'Go call your husband?' (4.16) as the primary purpose of this encounter.

The woman responds that she currently has no husband (4.17). Jesus' approves her answer and then provides information that she has in fact had six prior relationships – five previous husbands and the man she now has who is not her husband (4.18). At these words, those who treat this encounter in a literal, historical manner will miss the point of the Johannine symbolism within this exchange.[33] Some see in the reference to the five husbands an allegorical presentation of the former history of the Samaritans, alluding to the five foreign nations and their gods who were brought into Samaria following the Assyrian conquest in 721 BCE (2 Kgs 17.19-34).[34] This analogy breaks down however, since there are seven imported gods which were worshipped alongside YHWH (2 Kgs 17.30-32). A further consideration is that 'The Evangelist does not use allegorization, but rather symbolic representation as his main literary device.'[35]

In the prophetic literature, the infidelity of Samaria, and their worshipping of foreign gods (*ba'alim*), is depicted as adultery (Hos. 2.2-5), where there is a play on the double meaning of the word *ba'al*, which means both a pagan god and husband in Hebrew.[36] Israel/Samaria's true husband is God. The prophet

---

stress that the life Jesus offers is a different quality of life; it is a participation in the life of God in eternity.

33   Those who take this exchange literally explain its relevance as an indicator of Jesus' prophetic knowledge. See, for example, Barnabas Lindars, *The Gospel of John* (NCB; London: Oliphants, 1972), p. 184; Rudolph Bultmann, *The Gospel of John: A Commentary* (trans. G. R. Beasley Murray, et al.; Oxford: Blackwell, 1971), p. 187; Brown, *The Gospel According to John*, Vol. 1, p. 171.

34   So Manns, *L'Evangile de Jean à la lumière du judaïsme*, p. 135; Edwyn C. Hoskyns, *The Fourth Gospel* (F. N. Davis [ed.]; London: Faber & Faber, 1947), p. 243; Birger Olsson, *Structure and Meaning in the Fourth Gospel: A Text-linguistic Analysis of John 2.1-11 and 4.1-42* (ConBNT, 6; Lund: Gleerup, 1974), p. 186.

35   Bultmann, *The Gospel of John: A Commentary*, p. 188, n. 3.

36   Brown, *The Gospel According to John*, Vol. 1, p. 171.

Hosea, speaking to the Northern Kingdom of Israel, uses marital imagery to call Israel to fidelity to the covenant. Hosea speaks of Israel being led out into the wilderness again, and there entering again into a betrothal (Hos. 2.14-15). 'Jesus' declaration that Samaria "has no husband" is a classic prophetic denunciation of false worship.'[37] The five previous husbands plus her current one give a total of six, which symbolically indicates the inadequacy of Samaritan worship just as at the wedding in Cana, in a Jewish context, the six jars of water symbolized the lack of perfection of Jewish rituals. Jesus, the divine Bridegroom of Israel, now stands before her.[38] How will this woman respond?

Although a modern reader, not familiar with Israel's traditions and scriptures, finds the dialogue difficult to follow, the Samaritan woman emerges as a perfect dialogue partner with Jesus. She is able to follow the deeper, symbolic logic of this encounter. She knows the prophetic tradition and the use of marital language to speak of Israel's relationship with God. She realizes that at the heart of this dialogue is the question of worship. As the prophet Elijah declared to the Samaritans during the reign of Ahab, 'If YHWH is God, follow him; but if *Ba'al*, then follow him' (1 Kgs 18.21). She now perceives that Jesus, also, might be a prophet (4.19) and so asks where is the right place of worship. Where can we encounter the God of the covenant, the true bridegroom of Israel? She asks about the Temple Mount in Jerusalem and about the Samaritan place of worship on Mount Gerizim (4.20). Jesus replies that both are inadequate – neither on this mountain nor in Jerusalem will one encounter God (4.21). Since God is Spirit, the place to meet God can only be 'in Spirit': 'But the hour is coming, and now is, when the true worshippers will worship the Father in spirit and truth' (4.23). Jesus' answer indicates that this place of worship is a present reality. Because Jesus is the living temple of God, true worship can only happen in him.

Jesus' words about worship 'in spirit' lead the woman to speak of the Messiah, since the outpouring of the Spirit is associated with the end-time and the messianic days.[39] Because Jesus speaks of the Spirit as a present reality

---

37   Sandra M. Schneiders, *The Revelatory Text: Interpreting the New Testament as Sacred Scripture* (San Francisco: HarperCollins, 1991), p. 191.

38   'Such implications are realistic options here. In the language of the Gospel, John the Baptist has already acknowledged that Jesus, who has the bride, is the bridegroom (3.29). Jesus, moreover, has attended a marriage feast (2.1-11) where he replaced the waters of purification with his own superb wine.' See Jerome H. Neyrey, 'Jacob Traditions and the Interpretation of John 4.10-26', *CBQ* 41 (1979), pp. 419–37 (426). Within Semitic traditions the number seven took on cosmic and religious significance to represent a state of completion or perfection and by analogy six represented less than perfect. 'The number seven thus bears the character of totality, i.e., of the totality desired and ordained by God.' See Karl Heinrich Rengstorf, 'ἑπτά', in *TDNT*, Vol. 2, pp. 627–35 (628).

39   In the 'end times' the Messiah will be endowed with the Spirit (Isa. 11.2; 28.5; 42.1; 61.1) as will the people (Ezek. 36.27; 37.14; 39.29; Joel 3.1, 2; Isa. 32.15; Zech. 12.10; Hag. 2.5). The intertestamental literature and the Dead Sea Scrolls also provide evidence of this expectation (*Pss. Sol.* 17.37; 18.7; *1 En.* 49.3; 62.2; *T. Levi* 18.7; *T. Jud.* 24.2; 1QS Col. iv: 20-23; 1QS Sb 5.24, 25; 11QMelch 18). See F. W. Horn, 'Holy Spirit', *ABD*, Vol. 3, p. 265.

and he has revealed things to her about the true worship of God, she wonders if Jesus could be 'a Messiah' (4.25). According to Josephus (*Ant.* xviii, 85-8) the Samaritans, like the Jews, had messianic hopes, but the Samaritan hopes centred on a 'prophet-like-Moses' figure rather than a Davidic king. According to a later document, the *Memar Marqah*, this figure was to be a revealer who would uncover the hidden sanctuary on Mount Gerizim where the priest Eli had hidden the Ark of the Covenant.[40] 'The woman said to him, "I know that [a] Messiah is coming (he who is called Christ); when he comes, he will show us all things"' (4.25). Jesus responds in words that far surpass any messianic expectations. He reveals himself as 'I AM' (4.26), thus naming himself in the same way that Israel's God was named in the scriptures ('Εγώ Εἰμι – LXX). The woman of Samaria is the first in the Gospel to receive this revelation.

With the return of the disciples, the woman leaves her water pot (4.28) and returns to the village, inviting the villagers to 'Come, see . . .' (4.29). There is speculation about the woman leaving her water jar behind. Some consider it a sign of discipleship. Although the language of leaving everything behind is more a Synoptic image, I think this is an accurate interpretation, but it is discipleship in Johannine terms. Earlier in the conversation she had asked for the water that Jesus offered so that she would not need to come to the well (v. 15); in leaving her jar, I suggest that she has received this gift of living water and so no longer needs her water jar. It is also significant that her invitation to the villagers is similar to Jesus' invitation to John's disciples, and Philip's invitation to Nathanael: 'Come, see . . .' (4.29; cf. 1.39, 46). Just as the first disciples of Jesus went and invited others to him, now this woman-disciple invites the people of her village to him. She speaks of Jesus first as a revealer, and then poses a question, 'Perhaps he is the Christ/Messiah?'[41] In response to her words, the Samaritans go and invite Jesus to dwell with them and he dwells there for two days (4.40).

40   The *Memar Marqah* is dated to the fourth century and its late dating makes it difficult to make precise claims about Samaritan beliefs in the first century. The anarthrous use of the term Messiah and the woman's emphasis that the Messiah 'will reveal all things' (4.25) suggest that this tradition about the *Taheb* does influence first-century Samaritan traditions. See Brown, *The Gospel According to John*, Vol. 1, p. 72; R. Lowe, '"Salvation" is Not of the Jews', *JTS* 32 (1981), pp. 341–68 (342); Koester, *The Dwelling of God*, pp. 55–9.

41   While some interpret her question as a form of doubt (e.g. Brown, *The Gospel According to John*, Vol. 1, p. 173; Moloney, *John*, p. 131; and Rudolph Schnackenburg, *The Gospel According to St John*, Vol. 1 [trans. K. Smyth, et al.; HTCNT; London: Burns & Oates, 1968–82], p. 444), I believe it is a rhetorical device allowing the villagers to hear her words as an invitation and to make their own journey towards faith in Jesus. Teresa Okure suggests that her comments are 'a veiled confession couched in the form of a question in order to appeal to the personal judgment of the Samaritans, get them to reflect, and so arouse their interest in Jesus'. See Teresa Okure, *The Johannine Approach to Mission: A Contextual Study of John 4.1-42* (WUNT, II/32; Tübingen: J.C.B. Mohr [Paul Siebeck], 1988), p. 174. Also, a woman in that cultural context is not considered to be a reliable witness. On the issue of the role of women in Jewish legal testimony see R. G. Maccini, *Her Testimony is True: Women as Witnesses according to John* (JSNTSup, 125; Sheffield: Sheffield Academic Press, 1996), esp. ch. 3.

Through this intense theological dialogue, the woman has been able to shift her perspective, to remain open and receptive to Jesus' words, to continue to ask questions for further understanding, and to follow the theological thinking that maintains a logical thread throughout the dialogue which flows from water, to husbands, to worship, to messianic expectations. Through this woman of Samaria, her people welcome Jesus and come to acknowledge him as 'the saviour of the world' (4.42).

IV. The Woman's Characterization and its Narrative Significance

At the beginning of this essay I expressed my indebtedness to the narrative studies of Petri Merenlahti and James Resseguie, and I noted the words of Shimon Bar-Efrat on the importance of the characters for understanding the ideological purpose of a narrative: it is the characters 'who transmit the significance and values of the narrative to the readers'.[42] Following the discussion of my approach I began with the consideration of John and Jesus across the first three chapters, and the way the narrative develops the identity of Jesus through the symbolism of the bridegroom and the temple. These first chapters are situated within the world of Judaism. In chapter 4 the narrative moves beyond the world of Orthodox Judaism into the geographical location of Samaria with its complex historical and theological alienation from Judaism. In the above discussion of the episode in Samaria the two symbols of temple and bridegroom have continued to play an important part in the dialogue with the Samaritan woman. These symbols of Jesus' identity are part of the deeper narrative structure that enables a discerning reader to follow the logic of this complex passage. In this final section I return to the questions posed at the beginning of this essay about how this episode, and in particular, how the characterization of the woman of Samaria, furthers the plot and the ideological purpose of the Gospel.

A passage from Ezekiel can help elucidate the deeper significance of the meeting between Jesus, a man from Judaea, and the unnamed woman of Samaria. In Ezekiel 37, the prophet is told:

> Son of man, take a stick and write on it, 'For Judah, and the children of Israel associated with him'; then take another stick and write upon it, 'For Joseph (the stick of Ephraim) and all the house of Israel associated with him'; and join them together into one stick, that they may become one in your hand. (Ezek. 37.16-17)

Following this action, the prophetic sign is explained:

> Behold, I will take the people of Israel from the nations among which they have gone, and will gather them from all sides, and bring them to their own land; and I will make them one nation in the land, upon the mountains of Israel; and one king

---

42   Bar-Efrat, *Narrative Art in the Bible*, p. 47.

shall be king over them all; and they shall be no longer two nations, and no longer divided into two kingdoms. (Ezek. 37.21-22)

The passage from Ezekiel, addressed to the Exiles in Babylon, looks to a future when the divided kingdoms will be joined and Israel will be reconstituted as one. One stick is named 'for Joseph (the stick of Ephraim)'. After the Exodus, when the Israelites move into the land of Canaan, Moses is reputed to have divided the land among the 12 ancient tribes; in this division the tribe of Levi was not allocated a portion; instead the tribe of Joseph was allocated a double settlement named after his two sons, Ephraim and Manasseh (Josh. 14.3-4). The Samaritans consider themselves to be the direct descendants of these two tribes, Ephraim and Manasseh.[43] At the time, when Judah and Israel are reunited, then the promise is made that the covenant will be renewed: 'I will save them from all the backslidings in which they have sinned, and will cleanse them; and they shall be my people, and I will be their God' (Ezek. 37.23).

The episode by the well of Jacob symbolically presents the fulfilment of Ezekiel's prophetic action. Jesus, a man from Judaea, has come to a well, which was a typical meeting place for a betrothal; and the narrative has already established Jesus' identity as a 'bridegroom'. With strong echoes of the meeting with Jacob and Rachel,[44] Jesus meets a woman of Samaria and in this meeting he reveals himself as one 'greater than our father Jacob'. Without needing a bucket, Jesus is able to offer the woman waters welling up to eternity life. When the woman responds positively to his offer, the conversation moves to speak of her husbands. At this point it becomes clear that that woman has been in six relationships prior to meeting Jesus; this number suggests both the inadequacy of these prior relationships and the arrival of the 'seventh' bridegroom – Jesus. The symbolism of marriage, which runs through this entire encounter, recalls the OT covenant relationship between God and Israel, which was frequently likened to a marriage. In this 'betrothal-type' meeting between a Judaean man and a Samaritan woman, Judah and Samaria are once again united into one covenant people of God.

The dialogue then shifts to speak of the right place of worship and the necessity to worship 'in Spirit'. The mention of the Spirit leads the woman to consider if Jesus could be the Messiah associated with the end-time outpouring of the Spirit and the one who, according to Samaritan traditions, would reveal the hidden sanctuary.

Once again, the passage from Ezekiel 37 provides the theological background to the flow of this dialogue. In Ezekiel, when the two kingdoms are once again united then God will dwell with them.

---

43   Anderson, 'Samaritans', p. 941.
44   Jesus meets the woman at the sixth hour, the same time of Jacob's meeting with Rachel; also Jacob is explicitly named a number of times in this encounter and the woman compares Jesus' to Jacob (4.12).

I will make a covenant of peace with them; it shall be an everlasting covenant with them; and I will bless them and multiply them, and will set my sanctuary in the midst of them for evermore. My dwelling place (κατασκήνωσίς) shall be with them;[45] and I will be their God, and they shall be my people. (Ezek. 37.26-27)

In the final scene with the Samaritan villagers, Jesus is present to them as the covenant God ('Εγώ Εἰμι), the bridegroom of Israel, and the temple, the dwelling place of God. When the Samaritans come to Jesus we are told 'they asked him to dwell (μεῖνα) with them; and he dwelt (ἔμεινεν) there two days' (4.40). In the Last Discourse the verb 'to dwell (μένω)' takes on a rich theological meaning and this verb is used to describe the mutual indwelling of the Father, Son, Spirit and believer. The rich theology of divine/human intimacy, which is the basis for the logic across these final chapters (esp. 14.1–15.17) is sustained by this verb 'to dwell'. In looking at the many places where this word is employed across the entire Gospel, Klaus Scholtissek identifies only six places where μένω is used in a local sense meaning 'stay' (2.12; 4.40; 7.9; 10.40; 11.6; 19.31) compared to 32 times in a theological sense.[46] Although Scholtissek considers its use in 4.40 to have a neutral sense, given the symbolism of the entire passage, particularly the temple and marital symbolism, and in the light of Ezekiel 37, I would add 4.40 to the list of places where 'dwell' has a rich theological sense. Within this covenant-temple symbolic context, the 'two days' may allude to the glory cloud that hovered over the tabernacle during the time of Israel's wandering in the Sinai wilderness.[47]

The entire chapter is a symbolic enactment of the words of Ezekiel – Samaria and Judaea are joined as one covenant people and God's temple dwells in their midst. For these prophetic words to be fulfilled the woman of Samaria is essential for the narrative plot. The marital symbolism can only be evoked by the meeting between a *man* and a *woman* at the well. The unification of the divided kingdoms can only be evoked if the encounter is between a *Judaean* and a *Samaritan*. The Samaritan woman is thus an essential character at this

---

45   The term used to speak of God's dwelling place (κατασκήνωσίς) is related to the verb σκηνόω, which is the verb used in the Fourth Gospel to describe the flesh-taking of the Word in John 1.14: 'And the Word became flesh and dwelt (ἐσκήνωσεν) among us.'

46   See Klaus Scholtissek, *In Ihm Sein und Bleiben: Die Sprache der Immanenz un den Johanneischen Schriften* (Herder's Biblical Studies, 21; Freiburg: Herder, 2000), pp. 155–6. For the theological sense he identifies: 1.32, 33, 38, 39^{x2}; 3.36; 5.38; 6.27, 56; 8.31, 35^{x2}; 9.41; 12.24, 34, 46; 14.10, 17, 25; 15.4^{x3}, 5, 6, 7^{x2}, 9, 10^{x2}, 16; 21.22, 23. I would also add the use of μοναί (14.2) and μονὴν (14.23). On the theological sense of the verb 'to dwell', see also the articles by Dorothy A. Lee, 'Abiding in the Fourth Gospel: A Case-study in Feminist Biblical Theology', *Pac* 10 (1997), pp. 123–36, and Ignace de la Potterie, 'Le verbe «demeurer» dans la mystique johannique', *NRT* 117 (1995), pp. 843–59.

47   'And sometimes the cloud remained from evening until morning; and when the cloud was taken up in the morning, they set out, or if it continued for a day and a night, when the cloud was taken up they set out. Whether it was two days, or a month, or a longer time, that the cloud continued over the tabernacle, abiding there, the people of Israel remained in camp and did not set out; but when it was taken up they set out' (Num. 9.21-22).

point in the narrative to convey the ideological point of view of the evangelist. In the first three chapters Jesus came as the bridegroom/temple for the Jews. In chapter 4 he comes to those beyond Judaism.

Here in Samaria Jesus is recognized not simply in terms of Jewish or Samaritan messianic hopes but in terms of his divine purpose for all people: 'God sent the Son into the world, not to condemn the world, but that the *world* might be saved through him' (3.17). The Samaritans come to believe that he is 'the saviour of the world' (4.42). Such faith is the aim of the Gospel's ideological discourse (20.30-31), and such faith is only possible because of the openness, theological insight and words of this woman of Samaria (cf. 4.42).

Chapter 12

MARTHA AND MARY: LEVELS OF CHARACTERIZATION IN LUKE AND JOHN

Dorothy A. Lee

I. Introduction

Characterization has become an important focus in literary studies of the Bible. In this area, characters are analysed by two criteria: whether they are flat or round (types or individuals with a distinctive identity); and whether they are dynamic or static (developed or undeveloped).[1] Such characterization is apt to be sparse and understated in the Bible, creating gaps that invite the reader's participation: 'The silence of the text encourages the reader to fill the gaps.'[2] The same sparseness of detail, which so readily engages the reader, gives a sense of ambiguity and un-finality to human character in the world of the Bible which is profoundly shaped by the theological outlook of the biblical author. Characters do change in biblical narrative: the few, sketchy details are often strategic and pithy enough to create a real sense of movement and development.[3]

This essay is particularly concerned with two characters from the Gospels, Martha and Mary, who emerge from Luke and John as distinct and dynamic, if minor, characters.[4] Gospel studies in the past have tended to assume that the

---

1   According to Fred W. Burnett, biblical characters fall somewhere on the continuum between 'type and individuality' ('Characterization and Reader Construction of Characters in the Gospels', *Semeia* 63 [1993], p. 15).

2   Petri Merenlahti, 'Characters in the Making', in *Poetics for the Gospels? Rethinking Narrative Criticism* (London: T&T Clark, 2002), p. 80. The same article is reprinted as 'Characters in the Making: Individuality and Ideology in the Gospels', in David Rhoads and Kari Syreeni (eds), *Characterization in the Gospels: Reconceiving Narrative Criticism* (JSNTSup, 184; London, T&T Clark, 1999), pp. 49–72.

3   Witness, for example, the mother of the sons of Zebedee in the Gospel of Matthew who, after demanding positions of power for her two sons, is later found with the holy women at the crucifixion, in contrast to her sons (Matt. 20.20-21; 27.56; see Elisabeth Moltmann-Wendel, *The Women Around Jesus: Reflections on Authentic Personhood* (trans. John Bowden; London: SCM, 1982), pp. 119–27.

4   On the minor characters of the Fourth Gospel in six of the Johannine 'signs', each of whom is a model of faith and changes in the course of the narrative, see especially James M. Howard, 'The Significance of Minor Characters in the Gospel of John', *BSac* 163 (2006), pp.

characterization of such figures is flat, and that rounded, developed characters who change in mindset and behaviour throughout the narrative are a feature of modern, post-Enlightenment fiction rather than of epic, drama, or novel in the ancient world.[5] This view includes awareness of the symbolic role which characters play in the Gospels, where their illustrative role is a significant part of their presentation, particularly in the Fourth Gospel, and is dependent on theological meaning. Yet there is more to be said of characters than their representation. It is also the case that Gospel characters – even minor ones such as Martha and Mary – have distinct, personality traits, so that they prove to be much more than ideological ciphers.

Of the studies of characterization and the Gospels which have appeared in recent years, the work of Cornelis Bennema is of particular interest. Bennema has propounded a coherent theory of characterization, and has examined the individual characters who appear in the Gospel of John. He argues helpfully that round and flat characters are found in both ancient and modern literature, and that the differences between characters in modern fiction and drama, as against ancient, or between biblical and classical Graeco-Roman characters, is one of degree rather than strict alternative.[6] Bennema sees three aspects to understanding characterization in the Fourth Gospel: their appearance in text and context, including their interpretative portrayal by the Fourth Evangelist; their classification according to criteria of complexity, development or change, and insights into their inner life (which can be charted); and their individual responses to the Johannine Jesus.[7] Using this model, Bennema outlines the characters of the Fourth Gospel, including groups as well as individuals, making a case for seeing at least some of them as complex, developing, and rounded.

63–78 (75–7). See also Colleen M. Conway, 'Speaking through Ambiguity: Minor Characters in the Fourth Gospel', *BibInt* 10 (2002), pp. 324–41, who challenges the notion that the minor characters are only flat types.

5   Philip F. Esler and Ronald A. Piper warn against the danger of expecting from the ancient Mediterranean world the kind of characterization we find in the modern novel: 'In a culture such as this, the important thing was to live in accordance with group values and behaviour, not to carve out a distinctive new mode of existence for oneself . . .' (*Lazarus, Mary and Martha: A Social-Scientific and Theological Reading of John* [London: SCM, 2006], p. 19).

6   Biblical character is often contrasted with characterization in Graeco-Roman literature, where characters are said to be flat by modern standards, with typical rather than individual characteristics. Whether this is fair to ancient literature is a moot question. Consider the character of Achilles, for example, in the *Iliad*, and the rage that drives the plot to its unexpected resolution in the final book; or the characteristics of Antigone in Sophocles' play, and her costly unyielding defiance of royal decree. Many characters in ancient literature are flat, and their role is constrained to serving the narrative in specific ways. But not all characters in the ancient world fit within such constraints.

7   Cornelis Bennema, *Encountering Jesus: Character Studies in the Gospel of* John (Milton Keynes: Paternoster, 2009), pp. 12–21; also Cornelis Bennema, 'A Theory of Character in the Fourth Gospel with Reference to Ancient and Modern Literature', *BibInt* 17 (2009), pp. 375–421.

At the same time, we are also dealing in the Gospels with non-fictional narrative, whatever we make of the Gospels' relationship to history (which will depend, in part, on our understanding of their literary genre). This means that we are analysing characters who have an historical existence outside the bounds of the text. Here historical questions overlap with questions of sources and the complex relationship between the Gospels, as well as with the oral tradition which encircles them. Thus a Gospel character can exist in more than one Gospel, as well as having an existence in the history beyond the text. While we have no direct access to the historical life of these characters outside the Gospels, we can observe the ways they are depicted within and across texts, especially in different traditions, and draw conclusions – however tentative – about their historical features.

We can thus speak of a threefold world to which the characterization of Martha and Mary – along with other Gospels characters – belongs. First, their characterization belongs most perceptibly in the narrative world of the text, as an essential and integral aspect of the text; here their individual characterization and its contours have significance. Second, and linked to ideas of representation, the characters belong in the symbolic world of the text, in the representative role they play. In both aspects, we are dealing with the world of the text itself. Third, characterization is also implied as belonging in the historical world – that is, the world behind the text. But there is also a fourth world. To complete the picture, characterization also belongs in the world before the text, in the reception history of ensuing generations. From this viewpoint, the characterization of the two sisters projects itself into the world beyond the text, forming a meeting place with future readers, the contours of which are unpredictable and variegated. Reception history concerns itself, moreover, with subsequent and reflective 'texts' of all kinds, iconic and artistic as well as liturgical and discursive.

II. The World within the Text: The Narrative World

We begin with the narrative world from which the characterization of Martha and Mary emerges. In the Johannine account, the sisters form part of a chiastic narrative in seven scenes, stretching from John 11.1–12.11. The reference to the anointing at 11.2, while it speaks of an event that has not yet taken place, acts as a kind of prolepsis, pointing the reader forward to the anointing as integral to the Lazarus story. His life under threat of death forms the frame of the narrative, with his raising from the dead as the centre-piece, flanked on either side by the sisters' very different responses, along with those of the Jewish mourners:[8]

---

8   See Dorothy A. Lee, *Flesh and Glory: Symbol, Gender and Theology in the Gospel of John* (New York: Crossroad, 2004), p. 199; also Francis J. Moloney, 'Can Everyone Be Wrong? A Reading of John 11.1–12.8', *NTS* 49 (2003), pp. 505–27, and Satoko Yamaguchi, *Mary & Martha: Women in the World of Jesus* (Maryknoll: Orbis, 2002), pp. 114–15.

Scene 1. Threat to Lazarus　　　　　　*Scene 7. Threat to Lazarus*
11.1-16　　　　　　　　　　　　　*12.9-11*
Scene 2. Martha and Jesus　　　　　　　*Scene 6. Mary and Jesus*
11.17-27　　　　　　　　　　　　*12.1-8*
Scene 3. Belief and unbelief of 'Jews'　　*Scene 5. Belief and unbelief of 'Jews'*
11.28-37　　　　　　　　　　　　*11.45-52*

Scene 4. The raising of Lazarus
11.38-44

The narrative acts as a bridge between Jesus' ministry and his passion and death, bringing the first half of the Gospel to its climax and setting the second half in motion; it is 'not only the conclusion of Jesus' public life but, as the greatest sign, its culmination as well'.[9] The sisters play vitally important roles in relation to faith and discipleship in this hinge narrative, which lies at the core not only of this story but of the Gospel as a whole. Martha and Mary are among Jesus' friends and disciples; and, throughout the illness and death of their brother, they come to understand and reveal Jesus' identity and the significance of his mission. While they are technically minor characters, their key roles in the central narrative of John's Gospel give them greater force as Johannine characters.

Luke's narrative, by contrast, takes place earlier in Jesus' ministry, on the journey to Jerusalem, and the village, being unnamed ('a certain village', Lk. 10.38), is given no locale. The response of the two women, with Jesus at its centre, forms the structure of the narrative:

Part 1. Martha welcomes Jesus and Mary sits at his feet (10.38-39) A
Part 2. Martha complains to Jesus against Mary (10.40) B
Par 3. Jesus rebukes Martha and defends Mary (10.41-42) B¹

In the Lukan version, Jesus is invited into Martha's home, implying that she is in effect in charge of the household (10.38).[10] There is no mention of a brother in this narrative. Nor is the context related specifically to Passover and Jesus' impending death, except inasmuch as the Lukan journey from Galilee to Judaea has Jerusalem (the place of Jesus' death, resurrection, ascension, and descent of the Spirit) as its fixed point.

The scene lies between the parable of the Good Samaritan, with its focus on radical love of neighbour (10.25-37), and Jesus' teachings on prayer, which includes Luke's version of the Lord's Prayer (11.1-13).[11] The Martha-Mary

9　　Raimo Hakola, 'A Character Resurrected: Lazarus in the Fourth Gospel and Afterwards', in Rhoads and Syreeni (eds), *Characterization in the Gospels*, p. 228.

10　　It is difficult to know how to interpret this statement. The fact that Martha manages the home – due to force of personality and organizational gifts – need not mean that she is literally or technically the head of the household.

11　　On the significance of this pericope within its Lukan literary context, see, e.g., Joel B. Green, *The Gospel of Luke* (NICNT; Grand Rapids: Eerdmans, 1997), pp. 433–8, and John Nolland, *Luke 9:21–18:34* (WBC, 35B; Dallas: Word, 1993), pp. 605–6.

episode takes us from the one to the other, from the Samaritan as a model of authentic service to emphasis on the necessity and centrality of prayer; it also relates back to the sending out of the Seventy and the theme of receiving hospitably the messengers of the kingdom (10.5-9; cf. 9.53).[12] In doing so Luke qualifies the meaning of service and aligns the relationship between neighbourly love and prayer in a way that sets the one in the context of the other.[13] Love of neighbour follows and flows from love of God (10.27-28).[14] While there is considerable disagreement over the meaning of Luke 10.38-42, the narrative setting indicates a priority to listening to 'the word' (τὸν λόγον, 10.39) of Jesus.[15]

The more immediate question here is whether the divergences between Luke and John rule out the possibility that the characterization of the two women coheres in the two traditions. In Bennema's study, Martha and Mary (along with Lazarus) are treated separately.[16] Martha's character is regarded as somewhat complex, with some insight into her thoughts and suggestion of growth, though not a great deal. Mary likewise is seen to possess a degree of complexity but there is no character development and no glimpse into her inner life. In the Johannine account, says Bennema, she is closer to being a type, a flat character, than Martha. In a footnote reference to the Lukan depiction of the sisters, Bennema adds that Mary in Luke's version is the more positive of the two, in contrast to John's account where Martha is the more complete and affirmed character.[17] While aspects of this description are questionable, the overall point of a degree of complexity, and thus characterization, for both women is significant.

Different though the narratives may be, the essential characteristics of Martha are consistent in both traditions. The Johannine Martha is depicted as a round character, not flat, since her characterization has distinct traits and there is real development in her faith. Her initial scepticism changes, within the one scene, to a ringing affirmation of Jesus' self-revelation as ἡ ἀνάστασις καὶ ἡ ζωή (John 11.25-26). The Lukan Martha likewise has a close relationship

---

12 Robert C. Tannehill, *Luke* (ANTC; Nashville: Abingdon, 1996), p. 187.

13 Luke Timothy Johnson puts the two stories together, seeing the second (Martha and Mary) as a positive story in a hostile context (*The Gospel of Luke* [SP, 3; Collegeville, MN: Liturgical, 1991], pp. 171–6); see also Charles H. Talbert, *Reading Luke: A Literary and Theological Commentary on the Third Gospel* (Macon, GA: Smyth and Helwys, rev. edn, 2002), pp. 127–32.

14 Talbert, *Reading Luke*, pp. 131–2.

15 Elisabeth Schüssler Fiorenza argues that the context of Luke's story is the church rather than just the home ('The Practice of Biblical Interpretation: Luke 10.38-42', in Norman K. Gottwald and Richard A. Horsley [eds], *The Bible and Liberation: Political and Social Hermeneutics* [Maryknoll: Orbis, 1993], pp. 172–97). Allie M. Ernst believes there is more than one reading to this text, and that it served a number of rhetorical purposes in the early Church, not all of them linked to gender (*Martha from the Margins: The Authority of Martha in Early Christian Tradition* [Leiden and Boston: Brill, 2009], pp. 204–23).

16 Bennema, *Encountering Jesus*, pp. 145–50, and pp. 151–6; Lazarus is correctly seen as a flat character without moral or spiritual development (pp. 157–63).

17 Bennema, *Encountering Jesus*, p. 148, n. 17.

with Jesus, who is her guest at a banquet and to whom she extends hospitality (10.38b; 12.2). Martha's service in the Lukan story is paralleled in the banquet following the raising of Lazarus in the Johannine narrative, where she is described as 'serving' at the table (διηκόνει, John 12.2). In both narratives Martha is depicted as a woman of faith and kindness, who knows and respects the demands of hospitality. She is a disciple in both Gospels, indicated in Luke by her desire to provide hospitality and in John by the language of love which, in this Gospel, is indicative of discipleship.[18] In both narratives, she 'serves' Jesus, engaging in that διακονία which lies at the heart of Christian discipleship and ministry.[19] Believing and service are two of the main traits of Martha in the Johannine and Lukan accounts.

There are also a number of other personality traits that Martha possesses across the two narratives. In both Luke and John, she is confident, blunt in her opinions and articulate in stating them. In the Johannine account, she reproaches Jesus for his failure to reach Lazarus's sickbed in time (11.21). It is true that the same reproach is uttered by Mary in the next scene (11.32), but Mary's words are accompanied by prostration, giving it a rather different, and somehow less assertive, feel. In the Lukan account, Martha reproaches Jesus for indifference to her plight (οὐ μέλει σοι, 10.40), demanding that he support her against her sister. In both these statements, Martha displays boldness and outspokenness in confronting him. No question of shame prevents her speaking her mind, and speaking it forthrightly.[20] From this alone, we may conclude that Martha is a force to be reckoned with in both Gospels.

While being a woman of faith and a disciple of Jesus, Martha is also portrayed as limited in faith in the two accounts. This is hardly an unfamiliar motif in the presentation of disciples in the Gospels. Both sides of discipleship – the believing and the unbelieving, the faith and the doubt – are strongly, if confusingly, present in Martha's opening words to Jesus, when she first meets him outside the village: the reproach (εἰ ἦς ὧδε, 11.21) tempered somewhat by hope (καὶ νῦν οἶδα, 11.22). The same bewildering combination of faith and unfaith is apparent at the tomb of her brother where, faithfully following the one she has confessed to be resurrection and life, she resists the opening of the tomb,[21] taking death and its stench to be an insuperable barrier, the last word

---

18   Against this interpretation of the love-language, see Esler and Piper, *Lazarus, Mary and Martha*, pp. 81–2. They seem to have left 15.9-17, especially vv. 14-15, out of the equation; there, the Johannine Jesus defines discipleship in terms of love and friendship rather than of servitude and bondage. See Dorothy A. Lee, *Hallowed in Truth and Love: Spirituality in the Johannine Literature* (Melbourne: Mosaic Resources; Eugene, OR: Wipf & Stock, 2012), pp. 149–55.

19   On the link with *diakonia* in the early Church, especially associated with the figure of Martha, see Ernst, *Martha from the Margins*, pp. 177–223.

20   'Neither the honour/shame code nor the public/private code seems to affect Martha and Mary' (Yamaguchi, *Mary & Martha*, p. 136).

21   Martha's 'horrified response in 11:39 to Jesus' command to open the tomb amply demonstrates that she has so far harboured no thoughts of Lazarus' revival' (Wendy E. Sproston North, *The Lazarus Story within the Johannine Tradition* [JSNTSup, 212; Sheffield: Sheffield Academic Press, 2001], p. 106).

in human life (κύριε, ἤδη ὄζει, τεταρταῖος γάρ ἐστιν, 11.39). Her irresolute faith 'is enough to introduce tension and dimension to her characterization'.[22] At the same time, her faith, in the Johannine account, is not only ambiguous but also conventional. She believes in the future resurrection of the dead (οἶδα, 'I know', 11.24) and does not doubt the ultimate well-being of her brother. What she lacks is a Johannine perspective, an awareness of Jesus as the ἐγώ εἰμι whose presence forestalls death and pre-empts the resurrection of the last day – whose voice can pierce the cold, stone walls of human mortality.

For some, this seeming ambiguity suggests that the Johannine Martha is a woman of deficient faith, whose confession of faith at 11.27 is inadequate in the terms in which it is couched.[23] For others, her faith is strong and unwavering: why should she anticipate the raising of her brother because of Jesus' self-revelation?[24] These opposing conclusions are reached by ignoring the ambivalence of Martha's response to Jesus and the raising of her brother. Most commentators rightly regard the Johannine Martha's confession of faith as the expression of authentic faith (John 11.27).[25] The words of Martha's confession are used elsewhere in the Fourth Gospel, and on those grounds alone there is no reason to doubt the authenticity of her Christological understanding at this point. Her emphatic 'yes, Lord' (ναὶ κύριε), her confident 'I myself have come to believe' (ἐγώ πεπίστευκα), and the threefold title she confers (ὁ χριστὸς ὁ υἱὸς τοῦ θεοῦ ὁ εἰς τὸν κόσμον ἐρχόμενος, cf. 1.9, 14, 18, 34; 20.31), indicate considerable advance from her opening words. Moreover, while we may think Martha need not assume the raising of her brother, the Johannine evangelist has depicted Jesus as the one who can do precisely that, making present in the here-and-now the eschatological events of God's future (e.g. 3.18-21; 5.24-25).

If we put these two points together, it is most likely that what we find in the Johannine Martha is a growing but still limited faith. The parallel with Peter in the Synoptic tradition at Caesarea Philippi is hard to miss: in both cases, the central character – Peter, Martha – makes the core Christian confession, while immediately afterwards failing to understand the significance of their own utterance (Mk 8.27-33/pars). Like Peter in the Synoptic accounts of Jesus' declaration of his suffering, death and resurrection at Caesarea Philippi, there is a level of understanding present (especially at Matt. 16.17) which in the very next moment turns to misunderstanding.[26] Martha's faith, like that of Peter, is

22   Conway, 'Minor Characters', p. 335.
23   See, e.g., Francis J. Moloney, *The Gospel of John* (SP, 4; Collegeville. MN: Liturgical, 1998), pp. 327–9, and 'Can Everyone Be Wrong?', pp. 505–27.
24   Sandra M. Schneiders, *Written That You May Believe: Encountering Jesus in the Fourth Gospel* (New York: Herder & Herder, 1999), pp. 104–7.
25   See, e.g., Craig R. Koester, *Symbolism in the Fourth* Gospel (Minneapolis: Fortress, 1995), p. 67.
26   Raymond E. Brown, 'Roles of Women in the Fourth Gospel', in *The Community of the Beloved Disciple: The Life, Loves, and Hates of an Individual Church in New Testament Times* (New York: Paulist, 1979), Appendix II, pp. 190–2, and Schneiders, *Written That You May Believe*, p. 106. See also Kari Syreeni, 'Peter as Character and Symbol', in Rhoads and Syreeni

developing but incomplete. Her Christology, up to a point, is insightful and believing in Johannine terms; what remains incomplete is her eschatology.

The Lukan Martha is even more patently a woman of limited faith. Despite the warmth and extravagance of the hospitality she seeks to offer, her complaint introduces a sour note into the intimacy of the family circle. The guest is put in the embarrassing position of having to adjudicate between his hosts.[27] Martha resents the role Mary has chosen. Yet the reproach against Mary is also a criticism of Jesus for permitting Mary to play so seemingly passive a role while she honours the social obligations by herself. At the end of the Lukan narrative, it is not Martha's generosity or hospitality which is chided. Luke does not say simply that she is 'serving' but that she is '*distracted* by *much* service' (περιεσπᾶτο περὶ πολλὴν διακονίαν, 10.40), implying that there is something amiss with her attitude to what she is doing.[28] The verb περισπάω has the basic sense of 'draw or drag around/away', suggesting that Martha has somehow been drawn away from 'the word' to which Mary, by contrast, has firmly attached herself. Jesus' response to Martha is sympathetic rather than judgemental, as indicated by the repetition of her name.[29] He interprets the source of the problem as being her anxiety, implying that what she is offering is excessive for the occasion, especially since it leads to disquiet (πολλὴν διακονίαν). This may seem to contradict the picture of the Good Samaritan in the previous scene, whose service to the wounded traveller is generous to a fault (10.33-35), but the problem with Martha is her antipathy – the peevish dissatisfaction with her own role in comparison to that of Mary, and the fussiness and anxiety of her preparations.[30] Martha's limitations make themselves apparent in the demand that Mary assist with the 'much service'. The real problem is her criticism and discontent, not her serving of Jesus: '[T]he fundamental antithesis is not between hearing and serving, but between hearing and agitated toil. What truly causes the problem is that Martha, in her agitated toil with so many things, demands her sister's assistance . . . Martha represents a threat that Mary's part can be taken from her.'[31] It is this threat to

(eds), *Characterization in the Gospels*, pp. 112–16. On Peter generally in the Fourth Gospel, see Bradford B. Blaine, *Peter in the Gospel of John: The Making of an Authentic Disciple* (AcBib, 27; Atlanta: Society of Biblical Literature, 2007).

27　　Johnson, *Gospel of Luke*, pp. 175–6.

28　　Against this, cf. Barbara Reid, who sees the narrative as full of tensions and inconsistencies which, she argues, most commentators attempt to smooth over and ignore (*Choosing the Better Part? Women in the Gospel of Luke* [Collegeville, MN: Liturgical, 1996], pp. 144–62.

29　　I. Howard Marshall, *The Gospel of Luke: A Commentary on the Greek Text* (NIGTC; Grand Rapids: Eerdmans, 1978), p. 452.

30　　So Jacques Dupont, 'De quoi est-il besoin (Lc x.42)?', in Ernest Best and Robert McLachlan Wilson (eds), *Text and Interpretation: Studies in the New Testament Presented to Matthew Black* (Cambridge, UK: Cambridge University Press, 1979), pp. 115–20; see also Green, *Gospel of Luke*, p. 436, n. 143.

31　　Turid Karlsen Seim, 'The Gospel of Luke', in Elisabeth Schüssler Fiorenza (ed.), *Searching the Scriptures. Vol. 2: A Feminist Commentary* (New York: Crossroad, 1994), pp. 746–7.

Mary that constitutes the problem, at the basis of which lies resentment.[32] In both Gospels, Martha's faith is presented as in some sense ambiguous.

The real difference between the Lukan and the Johannine characterizations of Martha is that, in the much longer version in John, Martha is presented as moving forward in her understanding. Characters in Johannine narratives generally move in one direction or another in dialogue with Jesus: towards either a deeper understanding or an increasing alienation. This movement happens, usually, through several distinctive phases in colloquy between the two characters (or groups).[33] This faith development is a unique feature of the Fourth Gospel, particularly in the first half of the Gospel.[34] In John, Martha moves from scepticism to a level of authentic, Johannine faith. Luke's succinct narrative, by contrast, makes no allowances for such development – the censure of Martha and concomitant support of Mary ends, indeed climaxes, the story.[35]

As we have observed, Bennema sees the Johannine Mary as a flat character in comparison with her sister – more a type than a developed personality. His assessment is overly sceptical. Although the development is not as dramatic or striking – or at least not as articulate – as that of Martha, there is a change in Mary on the two occasions we encounter her in the Johannine narrative.[36]

---

32   The textual and exegetical confusion in Jesus' response to Martha is notorious. Does the text read 'you are anxious and troubled' (μεριμνᾶς καὶ θορυβάζῃ) or simply 'anxious'? And is it 'of one thing there is need' (ἑνὸς δέ ἐστιν χρεία) or 'a few things', and to what might that refer? The first does not materially alter the meaning, but the second is more significant. 'One thing' is the more likely reading, given the manuscript evidence and the balanced contrast between 'one thing' and 'many things', but it is still not clear what the 'one thing' is. If it refers to the number of dishes, it seems a little banal, although it does make sense of the narrative from a domestic point of view. If it refers more broadly to ministry – the 'one thing' referring to hearing the word – it seems to make a nonsense, if taken literally, of the Lukan theological insistence on service as integral to discipleship. See Bruce M. Metzger, *A Textual Commentary on the Greek New Testament* (New York: United Bible Societies, 4th edn, 1994), p. 129; and Joseph A. Fitzmyer, *The Gospel According to Luke X–XXIV: A New Translation with Introduction and Commentary* (AB, 28A; New York: Doubleday, 1985), pp. 891–4 and Marshall, *Gospel of Luke*, pp. 452–4. In all the textual confusion, and taking the broad perspective, it would seem that Luke is emphasizing, albeit clumsily, the priority of love of God, without wanting to deny also the necessity of love of neighbour/service.

33   The exception is Nicodemus, who seems to stand still, at least in his first appearance, and fades from the narrative – yet a narrative that remains unfinished (John 3.1-11; cf. 7.50-52; 19.38-42).

34   See Dorothy A. Lee, *The Symbolic Narratives of the Fourth Gospel: The Interplay of Form and Meaning* (JSNTSup, 95; Sheffield: JSOT Press, 1994).

35   Noting the parallels between the two stories, Hartwig Thyen argues that the Johannine account is a kind of 'palimpsest' of the Lukan, a deliberate rewriting of the narrative ('Die Erzuählung von den Bethanischen Geschwistern (Joh 11,1-12,19) als "Palimpsest" über Synoptishcen Texten', in F. Van Segbroeck, C. M. Tuckett, G. van Belle and J. Verheyden [eds], *The Four Gospels 1992: Festschrift F. Neirynck*, Vol. 3 [Leuven: University Press, 1992], pp. 2021–50).

36   Conway argues strongly that Mary is a vitally important character in the Lazarus story and not just a shadow of her sister, as is often assumed (*Men and Women*, pp. 143–9).

Along with the mourners, Mary is still grieving over her brother's death and Jesus' absence, the two of which are causally linked in her mind. The presence of others, with their own speculations and censures, takes this conversation in a different direction from the one it takes with Martha. What comes to the fore in this scene is a kind of paroxysm of grief: Mary's, the mourners', and Jesus' own complex emotional disturbance brought on by the sight of their grief.[37]

On the second occasion of Mary's meeting with Jesus, the location and setting of the banquet are unclear, the wording of 'they' and 'there' being unspecific (ἐποίησαν οὖν αὐτῷ δεῖπνον ἐκεῖ, 12.2). This vague reference, however, is immediately followed by mention of Martha serving (καὶ ἡ Μάρθα διηκόνει). There is no reason to mention Martha's presence or activity, given that the focus will be on Mary in this scene, unless we are to infer that the home is hers. If this is the case, we find Martha, as in the Lukan narrative, welcoming Jesus to a meal in her home. That this episode is part of the wider narrative of the raising of Lazarus is made clear by the prolepsis at 11.2, where, as we have seen, Mary is identified as the woman of the anointing (perhaps among a plethora of Marys!). Her anointing of Jesus' feet suggests a distinct level of characterization, apparent in the contrast between her first and second meeting with Jesus. Whereas she first falls at Jesus' feet in grief and disappointment (αὐτοῦ πρὸς τοὺς πόδας, John 11.32), she now places herself at his feet (τοὺς πόδας τοῦ Ἰησοῦ, 12.3) from a very different motivation: gratitude, devotion, costly generosity, and realization of the repercussions of Jesus' action.

The same pattern – though in a different setting – emerges from the Lukan narrative. Here, too, Mary sits at Jesus' feet (πρὸς τοὺς πόδας τοῦ κυρίου, 10.39); here too she is silent and makes no effort to defend herself in the face of criticism; here too she is supported by Jesus against the accusations of another disciple. Admittedly, in the Lukan account, there is no room for character development: Mary's faith remains constant in this one, short scene. Nonetheless, the parallels between the two different scenes support a similarity of characterization, even if it does not develop. In both Gospels, Mary's character is portrayed – sketchily rather than fulsomely – as quiet, intense and devout; she is present in both stories as a woman of few words who is sensitive to the symbolic gesture, the illustrative pose. In both she is a dedicated disciple of Jesus, with a deeper level of awareness than those around her.

The striking dissimilarity in characterization lies in the relationship between the sisters. In the Lukan account, the two are in conflict – at least from Martha's side. Each has chosen a different response to the presence of Jesus and, whereas Martha is chided for her disapproval of Mary's choice, Mary is commended for choosing 'the good portion' (τὴν ἀγαθὴν μερίδα, 10.42). In John's account, by contrast, the sisters are presented harmoniously, their response to Jesus differing in some respects, while united in reproach

---

37   On the emotions of Jesus at this point, and their link to the cross, see Lee, *Symbolic Narratives*, pp. 208–12.

of Jesus, and without any hint of competition or resentment. In Martha's service at the banquet there are no overtones of fretfulness or dissatisfaction; she acts appropriately. Indeed, her presence and activity indicate, if anything, consolidation of her faith in Jesus as resurrection and life.

III. The World within the Text: The Symbolic World

The second aspect, which is also part of the world of the text, is the representative role which Martha and Mary play. In many respects, this feature of Gospel narrative has been well traversed, particularly in Johannine scholarship where characters are often identified as possessing a representative function within the narrative.[38] The Samaritan woman, for example, may be seen as representing outsiders who respond positively and unexpectedly to the Christian message; Nicodemus represents those whose response to Jesus remains ambivalent; while the man born blind signifies those who come to faith in a context of opposition.[39] Behind these, and other, representations in the Fourth Gospel (whatever their representational value) stands the figure of the Johannine Jesus, who represents God *par excellence*: whose face he makes visible, whose voice audible, whose glory tangible. The Johannine Martha and Mary, in different ways, point to Jesus as the one who possesses divine authority over life and death, including his own. The characters of Luke's Gospel also play something of a representative role in relation to Jesus. His visit to the home of Martha and Mary is one small scene in the great drama of divine hospitality and salvation, embodied in the Lukan Jesus, around which the plot of the Gospel turns (cf. ἐπεσκέψατο καὶ ἐποίησεν λύτρωσιν τῷ λαῷ αὐτοῦ, 1.68).[40] The hospitality of the Lukan Martha and devotion of the Lukan Mary both attest to Jesus – each sister, in her own way, acknowledging his identity.[41]

At the same time, Martha and Mary have a representational or symbolic function in their own right, and not just in relation to the revelation of Jesus's identity. A symbol is not simply a signpost which points elsewhere and has no intrinsic value.[42] As symbols, the sisters embody in themselves the message

---

38   See Raymond F. Collins, *These Things Have Been Written: Studies on the Fourth Gospel* (LPTM, 2; Leuven: Peeters Press, 1990), pp. 1–45; cf. Esler and Piper, who prefer to speak, in social-scientific terms, of the Bethany family as 'prototypes', providing access to a shared group identity, in this case, of Jesus' 'own people' (*Lazarus, Mary and Martha*, pp. 75–103). On the problems with the representational approach, see especially Conway, 'Minor Characters', pp. 326–30.

39   For a summary outline of Johannine characters and what they represent, see Table 3 in Bennema, *Encountering Jesus*, pp. 209–10. Bennema's representations are based around qualities and characteristics of individuals rather than socio-contextual equivalence.

40   See Brendan Byrne, *The Hospitality of God: A Reading of Luke's Gospel* (Strathfield, NSW: St Paul's, 2000), pp. 4–5, 102–3, and Tannehill, *Luke*, pp. 185–7.

41   For a succinct summary of Luke's Christology, see Christopher M. Tuckett, *Luke* (NTG; Sheffield: Sheffield Academic Press, 1996), pp. 76–89.

42   For a definition of symbol, see Lee, *Flesh and Glory*, pp. 9–28.

of the Gospel. The Johannine Martha may be said to represent the believer,[43] the friend of Jesus, who struggles with the tragedy of death in the light of faith,[44] and who 'exemplifies for the reader the substance of the Gospel's overriding purpose (20.31)'.[45] She stands for the typical disciple, whose faith is open to development, who believes yet does not fully comprehend, and whose faith needs to grow in strength. The symbolic function of the Lukan Martha is more complex. She is a woman of faith, as we have noted, but more fallible and misguided in her response to Jesus, despite her good intentions. Debate over the symbolic function of Luke's Martha is no new thing. In older traditions, she is seen to represent the active, as against the contemplative, life. In feminist circles, she stands for the feisty, outspoken woman who, daring to raise her voice, is put back firmly in her place by the evangelist.[46]

Martha's Lukan significance has to be seen within the Gospel as a whole. At the beginning of the story, it is plain that, although not a literal follower of Jesus, she belongs in the company of the women who minister to Jesus, supporting him with their generosity and wealth (διακονέω, 4.39; 8.1-3; 23.55–24.10). Her service, however defective in one sense, represents true Christian ministry and hospitality in another.[47] Martha's initial welcome of Jesus is the appropriate response of a disciple. She ministers to Jesus, mirroring the servant life and death of Jesus himself in this Gospel (22.27).[48] Yet her service is in some way distorted, as we have seen – largely because it leads her to disdain Mary's choice. Martha symbolizes the flawed disciple,

---

43   According to Ernst, Martha 'represents the Johannine believer' (*Martha from the Margins*, p. 33); see also Colleen M. Conway, *Men and Women in the Fourth Gospel: Gender and Johannine Characterization* (SBLDS, 167; Atlanta: Society of Biblical Literature, 1999), pp. 139–43, and Holly E. Hearon, *The Mary Magdalene Tradition: Witness and Counter-Witness in Early Christian Communities* (Collegeville, MN: Liturgical Press, 2004), pp. 176–9.

44   See Schneiders, *Written That You May Believe*, pp. 152–61, who argues that the death of believers is the religious context behind the narrative, and the reason for its inclusion in the Fourth Gospel.

45   Margaret M. Beirne, *Women and Men in the Fourth Gospel: A Genuine Discipleship of Equals* (JSNTSup, 242; Sheffield: Sheffield Academic Press, 2003), p. 127. Beirne sees gender pairing in John's Gospel, Martha paired with the man born blind in John 9, and Mary paired (negatively) with Judas (pp. 105–69).

46   See, e.g., Jane Schaberg, 'Luke', in Carol A. Newsom and Sharon H. Ringe (eds), *The Women's Bible Commentary* (London: SPCK, 1992), pp. 288–9, Elisabeth Schüssler Fiorenza, *But She Said: Feminist Practices of Biblical Interpretation* (Boston: Beacon Press, 1992), pp. 55–76, and Sharon H. Ringe, *Luke* (Louisville: Westminster John Knox Press, 1995), pp. 160–2. It is not at all clear that the Lukan focus of the passage is one of gender (see Byrne, *Hospitality of God*, pp. 102–3). One problem with regarding female-centred narratives as focused on female gender, while male-centred narratives are representative of men and women, is that it reinforces the view that female characters cannot play a universal role in biblical narrative.

47   Turid Karlsen Seim sees Martha as a patroness, 'one of a number of relatively well-off and autonomous women who have their own house and place it at the disposition of others, whether the community or itinerant preachers' (*The Double Message: Patterns of Gender in Luke & Acts* [Nashville: Abingdon, 1994], p. 101).

48   The parallels are not only with those who 'serve' Jesus in Luke; the older brother in the parable of the lost son complains of having 'served' his father without reward (15.29).

who plays her part while resenting that of another. She stands for the typical disciple who knows and loves, but yet whose knowledge and love are limited and partial, overshadowed by anxiety and resentment.

Mary's symbolic role in both Gospels is one of unqualified faith and love. In the Johannine account of the banquet, her place at Jesus' feet and her anointing both have symbolic value. Her posture now signifies faith and devotion, in contrast to the grief and despair which it first denoted (John 11.32). Mary replaces the odour of death at the tomb with the fragrance of life: the smell of decay exchanged for the aroma of love.[49] With the costly outpouring of the myrrh, Mary mirrors the costliness of what Jesus has done in pouring out his life for her brother. She stands for the true disciple, in contrast to Judas Iscariot, the false disciple. But the anointing turns out to be also prophetic, pointing to the death of Jesus and the anointing of his body in burial (John 19.38-42). Mary's symbolic act intimates that the raising of Lazarus has, at its centre, the cross.

A similar pattern is present in Luke's narrative, though without explicit connection to the Passion.[50] Here too Mary sits at Jesus' feet, a place of honour and insight in this Gospel (5.8; 7.38; 8.35, 41; 17.16; cf. Acts 22.3), a role not normally assigned to women; she is listening to his word (ἤκουεν τὸν λόγον αὐτοῦ, 10.39), signifying that she has 'joined the road of discipleship'.[51] Here too she is silent and makes no effort to defend herself. Here too she is supported by Jesus against accusation. These parallels suggest a similarity of symbolic function. In both Gospels, as we have seen, Mary's character is depicted as introverted and intense. In the Johannine account, she symbolizes what it means to be an authentic disciple and friend of Jesus, responding to him with costly love. Her place at Jesus' feet, whether listening or anointing, represents for the evangelist the open-hearted, self-giving love of the true disciple.

Moreover, and particularly in John's Gospel, Martha and Mary represent, not simply individual believers, but also the apostolic community. Martha's confident words in confessing her faith indicate the Christian leader (John 11.27), who makes the core confession of faith on behalf of the believing community.[52] Mary's faith, by contrast, is expressed in symbolic action, as we have seen: her stance at the feet of Jesus and her anointing acknowledge, by implication, his identity and his saving death. The Johannine Martha and Mary, in other words, act in counterpart to confess the faith of the believing community. Martha's confession is in *word*, in the 'I believe' of her response

---

49   On the contrast between the two odours, see Lee, *Symbolic Narrative*, p. 222, n. 2; idem, 'The Gospel of John and the Five Senses', *JBL* 129 (2010), pp. 115–27 (124–5); and Gail R. O'Day, 'John', in Carol A. Newsom and Sharon H. Ringe (eds), *The Women's Bible Commentary* (London: SPCK, 1992), p. 299.

50   Luke's version of the anointing likewise has no overt connection to the Passion (7.36-50).

51   Green, *Gospel of Luke*, p. 435.

52   Schneiders, *Written That You May Believe*, p. 158.

to Jesus' self-disclosure, while Mary's is in *deed*, in the anointing of his feet, with all its implications of dedication and love.[53] Together the two women disclose the community's belief in Jesus. They are not in conflict as they are in Luke, but rather act in parallel.[54] In the end, the two confessions mirror each other and together serve to reveal the Johannine Jesus as the source of life, mortal and immortal – the one who gives his life in order to give life to others.

IV. The World Behind the Text: The Historical World

Martha and Mary also belong in the world behind the text, the historical world. The fact that we find them in two different Gospel traditions – the Synoptic and the Johannine – confirms that they belong within the ministry of Jesus. Not all of Jesus' disciples literally followed him, particularly on his last journey to Jerusalem, and the Gospels speak of a number of people, named and unnamed, who counted themselves among his supporters. This group included a number of women. While some of these women followed Jesus to Jerusalem – itself a counter-cultural act – other people, both women and men, expressed their discipleship through more general friendship, support and hospitality. Martha and Mary most likely belonged within this latter group.

The historical issue is complicated by two factors. In the first place, Lazarus is not mentioned in Luke's account. It could be that Luke does not know of Lazarus's existence or that John has added him to his own story. But it may also be the case that his presence is unimportant to the Lukan tale, as is also the case with the disciples who are following Jesus to Jerusalem. The problem is that arguments from silence are not persuasive: absence may just as well mean narrative irrelevance as ignorance on the part of the narrator.[55] The second historical difficulty is the question of location: Luke seems to suggest Galilee, whereas John is clear that it is located in Judaea.[56] It is true that none of the Gospel accounts are strictly chronological or precise geographically. Given that Luke is vague on the geography, it is likely that John is the more accurate in setting the location in Judaea.

Despite these difficulties, the characteristics of the two women are, as we have seen, consistent between the two Gospels. It may be that John is aware of Luke's account and has drawn his characterization from Luke, as is often suggested. It is also possible that this consistency of characterization is

---

53   Lee, *Flesh and Glory*, pp. 197–219.

54   See, for example, Turid Karlsen Seim, 'Roles of Women in the Gospel of John', in Lars Hartman and Birger Olsson (eds), *Aspects on the Johannine Literature* (Uppsala: Almquist & Wiksell, 1987), p. 73, and Conway, *Men and Women*, pp. 143–9.

55   Richard Bauckham, *The Testimony of the Beloved Disciple: Narrative, History, and Theology in the Gospel of John* (Grand Rapids: Baker Academic, 2007), p. 178.

56   Although Barbara Shellard argues that Jesus has left Galilee by this stage; she sees the Good Samaritan and the Martha-Mary story as based in Judaea (*New Light on Luke: Its Purpose, Sources and Literary Context* [JSNTSup, 215; Sheffield: Sheffield Academic Press, 2002], pp. 98–9).

grounded in historical tradition rather than being a literary fabrication of one or other of the evangelists.[57] It is true that realistic characterization need not imply historical authenticity; it may just as well be the product of narrative creativity. Nonetheless, there is no evidence of sustained Johannine use of Lukan traditions elsewhere in the Fourth Gospel, despite the common traditions between them, as would be the case if John had borrowed his characterization directly from Luke. If John has no direct access to Luke but shares common traditions, the case is even stronger for arguing that the characterization of the sisters belongs within traditions going back to the ministry of Jesus. The coherent characterization of the women in two Gospel traditions which, in some respects, are independent of each other tends, if anything, to support the historical view.[58] In this sense, it is more likely that the shared characterization has its origins in tradition history than in literary imitation.

A further factor reinforcing the historical underpinnings of the stories is that of birth order. Although controversial in some circles, many psychologists see birth order as an important factor in personality development.[59] Psychologist Alfred Adler (1870–1937) was the first to argue that birth order affects the personalities, cognitive development and self-esteem of children within the family; in other words, children are influenced not just by their parents but also by their siblings and the order in which they are born.[60] In birth order theory, the eldest child tends to bear the weight of parental expectation, and is often given greater responsibility and expected to perform at a higher standard and set an example to younger siblings; he or she is well organized and approves of authority, yet is also susceptible to stress. Middle children tend to have fewer problems and fewer common characteristics, but they are often sociable and flexible, people-oriented rather than task-oriented. Youngest children are empathetic, relaxed, creative, and good at initiating; they tend to act as they choose, without necessarily considering the effects on others.[61]

---

57   Ringe, *Luke*, p. 161.

58   For further on the historicity of Martha, Mary and Lazarus, see Bauckham, *The Testimony of the Beloved Disciple*, pp. 172–89; reprinted in Paul N. Anderson, Felix Just and Tom Thatcher (eds), *John, Jesus, and History – Volume 2: Aspects of Historicity in the Fourth Gospel* (Atlanta: Society of Biblical Literature, 2009), pp. 185–201. Bauckham argues that the consistency of characterization is not caused by John's dependence on Luke, but by the historical nature of the traditions; see also J. N. Sanders, '"Those Whom Jesus Loved" (John xi.5)', *NTS* 1 (1954–55), pp. 29–41, and Craig L. Blomberg, *The Historical Reliability of John's Gospel: Issues and Commentary* (Downers Grove, IL: InterVarsity Press, 2001), pp. 164–79.

59   J. Kluger, 'The Power of Birth Order', *Time*, Wed. 17 Oct. 2007, http://www.time.com/time/health/article/0,8599,1672715-1,00.html. Accessed June 2011.

60   C. G. Boeree, 'Personality Theories: Alfred Adler', http://webspace.ship.edu/cgboer/adler.html. Accessed June 2011.

61   See Renee M. Schilling, 'The Effects of Birth Order on Interpersonal Relationships', http://faculty.mckendree.edu/scholars/2001/schilling.htm. Accessed June 2011.

One criticism of birth order theory is that it is only one factor in personality development and that other factors too need to be taken into account. Another criticism is that people only live in their family of origin for a limited percentage of their lives, and that their personalities continue to develop beyond childhood. Widely different from our own as the ancient world is, birth order may have had a larger effect than in modern Western culture, since family identity held greater import and impact than individual identity, and families lived closely together.[62] Birth order theory may only be one in a number of significant determinants on character development within families, but it is an important factor. Exploring biblical characterization from this angle may lead to insights into sibling relationships within the familial context of the ancient world.

To ask about the relevance of birth order theory to the characterizations of Martha and Mary (and Lazarus) requires knowing their actual birth order within the family. It is apparent from the Lukan narrative that Martha is the elder sister; the fact that she welcomes Jesus (Lk. 10.38) suggests that it is she who manages the household into which Jesus is invited, as we have already observed. In the Johannine narrative, the order of names varies and depends partly on the immediate narrative context. Of the seven scenes in the story of the raising of Lazarus, there are different orders of names when the three siblings are grouped together: Lazarus – Mary – Martha (John 11.1); Martha – Mary – Lazarus (twice, John 11.5-6, 11.19); and Martha – Lazarus – Mary (John 12.2). The question is whether the ordering in any of these reflects birth order. Other criteria for ordering names include narrative considerations (e.g. Lazarus's illness, in the first instance, which is the springboard for the plot), the patriarchal propensity to place the male figure first, and the tendency to group sisters together. Where the two women alone are mentioned, the order is generally Martha – Mary (John 11.20, 28). In other words, Martha is almost always mentioned before Mary. The exception is the initial order of names, where Mary takes precedence over her sister, due to the proleptic reference to the anointing (John 11.2).

What can we conclude from this? It can hardly be doubted that Martha is the elder of the two sisters,[63] since her name is almost always placed in advance of her sister Mary. Moreover, as we have seen, both sisters have equal stress in the Johannine narrative, confessing their faith in either word or deed: Christological confession or symbolic action. The order of names must therefore reflect birth order. More difficult to assess is the place which Lazarus occupies in the family. The following relationship between the siblings makes some sense of the narrative: the order at 11.1 is dictated by the narrative in placing Lazarus first in the list; the order at 11.5-6 and 11.19 is shaped by the narrative requirement to hold together the two sisters, given that the following scenes depict their consecutive meetings with Jesus; and 12.2 reflects the birth

---

62   'Mediterranean persons . . . are collectivists' (Joan Cecilia Campbell, *Kinship Relations in the Gospel of John* [CBQMS, 42; Washington, DC: Catholic Biblical Association of America, 2007], p. 87).

63   Bauckham, *Testimony of the Beloved Disciple*, pp. 178–9.

order of the family, since it is not dictated by any particular narrative concern (if it was, Mary would be placed first, not Martha). If so, then Martha is the elder sister, Lazarus is the second sibling, and Mary is the youngest of the family.

If we apply birth order theory to this ordering of the three siblings, it makes some sense. Martha betrays the characteristics of an eldest child. She is assertive, and takes responsibility in both the Lukan and Johannine meals (γυνὴ δὲ τις ὀνόματι Μάρθα ὑπεδέξατο αὐτόν, Lk. 10.38; ἡ Μάρθα διηκόνει, John 12.2). She has a strong sense of duty and authority. She seems to betray a conservative attitude in her values, both theological and social: her conventional belief in the resurrection in John, and her attitude towards the social demands of hospitality. We may well imagine Martha possessing high expectations, both of herself and others. These latter two qualities are particularly associated with the Lukan account, but there is nothing in the Johannine depiction that suggests otherwise. On the contrary, Martha's meeting with Jesus is made at her initiative (11.20a); she organizes Jesus' meeting with her sister (11.28); and at the mouth of the tomb she is the one who objects (11.39). In both Gospels, as we have seen, Martha is outspoken in her criticisms, which are based on her sense of what is right and proper. In other words, Martha possesses many of the characteristics of an eldest sibling in her relationship to her sister and also, in John, her brother.

It is more tenuous to speak of the other two in relation to birth order theory. However, while there are practically no personality characteristics which emerge from Lazarus in the Johannine account (for obvious reasons!),[64] Mary betrays the qualities of a youngest born. She is intense, quiet, focused, capable of intimacy and of acting in unconventional ways. The 'rebel' streak is apparent in her choosing 'the good part' in Luke, sitting at the feet of the teacher, a part not normally allotted to women in the ancient world; and in the unbinding of her hair in John, where she is unashamed of her intense devotion to Jesus and unconcerned at the effect this might have on others. Mary has the appearance of a youngest child in her intensity and unconventionality. If birth order theory does anything, it is to illuminate the similarities of characterization between the two accounts, and point to their historical reality beyond the borders of the text. Birth order theory substantiates the striking similarities of characterization between both women in Luke and John, a characterization most likely grounded in the historical traditions of Jesus' ministry.

---

64   Hakola points out that Lazarus is named in the story, which is unusual in so minor a character, and emphasis is given to Jesus' love for him and the intimacy of their relationship ('A Character Resurrected', pp. 235–47); see also Sproston North, *The Lazarus Story*, pp. 41–57.

V. The World Before the Text: The World of Reception

The journey of Martha and Mary as characters beyond the text, as they enter into the world of subsequent readers and hearers, is an intricate one. This is the world real readers or hearers enter when they are influenced by the text, whenever they stand in the space opened up by the text (*Wirkungsgeschichte*).[65] In this liminal place, Mary and Martha belong also to the receivers of the text, those who have inherited and passed on Gospel traditions – often, in the process, changing them to fit the shape and contours of their own context. This world includes, not just that of exegesis, but also homiletical interpretation, spiritual reflection, liturgy, and legend.[66] Another area, often omitted in reception history, is that of art and icon, which comprise a distinctive form of interpretation. Here we are exploring 'how [the text] is received and actualized in media other than commentaries'.[67] The three examples below come from Renaissance painting, which depict and interpret the figures of Martha and Mary in the two Gospels.

The first example is from the early Renaissance. Duccio's painting of the raising of Lazarus captures vividly the dramatic scene at the tomb:

Duccio di Buoninsegna, *Resurrection of Lazarus*, 1308–11
Tempera on wood, 43.5 x 46 cm, Kimbell Art Museum, Fort Worth[68]

65　　For an outline of this approach to the text, see especially the introduction by Ulrich Luz, *Matthew 1–7* (Hermeneia; Minneapolis: Fortress, 2007), pp. 60–6.

66　　Later legend tells that Martha, Mary and Lazarus travelled to Gaul where they worked in evangelism, Lazarus becoming a bishop, and Martha slaying a dragon. For further on these legends, particularly concerning Martha as dragon-slayer (which may reflect her strength of character in the Gospel accounts), see Moltmann-Wendel, *The Women Around Jesus*, pp. 39–48.

67　　Luz, *Matthew 1–7*, p. 61.

68　　Web Gallery of Art, http://www.wga.hu/index1.html. Last accessed November 2011.

In the centre of the tableau stand the figures of Jesus and Martha, the latter with a worried frown on her face. Jesus holds out his right hand towards the rock-hewn tomb, from which Lazarus is (rather awkwardly) emerging, summoned by the imperious hand which signifies Jesus' voice. One of the bystanders covers his nose with his left hand against the smell of death and decay. On the ground, at the feet of Jesus, crouches Mary, her red cloak identifying her with Mary Magdalene. The disciples (prominent among them being Peter, immediately to Jesus' right, in a green cloak) cluster around Jesus and the sisters. The two women are in a direct line, one above the other.[69]

Although the painting presents the central scene at the tomb, it suggests also the earlier conversation between Martha and Jesus, the previous meeting between Jesus and Mary, and even the subsequent anointing where she is again found at Jesus' feet. Mary's abject pose in this interpretation may suggest penitence (in line with Western traditions about Mary Magdalene as the penitent prostitute[70]) but it also indicates her initial despair (John 11.32). The fact that both women are turned towards Jesus and away from the emerging Lazarus suggests also their assumption of the improbability of their brother being restored to life – their lack of understanding that the voice of the Son of God can pierce the grave. Hermeneutically, the scene depicts the human anxiety over death and its overpowering by the authoritative hand (i.e. voice) of the Son of God.

The second and third examples comprise two paintings from the later Renaissance based on the Lukan story, a popular topic of art in the high Renaissance period. The contrast between the paintings illustrates the difficulty and diversity of interpretation. On the one hand, Vermeer's famous depiction of Jesus' visit to the home of the sisters is harmonious and balanced. Vermeer's interpretation has a much less 'iconic' quality than Duccio's and is more vivid in its depiction of individual human physiognomy and character.

---

69   For further on the painting, especially in relation to other paintings in Duccio's Maestá, see Cecilia Jannella, *Duccio di Buoninsegna* (Florence: SCALA, 1991), pp. 22, 42–3.

70   For further on Western depiction of Mary Magdalene, see especially Susan Haskins, *Mary Magdalen: Myth and Metaphor* (London: HarperCollins, 1993).

Johannes Vermeer, *Christ in the House of Martha and Mary*, 1654–55(?)
Oil on canvas, 160 x 142 cm, National Gallery of Scotland, Edinburgh[71]

Vermeer's portrayal has a particular gentleness and intimacy to it. The three characters form a ring composition, beautifully balanced, and a three-way line can be drawn from each to the other two (interestingly, as in Duccio, with Martha above Mary). The moment it encapsulates is the conversation between Martha and Jesus: Martha offers hospitality with a loaf of bread while Jesus points to Mary, perched on a low stool at his feet, her pose intense and concentrated. Neither sister looks at the other but, as with Duccio, both are intent upon Jesus who, in this depiction, is seated entirely at his ease, stretched out between the two women. What is particularly significant about Vermeer's interpretation is the lack of anger in the scene: Jesus is explaining, no more, and Martha is listening closely to what he says, with Mary somewhat disengaged from the topic of conversation, her mind on higher things. Martha is not presented in negative terms, nor is Jesus obviously rebuking her. The interpretation is a kinder and softer retelling of the Lukan tale which, while obviously commending Mary's choice (and its representation of the contemplative life),

---

71   http://www.wga.hu/index1.html. Last accessed November 2011.

is nonetheless sympathetic towards the active life of compassion and service chosen by Martha, not to mention her misunderstanding.[72]

On the other hand, the Spanish painting by Velázquez of the same scene offers a very different reading. In this depiction, the painting is divided into two unequal scenarios. Martha is foregrounded in the kitchen occupying the left (and larger) side of the painting, as well as the bottom right, while the right upper side, which is presented as background and has almost the appearance of a painting or mirror on the wall, shows the scene with Mary at Jesus' feet. It is a painting in the tradition of the *Bodegón* or still life:

Diego Rodriguez de Silva y Velázquez, *Christ in the House of Mary and Martha*, c. 1620. Oil on canvas, 60 x 103.5 cm, National Gallery, London[73]

Martha's round face gazes mournfully and unhappily at the viewer; she is on the brink of tears. On the table before her are the domestic provisions, vividly portrayed: the fish, the eggs, paprika and garlic, while Martha works away with a mortar and pestle, urged on by an old woman immediately beside her. The miniature scene between Christ, who is clearly teaching (indicated by his raised right hand), and the adoring Mary at his feet, bathed in peaceful light, seems remote and almost unreal, as if Martha's intervention in that scene has been useless and she is again relegated to the kitchen. The sympathies of this painting are emphatically with Martha. Jesus and Mary, by comparison, seem unaware of, if not actually indifferent to, Martha's misery. This painting is more troubling than the serene portrayal of Vermeer – just as appealing in its own way, but more disturbing for the viewer. In the confusion of interpretation

72   See the discussion of the painting on the Vermeer website, http://www.essentialvermeer. com/catalogue/christ_in_the_house_of_mary_and_martha.html. Last accessed November 2011.

73   Web Gallery of Art, http://www.wga.hu/index1.html. Last accessed October 2011.

in reception history, it depicts, perhaps more accurately, the widespread tendency to sympathize with the figure of Martha and to feel that she is poorly treated by Luke.[74]

There is also an iconic tradition depicting Martha and Mary as saints in the Orthodox tradition, sometimes including the figure of Lazarus. In these icons the focus on the two female characters is explicitly mystical, the purpose of the icon being to offer 'a glimpse of the divine',[75] which is aimed at enabling the viewer to enter the celestial realm. The two women either stand together united, of equal height and significance, facing the viewer directly,[76] or they flank, on either side, their brother.[77] Martha is often identified by a scroll in her hand, signifying the gospel which she proclaims; her right hand may be raised in blessing. Mary usually clasps a flask of oil in one hand, recalling the anointing. The depiction is mostly Johannine, with the added reference to Lazarus in between, but it does not rule out an allusion to the Lukan account. The feast of Mary and Martha is on June 4, and the troparion (a short hymn in the Byzantine musical tradition) set for the day in Orthodox liturgy is also an interpretation of the Gospel texts:

> You fervently believed in Christ and His marvellous acts,
> O Martha and Mary, sisters of Lazarus.
> You were adorned with radiant virtues
> and were found worthy to be numbered with the Saints;
> together with holy Lazarus pray to God for us.

In this reading, Martha and Mary belong securely in the divine realm. They are the objects of veneration and accessible to the viewer; their enduring presence is confirmed by the iconic representation which parallels, and makes visual, the primary (biblical) text. What is unimportant are the features denoting personality traits or specific characterizations. Instead of the human warmth of

---

74   This sympathetic attitude to Martha is sharply delineated in the satirical poem of Rudyard Kipling (1907), 'The Sons of Martha', where the descendants of Martha are identified as those in society who carry out the labour on behalf of the descendants of Mary, the wealthy and leisured classes: 'They sit at the feet—they hear the Word—they see how truly the Promise runs. / They have cast their burden upon the Lord, and—the Lord He lays it on Martha's Sons!' (stanza 8, lines 3-4). Martha is aptly described as she 'of the careful soul and the troubled heart' (stanza 1, line 2). See http://www.online-literature.com/donne/920/. Last accessed December 2011.

75   See Solrunn Nes, *The Mystical Language of Icons* (London: St Paul's, 2000), pp. 7–21. Further on the role of icons in Orthodox spirituality, see L. Ouspensky, 'The Meaning and Language of Icons', in L. Ouspensky and V. Lossky (eds), *The Meaning of Icons* (New York: St Vladimir's Seminary Press, 1989), pp. 23–49.

76   See the icon of Saints Mary and Martha, Orthodox Monastery Wagener SC; http://www.saintsmaryandmarthaorthodoxmonastery.org/about.html. Last accessed November 2011.

77   For example, 'St Lazarus, St Martha and St Mary. Icon for Church in Bethany'; http://www.iconsnunanastasia.com/img56.html. Last accessed June 2012.

Vermeer's or Velázquez's depiction, iconic depictions present the women with what seem to be expressionless faces, but within the tradition this aspect is intended to convey a sense of peace and permanence: the abode of the eternal, as against the temporal and transient. As saints, Martha and Mary's intercession is available to the viewer in this tradition, and their blessing assured. In the iconic reception, biblical characterization becomes contemporary to each new generation of readers/viewers, who participate, through textual and iconic media, in the celestial realm.

These depictions illustrate something of the way in which biblical characters are presented in reception history and the purposes for which they are used. Each, in its own way, is intended both to tell and to interpret the story for the viewers of their day: for a liturgical context (Duccio), for personal edification (Vermeer, Velázquez), for prayer (the icons). Each portrays Martha and Mary as religious and representative figures with ongoing significance for the Christian community. Of the two paintings, Duccio's is the more formal in its presentation of the sisters, a presentation influenced as much by later tradition as by the biblical narrative itself, whereas Vermeer's is the more personal and familial, depicting the scene as one of mutuality in ministry rather than conflict; Velázquez is also personal in his vivid portrait of Martha's distress. Both Vermeer and Velázquez have a greater degree of intimacy than the representation by Duccio, with its stilted figure emerging from the rock and the anxiety and grief conveyed by the sisters. The iconic depictions set the narratives and characters within the context of prayer and contemplation. Each example is a powerful and perennial depiction of the Lukan and Johannine stories and of the characters which dominate them, drawing them into new contexts and new articulations of their symbolic power.

VI. Conclusion

As characters, Martha and Mary belong in four worlds: the narrative and the symbolic worlds within the text, the historical world behind it, and the world (and tradition) before it. The sisters have, independently, a similar characterization in both the Lukan and Johannine stories, for all the differences between the two narratives. Martha is the stronger and more dominant of the two, conservative in her attitudes yet also outspoken and with a strong sense of responsibility. In birth order, Martha is typical of an eldest sibling, betraying many of the characteristics identified in modern psychological theory. Mary seems to act as the youngest child in her capacity for relationship, her intensity, and her relative freedom from convention. Both are depicted as women of faith, and even exemplary faith. This coherence of characterization suggests that the sisters form part of the authentic traditions of Jesus' ministry. Martha and Mary are not just the literary constructions of the evangelists, but have their own place, and their own characterization, within the Jesus traditions of the earliest communities. These traditions, captured in the two Gospels, continue beyond the text and its immediate world into the reception history of the generations that followed, with their own readings of the biblical text and their own depictions of its leading characters.

Chapter 13

'WHOM JESUS LOVED': ANONYMITY AND IDENTITY. BELIEF AND WITNESS IN THE FOURTH GOSPEL

David R. Beck

I. Introduction

Unpacking the characterization of the enigmatic disciple identified in the Fourth Gospel with the relative clause 'whom Jesus loved' is complex due to several interpretive issues surrounding his narrative presence. Two of these which continue to receive much scholarly attention are the anonymity of this figure and the understanding of his role within the narrative.[1] This essay will explore the link between anonymity and identity, specifically the anonymity of the disciple whom Jesus loved[2] and the identity of the One who is the focus of this narrative witness. It will then look to the role of belief in relation to that identity, and the requirement of witness to his identity subsequent to belief to emulate the discipleship modelled by the one whom Jesus loved. Finally, it will look at the necessity of veracity for the narrative witness to be successful and its stated purpose achieved.

II. Anonymity in the Fourth Gospel Revisited

The anonymity of the disciple whom Jesus loved is noted by all, but resisted by many and subverted by some. He is introduced without any name being offered the reader, but with a qualifying phrase with no explanation, which the author apparently deems sufficient. How this lack of a name functions in the narrative has been a focus of much inquiry. Were the first readers of this narrative expected to know his identity? Does he stand in the text as a non-historic representative

---

1   My earlier study on anonymity and discipleship in the Fourth Gospel, *The Discipleship Paradigm: Readers and Anonymous Characters in the Fourth Gospel* (BIS, 27; Leiden: Brill, 1997), focused on how anonymity functions in the reading process to assist readers in identifying with those characters who are offered by the narrative as models for discipleship to emulate. This current study of the disciple whom Jesus loved will focus primarily on the function of his anonymity in the unfolding of this Gospel.

2   This study will consistently refer to this figure with the relative clause 'whom Jesus loved' as it is the only narrated grammatical form used as his identifier in the Fourth Gospel.

figure for all who would become recipients of Jesus' love? Does this designation indicate he was loved by Jesus in a way the other disciples were not? Is the narrative hinting at an identity it will later reveal?

The subversion of his anonymity is reflected by the standard means for identifying this disciple among his interpreters. Every time his designation as 'the disciple whom Jesus loved' is replaced with 'Beloved Disciple', the capitalization converts it grammatically to a proper noun, which for all practical purposes makes a name of it. This is refreshingly admitted by Jo-Ann A. Brant: 'The narrator resists giving him a name; he draws him in circles by using a retrospective clause, "the disciple whom Jesus loved", which readers (including myself), for their own convenience, have turned into a name, "the Beloved Disciple".'[3] Even worse is referring to the disciple whom Jesus loved by his 'initials' as a scholarly shorthand, 'BD'.[4] Others speak of his identifying designation as a title,[5] which is grammatically just a step away from a name.

Scholarly attempts to discover the identity of the disciple whom Jesus loved have not abated. Recent examples range from an attempt to identify this figure as John, son of Zebedee, from the chiastic structuring of the text,[6] to an examination of various second-century traditions concerning beloved disciples in apocryphal gospels as evidence of the rich diversity of various communities' competing claims that their favourite authoritative disciple was the one whom Jesus loved most.[7] Ben Witherington has joined those readers who are convinced Lazarus is the only named character in the narrative who qualifies for this identification.[8] The shared unsubstantiated assumption of such attempts is that it is the intention of the narrative to give such an identification and that the disciple whom Jesus loved is one of the named characters in the narrative. Attridge notes that 'the plethora of suggestions about the identity and function of the Beloved disciple should itself give us pause'.[9]

Richard Bauckham, while making a compelling case for the narrative identification of the disciple whom Jesus loved as the author of the Fourth Gospel, undermines the narrative function of his anonymity. He claims that

3   Jo-Ann A. Brant, *Dialogue and Drama: Elements of Greek Tragedy in the Fourth Gospel* (Peabody, MA: Hendrickson, 2004), p. 199.

4   John W. Pryor, *John: Evangelist of the Covenant People: The Narrative & Themes of the Fourth Gospel* (Downers Grove, IL: InterVarsity, 1992), p. 185, *passim*.

5   'Peter does not enjoy the intimacy and loving relationship with Jesus that the Beloved Disciple (as his very title implies) enjoys', Kevin Quast, *Peter and the Beloved Disciple: Figures for a Community in Crisis* (JSNTSup, 32; Sheffield: JSOT Press, 1989), p. 69.

6   Daniel F. Stramara, Jr, 'The Chiastic Key to the Identity of the Beloved Disciple', *St. Vladimir's Theological Quarterly* 53.1 (2009), pp. 5–27 (25).

7   Marvin Meyer, 'Whom Did Jesus Love Most? Beloved Disciples in John and Other Gospels', in Tuomas Rasimus (ed.), *The Legacy of John: Second-Century Reception of the Fourth Gospel* (NovTSup, 132; Leiden/Boston: Brill, 2010), pp. 73–91.

8   Ben Witherington III, *What Have They Done to Jesus? Beyond Strange Theories and Bad History—Why We Can Trust the Bible* (San Francisco: HarperOne, 2006), p. 146.

9   Harold W. Attridge, 'The Restless Quest for the Beloved Disciple', in David H. Warren, Ann Graham Brock and David W. Pao (eds), *Early Christian Voices in Texts, Traditions, and Symbols: Essays in Honor of François Bovon* (BIS, 66; Leiden: Brill, 2003), pp. 71–80 (78).

by both his anonymity and his withholding from the reader his role as author until the conclusion of chapter 21, this disciple is in effect admitting 'he is not a disciple readers will know by name'.[10] This fails to recognize that the narrative function of his anonymity is completely unrelated to his name and identity. Rather, it is in response to the only One whose name and identity matters, The Word who became flesh and dwelt among us.

The reason that scholarly attempts to identify and name this disciple go unabated is not because such a knowledge is necessary for the narrative witness to be fully effective,[11] but rather because of modern readers' attempts to impose their own sensibilities upon the text, rather than let the narrative speak for itself. Charlesworth is wrong in his assertion that for the disciple whom Jesus loved, 'anonymity moves to an epithet and finally to a revelation of the identity of the Beloved Disciple . . . an enigma that is gradually disclosed'.[12] Instead, this narrative does just the opposite. As evidenced by the plethora of different identifications that result from these varied investigations, the narrative defies all attempts on the part of readers to make such an identification.[13]

The reason for the anonymity of this disciple is not that he was not well known to the readers and his name would not be recognized,[14] nor even that his naming is unnecessary because he is already known to the author and his readers.[15] The significance of his anonymity is rather to be found in the Fourth Gospel's revelation that there is only One whose name is significant and only One person whose identity matters.

III. The Identity of the Pre-incarnate Word in the Fourth Gospel

In this Gospel narrative, the One character whose identity has lasting significance is introduced in the Prologue as already existing in the beginning, whose existence is a coexistence with God, and who himself exists as God. His identity as God, the Word who became flesh, is the opening gambit of this narrative. The reader learns that through belief in him the life God offers is available. And this belief is specifically declared to be belief in his name (1.12), a name as yet unstated. This early declaration also introduces the essential Johannine concept of belief. The primacy of eliciting belief as the purpose for which this Gospel narrative is written is evidenced in the thematic promise of John 3.16-18. The purpose for which the Father sent the Son is that eternal life

---

10   Richard Bauckham, 'The Fourth Gospel as the Testimony of the Beloved Disciple', in Richard Bauckham and Carl Mosser (eds), *The Gospel of John and Christian Theology* (Grand Rapids: Eerdmans, 2008), pp. 120–39 (133).

11   *Contra* Attridge, 'Restless Quest', p. 78.

12   James H. Charlesworth, *The Beloved Disciple: Whose Witness Validates the Gospel of John?* (Valley Forge, PA: Trinity Press International, 1995), p. xv.

13   Derek Tovey, *Narrative Art and Act in the Fourth Gospel* (JSNTSup, 151; Sheffield, Sheffield Academic Press, 1997), p. 123.

14   *Contra* Bauckham, 'Fourth Gospel', p. 138.

15   Tovey, *Narrative Art*, p. 144.

might be accessed through believing in him. The purpose statement of 20.21 confirms that the *raison d'être* for this narrative's being written is identical with the Father's purpose in sending the Son. It is to produce belief in him, embracing his identity, resulting in the eternal life from the Father that he was sent to give.

The overwhelming significance of Jesus' identity as the One sent by the Father, making insignificant any other identity but his own, is highlighted by the Baptist's debate with the priests and Levites that immediately follows the Prologue. The appearance of John is the reader's first encounter with an historical character. His introduction anchors the supra-historical presence of the Word firmly in human history, in which the reader is a participant. When John is first encountered it is as the one sent from God to bear witness to the light, but who is not himself the light (1.7-8). His reappearance leads to a direct identity query, 'Who are you?' (1.19). John's answer to this straightforward question is significant to the reader's understanding of the issue of identity in the Fourth Gospel. An emphatic tripartite formula, 'He confessed, he did not deny, but confessed' (1.20) introduces a 'confession' that is not a confession, but a denial.[16] Instead of revealing his own identity, John vehemently denies that he is to be identified as the Christ.

The emphasis on John's role as a witness to Jesus offsets John's narrative priority, his appearance preceding Jesus' entry into the text. The simple inquiry into John's identity is answered only by denial, by whom he is not. His only positive statement of his own identity is as the one coming to prepare the way for the One coming after whose sandal he is unworthy even to untie. This emphasis on the identity of the One who was and is and becomes flesh establishes this as a narrative of identity crisis. The crisis occurs as the various figures, collectively and individually, encounter Jesus and are confronted with his identity already revealed in the Prologue. The content of that crisis is whether they will respond with belief as the narrative requires.

The narrative proceeds to the first of these encounters between various individuals and Jesus, the focus of which is always their success or failure at coming to terms with the Prologue's declaration of his identity. In light of this continued narrative focus on the only One whose identity has any value, the lack of a name or other identity descriptors except for his designation as the recipient of Jesus' love is appropriate for this disciple. It is not that the narrative is seeking to unveil a secret that is hidden, or reveal a fact assumed to be unknown. Instead, it reflects the consistent message of this narrative that his is not the identity that matters, that can bring life to those not yet born 'again/from above' (ἄνωθεν, 3.3).

---

16   Marinus de Jonge, 'John the Baptist and Elijah in the Fourth Gospel', in Robert T. Fortna and Beverly Gaventa (eds), *The Conversation Continues: Studies in Paul and John in Honor of J. Louis Martyn* (Nashville: Abingdon, 1990), pp. 299–308 (302).

IV. Narrative Portrayal of the Disciple Whom Jesus Loved

The first undisputed appearance of the disciple whom Jesus loved within the narrative of the Fourth Gospel occurs at the supper in chapter 13. As the scene begins, Jesus dialogues with Peter (13.1-11) as he washes the feet of the disciples, a conversation in which Peter fails to understand what Jesus says or is doing, prompting Jesus' teaching on servanthood and obedience (13.12-17). He next cites Psalm 41 (13.18) to predict his betrayal. For the benefit of Jesus' disciples – who in the Fourth Gospel are consistently unaware of the meaning of his words prior to his resurrection – (and of the uninformed reader), Jesus speaks plainly: 'One of you will betray me.' This leads to the scene in which the reader first encounters the disciple explicitly designated 'whom Jesus loved'. There is no explanation of who he is or where he came from. It is almost as if the reader is to assume he has been there all along, but with no indication he is to be identified with any particular disciple previously encountered. There is no introduction to detail anything of his personality traits, background, family, or the circumstances which led to his following Jesus. He is simply stated to be 'one of his disciples' (13.23).

The two most noteworthy items in his first narrative description are his designation as the disciple whom Jesus loved and his position in relation to Jesus. This statement of his position, ἐν τῷ κόλπῳ τοῦ Ἰησοῦ, 'on the breast of Jesus', precedes the descriptive phrase, 'the one whom Jesus loved'. The text is silent on this disciple's position at the table, focusing instead on his *position toward Jesus*. Instead of providing information concerning this disciple's honoured position among the disciples, the Fourth Gospel guides the reader to an understanding about his role as the special recipient of Jesus' love. The description of the disciple whom Jesus loved – ἐν τῷ κόλπῳ τοῦ Ἰησοῦ (13.23) – echoes the earlier description of Jesus – ὁ ὢν εἰς τὸν κόλπον τοῦ πατρός (1.18) – and 'implies that Jesus' relationship to the Father was a model for the Beloved Disciple's relationship to Jesus'.[17] No one else in the Gospel is described by this phrase.

The intimate position and designation as the disciple whom Jesus loved is viewed by Rekha M. Chennattu as representative of the new covenant relationship 'that is expected from the disciples and the subsequent readers of the Gospel (15.4-10), those who are summoned to be like the Beloved Disciple (20.3-10) by believing without seeing Jesus (20.29)'.[18] In the parallel occurrence of this description of Jesus' position with the Father in the Prologue, the reader is informed that Jesus is not only eternally with God, and

---

17   R. Alan Culpepper, *John, the Son of Zebedee: The Life of a Legend* (Studies on Personalities of the New Testament; Columbia, SC: University of South Carolina Press, 1994), p. 60; David J. Hawkin, *The Johannine World: Reflections on the Theology of the Fourth Gospel and Contemporary Society* (SUNY Series in Religious Studies; Albany: State University of New York Press, 1996), pp. 82, 142; Quast, 'Peter', p. 58.

18   Rekha M. Chennattu, *Johannine Discipleship as Covenant Relationship* (Peabody, MA: Hendrickson, 2006), p. 101.

also God in the flesh, but his incarnation is a manifestation of the Father (1.18). Just as the final chapter will assign the narrative's reliable witness to Jesus to the disciple whom Jesus loved, this first chapter portrays Jesus as the earthly witness to the Father. Mark Stibbe's recent study of the characterization of the Father in the Fourth Gospel asserts that 'outside the narrator, the only reliable witness to the Father's character occurs on the lips of the Son'.[19]

This parallel of the description of Jesus' position with the disciple whom Jesus loved echoes the Prologue and guides the reader back to chapter 1 with its subsequent account of the presence of two disciples of John in 1.35, one of whom will be identified as Andrew. The other remains unnamed, but Bauckham finds compelling narrative parallels with the disciple whom Jesus loved, leading to the reader's recognition that they are one and the same. Their initial activity toward Jesus is following, ἀκολυθέω. Each is stated to remain with Jesus, at least temporarily, using the same verb, μένω. This qualifies the disciple whom Jesus loved to give witness to Jesus, as he fulfils the qualification given by Jesus himself in 15.27: 'You will testify also because you have been with me from the beginning.'[20] Observation of these textual parallels raises awareness that the first explicit identification of this disciple as the one whom Jesus loved is not his first appearance in the narrative.

The indeterminacy of the narrative portrayal of this disciple is reinforced in the supper scene of chapter 13 in that the portrayal of his character is not by description or dialogue, but instead the narrative is content to reveal him through his interaction with and contrast to other named characters surrounding him. In this first occurrence of his textual juxtaposition with Peter, he is portrayed as Peter's means of querying Jesus concerning a question of identity, that of the betrayer. These two brief statements of his position towards Jesus and his relaying of Peter's question are the only information narrated concerning him in this briefest of glimpses that initiates the explicitly stated narrative presence of this enigmatic figure, the disciple whom Jesus loved.

Many questions are left unanswered. Does he understand Jesus' identification of Judas as the betrayer? Some interpreters insist that he must,[21] but this is specifically refuted by the clear statement in v. 28, 'no one at the table knew why Jesus had said this to him'. The narrator says 'no one' and this includes the disciple whom Jesus loved. To understand 'why' as referring to anything other than the significance of Jesus' action as an answer to their request for the betrayer's identity is without textual support. Does the disciple whom Jesus loved relay any information to Peter, who prompted his initial query to Jesus?

19   Mark Stibbe, 'Telling the Father's Story: The Gospel of John as Narrative Theology', in John Lierman (ed.), *Challenging Perspectives on the Gospel of John* (Tübingen: Mohr Siebeck, 2006), pp. 170–93 (178).

20   Bauckham, 'Fourth Gospel', pp. 133–4; cf. Tovey, *Narrative Art*, p. 132.

21   Hawkin, *The Johannine World*, p. 82; D. A. Carson, *The Gospel According to John* (PNTC; Grand Rapids: Eerdmans, 1991), p. 474.

The text refuses to fill this gap, requiring readers to fill it from their own external knowledge or live with the ambiguity.[22]

The supper episode (13.21-30) does not portray a mediating role for the disciple whom Jesus loved, not for Peter or any other of the disciples, because he is narratively portrayed mediating nothing.[23] Instead, the indeterminacy of this scene raises the issue of utmost import for the reader. The statement by Jesus that one of his *disciples* will betray him, together with the indeterminacy of this introduction to the disciple whom Jesus loved, addresses each reader with her/his loyalty to and relationship with Jesus. As Brodie states, 'The phrasing, as well as being open-ended, is also overlapping (from betrayer to beloved) and it all indicates a single idea: any of them could be the betrayer and any of them could be the beloved.'[24]

The next certain appearance of this disciple is the scene at the foot of the cross with the also unnamed mother of Jesus in chapter 19. This is his only explicitly designated appearance without Peter alongside him. Instead he appears here beside the mother of Jesus, whose initial encounter with Jesus was narrated in chapter 2. The narrative entrance of both of them is abrupt, offering no explanation of how, or why, they are present 'standing by the cross' (19.25-27). The appearance is again notably brief. Jesus addresses them both, directing his mother to consider the disciple whom Jesus loved as her son, while instructing him to consider her as his mother. This is followed by the information of the immediacy of the disciple's obedience; 'from that hour he took her into his own household' (v. 27). What are we to make of this second and equally brief appearance of the disciple whom Jesus loved?

The symbolic understandings of this scene are numerous. Older interpretations include Jesus' mother as the representative of Jewish Christianity while the disciple whom Jesus loved represents Gentile Christianity, which incorporated what had been a Jewish sectarian movement into its fold; or the understanding of the mother of Jesus as the church who now has oversight of the Christian, represented by the disciple.[25] Writing from her identified perspective of a first-generation Asian immigrant, Sophia Park interprets this scene as an empowerment for displaced persons.[26] She understands these words of Jesus as the language of adoption in the context of the character configuration at the foot of the cross. The setting is remarkable for its contrasting character groupings. These include the soldiers and the disciples, the disciples and Jesus on the cross, the mother of Jesus with other

---

22   Culpepper, *John*, p. 60.
23   David J. Hawkin, 'The Function of the Beloved Disciple Motif in the Johannine Redaction', *Laval Theologique et Philosophique* 33 (1977), pp. 135–50 (143).
24   Thomas Brodie, *The Gospel According to John: A Literary and Theological Commentary* (New York: Oxford University Press, 1993), p. 453.
25   Rudolf Bultmann, *The Gospel of John: A Commentary* (trans. G. R. Beasley-Murray, et al.; Philadelphia: Westminster, 1971), p. 673; Raymond E. Brown, *The Gospel According to John* (AB, 29a; Garden City, NY: Doubleday, 1970), p. 926.
26   Sophia Park, 'The Galilean Jesus: Creating a Borderland at the Foot of the Cross (John 19:23-30)', *TS* 70 (2009), pp. 419–36.

women disciples, the women with the disciple whom Jesus loved, and the mother of Jesus with the disciple whom Jesus loved. Within this context, Jesus' words and the immediate obedient response on the part of the disciple whom Jesus loved invite the displaced and dislocated to cross over into a place of belonging within his community of disciples.[27]

The familial adoption language at the foot of the cross echoes the previous occurrence of the mother of Jesus in chapter 2, where I have argued Jesus challenges her to a new understanding of her relationship to him apart from the familial mother/son.[28] Here we have a narrative portrayal of her presence with the disciple whom Jesus loved on an equal footing with him in the presence of Jesus, as she necessarily stands before the cross not as Jesus' mother, but as his disciple.[29] The entrusting of her care to the disciple reinforces the intimacy of his relationship with Jesus, whose mother is to become his mother.[30] The presence of the disciple whom Jesus loved at the cross is also a narrative affirmation of the eyewitness claim made in v. 35, a claim upon which the veracity and authenticity of his witness rests.

The familial adoption language inaugurating the new relationship of the disciple whom Jesus loved to Jesus' mother in the scene at the foot of the cross has also been suggested to reinforce the authentication of his witness. Even as this disciple whom Jesus loved is revealed to have 'insider' status, and is uniquely positioned by his presence in the narrative from the very beginning, the addition of Jesus' mother to his family, fully embodied within the community of believers, allows her testimony to reinforce theirs, and especially that of the one whose witness 'we know to be true' (19.35).[31]

While there is no intervening explicitly designated appearance of the disciple whom Jesus loved between the scenes at the supper and those at the cross, a much-discussed possible appearance occurs in the trial scene of chapter 18. What assessment can be made concerning the 'other disciple' with Peter in the high priest's courtyard? Is this the disciple whom Jesus loved? The lack of this specific designation to identify the 'other disciple' with Peter as the disciple whom Jesus loved makes equating the two speculative, with certainty perhaps unattainable. Yet the possibility is enticing and the evidence is compelling, even if it falls short of conclusive. The bases for the identification include his association with Peter and the notable parallel literary construction in 18.15-16 and 20.3-8. In chapter 18 at the place of Jesus' trial Peter is on the outside looking in and the other disciple has entered. In chapter 20 at the

27   Park, 'Galilean Jesus', p. 436.

28   Beck, *Discipleship Paradigm*, pp. 54–61.

29   Carson, *John*, p. 619.

30   C. K. Barrett, *The Gospel According to St John: An Introduction with Commentary and Notes on the Greek Text* (Philadelphia: Westminster, 2nd edn, 1978), p. 552.

31   Joan Cecelia Campbell, *Kinship Relations in the Gospel of John* (CBQMS, 42; Washington, DC: Catholic Biblical Association of America, 2007), pp. 43–4.

place of Jesus' burial, the disciple whom Jesus loved is narrated on the outside looking in at Peter who has already entered.[32]

Unlike with the 'other disciple' of chapter 1, by this stage of the narrative the reader is already familiar with the disciple whom Jesus loved through his explicit introduction at the supper in chapter 13. Combined with his companionship with Peter, it can be said that this identification is highly probable. But since the disciple whom Jesus loved has already been introduced by his identifying clause in chapter 13 there is no compelling reason why he should not be identified by it here, if this is indeed he. However, identifying him with any other specific figure from the Fourth Gospel narrative is equally as problematic, and subject to the same criticisms. If the anonymous disciple in chapter 18 is to be identified with the disciple whom Jesus loved, then Culpepper rightly notes that this is the only reference to him that reveals anything 'apart from his relationship to Jesus, Peter, Jesus' mother, or the later Christian community',[33] specifically his acquaintance with the high priest, allowing him to be Peter's access to the courtyard. He stands in the high priest's courtyard as an anonymous disciple, a figure who seems somewhat familiar to readers as if they have met him somewhere before.

It is in the third scene where the disciple whom Jesus loved is explicitly designated as present that he is first said to believe. As he arrives at the empty tomb he is once more in the company of Peter. They are informed by Mary that things are not as expected. The narrative quotes her as saying, 'They have taken the Lord out of the tomb, and we do not know where they have laid him' (20.2). The use of 'we' may indicate she is a spokesperson for a larger group; narratively it suggests she speaks not only for herself, but 'as though she represented others'.[34]

The symbolism to be found in the disciple whom Jesus loved outpacing Peter to the tomb, yet not going in, while Peter enters without hesitating is dependent on what interpreters who discover symbolism here import from outside the text. There is no suggestion offered within the narrative for the significance of the priority of arrival or entrance. This is also true for the varied symbolic interpretations of the detail of the burial linen lying separate from the face-cloth. The report of the priority of arrival and entry does serve to contrast the disciple whom Jesus loved with Peter. If 'competitors' is too strong a description for this contrast, they nonetheless stand in contrast. Instead of their actions being simultaneous – they ran, they arrived, they went in – we have two distinct sets of actions narrated. This prepares the reader for the distinctiveness of their responses. The only verbs describing Peter's response are 'went in' and 'saw' (20.6). An additional verb is employed to narrate the response of the disciple whom Jesus loved. He also 'went in' and 'saw', but his response goes further than Peter's: he also 'believed' (ἐπίστευσεν, 20.8).

---

32   Frans Neirynck, 'The "Other Disciple" in Jn 18:15-16', *EThL* 51 (1975), pp. 113–41 (139–40).

33   Culpepper, *John*, p. 61.

34   Brodie, *John*, p. 561.

While his belief is explicitly narrated in 20.8, the exact content of that belief, as well as what prompted it, is not. It has been suggested that what is narrated in v. 8 is an incomplete faith on the part of the disciple whom Jesus loved that will be developed further as the narrative advances.[35] Barrett understands the statement as an explanation that, unlike the community of the first readers, the disciple whom Jesus loved had a faith based only on what he saw at the tomb, not a conviction concerning what the scripture had foretold concerning Jesus.[36]

The specific content of the narratively declared belief of the disciple whom Jesus loved has recently been examined by Craig Koester. This disciple is consistently portrayed as insightful as well as possessing 'insider' status. He shares intimacy with Jesus at the supper, he is in all probability the insider who can access the high priest's courtyard, he is the only male disciple at the cross, and in the resurrection appearance narrated in chapter 21, he is the first to recognize the risen Jesus. Accordingly, the belief with which he is credited in 20.8 is best understood as just that, genuine belief that Jesus has escaped the bonds of death. The statement of his failure to understand the scriptures that follows in v. 9 does not indicate his faith is anything less than genuine, because 'the gospel assumes that understanding comes through faith, not prior to faith'.[37]

Only one of these two disciples is unambiguously portrayed as coming to faith: the disciple whom Jesus loved. His is a belief without the prerequisite of a sign, a belief produced precisely by that which is not seen. The significance of the empty tomb is not what was seen, but what was absent. Brendan Byrne identifies a link between 20.9 and 20.29 where 'the point is not that of "not seeing and yet believing", but rather of "not seeing *Jesus* and yet believing"'.[38] The narrative offers the disciple whom Jesus loved as a model of faith response 'for the purpose of encouraging the readers to respond in a similar act of faith'.[39]

The final scene in which the disciple whom Jesus loved is explicitly identified is in the resurrection appearance to the seven in chapter 21. This chapter has long been the subject of exegetical debate concerning its place in the Fourth Gospel and its authorship in relation to the rest of the Gospel. The arguments for and against the authenticity of chapter 21 as an original part of the Fourth Gospel by the same author have been thoroughly reviewed by Stanley Porter. After a detailed examination of the MSS evidence, grammar and vocabulary, thematic unity, and the function of 20.30-31 and 21.24-25

---

35   Brown, *John*, Vol. 2, p. 987.

36   Barrett, *St John*, p. 564.

37   Craig R. Koester, 'Jesus' Resurrection, the Signs, and the Dynamics of Faith in the Gospel of John', in Craig R. Koester and Reimund Bieringer (eds), *The Resurrection of Jesus in the Gospel of John* (WUNT, 222; Tübingen: Mohr Siebeck, 2008), pp. 47–74 (68).

38   Brendan Byrne, 'The Faith of the Beloved Disciple and the Community in John 20', *JSNT* 23 (1985), pp. 83–97 (90).

39   Quast, *Peter*, p. 120.

as two closings, he makes a compelling case that chapter 21 was authored by the same hand as chapters 1–20. He is willing to consider the possibility it could have been a later addition, but if so it was added so early as to leave no manuscript evidence to the Gospel ever being published and circulated without it.[40] It is this reality of the history of the text that makes it a part of the reading experience of every reader who does not choose to alter the form of the text as it has been received.

In the beginning of chapter 21 seven disciples are listed; two anonymous 'other disciples' conclude the list. The reader is led by the narrative to conclude that the disciple whom Jesus loved is one of the four unnamed disciples in this list. He is either one of the sons of Zebedee, mentioned only here in the Fourth Gospel, or one of the two 'other disciples'. Not until v. 7 is the reader informed that the disciple whom Jesus loved is among this group fishing. He again is in the company of Peter, this time informing Peter that the one whose spoken word has just provided an overwhelming catch is the one whose empty tomb they have so recently visited. 'It is the Lord!' The significance of the disciple's identification of Jesus is not specified. The obvious impact on the reader is that it is this disciple whom Jesus loved who is best able to recognize Jesus when he is encountered. Furthermore, it is a confirmation of the declaration already encountered in 19.35 and soon to be restated in 21.24. The witness of this disciple is trustworthy and reliable. A person can base his/her life's response on it, as Peter does here, plunging into the sea to rush into the presence of his Lord.

The latter part of this chapter contains the final appearance of the disciple whom Jesus loved, as Peter sees him 'following' (ἀκολυθοῦντα, 21.20), the Johannine 'term par excellence for the dedication of discipleship'.[41] Immediately preceding the narrative appearance of the disciple whom Jesus loved, Jesus concluded his comments to Peter with the command, 'Follow me' (ἀκολύθει μοι, 20.19). After Jesus rebukes Peter's inappropriate concern for the consequences of someone else's discipleship, the reader is confronted with the final words Jesus speaks in this Gospel, the repetition of this command to Peter, 'Follow me!' (σύ μοι ἀκολύθει, 21.22). Interpolated between the two admonitions to Peter emphasizing the content of discipleship, the disciple whom Jesus loved is portrayed doing exactly that, with a reminder of both his designation as one loved by Jesus and the intimacy of his position toward Jesus, 'who had lain upon his breast' (21.20).[42] The closing verses of this Gospel testify to the role of the disciple as the witness *par excellence* to Jesus.

40   Stanley E. Porter, 'The Ending of John's Gospel', in William H. Brackney and Craig A. Evans (eds), *From Biblical Criticism to Biblical Faith: Essays in Honor of Lee Martin McDonald* (Macon, GA: Mercer University Press, 2007), pp. 55–73.

41   Brown, *John*, Vol. 1, p. 78.

42   Carson, *John*, p. 681.

V. The Historicity of an Ideal Disciple

The important question of the historicity of this figure has garnered much attention. Is he only a representative figure comparable to 'Christian' in Bunyan's *Pilgrim's Progress*? Is he an historical follower of Jesus who is the eyewitness guarantor of the veracity of the narrative, if not the author himself? Are the two functions mutually exclusive? Ismo Dunderberg has recently argued against his historicity, claiming that the historical context in which this disciple appears is a polemic against the brothers of Jesus and possible other 'dynastic' claims, and that this 'gave rise to the invention of the Beloved Disciple . . . and the designation "the disciple whom Jesus loved"'.[43] However, the majority of scholars do not reject his reality as an actual person, but focus on his function within the narrative.

In Raymond Collins' interpretation of the disciple whom Jesus loved as a representative figure, he is 'the epitome of discipleship; he is the disciple par excellence'.[44] Collins denies that this function undermines his reality as an historical person, declaring that he 'is not a figment of the imagination of the evangelist who wrote the Fourth Gospel. He is a real individual.'[45] Bauckham goes further than this, arguing from the narrative declaration of 21.24-25 that the disciple whom Jesus loved is the narratively identified author of the Fourth Gospel.[46] But for him, this precludes his function as an ideal disciple. 'If this means that he represents, as a model for others, the ideal of discipleship, it is certainly misleading. The beloved disciple may sometimes function in this way, just as other disciples . . . but such a function cannot adequately account for most of what is said about him.'[47] Bauckham believes that in chapter 21 Peter is portrayed as an ideal model of discipleship, being appointed Jesus' chief undershepherd.[48] Cornelis Bennema concurs with this assessment, maintaining that while the disciple whom Jesus loved is the ideal eyewitness, he is not the ideal disciple.[49] What is overlooked in this evaluation of this disciple as the model of discipleship is the narratively revealed content of that discipleship. It is not to become a shepherd of God's flock, a biblical role limited to only a few. It is instead to believe and to bear witness to the life-changing nature of that belief.

---

43   Ismo Dunderberg, 'The Beloved Disciple in John: Ideal Figure in an Early Christian Controversy', in Ismo Dunderberg and Christopher Tuckett (eds), *Fair Play: Diversity and Conflicts in Early Christianity – Essays in Honor of Heikki Räisänen* (NovTSup, 132; Leiden/Boston/Köln: Brill, 2002), pp. 243–69 (269).

44   Raymond Collins, 'From John to the Beloved Disciple: An Essay on Johannine Characters', *Int* 49 (1995), pp. 359–69 (367).

45   Raymond Collins, 'Representative Figures in the Fourth Gospel', *DRev* 94 (1976), pp. 26–46, 118–32 (131).

46   Bauckham, 'Fourth Gospel', pp. 126–31.

47   Richard Bauckham, *The Testimony of the Beloved Disciple* (Grand Rapids: Baker Academic, 2007), p. 82.

48   Bauckham, *Testimony*, p. 86.

49   Cornelis Bennema, *Encountering Jesus: Character Studies in the Gospel of John* (Milton Keynes: Paternoster, 2009), p. 174.

VI. '... *In Order That You Might Believe* ...'

As has already been noted, generating belief is the stated purpose of this narrative. Besides the explicit purpose statement of 20.31, the theme of belief stands out throughout the narrative. Well before the initial portrayal of the coming to belief of the disciple whom Jesus loved in chapter 20, the narrative has presented the primacy of belief for discipleship. It is God's stated purpose in sending his Son 3.16-18, 5.24; it is the identified response of the Samaritan villagers in 4.39-41; it is what is required from those with whom Jesus disputes in 5.46 and 8.46; it is the response requested of the formerly blind man in 9.35-38. After Martha in chapter 11 seemingly backs away from her initial faith declaration, 'Even now I know that whatever you ask of God, God will give you', Jesus simply yet powerfully states, 'Your brother will rise again', to which she hesitantly responds, 'I know he will rise again in the resurrection on the last day.' To this weak response Jesus proclaims, 'I am the resurrection and the life; he who *believes* in me will live even if he dies, and everyone who lives and *believes* in me will never die.' Then he adds the all-important query, 'Do you *believe* this?' (11.22-26).

This is not to say that belief is a simple concept in the Fourth Gospel. In Jesus' encounter with the royal official (βασιλικός), the narrative states that after Jesus declared that his son lived, the man believed (ἐπίστευσεν) Jesus' word and went as he was told (4.50). In the midst of his obedience, he meets his servants. They bring the news of the boy's healing and confirmation of Jesus' word. In response to the report, it is stated again in v. 53 that the man 'believed' (ἐπίστευσεν). Are we to understand ἐπίστευσεν in v. 50 somehow differently than in v. 53? Various answers have been given and the textual ambiguity is such as to allow them. However this parallel/progression of belief is understood, it is explicitly narrated that after the second occurrence his belief 'spreads outward and his entire household is able to share it'.[50]

The play on words that ends chapter 2 raises the issue that in this narrative not all belief is trustworthy. There it is stated that 'many believed (ἐπίστευσεν) in his name when they saw the signs which he did; but Jesus did not trust (οὐκ ἐπίστευσεν) himself to them' (2.23-24). In a recent article Debbie Hunn has pointed out that it is not just that they believed, but they believed in his name. There are four other occurrences in the New Testament where the verb πιστεύω is linked with εἰς τὸ ὄνομα, 'in the name' of Jesus. Two of these are in this Gospel – 1.12 and 3.18 – neither of which is descriptive of the belief of narrative characters; instead they are the narrator's voice urging the readers to embrace his call to believe. The others occur in 1 John 3.23 and 5.13 and again are unambiguously urging the readers to belief in his name.[51]

---

50   A. G. Van Aarde, 'Narrative Criticism Applied to John 4:43-54', in P. Hartin and J. Petzer (eds), *Text & Interpretation: New Approaches in the Criticism of the New Testament* (NTTS, 15; Leiden: Brill, 1991), pp. 101–28 (124–6).

51   Debbie Hunn, 'The Believers Jesus Doubted: John 2:23-25', *TrinJ* 25 (2004), pp. 15–25 (17).

This casts a shadow on the traditional understanding of the inadequacy of the belief expressed by these inhabitants of Jerusalem in 2.23. Without an easy explanation for Jesus' mistrust, by the contrasting uses of πιστεύω the narrative alerts readers to the elusive nature of what constitutes sufficient, adequate belief. In Brodie's words 'πιστεύω is the heartbeat of the gospel, and the negating of that verb – for the first time in the gospel, and by Jesus! – means that in some sense the heart has missed a beat.'[52]

Even more troublesome for a simplistic understanding of belief in this Gospel are the events narrated in Jesus' disputation with 'the Jews' in chapter 8 as the exchange grows increasingly heated. They accuse him of false testimony (v. 13); he accuses them of wanting to kill him (v. 40) and being children of the devil (v. 44). They in turn accuse him of being a Samaritan and demon possessed (v. 48) and in the end they pick up stones to kill him (v. 59). What makes this troublesome for the concept of belief in this Gospel is that at the beginning of this dialogue they are identified as 'Jews who had believed (πεπιστευκότας) him' (v. 31).

Belief is portrayed as a process, not a singular event, and as being more than it might at first appear. As Kelli O'Brien writes, it 'goes beyond intellectual content to something more fundamental: acceptance of Jesus and willingness to remain with him despite difficulties of all kinds, including uncertainty about precisely what it is that Jesus is revealing'.[53] Yet the complexity of belief does not alter the fact that eliciting belief is the stated purpose of the Fourth Gospel narrative: 'These things are written in order that you might believe (ἵνα πιστεύ[σ]ητε) that Jesus is the Christ the Son of God, and that believing (ἵνα πιστεύοντες) you might have life in his name' (20.31).

Furthermore, belief is the narrated response of the disciple whom Jesus loved. Recognizing his presence from the very beginning of this narrative, in 1.35 he believes John's witness and begins following Jesus. He is numbered among the disciples who believed in response to Jesus' first sign at the wedding in Cana (2.11). At the empty tomb his is the first recorded belief after Jesus' resurrection (20.8). Again, the belief narrated here is enigmatic and complex, qualified as it is by the statement in v. 9 that 'as yet they did not understand the scripture, that he must rise again from the dead'. Charlesworth provides a detailed examination of 20.8 that focuses on exactly what the narrative does and does not say. He rightly notes that the narrative never states the content of what the disciple came to believe. He points out that morphologically, the most common (36 occurrences) pattern for this verb in the Fourth Gospel is πιστεύειν εἰς, to believe in something. The evangelist could easily have written that the disciple whom Jesus loved believed in Jesus' resurrection. 'He chose not to do so.'[54] Charlesworth suggests that rather than read into the text a preconceived idea of this disciple's experience, it

---

52   Brodie, *John*, p. 192.

53   Kelli S. O'Brien, 'Written That You May Believe: John 20 and Narrative Rhetoric', *CBQ* 67 (2005), pp. 284–302 (291); cf. Susan E. Hylen, *Imperfect Believers: Ambiguous Characters in the Gospel of John* (Louisville: Westminster John Knox, 2009), p. 158.

54   Charlesworth, *Beloved Disciple*, p. 93.

is more faithful to the narrative to understand ἐπίστευσεν as an inceptive aorist, 'implying that the Beloved Disciple, as he went into the empty tomb and saw the clothes and face-cloth, began to develop a belief that culminated in a full awareness that Jesus had been raised'.[55]

Life-giving belief generated within readers is the reason for which this narrative has been written. But even this declaration is placed in immediate juxtaposition to a final dialogue of Jesus revealing the complexity of life-giving belief: Jesus' dialogue with Thomas. Thomas's confession is limited to a verbal statement of belief. His confession exemplifies a belief that requires first-hand observation. Thomas's confession is a Christological apex in this narrative, explicitly identifying Jesus as both Lord and God (ὁ κυριός μου καὶ ὁ θεός μου). The inadequacy is not with the confession itself but with the prerequisite of 'seeing' before he could believe. Jesus' response to Thomas's confession suggests he is unimpressed with its prerequisite. Jesus never declares Thomas or his confession blessed; it is those textually absent ones who are not eyewitnesses (i.e. potentially all future readers?) but yet believe whose confessions prompt Jesus to approvingly designate them as blessed (μακάριοι). As Collins states, 'the reader of the Fourth Gospel knows that he has encountered in Thomas a leading disciple who epitomizes both the bravado and the ignorance of the disciples'.[56]

VII. 'These Things Have Been Written ...'

An equally important concept in this Gospel is that of witness. The narrative begins with the Baptist's witness to Jesus. First his role as witness is declared in the Prologue (1.6-8), then spoken of in his dialogue with the ones sent to him by the Pharisees (1.19-34), and it bears fruit in the two of his disciples who hear him testify 'Behold the Lamb of God' (1.36) and immediately become the first to 'follow' (ἀκολυθέω) Jesus. The attention given to John's portrayal as witness to Jesus indicates the essential nature of witness in this narrative for comprehending the origin and identity of Jesus,[57] and installs 'witness' as an element of appropriate response to Jesus' identity.

The theme of witness is constant through the Fourth Gospel narrative. The corroborative testimony of the three primary witnesses to the identity of Jesus in the Gospel – John (chs 1–3), the Holy Spirit (chs 14 and 16), and the Father (chs 5–8, 10, 12, 15, 17) – appears together in 1.29-34.[58] Just as John chronologically preceded Jesus, his witness precedes that of the other

---

55   Charlesworth, *Beloved Disciple*, p. 95.

56   Collins, 'Representative Figures', p. 125.

57   Francis X. D'Sa, 'The Language of God and the God of Language: The Relation between God, Human Beings, the World and Language in Saint John', in Robert P. Scharlemann and Gilbert E. M. Ogutu (eds), *God in Language* (New York: Paragon House, 1987), pp. 35–59 (40).

58   J. Daryl Charles, '"Will the Court Please Call in the Prime Witness?" John 1:29-34 and the "Witness"-Motif', *TrinJ* 10 (1989), pp. 71–83 (71).

two. The primacy of witness for understanding Jesus' identity and responding appropriately to him is confirmed. In chapter 5 Jesus declares that his witness is not a self-witness. There is the witness of John, the witness of his works, the witness of his Father, and the witness of scripture (5.33-47). Fully realized discipleship is to believe and to witness.[59]

It has been argued elsewhere that the paradigmatic understanding of discipleship established by the narrative strategy of anonymity in the Fourth Gospel is that of belief that does not necessitate seeing or signs (σημεια), and results in bearing witness concerning Jesus and the efficacy of his words.[60] But in the narrative, the disciple whom Jesus loved remains relatively quiet, and when he speaks it is seemingly innocuous. In 13.25, in response to Peter's beckoning, he asks Jesus who the betrayer is. In his possible appearance in chapter 18 his speaking is not narrated but his insider status gains Peter access to the high priest's courtyard, which for Peter becomes his place of discipleship failure through denial. At the cross he responds in obedience to Jesus' command to become a son to Jesus' mother, but he bears no witness. Inside the empty tomb he is narratively portrayed coming to belief, then anti-climatically he goes home, the reader having been informed he did not understand the scripture.

His final appearance in the conclusion of this narrative finally reveals the disciple whom Jesus loved bearing witness to Jesus. He again is in the company of Peter, this time informing Peter, 'It is the Lord!' The significance of the disciple's identification of Jesus is not made explicit. However, it is in stark contrast to Peter's jarringly mundane announcement, 'I am going fishing' (21.3). Peter's first post-resurrection utterance concerns fishing, while the disciple whom Jesus loved speaks recognition of Jesus, and bears witness of his presence to others: 'It is the Lord!' (21.7).

It is this disciple whom Jesus loved who is shown as best able to recognize Jesus when he is encountered. Furthermore, it is a confirmation of the declaration already encountered in 19.35 and soon to be restated in 21.24. The witness of this disciple is trustworthy and reliable. Despite the mostly silent portrayal of the disciple singled out as a special recipient of Jesus' love, the reader is informed in the final verses that his testimony is heard throughout the text from the Prologue onward (21.24). The witness of the disciple whom Jesus loved stands as the backdrop to, basis for, and content of the entire narrative portrayal of Jesus in the Fourth Gospel. The reader is given *his* testimony in each episode of Jesus' encounter with various characters, in every dialogue and discourse. The disciple's identification of Jesus for Peter, and presumably for the other disciples in 21.7, can be seen to narratively initiate his witnessing function.[61] But it is not in the role of mediator between Jesus and Peter, or the other disciples, that the disciple whom Jesus loved has his primary witness. 'Rather he is represented as the disciple who was so related to Jesus and the

---

59   O'Brien, 'Written That You May Believe', p. 297.

60   Beck, *Discipleship Paradigm*, p. 137.

61   Sjef van Tilborg, *Imaginative Love in John* (BIS, 2; Leiden: Brill, 1993), p. 104.

events of Jesus' story that he can bear witness *to the readers/hearers of the Gospel.*'[62]

VIII. '. . . And We Know His Witness is True'

Exactly what the statement of 21.24 reveals about authorship is an area of scholarly disagreement. Culpepper states that 'the author attributed a prior and formative role to the Beloved Disciple', while Bauckham claims '21.24 designates this disciple whom Jesus loved as the *author* of the Gospel', not just the guarantor of the tradition.[63] Furthermore the text claims that the veracity of his witness is without question; it is truth (ἀληθής, 21.24). Tovey observes the truth claims of this Gospel witness, and notes that the narrative deliberately portrays the disciple whom Jesus loved in a manner which uniquely qualifies him as the reliable guarantor of the truth of his testimony which is the Fourth Gospel narrative.[64] These include his identification as the one 'whom Jesus loved', his identity as a μαθητής, and his connection with Peter. James Resseguie also acknowledges the Fourth Gospel's presentation of the disciple whom Jesus loved as the reliable and truthful witness whose testimony constitutes this narrative. 'Several traits blend together to portray the beloved disciple as the one who has the ideal point of view of the gospel; his intimacy with Jesus; his fidelity; his ability to see what others apparently do not perceive.'[65]

Another narrative strategy to accomplish the author's purpose to elicit faith in his readers through their acceptance of the truthfulness of his witness is the adoption of what Howard Jackson asserts is a documented ancient formulaic statement of veracity in 21.24. On the function of this third-person truth claim Jackson asserts, 'The author wants his narrative accepted as a factual and accurate presentation of events in which he himself participated or to which he himself was an eyewitness; his anti-docetic programme demands that it be accepted as such, for otherwise his testimony to the earthly, fleshly Jesus is not credible.'[66]

Andrew Lincoln recognizes that 'historicity clearly impinges on the truth claims of the Fourth Gospel'.[67] Yet he issues a caution based on an investigation

---

62   Richard Bauckham, 'The Beloved Disciple as Ideal Author', *JSNT* 49 (1993), pp. 21–44 (39).

63   Culpepper, *John*, p. 71; Bauckham, 'Ideal Author', p. 29; cf. Tovey, *Narrative Art*, p. 138.

64   Tovey, *Narrative Art*, p. 129.

65   James L. Resseguie, *The Strange Gospel: Narrative Design and Point of View in John* (BIS, 56; Leiden: Brill, 2001), p. 162.

66   Howard M. Jackson, 'Ancient Self-Referential Conventions and Their Implications for the Authorship and Integrity of the Gospel of John', *JTS* 50 (1999), pp. 1–34 (29).

67   Andrew T. Lincoln, '"We Know That His Testimony Is True": Johannnine Truth Claims and Historicity', in Paul N. Anderson, Felix Just and Tom Thatcher (eds), *John, Jesus, and History – Volume 1: Critical Appraisals of Critical Views* (SBLSymS, 44; Atlanta: Society of Biblical Literature, 2007), pp. 179–97 (179).

of the genres of ancient historiography and particularly ancient biography: 'To assume that Johannine truth claims refer to historicity in terms of detailed historical accuracy is simply to make a category mistake.'[68] He concludes that the purposes of these truth claims are found in what God is accomplishing in the person of the Messiah. For Lincoln, a proper understanding of these statements will preclude the use of questions of detailed factual accuracy to 'provide the determinative truth by which they judge this Gospel'.[69]

An examination of the use and background of the ἀλήθεια word group in the Fourth Gospel has been offered by Dennis Lindsay. He contends that this concept in the Fourth Gospel is best understood as synonymous with the Hebrew אמת and functions as the opposite of what is false.[70] The narrative indicates that the veracity claims of the disciple's witness in chapter 21 are essential to its narrative success in fulfilling its stated purpose. As noted by Merenlahti and Hakola, 'In the case of a non-fictional narrative, the authors commit themselves strictly to the story by guaranteeing its veracity. The authors assume that the reader takes the story seriously and believes it.'[71] Its purpose cannot be achieved if readers 'doubt the author's basic truth claims'.[72]

IX. Conclusion

This revisiting of the characterization of the disciple whom Jesus loved has confirmed that to allow the text to be the text and speak its own witness is to preserve the anonymity of the specially designated disciple whom Jesus loved, so that the identity of the One whose intimacy he shares can be the focus of his narrative witness. He writes with a singleness of purpose: that his witness might lead to life-giving belief in the name of the One who was, and is God, and dwelt among us. A necessary component of that witness is its veracity, as indicated by the testimony of 19.35 and 21.24, and the narrative frequency and prominence given to the word group ἀλήθεια in this Gospel.

His anonymity further serves to assist readers' identification in both envisioning themselves as Jesus' disciples, coming to believe in Jesus, and then experiencing the reality of becoming a disciple whom Jesus loved, by emulating the discipleship he portrays in this narrative. The content of this discipleship includes belief and truthful witness to the content of that belief

---

68   Lincoln, 'We Know', p. 184. For a vigorous defence of the historicity and detailed veracity of each episode of this narrative see Craig L. Blomberg, *The Historical Reliability of John's Gospel: Issues and Commentary* (Downers Grove, IL: InterVarsity, 2001).

69   Lincoln, 'We Know', p. 197.

70   See Dennis R. Lindsay, '"What is Truth?" ᾿Αλήθεια in the Gospel of John', *ResQ* 35 (1993), pp. 129–45.

71   Petri Merenlahti and Raimo Hakola, 'Reconceiving Narrative Criticism', in David Rhoads and Karen Syreeni, *Characterization in the Gospels: Reconceiving Narrative Criticism* (JSNTSup, 184; Sheffield: Sheffield Academic Press, 1999), pp. 13–48 (35).

72   Merenlahti and Hakola, 'Reconceiving', p. 38.

embodied in the identity of the One who was in the beginning with God, and who was himself God, but who became flesh and dwelt among us (1.14).

A careful reading of the narrative portrayal of the disciple whom Jesus loved will not reveal his name to the reader. Nor will it inform the reader of background details concerning his life and circumstances. Instead, as Attridge summarizes, 'The Beloved Disciple's anonymity, *qua* witness, *qua* author of this story, performs primarily a *literary* role, re-engaging the reader, drawing her back time and again to a potential encounter with the one Witness sent by the Father.'[73]

73   Attridge, 'Restless Quest', p. 80.

Chapter 14

THE CHARACTER OF PILATE IN THE GOSPEL OF JOHN

Cornelis Bennema

I. Introduction

Pontius Pilate was Rome's representative in Judaea from 26 until 36/37 CE. Although Pilate is given no title in the Gospel of John, other sources designate him as 'procurator' (a financial officer of a province; Josephus, *Jewish War* 2.169; Philo, *Embassy to Gaius* 1.299), 'prefect' (a military commander; according to an inscription at Caesarea, discovered in 1961) and 'governor' (a generic title for a leader; Matt. 27.2; Lk. 3.1; Josephus, *Antiquities* 18.55). As Rome's appointed agent in Judaea, Pilate was in charge of the Roman auxiliary troops, stationed in Caesarea (Galilee) with a detachment (one cohort) in Jerusalem. Although his headquarters were in Caesarea, he sometimes stayed in Jerusalem (e.g. during the Passover, to ensure order). Pilate had the final say on cases of capital punishment, and could reverse death sentences that the Sanhedrin submitted to him for ratification. Pilate's verdict was legally binding and he was accountable only to the emperor.

My method of character analysis for Pilate in John's Gospel consists of three aspects.[1] First, I study character in text and context, using information in the Johannine narrative and other sources. Pilate has been variously characterized: from being weak, indecisive and accommodating to being tough, cruel and prone to flaunting his authority. This may be due to the seemingly disparate representations of Pilate in the Gospels (pathetic or sympathetic) and in Philo and Josephus (strong and able).[2] We must examine whether the Johannine Pilate is indeed weak, indecisive and accommodating or more in keeping with the Pilate portrayed in Philo and Josephus. Besides considering the works of

---

1   For a detailed explanation, see my essay 'A Comprehensive Approach to Understanding Character in the Gospel of John' in chapter three of this volume. For an earlier version of my theory of character, see Cornelis Bennema, 'A Theory of Character in the Fourth Gospel with Reference to Ancient and Modern Literature', *BibInt* 17 (2009), pp. 375–421.

2   Brian Charles McGing, 'Pontius Pilate and the Sources', *CBQ* 53 (1991), pp. 416–38 (416–17); Helen K. Bond, *Pontius Pilate in History and Interpretation* (SNTSMS 100; Cambridge, UK: Cambridge University Press, 1998), pp. 174–5; Colleen M. Conway, 'Speaking through Ambiguity: Minor Characters in the Fourth Gospel', *BibInt* 10 (2002), p. 333; Jerome H. Neyrey, *The Gospel of John* (NCBC; Cambridge, UK: Cambridge University Press, 2007), p. 305.

Josephus and Philo, we should also look at the Synoptic portrayal of Pilate, especially since some have made a good case that the Johannine author knew Mark's Gospel.[3] This does not mean that I will look at the Johannine Pilate through a Markan lens. Instead, I assume that the Johannine author knew Mark's characterization of Pilate, and either confirms or augments his portrayal. This invites a comparison of how the various sources portray Pilate. Hence, I start by examining the Johannine text to reconstruct Pilate in section II; then, in section IV, I investigate the characterizations of Pilate in the other sources and compare these with our portrayal of the Johannine Pilate.

The second aspect of my method to reconstruct Pilate's character is an analysis and classification of the Johannine Pilate along three continua (complexity, development, inner life). This will be dealt with in section III, along with plotting of the resulting character on a continuum of degree of characterization (from agent to type to personality to individuality).[4] The final aspect of my method, in section V, includes the evaluation of the Johannine Pilate in terms of his response to Jesus, in relation to the author's point of view, purpose and dualistic worldview. I will also determine Pilate's role in the plot. After I arrive at a comprehensive understanding of the Johannine Pilate, I shall seek to determine his representative value for today.

II. Pilate's Interactions with Jesus and 'the Jews'

The Johannine Pilate occurs only in the passion narratives (Jn 18–19), where he interacts with Jesus and 'the Jews' who bring Jesus to trial. Regarding Jesus' trial in 18.28–19.16a, the author has organized the exchanges between Pilate and 'the Jews', and between Pilate and Jesus such that they alternate with each other. Structurally, this episode consists of seven rounds, with Pilate moving in and out of the palace with each round.[5] In rounds one, three, five and seven, Pilate comes *out of* the palace to interact with 'the Jews' (18.29; 18.38b; 19.4; 19.13); in rounds two, four and six, he goes *into* the palace to interact with Jesus (18.33; 19.1; 19.9).[6] I shall follow this structure to analyse

---

3   Cf. Richard Bauckham, 'John for Readers of Mark', in idem, *The Gospels for All Christians: Rethinking the Gospel Audiences* (Grand Rapids: Eerdmans, 1998), pp. 147–71; Paul N. Anderson, *The Riddles of the Fourth Gospel: An Introduction to John* (Minneapolis: Fortress, 2011), pp. 126–9.

4   Regarding classifying ancient characters, the categories 'personality' and 'individuality' refer to a 'collectivist identity' or 'group-oriented personality', where the person's identity is *embedded* in a larger group or community, rather than to a modern autonomous individual (cf. Bruce J. Malina, *The New Testament World: Insights from Cultural Anthropology* [Louisville: Westminster John Knox, 3rd edn, 2001], pp. 60–7).

5   The praetorium in 18.28 may well have been Herod's palace, adjacent to the temple, which Pilate used when he was in Jerusalem.

6   Many scholars have observed this structure. For an alternative structure, see Charles Homer Giblin, 'John's Narration of the Hearing before Pilate (John 18,28–19,16a)', *Bib* 67 (1986), pp. 221–39 (221–4).

Pilate, and this analysis will prepare for the reconstruction of Pilate's character in section III.

Round One (18.28-32)

While presenting Jesus to Pilate, 'the Jews' do not enter the palace since that would render them ritually unclean and disqualify them from participating in the Passover meal (18.28). Ironically, their actions concerning Jesus make them spiritually 'unclean' and prevent them from partaking in the real Passover meal on the cross (cf. 1.29; 6.51-55). When Pilate comes out to inquire about the charges (18.29), his question is surprising since he must have known why 'the Jews' brought Jesus to him.[7] The Roman cohort could only have been present at Jesus' arrest (18.3) with Pilate's consent, implying that 'the Jews' had contacted Pilate earlier and probably informed him about their scheme to kill Jesus (cf. 11.47-53).[8] The reply of 'the Jews' that Jesus is an evildoer is not a legal charge and reveals some of their perplexity about Pilate's question (18.30). Pilate does not, however, humour 'the Jews' and, knowing that they want Jesus' death, he taunts them, flaunting his authority (18.31).[9]

Round Two (18.33-38a)

Entering the palace, Pilate asks Jesus whether he is the king of the Jews (18.33). Pilate's question reveals that he has had contact with 'the Jews' prior to Jesus' arrest, when they had probably told him that Jesus claimed to be a king – a political charge of insurrection against Rome (cf. 19.12). This explains Jesus' counter-question in 18.34, but Pilate is quick to distance himself from 'the Jews' (18.35). Pilate may have assisted 'the Jews' in arresting Jesus – any potential insurrection needed to be investigated – but he does not side with them and probably wants to examine the case for himself.[10] Going back to Pilate's earlier question about kingship, Jesus asserts that his kingdom is not from this world (18.36). This is a political statement because Jesus acknowledges that he has a kingdom – and hence is a king – and although his kingdom is 'from above' it exists and operates *in* this world. Besides, it is impossible to be loyal to both Jesus and his kingdom, and to the Roman emperor and his empire.[11] Although,

---

7   It is unclear whether Pilate's coming out indicates that he is forced from the beginning to comply with the demands of 'the Jews' (R. Alan Culpepper, *Anatomy of the Fourth Gospel: A Study in Literary Design* [Philadelphia: Fortress, 1983], p. 142) or whether he shows tact and courtesy (Bond, *Pilate*, p. 175).

8   Cf. Bond, *Pilate*, p. 167.

9   Some claim that John is historically inaccurate in 18.31b since there is not enough evidence that the Sanhedrin had the authority to hand down death sentences in case of offences against Jewish religious law prior to 70 CE (e.g. Tibor Horvath, 'Why Was Jesus Brought to Pilate?', *NovT* 11 [1969], pp. 174–84 [176–9]).

10   *Contra* Warren Carter who contends that Pilate had allied himself with 'the Jews' to remove Jesus (*Pontius Pilate: Portraits of a Roman Governor* [Collegeville, MN: Liturgical, 2003], pp. 141–2).

11   Cf. Cornelis Bennema, 'The Sword of the Messiah and the Concept of Liberation in the Fourth Gospel', *Bib* 86 (2005), pp. 35–58 (54–7).

in Greek, Pilate's question in 18.37 expects the answer 'yes', he has probably concluded that Jesus' kingdom is not a threat to Rome. Hence, his statement seems condescending – 'You are a king then!'[12] Perhaps knowing that Pilate is searching for truth, Jesus extends an implicit invitation to discover truth – saving truth about the divine reality present in Jesus' teaching.[13] Pilate's 'What is truth?' is not an earnest question (for he leaves immediately) but a dismissive remark. This indicates that he does not take Jesus seriously and is probably irritated with Jesus' responses and his own lack of success in cracking the case. Not understanding Jesus, Pilate implicitly rejects him and his invitation.

Round Three (18.38b-40)

Coming out of the palace, Pilate informs 'the Jews' that the charges against Jesus are baseless (18.38b). Although Pilate appears honest, he is also taunting 'the Jews'. This becomes more evident in 18.39 where Pilate, by referring to Jesus as 'the king of the Jews', is most likely mocking 'the Jews' about their nationalistic hopes. He does not seriously seek Jesus' release. If he had seriously considered Jesus a king, he would never have offered to release him.[14] Pilate has known since before Jesus' arrest that 'the Jews' wanted Jesus' death (cf. 18.31) – and he uses this knowledge to taunt 'the Jews' and flaunt his authority. In desperation and frustration, 'the Jews' shout out not to release Jesus (18.40).

Round Four (19.1-3)

Pilate, though not convinced that Jesus poses a threat to Rome, resorts to cruel and calculated measures to extract truth from Jesus (19.1). Jennifer Glancy makes a good case for understanding the scourging as an act of judicial rather than punitive torture, a means of interrogation to extract truth.[15] Pilate may

---

12   Cf. Bart D. Ehrman, 'Jesus' Trial before Pilate: John 18.28–19.16', *BTB* 13 (1983), pp. 124–31 (128); Thomas W. Gillespie, 'The Trial of Politics and Religion: John 18.28–19.16', *Ex Auditu* 2 (1986), pp. 69–73 (71).

13   For the concept of saving truth, see Cornelis Bennema, *The Power of Saving Wisdom: An Investigation of Spirit and Wisdom in Relation to the Soteriology of the Fourth Gospel* (WUNT, II/148; Tübingen: Mohr Siebeck, 2002), pp. 121–2; idem, 'Christ, the Spirit and the Knowledge of God: A Study in Johannine Epistemology', in Mary Healy and Robin Parry (eds), *The Bible and Epistemology: Biblical Soundings on the Knowledge of God* (Milton Keynes: Paternoster, 2007), p. 114.

14   Cf. Bond, *Pilate*, pp. 181–2.

15   Jennifer A. Glancy, 'Torture: Flesh, Truth, and the Fourth Gospel', *BibInt* 13 (2005), pp. 107–36. Most scholars perceive the scourging to be punitive torture, aimed to inflict pain as punishment (e.g. Culpepper, *Anatomy*, p. 142; David K. Rensberger, *Overcoming the World: Politics and Community in the Gospel of John* [London: SPCK, 1988], p. 93; Neyrey, *Gospel of John*, p. 300; cf. the scholars mentioned by Glancy, 'Torture', pp. 121–2, n. 48), but this is unlikely in the *middle* of an interrogation. Convinced that the scourging is punitive and hence should come after the trial is over, Barnabas Lindars concludes that John is unhistorical and has deliberately displaced this scene (*The Gospel of John* [NCB; London: Oliphants, 1972], pp. 553–4, 563–4).

not know the truth (cf. 18.38a), but he thinks he can get it out of Jesus: using a *mastix*, a whip studded with lumps of bone or metal, Pilate has Jesus tortured in order to extract a confession.[16]

Round Five (19.4-7)

Pilate is now convinced that there is no real case and that Jesus is innocent (19.4; cf. 18.38), but he also knows that 'the Jews' are determined to have Jesus killed.[17] For those who view the scourging as a punishment, the phrase 'to let you know that I find no case against him' is problematic. However, Pilate's statement makes perfect sense when the flogging is seen as judicial torture to extract truth. Pilate demonstrates to 'the Jews' that despite having Jesus whipped he gets no admission of guilt, and hence Jesus' flogged body testifies to guiltlessness.[18] With his exclamation – 'See the man!' – Pilate scoffs at 'the Jews' about this pathetic figure whom he considers innocent and harmless (19.5).[19] Aggravated, 'the Jews' demand Jesus' crucifixion but Pilate continues to taunt them (19.6). For the first time, 'the Jews' level a (religious) charge: Jesus has blasphemed by equating himself with God (19.7; cf. 5.18; 10.33) – a capital offence according to the Mosaic law (Lev. 24.16).[20]

Round Six (19.8-11)

Pilate becomes rather afraid, perhaps driven by a superstitious belief about divine matters, and wants to know Jesus' origin (19.8-9).[21] Annoyed by Jesus' silence, Pilate tries to assert his authority and fails; instead, Jesus points out that Pilate's authority is God-given (literally, 'given from above') (19.10-11).[22] Jesus' remark that the one who handed him over to Pilate (either Judas

---

16　　Glancy, 'Torture', pp. 121–2.

17　　Neyrey comments that instead of the verdict and sentence, Jesus' trial goes through a completely new cycle in 19.5-16 (*Gospel of John*, p. 300).

18　　Glancy, 'Torture', p. 125.

19　　The author may be alluding to Jesus' humanity or to his title 'Son of Man' (cf. Bond, *Pilate*, pp. 185–6). Dieter Böhler understands the phrase as a royal proclamation, echoing 1 Sam. 9.17 ('"Ecce Homo!" (Joh 19,5) ein Zitat aus dem Alten Testament', *BZ* 39 [1995], pp. 104–8).

20　　David W. Wead argues that 'the Jews' also accuse Jesus of being a false prophet who led people away from the Mosaic law, another offence warranting the death penalty (Deut. 13.1-5) ('We Have a Law', *NovT* 11 [1969], pp. 185–9).

21　　Cf. Rudolf Bultmann, *The Gospel of John* (trans. George R. Beasley-Murray; Philadelphia: Westminster, 1971), p. 661; Mark W. G. Stibbe, *John as Storyteller: Narrative Criticism and the Fourth Gospel* (SNTSMS, 73; Cambridge, UK: Cambridge University Press, 1992), p. 108; Giblin, 'Narration', p. 231; Bond, *Pilate*, p. 187. 'Rather afraid' makes more sense than 'even more afraid' (NIV) or 'more afraid than ever' (NRSV) since Pilate has not shown fear previously. Francis J. Moloney observes that Pilate asks 'the fundamental question of Johannine Christology: "Where are you from?"' (*The Gospel of John* [SP, 4; Collegeville, MN: Liturgical, 1998], p. 495).

22　　Jesus probably refers to the power God has given Pilate for this particular moment (Bultmann, *Gospel*, p. 662; Raymond E. Brown, *The Gospel According to John* [AB, 29A; New York: Doubleday, 1970], pp. 892–3) rather than to a possible God-given authority of the state (cf. Rom. 13.1). For a critique of this latter concept, see John Howard Yoder, *The Politics of Jesus*

or Caiaphas/'the Jews') is guilty of a greater sin does not mean Pilate himself is guiltless – he rejects Jesus, does not use his God-given authority to do justice, and will hand Jesus over to 'the Jews' (19.16a).[23]

Round Seven (19.12-16a)

A mixture of belief in Jesus' innocence, superstitious fear and Jesus' words in 19.11 drives Pilate to make his first real attempt to release Jesus. It comes too late however, for 'the Jews' play their trump card. They skilfully manipulate Pilate by modifying their allegation from a religious (19.7) to a political one (19.12). By questioning Pilate's loyalty to the emperor, they corner him, denying him the option of releasing Jesus. Hearing their words, Pilate sits on the judge's bench to demonstrate his authority over 'the Jews'.[24] Pilate knows what 'the Jews' want and while he realizes they have forced his hand, he too has a card up his sleeve. He taunts them saying, 'See your king!', causing the exasperated 'Jews' to demand Jesus' crucifixion (19.14b-15a). Pilate now plays *his* trump card. With his 'Shall I crucify your king?' Pilate shrewdly manipulates 'the Jews' into admitting their allegiance to Rome and denying their religious loyalties (19.15).[25] Having secured this victory, Pilate hands Jesus over to 'the Jews' to be crucified (19.16a).

Beyond the Trial

After Jesus' trial, Pilate's power play continues. In 19.19-22, Pilate mocks the nationalistic, messianic hopes of 'the Jews' with the inscription 'Jesus the Nazarene, the king of the Jews' on the cross. He then flaunts his authority by refusing the alteration that 'the Jews' suggest. Pilate's power over the Jewish people is also apparent in 19.31 and 19.38 when they need his consent on a religious matter.[26]

(Grand Rapids: Eerdmans, 2nd edn, 1994), ch. 10. Ironically, Pilate presumes to have authority whereas in reality it is Jesus who does (1.12; 5.27; 10.18; 17.2).

23   Judas is most often the subject of the verb 'to hand over' in John, including in 18.2, 5. Here, the reference could be to 'the Jews' who hand Jesus over to Pilate (18.30, 35) (Jesus' use of the singular is perhaps generic) and/or to Caiaphas as the leader of 'the Jews' (although never related to the verb 'to hand over', he is the leading voice in 11.47-53). Whoever the subject, his/their sin is greater, because while Pilate has God-given authority, his/theirs comes from the devil (8.44; 13.2, 27).

24   Although it is possible to translate 19.13b as, 'and he [Pilate] seated him [Jesus] on the judge's seat', this is unlikely (cf. Bond, *Pilate*, p. 190; Colleen M. Conway, *Men and Women in the Fourth Gospel: Gender and Johannine Characterization* [SBLDS, 167; Atlanta: Society of Biblical Literature, 1999], p. 161; *contra* Gail R. O'Day, *The Gospel of John* [NIB, 9; Nashville: Abingdon, 1995], p. 822).

25   Cf. Culpepper, *Anatomy*, p. 143; Giblin, 'Narration', pp. 233, 238; Bond, *Pilate*, pp. 191–3; Conway, *Men and Women*, p. 162; Carter, *Pilate*, pp. 150–1. As Rudolf Schnackenburg observes, both 'the Jews' and Pilate sacrifice their convictions – 'the Jews' their theological convictions and Pilate his conviction of justice (*The Gospel According to St. John*, Vol. 3 [trans. Kevin Smyth, et al.; HTCNT, 3 vols; London: Burns & Oates, 1968–82], p. 266).

26   *Contra* Culpepper, who contends that these are all Pilate's efforts to atone for his concession to 'the Jews' (*Anatomy*, p. 143).

III. Character Analysis and Classification of Pilate

Instead of placing characters in fixed categories – flat/round, static/dynamic, simple/complex – as most scholars do, I suggest that they move along a continuum and thus display degrees of characterization. Using the non-reductionist model of Joseph Ewen, I therefore analyse the Johannine Pilate by situating him on three continua or axes, namely complexity, development and inner life. After Pilate's character analysis, I will classify him on a continuum of degrees of characterization.[27]

a. Character Complexity

The degree of a character's complexity has to do with its traits. Characters range from those displaying a single trait to those displaying a complex web of traits, with varying degrees of complexity in between. Pilate is probably the most complex character in the Johannine narrative. In his dealing with Jesus, Pilate seeks to uncover the truth in his own cruel and efficient way. He misunderstands and disparages Jesus' kingship and rejects the (saving) truth he has to offer, but he is also convinced that Jesus is harmless and innocent (18.38; 19.4, 6) and tries to release him (19.12). At the same time, he uses Jesus to manipulate and taunt 'the Jews'. In his politically motivated game of mocking and manipulating 'the Jews' to admit their allegiance to Rome, he chooses to sacrifice the truth/Jesus. Pilate does not use his God-given authority to mete out justice; instead he rejects the truth/Jesus and thus condemns himself (cf. 3.20-21).[28] He knows what is true and just – Jesus is innocent and should be released – but he does not act accordingly. In the final evaluation, Pilate does not come to the light (cf. 3.20-21) and his response to Jesus falters and fails.[29]

Regarding 'the Jews', Pilate is cruel, taunting, condescending and manipulative. Knowing that they want to kill Jesus but need his approval, Pilate repeatedly taunts them and flaunts his authority. In return, 'the Jews' manage to manipulate Pilate when they realize he wants to release Jesus. Knowing he is cornered and must concede to their demands, Pilate extracts a high price – a declaration of their allegiance to Rome and a denial of their religious loyalties. A seemingly victorious Pilate becomes a victim of his own political game because he too pays a price for his victory – denying and perverting truth and justice. Indeed, it is a hollow victory.[30] Yet, at one point, on hearing the charge of 'the Jews' that Jesus claimed to be the Son of God,

---

27   For a more detailed explanation of this aspect of my theory, see Bennema, 'Comprehensive Approach', section III.b or Bennema, 'Theory of Character', pp. 392–3, 402–10.

28   In fact, Pilate is on trial and condemns himself (Ehrman, 'Trial', p. 128; Raymond E. Brown, 'The Passion according to John: Chapters 18 and 19', *Worship* 49 [1975], pp. 126–34 [129–30]).

29   Culpepper concludes that 'although he [Pilate] seems to glimpse the truth, a decision in Jesus' favor proves too costly for him' (*Anatomy*, p. 143). Cf. O'Day, *Gospel*, pp. 825–6.

30   Culpepper, *Anatomy*, p. 143.

Pilate also shows (superstitious) fear. In sum, our analysis reveals that Pilate is a complex character with multiple traits including being cruel, calculating, taunting, manipulative, provocative and afraid.

b. Character Development

Characters may vary from those who show no development to those who are fully developed. Character development is not simply the addition of a trait that the reader infers further along the text continuum, or a character's progress in his or her understanding of Jesus. Development is revealed in a character's ability to surprise the reader, when a newly found trait replaces another or does not fit neatly into the existing set of traits, implying that the character has changed. There are some indications of development in Pilate. First, although Pilate is convinced early on about Jesus' innocence, he does not attempt to release him, but surprisingly he tries fervently to release him later. Second, it is rather unexpected that Pilate, the calculating politician, is outwitted by 'the Jews' and is forced to yield. Third, it may surprise the reader that the strong Pilate shows fear on one occasion.

c. Character's Inner Life

The inner life of a character gives the reader insight into its thoughts, emotions and motivations, and is usually conveyed by the narrator and sometimes by other characters. Regarding penetration into the inner life, characters range from those who allow us a peek inside their minds to those whose minds remain opaque. The narrator reveals two aspects of Pilate's inner life: he is afraid (19.8) and he wants to release Jesus (19.12). Some scholars contend that the structure of the passage, in which Pilate alternately goes in and out of the palace, reflects his inner conflict – he goes back and forth in his mind, unable to take sides.[31] This picture seems incorrect. Pilate despises 'the Jews' and is clear about his strategy but he is also in search of the truth about Jesus. Although he tries to play both sides and fails, he is not indecisive: he ultimately opts for the emperor and his own political survival at the expense of truth and justice. Nevertheless, Pilate does go back and forth in his mind, constantly weighing his political options, and this is what the structure of the passage probably emphasizes.[32]

d. Characterization of Pilate

After this character analysis, we can classify Pilate by positioning his resulting character on a characterization continuum as (i) an agent; (ii) a type; (iii) a character with personality; or (iv) an individual or person. Considering his

---

31   E.g., Stibbe, *Storyteller*, pp. 106, 109.

32   Cf. Andrew T. Lincoln, *The Gospel According to Saint John* (BNTC, 4; London: Continuum and Peabody, MA: Hendrickson, 2005), p. 458. Thomas L. Brodie connects the inside/outside contrast with the idea of revelation: inside the praetorium Jesus gives revelation; 'the Jews' outside are without revelation (*The Gospel According to John: A Literary and Theological Commentary* [New York: Oxford University Press, 1993], p. 521).

location on the axes of complexity (complex, multiple traits), development (some) and inner life (some), I suggest to classify the character of Pilate as being beyond personality, towards an individual.[33] Next to Peter and Judas, Pilate is among the most complex characters in John's Gospel.[34]

IV. Characterization of Pilate in Other Sources

The writings of Josephus and Philo make it evident that Pilate did not like or understand the Jews. Four major incidents record Pilate's conflict with the Jews.[35] The first incident most probably occurred quite soon after Pilate's arrival in Judaea in 26 CE. Josephus records in *War* 2.169-74 and *Antiquities* 18.55-9 that Pilate brought Roman standards with embossed figures of the emperor into Jerusalem overnight. The Jews went to Caesarea to request Pilate to remove the images, but Pilate did not do anything for five days. When on the sixth day Pilate threatened the Jews with immediate death unless they backed down, it was in fact Pilate who backed down when he saw the determination of the Jews to be willing to die for their cause. And the standards were removed. McGing concludes that Pilate appears to be provocative, indecisive, stubborn and weak by giving in.[36] Based on *War* 2.169-74, Bond is milder in Josephus's description of Pilate: he is insensitive but not blatant when he introduces the iconic standards; he shows either patience or stubbornness in allowing the Jews to remain outside his house; the removal of the standards is not a sign of weakness but a willingness to heed public opinion and preserve peace in the province.[37] However, Bond admits that in *Antiquities* 18.55-9, Pilate appears insensitive, stubborn, aggressive and astounded by the Jewish resilience.[38]

On another occasion, Josephus records how Pilate seized funds from the temple treasury to construct an aqueduct in Jerusalem (*War* 2.175-7; *Ant.* 18.60-2). The Jews were infuriated and protested. Rather than openly employ troops, Pilate ordered an undercover operation in which soldiers in civilian dress infiltrated the protesting crowd, ready to hit rioters with clubs (rather than swords). However, at Pilate's signal, the troops went beyond their orders, killing a large number of Jews. According to McGing, Pilate's intention was not to spill blood or back down, but to use force without killing people. This could have been an effective, and yet not too brutal, means of controlling a disorderly demonstration, if it had not gone out of hand.[39]

---

33   We must not understand the character of Pilate in a modern individualistic sense but as a 'collectivist identity' or 'group-oriented personality', where Pilate's identity is embedded in a larger group (e.g. the Romans) (cf. n. 4).

34   See Bennema, *Encountering Jesus*, pp. 203–4.

35   McGing mentions a few more possible incidents in Pilate's career, but the four mentioned here are the most significant ones.

36   McGing, 'Pilate', p. 429.

37   Bond, *Pilate*, pp. 57–9.

38   Bond, *Pilate*, pp. 74–5.

39   McGing, 'Pilate', p. 430. Cf. Bond, *Pilate*, pp. 59–60.

A third incident occurred when Pilate had already been governor for some time (possibly in 32 CE), and is recorded by Philo (*Leg.* 299-305).[40] Pilate set up golden votive shields bearing the name (but not the image) of the emperor in Herod's palace in Jerusalem. When the Jews asked for the shields to be removed, Pilate stubbornly refused their petition for, Philo writes, 'he was a man of a very inflexible disposition, and very merciless as well as very obstinate'. When prominent Jews then wrote to the emperor, an angry Tiberius ordered that Pilate immediately take down the shields and transfer them to the temple of Augustus in Caesarea. According to Philo, Pilate's intention was not so much to honour the emperor as to annoy the Jews by intentionally violating their customs (*Leg.* 299-301). After hearing the petition of the Jews, Pilate was afraid however that they would report his conduct as governor to the emperor, which Philo describes in the worst of terms in *Legatio ad Gaium* 302:

> [H]e [Pilate] feared . . . they might in reality go on an embassy to the emperor, and might impeach him with respect to other particulars of his government, in respect of his corruption, and his acts of insolence, and his rapine, and his habit of insulting people, and his cruelty, and his continual murders of people untried and uncondemned, and his never ending, and gratuitous, and most grievous inhumanity.

Besides, in his determination not to back down this time or please the Jews, Pilate misjudged Tiberius (*Leg.* 303-5). Some scholars doubt the reliability of Philo's assessment of Pilate, since Philo uses similar rhetorical accusations for other Roman administrators in *In Flaccum* 105.[41] Nevertheless, Bond contends that behind Pilate's theological-political rhetoric the historical Pilate is just visible. She argues that Philo's description of the facts seems trustworthy but that Pilate's erection of the shields was not a deliberate act of aggression (as Philo maintains); Pilate simply wanted to demonstrate his loyalty to the emperor.[42]

The last incident of conflict with the Jews in Pilate's career is recorded in Josephus, *Antiquities* 18.85-9. A false prophet persuaded a crowd of Samaritans to go to Mount Gerizim to show them the sacred vessels buried by Moses. The Samaritans believed him and they came armed, planning to climb the mountain. Pilate violently subdued this small Samaritan rebellion, in which some were killed. The Samaritans complained to Vitellius, the prefect of Syria, telling him that they had fled to escape the violence of Pilate. Vitellius

---

40   Bond cautions that 'whilst Philo's account of Pilate doubtlessly contains a core of historical fact, his description of Pilate's character and intentions has very likely been influenced by his rhetorical objectives' (*Pilate*, p. 25). See further Tom Thatcher, 'Philo on Pilate: Rhetoric or Reality', *ResQ* 37 (1995), pp. 215–18.

41   McGing, 'Pilate', p. 433; Bond, *Pilate*, pp. 31–3. Bond contends that 'Philo's characterization of Pilate has been shaped by his theological outlook, in which . . . he depicts the prefect in stereotyped language reserved for those who act against the Jewish Law' (*Pilate*, p. 36).

42   Bond, *Pilate*, pp. 47–8. Differently, Joan E. Taylor explains this incident in the wider context of Pilate's determination to promote the Roman imperial cult in Judaea ('Pontius Pilate and the Imperial Cult in Roman Judaea', *NTS* 52 [2006], pp. 555–82 [575–82]).

then ordered Pilate to go to Rome to explain his actions to the emperor (either at the end of 36 CE or at the beginning of 37 CE). Tiberius however had died before Pilate reached Rome, and, according to Eusebius, Pilate committed suicide not long after that (*Hist. Eccl.* 2.7). *Contra* scholars who see this incident as Pilate being sacked from his job,[43] McGing offers an alternative explanation. He argues that a Roman governor who would not deal with a large, armed crowd in the Judaean countryside would be seriously failing in his duty, and it is hardly surprising that there should be bloodshed. Besides, it is not at all clear from Josephus's account that Vitellius necessarily thought that Pilate had acted wrongly. Finally, Pilate had already been in office for ten years, which was considered a very long period, and Tiberius's death and Pilate's return to Rome might well have been a suitable opportunity to end Pilate's long governorship.[44]

Based on Josephus and Philo, I derive the following portrait of Pilate. Although Pilate appears to have been a relatively competent governor, he provoked the Jews on various occasions. However, he may have done so unintentionally, being ignorant about and insensitive to the rigorous Jewish customs and laws.[45] In his conflicts with the Jews, Pilate could stubbornly and wilfully resist the Jews but also give in – especially when his loyalty to the emperor was questioned. He could be decisive but also be non-committal, use brute force or show restraint.[46] The Johannine portrait of Pilate does not differ greatly from those of Josephus and Philo.[47] In John's Gospel, Pilate refuses to give in to the demands of 'the Jews' and mocks them, but they find a way to compel Pilate into yielding. Similarly, Josephus and Philo record incidents where Pilate provokes the Jews and refuses to give in to their wishes but eventually has to concede. Whether in John's Gospel, Josephus or Philo, Pilate appears cruel, decisive, calculating and provocative. He appears to choose the course of action that is to his advantage and ensures his political survival.

We find a partially different story when we turn to the Synoptic Gospels. In Mark's Gospel, I do not see a radically different picture from that in John's Gospel. Realizing that the chief priests had handed Jesus over out of envy, Pilate's remark concerning whether he should release the king of the Jews appears an intentional mockery, sneering at their nationalistic hopes (15.9-

---

43   For example, Harold W. Hoehner, 'Pontius Pilate', in *DJG*, p. 616.

44   McGing, 'Pilate', pp. 433–4. Bond makes the same point (*Pilate*, pp. 92–3).

45   McGing, 'Pilate', pp. 434–5. Cf. Bond, *Pilate*, pp. 47–8, 93.

46   Cf. McGing, 'Pilate', p. 435; Bond, *Pilate*, pp. 47–8, 60, 62, 78, 93. Regarding Josephus, Bond argues that Pilate is described in more detail and much harsher terms in the *Antiquities* than in the *Jewish War*: a reasonably competent yet insensitive governor, deliberately setting himself against the Jewish law. She concludes that the historical Pilate behind Josephus's stories 'appears to fulfil his duty of effectively maintaining Roman order in the province without recourse to undue aggression' (*Pilate*, p. 93).

47   Cf. McGing, 'Pilate', pp. 437–8; Frances Taylor Gench, *Encounters with Jesus: Studies in the Gospel of John* (Louisville: Westminster John Knox, 2007), pp. 122–3. *Contra* Margaret Davies, *Rhetoric and Reference in the Fourth Gospel* (JSNTSup, 69; Sheffield: Sheffield Academic Press, 1992), pp. 314–15; Neyrey, *Gospel of John*, pp. 304–5.

10). Although his handing Jesus over to be crucified because he 'considered to satisfy the crowd' (15.15) may indicate weakness, it could equally point to Pilate's ability to be calculating. Perceiving the potential for a riot (15.11; cf. Matt. 27.24), Pilate may well have decided to give in on this occasion.[48] In contrast, Bond finds different portraits of Pilate in the Gospel of Matthew (less harsh and calculating, seeking exoneration) and the Gospel of Luke (weak, malleable, incompetent).[49] To account for these different portraits, Bond suggests that 'the community situation was the fundamental factor in determining the way in which each evangelist portrayed the prefect'.[50] Assuming the priority of Mark's Gospel, it is interesting that while Matthew and Luke altered or deviated from Mark, the Johannine author (who, in my view, also knew Mark) significantly expands on Mark's account and essentially agrees with his characterization of Pilate.

V. Evaluation and Representative Value of Pilate

In my reading of the Johannine Pilate, I differ from the majority of scholars who portray Pilate as weak and indecisive.[51] While I tend to agree with scholars who view Pilate as a strong character, they seem to overrate Pilate's control over the situation at the trial by downplaying the force of 19.12, where 'the Jews' finally get a grip on Pilate.[52] Pilate is a competent, calculating politician who wants to show 'the Jews' he is in charge while also trying to be professional in handling Jesus' case. But he is unable to achieve either aim because he underestimates the determination and shrewdness of 'the Jews'. He may have released the innocent Jesus had he not been manipulated into sacrificing the truth/Jesus to ensure his own political survival and triumph. He knows Jesus is innocent but does not use his God-given authority to bring justice for fear of losing the political game. Pilate ultimately chooses Caesar and the empire 'from below' instead of Jesus and his kingdom 'from above'.

48   Cf. Bond's analysis of Pilate in Mark's Gospel as skilful, manipulative and loyal to the emperor (*Pilate*, pp. 103–17).

49   Ibid., pp. 120–62.

50   Ibid., p. 206.

51   E.g. Brown, *Gospel*, p. 864 (the honest, well-disposed man who adopts a middle position); Culpepper, *Anatomy*, p. 143 (Pilate avoids making a decision); Stibbe, *Storyteller*, p. 109 (Pilate is indecisive, representing the 'impossibility of neutrality'). Although Martinus C. de Boer seeks to avoid the weak/strong dichotomy, he nevertheless characterizes Pilate as a reluctant participant in the drama who, seeking to release Jesus, is manipulated by 'the Jews' from beginning to end ('The Narrative Function of Pilate in John', in G. J. Brooke and J.-D. Kaestli [eds], *Narrativity in Biblical and Related Texts* [BETL, 149; Leuven: Peeters, 2000], pp. 143–4, 146, n. 24).

52   Rensberger, *World*, pp. 94–5; Bond, *Pilate*, pp. 190–2; Conway, *Men and Women*, p. 161; Carter, *Pilate*, pp. 127, 150. While Christopher M. Tuckett also views Pilate as a strong, pig-headed man, surprisingly he does not deal with 19.12 ('Pilate in John 18–19: A Narrative-Critical Approach', in Brooke and Kaestli [eds], *Narrativity*, p. 138). O'Day presents a more balanced view (*Gospel*, pp. 813–26).

Having analysed and classified Pilate, I use two criteria to evaluate Pilate's character: (i) his response to Jesus in relation to the author's evaluative point of view, purpose and worldview; (ii) his role in the plot. First, I consider Pilate's response to Jesus. Any meaningful communication, whether verbal or non-verbal, has a particular purpose – a message that the sender wants to get across to the receiver. In line with its salvific purpose (20.30-31), the Johannine author tells his story from a particular perspective called 'point of view'. The implication is that a narrative is not neutral since it has an inbuilt perspective that is communicated to the reader. Hence, we must evaluate Pilate's character in the light of the author's evaluative point of view. Considering Pilate's misunderstanding, rejection, compromise of truth and justice, and choosing Caesar rather than Jesus, I must conclude that Pilate's response to Jesus is inadequate. He searches for truth, is convinced of Jesus' innocence and tries to release him but he eventually sacrifices his convictions and Jesus.[53]

I now turn to Pilate's role in the plot. If 'plot' is the logical and causal sequence of events in the narrative, the plot of John's Gospel evolves around the revelation of the Father and Son in terms of their identity, character, mission and relationship, and people's response to this revelation. The Gospel's plot is affected by the author's strategy to persuade the reader to believe that Jesus is the Christ and the source of everlasting life or salvation (20.31).[54] Pilate significantly advances the plot in two ways. First, God's salvific plan for the world was to 'give' his Son (3.16), which he ultimately did at the cross. Jesus was constantly aware of this salvific mission: he said he would give his life for the life of the world (6.51) and lay down his life for the sheep (10.15). In his consent to have Jesus crucified, Pilate thus propels the Johannine plot to its climax. Second, since Pilate was the Roman prefect or procurator of Judaea, Jesus' trial is acted out before the Roman authorities, the greatest power of the then-known 'civilized' world. In line with the universal scope of John's Gospel, Jesus' trial must unfold on the world stage because he was sent into the world and his saving act on the cross will have cosmic consequences. Even Pilate's words on the cross assist the cosmic scope of Jesus' salvific mission since the phrase 'Jesus, the king of "the Jews"', written in Greek, Latin and Aramaic, the major languages of the then-known world, was for everyone to read.

Finally, we must consider Pilate's representative value for today. Since the author of John's Gospel seeks to persuade his readers of his perspective on Jesus through a broad array of characters that interact with Jesus, we must reflect on how these characters and their responses have representative value for readers in other contexts and eras. In contrast to many scholars who think that merely the character's belief-response is representative, I contend that the representative value of the Johannine characters across cultures and time lies in the *totality* of the character – traits, development *and* response. Without

---

53   Cf. de Boer's observation that for Pilate Jesus is not *his* king but remains the king *of 'the Jews'* ('Narrative Function', p. 150).

54   Cf. Culpepper, *Anatomy*, p. 98.

revisiting all Pilate's traits and responses, lest I appear to be searching for his exact, modern *doppelgänger*, I merely sketch a general (hopefully not too general) profile. I suggest that Pilate represents those in positions of authority who compromise truth and justice to safeguard their career and ensure survival; those who start well on a quest for truth but eventually abandon it because other things (career, image, and so on) take precedence.

BIBLIOGRAPHY

Abbott, H. Porter, *The Cambridge Introduction to Narrative* (Cambridge, UK: Cambridge University Press, 2002).

Abrams, M. H., *A Glossary of Literary Terms* (New York: Harcourt Brace College Publishers, 7th edn, 1999).

Abrams, M. H. and Geoffrey Galt Harpham, *A Glossary of Literary Terms* (Boston: Wadsworth Cengage Learning, 2009).

Allport, G. W. and H. S. Odbert, *Trait-Names: A Psycholexical Study*, *Psychological Monographs* 47 (1936), pp. 1–171.

Allport, Gordon W. and Leo Joseph Postman, *The Psychology of Rumor* (New York: Henry Holt and Co., 1947).

Alter, Robert, *The Art of Biblical Narrative* (New York: Basic Books, 1981).

Anderson, Paul N., *The Fourth Gospel and the Quest for Jesus: Modern Foundations Reconsidered* (London: T&T Clark, 2006).

——— *The Riddles of the Fourth Gospel: An Introduction to John* (Minneapolis: Fortress, 2011).

Anderson, Paul N., Felix Just and Tom Thatcher (eds), *John, Jesus, and History – Volume 2: Aspects of Historicity in the Fourth Gospel* (Atlanta: Society of Biblical Literature, 2009).

Anderson, Robert T., 'Samaritans', in David Noel Freedman (ed.), *Anchor Bible Dictionary* (6 vols; New York: Doubleday, 1992), Vol. 6, pp. 940–7.

Arp, Thomas R., *Perrine's Story and Structure* (Fort Worth: Harcourt Brace College Publishers, 9th edn, 1998).

Ashton, John, 'The Identity and Function of the IOUDAIOI in the Fourth Gospel', *Novum Testamentum* 27 (1985), pp. 40–75.

——— 'The Transformation of Wisdom: A Study of the Prologue of John's Gospel', *New Testament Studies* 32 (1986), pp. 161–86.

Attridge, Harold W., 'The Restless Quest for the Beloved Disciple', in David H. Warren, Ann Graham Brock and David W. Pao (eds), *Early Christian Voices in Texts, Traditions, and Symbols: Essays in Honor of François Bovon* (BIS, 66; Leiden: Brill, 2003), 71–80.

Baarda, Tjitze, 'John 1:17b: The Origin of a Peshitta Reading', *Ephemerides theologicae lovaniensis* 77 (2001), pp. 153–62.

Bal, Mieke, *Narratology: Introduction to the Theory of Narrative* (Toronto: University of Toronto Press, 1985).

Baldensperger, Wilhelm, *Der Prolog des vierten Evangeliums: sein polemisch-apologetischer Zweck* (Tübingen: Mohr, 1898).

Bar-Efrat, Shimon, 'Some Observations on the Analysis of Structure in Biblical Narrative', *Vetus Testamentum* 30 (1980), pp. 154–73.

———— *Narrative Art in the Bible* (JSOTSup, 70; Sheffield: Sheffield Academic Press, 1992).

Barker, Margaret, *The Gate of Heaven: The History and Symbolism of the Temple in Jerusalem* (London: SPCK, 1991).

Barrett, C. K., *The Prologue of St John's Gospel* (London: Athlone, 1971).

———— *The Gospel According to St John: An Introduction with Commentary and Notes on the Greek Text* (Philadelphia: Westminster, 2nd edn, 1978).

Bassler, Jouette M., 'Mixed Signals: Nicodemus in the Fourth Gospel', *Journal of Biblical Literature* 108 (1989), pp. 635–46.

Bauckham, Richard, 'The Beloved Disciple as Ideal Author', *Journal for the Study of the New Testament* 49 (1993), pp. 21–44.

———— (ed.), *The Gospel for All Christians: Rethinking the Gospel Audiences* (Grand Rapids: Eerdmans, 1998).

———— 'John for Readers of Mark', in idem, *The Gospels for All Christians: Rethinking the Gospel Audiences* (Grand Rapids: Eerdmans, 1998), pp. 147–71.

———— *Jesus and the Eyewitnesses: The Gospels as Eyewitness Testimony* (Grand Rapids: Eerdmans, 2006).

———— 'Historiographical Characteristics of the Gospel of John', *New Testament Studies* 53 (2007), pp. 17–36.

———— *The Testimony of the Beloved Disciple: Narrative, History, and Theology in the Gospel of John* (Grand Rapids: Baker Academic, 2007).

———— 'Eyewitnesses and Critical History: A Response to Jens Schröter and Craig Evans', *Journal for the Study of the New Testament* 31 (2008), pp. 221–35.

———— 'The Fourth Gospel as the Testimony of the Beloved Disciple', in Richard Bauckham and Carl Mosser (eds), *The Gospel of John and Christian Theology* (Grand Rapids: Eerdmans, 2008), pp. 120–39.

———— 'In Response to My Respondents: *Jesus and the Eyewitnesses* in Review', *Journal for the Study of the Historical Jesus* 6 (2008), pp. 225–53.

———— 'The Transmission of the Gospel Traditions', *Revista catalana de teología* 33 (2008), pp. 377–94.

Bauckham, Richard and Carl Mosser (eds), *The Gospel of John and Christian Theology* (Grand Rapids: Eerdmans, 2008).

Bauer, Walter, *Das Johannesevangelium erklärt* (HKNT 6; Tübingen: J.C.B. Mohr, 1933).

Beck, David R., *The Discipleship Paradigm: Readers and Anonymous Characters in the Fourth Gospel* (BIS, 27; Leiden: Brill, 1997).

Beirne, Margaret M., *Women and Men in the Fourth Gospel: A Genuine Discipleship of Equals* (JSNTSup, 242; Sheffield: Sheffield Academic Press, 2003).

Bennema, Cornelis, *The Power of Saving Wisdom: An Investigation of Spirit and Wisdom in Relation to the Soteriology of the Fourth Gospel* (WUNT, II/148; Tübingen: Mohr Siebeck, 2002).

——— 'The Sword of the Messiah and the Concept of Liberation in the Fourth Gospel', *Biblica* 86 (2005), pp. 35–58.

——— 'Christ, the Spirit and the Knowledge of God: A Study in Johannine Epistemology', in Mary Healy and Robin Parry (eds), *The Bible and Epistemology: Biblical Soundings on the Knowledge of God* (Milton Keynes: Paternoster, 2007), pp. 107–33.

——— 'The Character of John in the Fourth Gospel', *Journal of the Evangelical Theological Society* 52 (2009), pp. 271–84.

——— *Encountering Jesus: Character Studies in the Gospel of John* (Milton Keynes: Paternoster, 2009).

——— 'The Identity and Composition of οἱ Ἰουδαῖοι in the Gospel of John', *Tyndale Bulletin* 60 (2009), pp. 239–63.

——— 'A Theory of Character in the Fourth Gospel with Reference to Ancient and Modern Literature', *Biblical Interpretation* 17 (2009), pp. 375–421.

Berlin, Adele, *Poetics and Interpretation of Biblical Narrative* (Sheffield: Almond Press, 1983).

——— 'Point of View in Biblical Narrative', in Stephen A. Geller (ed.), *A Sense of Text: The Art of Language in the Study of Biblical Literature* (Winona Lake: Eisenbrauns, 1983), pp. 71–113.

Berlin, Adele and Elizabeth Struthers Malbon (eds), *Semeia 63: Characterization in Biblical Literature* (Atlanta, GA: Society of Biblical Literature, 1993).

Bieringer, Reimund, Didier Pollefeyt and Frederique Vandecasteele-Vanneuville (eds), *Anti-Judaism and the Fourth Gospel* (Louisville: Westminster John Knox, 2001).

Bishop, Jonathan, 'Encounters in the New Testament', in Kenneth R. R. Gros Louis (ed.), *Literary Interpretations of Biblical Narratives* (2 vols; Nashville: Abingdon, 1974–82), Vol. 2, pp. 285–94.

Black, Matthew, 'Does an Aramaic Tradition Underlie John 1:16?', *Journal of Theological Studies* 42 (1941), pp. 69–70.

Blaine, Bradford B., *Peter in the Gospel of John: The Making of an Authentic Disciple* (AcBib, 27; Atlanta: Society of Biblical Literature, 2007).

Blomberg, Craig L., *The Historical Reliability of John's Gospel: Issues and Commentary* (Downers Grove, IL: InterVarsity, 2001).

Boeree, C.G., 'Personality Theories: Alfred Adler', http://webspace.ship.edu/cgboer/adler.html.

Böhler, Dieter '"Ecce Homo!" (Joh 19,5) ein Zität aus dem Alten Testament', *Biblische Zeitschrift* 39 (1995), pp. 104–8.

Boismard, Marie-Emile, *Du Baptême à Cana (Jean 1,19–2,11)* (LD 18; Paris: Cerf, 1956).

——— *Evangile de Jean: Etudes et Problemes* (RechBib, 3; Bruges: Desclée de Brouwer, 1958).

—— 'L'ami de l'Époux (Jo., 111, 29)', in A. Barucq, et al. (eds), *À la rencontre de Dieu: Mémorial Albert Gelin* (Bibliothèque de la Faculté catholique de théologie de Lyon, 8; Le Puy: Xavier Mappus, 1961), pp. 289–95.

Bolyki, János, 'Burial as an Ethical Task in the Book of Tobit, in the Bible and in the Greek Tragedies', in Géza G. Zeravits and József Zsengellér (eds), *The Book of Tobit: Text, Tradition, Theology* (Leiden: Brill, 2005), pp. 89–101.

Bond, Helen K., *Pontius Pilate in History and Interpretation* (SNTSMS, 100; Cambridge, UK: Cambridge University Press, 1998).

Bonney, William, *Caused to Believe: The Doubting Thomas Story as the Climax of John's Christological Narrative* (BIS, 62; Leiden: Brill, 2002).

Booth, Wayne, *The Rhetoric of Fiction* (Chicago: University of Chicago Press, 2nd edn, 1983).

Borgen, Peder, 'Observations on the Targumic Character of the Prologue of John', *New Testament Studies* 16 (1969), pp. 288–95.

—— 'Logos was the True Light: Contributions to the Interpretation of the Prologue of John', *Novum Testamentum* 14 (1972), pp. 115–30.

Bowen, Clayton R., 'Notes on the Fourth Gospel', *Journal of Biblical Literature* 43 (1924), pp. 22–7.

Boyarin, Daniel, 'The Gospel of the Memra: Jewish Binitarianism and the Prologue to John', *Harvard Theological Review* 94 (2001) pp. 243–84.

—— *Border Lines: The Partition of Judaeo-Christianity* (Philadelphia: University of Pennsylvania, 2004).

Brant, Jo-Ann A., *Dialogue and Drama: Elements of Greek Tragedy in the Fourth Gospel* (Peabody, MA: Hendrickson, 2004).

—— *John* (Paideia Commentaries on the New Testament; Grand Rapids: Baker, 2011).

Brodie, Thomas, *The Gospel According to John: A Literary and Theological Commentary* (New York: Oxford University Press, 1993).

Brown, Raymond E., 'Three Quotations from John the Baptist in the Gospel of John', *Catholic Biblical Quarterly* 22 (1960), pp. 292–8.

—— *The Gospel According to John* (AB, 29 and 29A; New York: Doubleday, 1966–70).

—— 'The Passion according to John: Chapters 18 and 19', *Worship* 49 (1975), pp. 126–34.

—— *The Community of the Beloved Disciple: The Life, Loves, and Hates of an Individual Church in New Testament Times* (New York: Paulist, 1979).

—— 'The Resurrection in John 20: A Series of Diverse Reactions', *Worship* 64 (1990), pp. 194–206.

—— *The Death of the Messiah: From Gethsemane to the Grave* (2 vols; ABRL; New York: Doubleday, 1994).

————— *An Introduction to the Gospel of John* (ed. Francis J. Moloney; ABRL; New York: Doubleday, 2003).

Brown, Roger and James Kulik, 'Flashbulb Memories', *Cognition* 5 (1977), pp. 73–99.

Bruner, Jerome S. and Leo Joseph Postman, 'On the Perception of Incongruity: A Paradigm', *Journal of Personality* 18 (1949), pp. 206–23.

Buckhout, Robert, 'Eyewitness Testimony', in Ulric Neisser (ed.), *Memory Observed: Remembering in Natural Contexts* (San Francisco: W.H. Freeman, 1982), pp. 116–25.

Bultmann, Rudolf, *Theology of the New Testament* (2 vols; New York: Charles Scribner's Sons, 1955).

————— *Das Evangelium des Johannes* (Göttingen: Vandenhoeck & Ruprecht, 18th edn, 1964).

————— *The Gospel of John* (Philadelphia: Westminster Press, 1971).

Burnett, Fred W., 'Characterization and Reader Construction of Characters in the Gospels', *Semeia* 63 (1993), pp. 3–28.

Burridge, R. A., *What Are the Gospels? A Comparison with Graeco-Roman Biography* (Grand Rapids: Eerdmans, 2004).

Byrne, Brendan, 'The Faith of the Beloved Disciple and the Community in John 20', *Journal for the Study of the New Testament* 23 (1985), pp. 83–97.

————— *The Hospitality of God: A Reading of Luke's Gospel* (Strathfield, NSW: St Paul's, 2000).

Byrskog, Samuel, *Story as History – History as Story: The Gospel Tradition in the Context of Ancient Oral History* (WUNT, 123; Tübingen: Mohr Siebeck, 2000).

Campbell, Joan Cecilia, *Kinship Relations in the Gospel of John* (CBQMS, 42; Washington: Catholic Biblical Association of America, 2007).

Campbell, Sue, 'Our Faithfulness to the Past: Reconstructing Memory Value', *Philosophical Psychology* 19 (3) (2006), pp. 361–80.

Carson, D. A., *The Gospel According to John* (PNTC; Grand Rapids: Eerdmans, 1991).

Carter, Warren, *Pontius Pilate: Portraits of a Roman Governor* (Collegeville, MN: Liturgical, 2003).

————— *John and Empire: Initial Explorations* (London and New York: T&T Clark, 2008).

Charles, J. Daryl, '"Will the Court Please Call in the Prime Witness?" John 1:29-34 and the "Witness"-Motif', *Trinity Journal* 10 (1989), pp. 71–83.

Charlesworth, James H., *The Beloved Disciple: Whose Witness Validates the Gospel of John?* (Valley Forge: Trinity Press International, 1995).

————— 'The Historical Jesus in the Fourth Gospel: A Paradigm Shift?', *Journal for the Study of the Historical Jesus* 8 (2010), pp. 3–46.

Chatman, Seymour, *Story and Discourse: Narrative Structure in Fiction and Film* (Ithaca, NY: Cornell University Press, 1978).

Chennattu, Rekha M., 'Women in the Mission of the Church: An Interpretation of John 4' (Paper presented at the Conference on 'Mission in Asia in the Third Millennium: Models for Integral Human Liberation', Sanata Dharma University, Yogyakarta, Indonesia, 14–17 April 1999).

——— *Johannine Discipleship as a Covenant Relationship* (Peabody, MA: Hendrickson, 2006).

Collins, Adela Yarbro, 'The Gospel of John and the Jews', *Review and Expositor* 84 (1987), pp. 273–88.

——— 'How on Earth Did Jesus Become a God? A Reply', in David B. Capes, April D. DeConick and Helen K. Bond (eds), *Israel's God and Rebecca's Children: Christology and Community in Early Judaism and Christianity* (Waco: Baylor University Press, 2007), pp. 55–66.

Collins, Raymond F., 'Representative Figures in the Fourth Gospel, Part I', *The Downside Review* 94 (1976), pp. 26–46.

——— 'Representative Figures in the Fourth Gospel, Part II', *The Downside Review* 94 (1976), pp. 118–32.

——— 'John's Gospel: A Passion Narrative?', *The Bible Today* 24 (1986), pp. 181–6.

——— 'The Twelve, Another Perspective: John 6,67-71', *Melita Theologica* 90 (1989), pp. 95–109.

——— *These Things Have Been Written: Studies on the Fourth Gospel* (LTPM, 2; Leuven/Grand Rapids: Peeters/Eerdmans, 1990).

——— '*Beatitudes*', in David Noel Freedman (ed.), *Anchor Bible Dictionary* (6 vols; New York: Doubleday, 1992), Vol. 1, pp. 629–31.

——— 'From John to the Beloved Disciple: An Essay on Johannine Characters', *Interpretation* 49 (1995), pp. 359–69.

——— 'Characters Proclaim the Good News', *Chicago Studies* 37 (1998), pp. 47–57.

——— '"Blessed Are Those Who Have Not Seen": John 20:29', in Rekha M. Chennattu and Mary L. Coloe, *Transcending Boundaries: Contemporary Readings of the New Testament* (Biblioteca di Scienze Religiose 187; Rome: LAS, 2005), pp. 173–90.

Coloe, Mary L., 'The Structure of the Johannine Prologue and Genesis 1', *Australian Biblical Review* 45 (1997), pp. 40–55.

——— *God Dwells with Us: Temple Symbolism in the Fourth Gospel* (Collegeville, MN: Liturgical, 2001).

——— 'Witness and Friend: Symbolism Associated with John the Baptiser', in Jörg Frey, Jan van der Watt and Ruben Zimmermann (eds), *Imagery in the Gospel of John: Terms, Forms, Themes and Theology of Figurative Language* (WUNT, 200; Tübingen: Mohr Siebeck, 2006), pp. 319–32.

——— *Dwelling in the Household of God: Johannine Ecclesiology and Spirituality* (Collegeville, MN: Liturgical, 2007).

——— 'The Johannine Pentecost: John 1.19–2.12', *Australian Biblical Review* 55 (2007), pp. 41–56.

Conway, Colleen M., *Men and Women in the Fourth Gospel: Gender and Johannine Characterization* (SBLDS, 167; Atlanta: Society of Biblical Literature, 1999).

———— 'Speaking through Ambiguity: Minor Characters in the Fourth Gospel', *Biblical Interpretation* 10 (2002), pp. 324–34.

Cullmann, Oscar, *Christology of the New Testament* (trans. Shirley Guthrie and Charles A. M. Hall; Philadelphia: Westminster Press, 1959).

Culpepper, R. Alan, 'The Pivot of John's Prologue', *New Testament Studies* 27 (1980), pp. 1–31.

———— *Anatomy of the Fourth Gospel* (Philadelphia: Fortress, 1983).

———— 'The Johannine *hypodeigma*: A Reading of John 13', *Semeia* 53 (1991), pp. 133–52.

———— 'John 5:1-18: A Sample of Narrative-Critical Commentary', in Mark W. G. Stibbe (ed.), *The Gospel of John as Literature* (Leiden: Brill, 1993), pp. 193–207.

———— *John, the Son of Zebedee: The Life of a Legend* (Studies on Personalities of the New Testament; Columbia, SC: University of South Carolina Press, 1994).

———— 'The Theology of the Johannine Passion Narrative: John 19:16b-30', *Neotestamentica* 31 (1997), pp. 21–37.

———— 'Designs for the Church in the Imagery of John 21:1-14', in Jörg Frey, Jan G. van der Watt and Ruben Zimmermann (eds), *Imagery in the Gospel of John: Terms, Forms, Themes and Theology of Figurative Language* (WUNT, 200; Tübingen: J.C.B. Mohr, 2006), pp. 369–402.

———— 'Peter as Exemplary Disciple in John 21:15-19', *Perspectives in Religious Studies* 37 (2010), pp. 165–78.

Culpepper, R. Alan and C. Clifton Black (eds), *Exploring the Gospel of John* (Louisville: Westminster John Knox, 1996).

Culy, Martin M., *Echoes of Friendship in the Gospel of John* (NTM, 30; Sheffield: Sheffield Phoenix Press, 2010).

Curci, Antonietta and Olivier Luminet, 'Follow-up of a Cross-National Comparison on Flashbulb and Event Memory for the September 11th Attacks', *Memory,* 14 (2006), pp. 329–44.

D'Sa, Francis X., 'The Language of God and the God of Language: The Relation between God, Human Beings, the World and Language in Saint John', in Robert P. Scharlemann and Gilbert E. M. Ogutu (eds), *God in Language* (New York: Paragon House Publishers, 1987), pp. 35–59.

Darr, John A., *Herod the Fox: Audience Criticism and Lukan Characterization* (JSNTSup, 163; Sheffield: Sheffield Academic Press, 1998).

Davies, Margaret, *Rhetoric and Reference in the Fourth Gospel* (JSNTSup, 69; Sheffield: Sheffield Academic Press, 1992).

Day, Janeth Norfleete, *The Woman at the Well: Interpretation of John 4:1-42 in Retrospect and Prospect* (BIS, 61; Leiden: Brill, 2002).

de Boer, Martinus C., 'Narrative Criticism, Historical Criticism, and the Gospel of John', *Journal for the Study of the New Testament* 47 (1992), pp. 35–48.

——— 'The Narrative Function of Pilate in John', in G. J. Brooke and J.-D. Kaestli (eds), *Narrativity in Biblical and Related Texts* (BETL, 149; Leuven: Peeters, 2000), pp. 141–58.

de la Potterie, Ignace, 'Le verbe «demeurer» dans la mystique johannique', *Nouvelle Revue Théologique* 117 (1995), pp. 843–59.

de Jonge, Marinus, 'Nicodemus and Jesus: Some Observations on Misunderstanding and Understanding in the Fourth Gospel', *Bulletin of the John Rylands Library* 53 (1971), pp. 337–59.

——— *Jesus, Stranger from Heaven and Son of God: Jesus Christ and the Christians in Johannine Perspective* (Missoula, MT: Scholars, 1977).

——— 'John the Baptist and Elijah in the Fourth Gospel', in Robert T. Fortna and Beverly Gaventa (eds), *The Conversation Continues: Studies in Paul and John in Honor of J. Louis Martyn* (Nashville: Abingdon, 1990), pp. 299–308.

Docherty, Thomas, *Reading (Absent) Character: Towards a Theory of Characterization in Fiction* (Oxford: Clarendon, 1983).

Dodd, C. H., *The Interpretation of the Fourth Gospel* (Cambridge, UK: Cambridge University Press, 1960).

——— *Historical Tradition in the Fourth Gospel* (London: Cambridge University Press, 1976).

Domeris, W. R., 'The Johannine Drama', *Journal of Theology for Southern Africa* 42 (1983), pp. 29–35.

Dschulnigg, Peter, *Jesus begegnen: Personen und ihre Bedeutung im Johannesevangelium* (Münster: Lit, 2002).

Droge, Arthur J., 'The Status of Peter in the Fourth Gospel: A Note on John 18:10-11', *Journal of Biblical Literature* 109 (1990), pp. 307–11.

Duke, Paul D., *Irony in the Fourth Gospel* (Atlanta: John Knox Press, 1985).

Dunderberg, Ismo, 'The Beloved Disciple in John: Ideal Figure in an Early Christian Controversy', in Ismo Dunderberg and Christopher M. Tuckett (eds), *Fair Play: Diversity and Conflicts in Early Christianity – Essays in Honor of Heikki Räisänen* (NovTSup 132; Leiden: Brill, 2002), pp. 243–69.

Dupont, J., 'De quoi est-il besoin (Lc x.42)?', in E. Best and R. M. Wilson (eds), *Text and Interpretation: Studies in the New Testament Presented to Matthew Black* (Cambridge, UK: Cambridge University Press, 1979), pp. 115–20.

du Rand, J. A., 'The Creation Motif in the Fourth Gospel: Perspectives on its Narratological Function within a Judaistic Background', in G. van Belle, J. G. van der Watt and P. J. Maritz (eds), *Theology and Christology in the Fourth Gospel* (Leuven: Peeters, 2005), pp. 21–46.

Easterling, Patricia E., 'Character in Sophocles', *Greece and Rome* 24 (1977), pp. 121–9.

Echterhoff, Gerald, William Hirst and Walter Hussy, 'How Eyewitnesses Resist Misinformation: Social Postwarnings and the Monitoring of Memory Characteristics', *Memory & Cognition* 33 (2005), pp. 770–82.

Edwards, Ruth B., *Discovering John* (London: SPCK, 2003).

———— '*Charin anti charitos* (John 1.16): Grace and Law in the Johannine Prologue', *Journal for the Study of the New Testament* 32 (1988), pp. 3–15.

Ehrman, Bart D., 'Jesus' Trial before Pilate: John 18.28–19.16', *Biblical Theology Bulletin* 13 (1983), pp. 124–31.

Elliot, J. K., 'Κηφᾶς, Σίμων Πέτρος, ὁ Πέτρος: An Examination of New Testament Usage', *Novum Testamentum* (1972), pp. 241–56.

Ernst, Allie M., *Martha from the Margins: The Authority of Martha in Early Christian Tradition* (Leiden and Boston: Brill, 2009).

Esler, Philip F. and R. A. Piper (eds), *Lazarus, Mary and Martha: A Social-Scientific and Theological Reading of John* (London: SCM, 2006).

Ewen, Joseph, 'The Theory of Character in Narrative Fiction' (in Hebrew), *Hasifrut* 3 (1971), pp. 1–30.

Farelly, Nicholas, *The Disciples in the Fourth Gospel: A Narrative Analysis of their Faith and Understanding* (WUNT, II/290; Tübingen: Mohr Siebeck, 2010).

Fehribach, Adeline, *The Women in the Life of the Bridegroom: A Feminist Historical-Literary Analysis of the Female Characters in the Fourth Gospel* (Collegeville, MN: Liturgical, 1998).

Feuillet, André, 'Les adieux de Christ à sa mere (Jn. 19,25-27) et la maternité spirituelle de Marie', *Nouvelle Revue Théologique* 86 (1964), pp. 469–83.

———— 'La signification fondamentale du premier miracle de Cana (Jo. II, 1-11) et le symbolisme johannique', *Revue thomiste* 65 (1965), pp. 517–35.

———— 'L'heure de la femme (Jn. 16-21) et l'heure de la Mère de Jésus (Jn. 19,25-27)', *Biblica* 47 (1966), pp. 169–84.

Fishbane, Michael, *Text and Texture: Close Readings of Selected Biblical Texts* (New York: Schocken, 1979).

Fitzmyer, Joseph A., *The Gospel According to Luke X–XXIV: A New Translation with Introduction and Commentary* (AB, 28A; New York: Doubleday, 1985).

Forster, E. M., *Aspects of the Novel* (New York: Harcourt, Brace and Company, 1927).

Fowler, Roger (ed.), *A Dictionary of Modern Critical Terms* (London: Routledge & Kegan Paul, rev. edn, 1987).

Freed, Edwin, '*Ego Eimi* in John 1:20 and 4:25', *Catholic Biblical Quarterly* 41 (1979) pp. 288–91.

Gench, Frances Taylor, *Back to the Well: Women's Encounters with Jesus in the Gospels* (Louisville: Westminster John Knox, 2004).

———— *Encounters with Jesus: Studies in the Gospel of John* (Louisville: Westminster John Knox, 2007).

Gibbons, Debbie, 'Nicodemus: Character Development, Irony and Repetition in the Fourth Gospel', *Proceedings: Eastern Great Lakes and Midwest Bible Societies* 11 (1991), pp. 116–28.

Giblin, Charles, 'Confrontations in John 18, 1-27', *Biblica* 65 (1984), pp. 210–31.

—— 'Two Complementary Literary Structures in John 1:1-18', *Journal of Biblical Literature* 104 (1985), pp. 87–103.

—— 'John's Narration of the Hearing before Pilate (John 18,28–19,16a)', *Biblica* 67 (1986), pp. 221–39.

Gilbert, Julian A. E. and Ronald P. Fisher, 'The Effects of Varied Retrieval Cues on Reminiscence in Eyewitness Memory', *Applied Cognitive Psychology* 20 (2006), pp. 723–39.

Gillespie, Thomas W., 'The Trial of Politics and Religion: John 18.28–19.16', *Ex Auditu* 2 (1986), pp. 69–73.

Glancy, Jennifer A., 'Torture: Flesh, Truth, and the Fourth Gospel', *Biblical Interpretation* 13 (2005), pp. 107–36.

Goethals, George R. and Richard F. Reckman, 'Recalling Previously Held Attitudes', *Journal of Experimental Social Psychology* 9 (1973), pp. 491–501.

Goldhill, Simon, 'Modern Critical Approaches to Greek Tragedy', in P. E. Easterling (ed.), *The Cambridge Companion to Greek Tragedy* (Cambridge, UK: Cambridge University Press, 1997), pp. 127–50.

Gowler, David B., *Host, Guest, Enemy and Friend: Portraits of the Pharisees in Luke and Acts* (ESEC, 2; New York: Peter Lang, 1991).

Green, Joel B., *The Gospel of Luke* (NICNT; Grand Rapids: Eerdmans, 1997).

Guardiola-Saenz, Leticia A., 'Border-Crossing and Its Redemptive Power in John 7:53–8:11: A Cultural Reading of Jesus and *the Accused*', in Ingrid R. Kitzberger (ed.), *Transformative Encounters: Jesus and Women Re-viewed* (Leiden: Brill, 1999), pp. 267–91.

Gutbrod, Walter, ''Ἰουδαῖος, 'Ἰσραήλ, 'Εβραῖος in Greek Hellenistic Literature', *Theological Dictionary of the New Testament*, Vol. 3, pp. 369–91.

Haber, Ralph Norman and Lyn Haber, 'Experiencing, Remembering and Reporting Events', *Psychology, Public Policy, and Law* 6 (2000), pp. 1057–97.

Hakola, Raimo, 'A Character Resurrected: Lazarus in the Fourth Gospel and Afterwards', in David Rhoads and Kari Syreeni (eds), *Characterization in the Gospels: Reconceiving Narrative Criticism* (JSNTSup, 184; Sheffield: Sheffield Academic Press, 1999), pp. 223–63.

—— 'The Johannine Community as Jewish Christians? Some Problems in Current Scholarly Consensus', in Matt Jackson-McCabe (ed.), *Jewish Christianity Reconsidered: Rethinking Ancient Groups and Texts* (Minneapolis: Fortress, 2007), pp. 181–201.

—— 'The Burden of Ambiguity: Nicodemus and the Social Identity of the Johannine Christians', *New Testament Studies* 55 (2009), pp. 438–55.

Hanson, A. T., 'John 1:14-18 and Exodus 34', *New Testament Studies* 23 (1977), pp. 90–101.

Harstine, Stan, *Moses as a Character in the Fourth Gospel* (JSNTSup, 229; London: Sheffield Academic Press, 2002).

Harvey, W. J., *Character and the Novel* (Ithaca, NY: Cornell University Press, 1965).

Haskins, Susan, *Mary Magdalen: Myth and Metaphor* (London: HarperCollins, 1993).

Hastorf, Albert H. and Hadley Cantril, 'They Saw a Game: A Case Study', *Journal of Abnormal and Social Psychology/Journal of Abnormal Psychology* 49 (1) (1954), pp. 129–34.

Hawkin, David J., 'The Function of the Beloved Disciple Motif in the Johannine Redaction', *Laval Theologique et Philosophique* 33 (1977), pp. 135–50.

———— *The Johannine World: Reflections on the Theology of the Fourth Gospel and Contemporary Society* (SUNY Series in Religious Studies; Albany: State University of New York Press, 1996).

Hearon, Holly E., *The Mary Magdalene Tradition: Witness and Counter-Witness in Early Christian Communities* (Collegeville, MN: Liturgical, 2004).

Hochman, Baruch, *Character in Literature* (Ithaca, NY: Cornell University Press, 1985).

Hoegen-Rohls, Christina, *Der Nachösterliche Johannes: Die Abschiedsreden Als Hermeneutischer Schlüssel Zum Vierten Evangelium* (WUNT, II/84; Tübingen: J.C.B. Mohr [Paul Siebeck], 1996).

Hoehner, Harold W., 'Pontius Pilate', in Joel B. Green, Scot McKnight and I. Howard Marshall (eds), *Dictionary of Jesus and the Gospels* (Downers Grove, IL: InterVarsity, 1992), p. 616.

Hooker, Morna, 'John the Baptist and the Johannine Prologue', *New Testament Studies* 16 (1970), pp. 354–8.

———— 'Johannine Prologue and the Messianic Secret', *New Testament Studies* 21 (1974), pp. 40–58.

———— *The Gospel According to St. Mark* (BNTC; Peabody, MA: Hendrickson, 1993).

———— *Beginnings: Keys That Open the Gospels* (Harrisburg, PA: Trinity Press International, 1997).

Horn, F. W., 'Holy Spirit', *Anchor Bible Dictionary* (6 vols; New York: Doubleday, 1992), Vol. 3, pp. 260–80.

Horvath, Tibor, 'Why Was Jesus Brought to Pilate?', *Novum Testamentum* 11 (1969), pp. 174–84.

Hoskyns, Edwyn C., *The Fourth Gospel* (F. N. Davis [ed.], London: Faber & Faber, 1947).

Howard, James M., 'The Significance of Minor Characters in the Gospel of John', *Bibliotheca Sacra* 163 (2006), pp. 63–78.

Hunn, Debbie, 'The Believers Jesus Doubted: John 2:23-25', *Trinity Journal* 25 (2004), pp. 15–25.

Hunt, Steven A., 'Nicodemus, Lazarus, and the Fear of "the Jews" in the Fourth Gospel', in G. van Belle, M. Labahn and P. Maritz (eds), *Repetitions and Variations in the Fourth Gospel: Style, Text, Interpretation* (BETL, 223; Leuven: Peeters, 2009), pp. 199–212.

Hunt, Steven A., Ruben Zimmermann and D. François Tolmie (eds), *Character Studies in the Fourth Gospel: Narrative Approaches to Fifty-Five Figures in John* (WUNT, I; Tübingen: Mohr Siebeck, forthcoming 2013).

Hylen, Susan E., *Allusion and Meaning in John 6* (BZNW, 137; Berlin: Walter de Gruyter, 2005).

——— *Imperfect Believers: Ambiguous Characters in the Gospel of John* (Louisville: Westminster John Knox, 2009).

Irigoin, Jean, 'La composition rythmique du prologue de Jean (I, 1-18)', *Revue Biblique* 98 (1991), pp. 5–50.

Iser, Wolfgang, 'The Reading Process: A Phenomenological Approach', *New Literary History* 3 (1972), pp. 279–99.

Iverson, Kelly R., *Gentiles in the Gospel of Mark: 'Even the Dogs Under the Table Eat the Children's Crumbs'* (LNTS, 339; London: T&T Clark, 2007).

Iverson, Kelly R. and Christopher W. Skinner (eds), *Mark as Story: Retrospect and Prospect* (SBLRBS, 65; Atlanta: Society of Biblical Literature, 2011).

Jackson, Howard M., 'Ancient Self-Referential Conventions and Their Implications for the Authorship and Integrity of the Gospel of John', *Journal of Theological Studies* 5 (1999), pp. 1–34.

James, Henry, 'The Art of Fiction', in Morris Roberts (ed.), *The Art of Fiction and Other Essays by Henry James* (New York: Oxford University Press, 1948), pp. 3–23.

Jannella, Cecilia, *Duccio di Buoninsegna* (Florence: SCALA, 1991).

Jeremias, Joachim, 'νύμφη, νυμφίος', *Theological Dictionary of the New Testament*, Vol. 4, pp. 1099–106.

Johnson, Luke Timothy, *The Gospel of Luke* (SP, 3; Collegeville, MN: Liturgical, 1991).

Johnson, Marcia K., Shahin Hashtroudi and D. Stephen Lindsay, 'Source Monitoring', *Psychological Bulletin* 114 (1) (1993), pp. 3–28.

Käsemann, Ernst, *New Testament Questions of Today* (London: SCM, 1969).

Katz, Steven T., 'Issues in the Separation of Judaism and Christianity after 70 C.E.: A Reconsideration', *Journal of Biblical Literature* 103 (1984), pp. 43–76.

Keener, Craig S., *The Gospel of John* (2 vols; Peabody, MA: Hendrickson, 2003).

Kelber, Werner, 'The Birth of a Beginning: John 1:1-18', *Semeia* 52 (1990), pp. 121–44.

Kelly, Andrew and Francis J. Moloney, *Experiencing God in the Gospel of John* (New York: Paulist Press, 2003).

Kermode, Frank, *The Genesis of Secrecy: On the Interpretation of Narrative* (Cambridge, MA: Harvard University Press, 1979).

———— 'St John as Poet', *Journal for the Study of the New Testament* 28 (1986) pp. 3–16.

Kierspel, Lars, *The Jews and the World in the Fourth Gospel: Parallelism, Function, and Context* (WUNT, II/220; Tübingen: Mohr Siebeck, 2006).

Kimelman, Reuven. '*Birkhat Ha-Minim* and the Lack of Evidence for an Anti-Christian Jewish Prayer in Late Antiquity', in E. P. Sanders (ed.), *Jewish and Christian Self-Definition* (Philadelphia: Fortress, 1981), pp. 226–44.

Kingsbury, Jack Dean, *Matthew as Story* (Minneapolis: Augsburg Fortress, 1988).

Kitzberger, Ingrid Rosa, 'Mary of Bethany and Mary of Magdala – Two Female Characters in the Johannine Passion Narrative: A Feminist, Narrative-Critical Reader-Response', *New Testament Studies* 41 (1995), pp. 564–86.

———— 'Synoptic Women in John: Interfigural Readings', in Ingrid R. Kitzberger (ed.), *Transformative Encounters: Jesus and Women Reviewed* (Leiden: Brill, 1999), pp. 77–111.

Klassen, William, *Judas: Betrayer or Friend of Jesus?* (Minneapolis: Fortress, 1996).

Kluger, J., 'The Power of Birth Order', *Time*, Wed. 17 Oct. 2007.

Koester, Craig R., *The Dwelling of God: The Tabernacle in the Old Testament, Intertestamental Jewish Literature, and the New Testament* (CBQMS, 22; Washington: Catholic Biblical Association of America, 1989).

———— *Symbolism in the Fourth Gospel: Meaning, Mystery, Community* (Minneapolis: Fortress, 1995).

———— 'Jesus' Resurrection, the Signs, and the Dynamics of Faith in the Gospel of John', in Craig R. Koester and Reimund Bieringer (eds), *The Resurrection of Jesus in the Gospel of John* (WUNT, 222; Tübingen: Mohr Siebeck, 2008), pp. 47–74.

Koester, Helmut, 'ΓΝΩΜΑΙ ΔΙΑΦΟΡΟΙ', in Helmut Koester and James M. Robinson, *Trajectories through Early Christianity* (Philadelphia: Fortress, 1971), pp. 114–57.

Köhler, Wilhelm, 'ἐπί', *Exegetical Dictionary of the New Testament*, Vol. 2, pp. 21–3.

Kollmann, Bernd and Ruben Zimmermann, *Hermeneutik der frühchristlichen Wundererzählungen* (WUNT I; Tübingen: Mohr Siebeck, forthcoming 2013).

Krafft, Eva, 'Die Personen des Johannesevangeliums', *Evangelische Theologie* 16 (1956), pp. 18–32.

Kragerud, A., *Der Lieblingsjünger im Johannesevangelium. Ein exegetischer Versuch* (Oslo: Universitätsverlag, 1959).

Kysar, Robert, 'John, The Gospel of', *Anchor Bible Dictionary* (New York: Doubleday, 1992), Vol. 3, pp. 912–31.

Lagrange, Marie-Josef, *Évangile selon Saint Jean* (EBib; Paris: Gabalda, 1936).

Lanser, Susan Sniader, *The Narrative Act: Point of View in Prose Fiction* (Princeton, NJ: Princeton University Press, 1981).

Lauterbach, Jacob (ed.), *Mekilta de Rabbi Ishmael* (3 vols; Philadelphia: Jewish Publication Society of America, 1961).

Lawrence, Louis J., *An Ethnography of the Gospel of Matthew: A Critical Assessment of the Use of the Honour and Shame Model in New Testament Studies* (WUNT, II/165; Tübingen: Mohr Siebeck, 2003).

Leal, Juan, 'El simbolismo histórico del iv Evangelio', *Estudios Biblicos* 19 (1960), pp. 329–48.

Lee, Dorothy A., *The Symbolic Narratives of the Fourth Gospel: The Interplay of Form and Meaning* (JSNTSup, 95; Sheffield: JSOT Press, 1994).

—————— 'Abiding in the Fourth Gospel: A Case-Study in Feminist Biblical Theology', *Pacifica* 10 (1997), pp. 123–36.

—————— *Flesh and Glory: Symbol, Gender and Theology in the Gospel of John* (New York: Crossroad, 2004).

—————— 'The Gospel of John and the Five Senses', *Journal of Biblical Literature* 129 (2010), pp. 115–27.

—————— *Hallowed in Truth and Love: Spirituality in the Johannine Literature* (Melbourne: Mosaic Resources; Eugene, OR: Wipf & Stock, 2012).

Levine, Amy-Jill and Marc Zvi Brettler (eds), *The Jewish Annotated New Testament: New Revised Standard Version Bible Translation* (Oxford and New York: Oxford University Press, 2011).

Licht, Jacob, *Storytelling in the Bible* (Jerusalem: Magnes, 1978).

Lieu, Judith, 'The Mother of the Son in the Fourth Gospel', *Journal of Biblical Literature* 117 (1998), pp. 61–77.

—————— *Neither Jew Nor Greek: Constructing Early Christianity* (New York: T&T Clark, 2002).

Lincoln, Andrew T., *Truth on Trial: The Lawsuit Motif in the Fourth Gospel* (Peabody, MA: Hendrickson, 2000).

—————— *The Gospel According to Saint John* (BNTC; London: Continuum and Peabody, MA: Hendrickson, 2005).

—————— '"We Know That His Testimony Is True": Johannnine Truth Claims and Historicity', in Paul N. Anderson, Felix Just and Tom Thatcher (eds), *John, Jesus, and History – Volume 1: Critical Appraisals of Critical Views* (SBLSymS, 44; Atlanta: Society of Biblical Literature, 2007), pp. 179–97.

—————— 'The Lazarus Story: A Literary Perspective', in Richard Bauckham and Carl Mosser (eds), *The Gospel of John and Christian Theology* (Grand Rapids: Eerdmans, 2008), pp. 211–32.

Lindars, Barnabas, *The Gospel of John* (NCB; London: Oliphants, 1972).

Lindsay, Dennis R., '"What is Truth?" Ἀλήθεια in the Gospel of John', *Restoration Quarterly* 35 (1993), pp. 129–45.

Loftus, Elizabeth F., *Eyewitness Testimony* (Cambridge, MA: Harvard University Press, 1979).

Loisy, Alfred, *Le quatrième Evangile. Les epîtres dites de Jean* (Paris: Emile Nourry, 1921).

Lowe, Malcolm, 'Who Were the IOUDAIOI?', *Novum Testamentum* 18 (1976), pp. 101–30.

Lowe, R., '"Salvation" is Not of the Jews', *Journal of Theological Studies* 32 (1981), pp. 341–68.

Lozada Jr, Francisco, *A Literary Reading of John 5: Text as Construction* (Studies in Biblical Literature, 20; New York: Peter Lang, 2000).

Luz, Ulrich, *Matthew 1–7* (Hermeneia; Minneapolis: Fortress, 2007).

Maccini, Robert G., 'A Reassessment of the Woman at the Well in John 4 in Light of the Samaritan Context', *Journal for the Study of the New Testament* 53 (1994), pp. 35–46.

——— *Her Testimony is True: Women as Witnesses according to John* (JSNTSup, 125; Sheffield: Sheffield Academic Press, 1996).

Malatesta, Edward, *Interiority and Covenant: A Study of* εἶναι ἐν *and* μένειν ἐν *in the First Letter of Saint John* (AnBib, 69; Rome: Biblical Institute Press, 1978).

Malbon, Elizabeth Struthers, 'Narrative Criticism: How Does the Story Mean?', in Janice Capel Anderson and Stephen D. Moore (eds), *Mark & Method: New Approaches in Biblical Studies* (Minneapolis: Fortress, 1992), pp. 23–49.

——— *In the Company of Jesus: Characters in Mark's Gospel* (Louisville: Westminster John Knox, 2000).

——— *Mark's Jesus: Characterization as Narrative Christology* (Waco: Baylor University Press, 2009).

——— 'Characters in Mark's Story: Changing Perspectives on the Narrative Process', in Kelly R. Iverson and Christopher W. Skinner (eds), *Mark as Story: Retrospect and Prospect* (SBLRBS, 65; Atlanta: Society of Biblical Literature, 2011), pp. 45–69.

Malina, Bruce J., *The New Testament World: Insights from Cultural Anthropology* (Louisville: Westminster John Knox, 3rd edn, 2001).

Malina, Bruce J. and Richard L. Rohrbaugh, *Social-Science Commentary on the Gospel of John* (Minneapolis: Fortress, 1998).

Manns, Frédéric, *Le symbole eau-esprit dans le judaïsme ancien* (SBFA, 19; Jerusalem: Franciscan Printing Press, 1983).

——— *L'Evangile de Jean à la lumière du judaïsme* (SBFA, 33; Jerusalem: Franciscan Printing Press, 1991).

Marguerat, Daniel and Yvan Bourquin, *How to Read Bible Stories: An Introduction to Narrative Criticism* (London: SCM, 1999).

Marrow, Stanley B., 'Κόσμος in John', *Catholic Biblical Quarterly* 64 (2002), pp. 90–102.

Marsh, Elizabeth J., 'Retelling is Not the Same as Recalling: Implications for Memory', *Current Directions in Psychological Science* 16 (2007), pp. 16–20.

Marshall, I. Howard, *The Gospel of Luke: A Commentary on the Greek Text* (NIGTC; Grand Rapids: Eerdmans, 1978).

Martin, Michael W., *Judas and the Rhetoric of Comparison in the Fourth Gospel* (NTM, 25; Sheffield: Sheffield Phoenix Press, 2010).

Martin, Wallace, *Recent Theories of Narrative* (Ithaca, NY: Cornell University Press, 1986).

Martyn, J. Louis, *History and Theology in the Fourth Gospel* (Nashville: Abingdon, 2nd edn, 1979).

Maynard, Arthur H., 'The Role of Peter in the Fourth Gospel', *New Testament Studies* 30 (1984), pp. 531–47.

McEvenue, Sean E., *The Narrative Style of the Priestly Writer* (AnBib, 50; Rome: Pontificio Istituto Biblico, 1971).

McGing, Brian Charles, 'Pontius Pilate and the Sources', *Catholic Biblical Quarterly* 53 (1991), pp. 416–38.

McIver, Robert K., *Memory, Jesus, and the Synoptic Gospels* (Atlanta: Society of Biblical Literature, 2011).

McNamara, Martin, 'Logos of the Fourth Gospel and Memra of the Palestinian Targum: Ex 12:42', *Expository Times* 79 (1968), pp. 115–17.

McWhirter, Jocelyn, *The Bridegroom Messiah and the People of God: Marriage in the Fourth Gospel* (SNTSMS, 138; Cambridge, UK: Cambridge University Press, 2006).

Meeks, Wayne A., 'The Man from Heaven in Johannine Sectarianism', *Journal of Biblical Literature* 91 (1972), pp. 44–72.

Meier, John P., *A Marginal Jew: Rethinking the Historical Jesus* (Vol. 1; New York: Doubleday, 1991).

Menken, Martinus J. J., 'The Quotation from Isa 40:3 in John 1:23', *Biblica* 66 (1985), pp. 190–205.

Merenlahti, Petri, 'Characters in the Making: Individuality and Ideology in the Gospels', in David Rhoads and Kari Syreeni (eds), *Characterization in the Gospels: Reconceiving Narrative Criticism* (JSNTSup, 184; Sheffield: Sheffield Academic Press, 1999), pp. 49–72.

Merenlahti, Petri and Raimo Hakola, 'Reconceiving Narrative Criticism', in David Rhoads and Kari Syreeni (eds), *Characterization in the Gospels: Reconceiving Narrative Criticism* (JSNTSup, 184; Sheffield: Sheffield Academic Press, 1999), pp. 13–48.

Metzger, Bruce M., *A Textual Commentary on the Greek New Testament* (London: United Bible Societies, 1975).

Metzner, Rainer, *Die Prominenten im Neuen Testament. Ein prosopographischer Kommentar* (NTOA 66. Göttingen: Vandenhoeck & Ruprecht, 2008).

Meyer, Marvin, 'Whom Did Jesus Love Most? Beloved Disciples in John and Other Gospels', in Tuomas Rasimus (ed.), *The Legacy of John: Second-Century Reception of the Fourth Gospel* (NovTSup, 132; Leiden: Brill, 2010), pp. 73–91.

Meyer, Paul W., '"The Father": The Presentation of God in the Fourth Gospel', in R. Alan Culpepper and C. Clifton Black (eds), *Exploring* the Gospel of John (Louisville: Westminster John Knox, 1996), pp. 255–73.

Michaelis, Wilhelm, 'σκηνή', *Theological Dictionary of the New Testament*, Vol. 7, pp. 368–94.

Michaels, J. Ramsey, *The Gospel of John* (NICNT; Grand Rapids: Eerdmans, 2010).

Miller, Susan, *Women in Mark's Gospel* (LNTS, 259; London: T&T Clark, 2004).

Minear, Paul S., '"We Don't Know Where . . ." John 20:2', *Interpretation* 30 (1976), pp. 125–39.

Miscall, Peter D., *The Workings of Old Testament Narrative* (Philadelphia: Fortress, 1983).

Mlakuzhyil, George, *The Christocentric Literary Structure of the Fourth Gospel* (AnBib, 117; Rome: Editrice Pontificio Istituto Biblico, 1987).

Moloney, Francis J., 'From Cana to Cana (Jn. 2.1–4.54) and the Fourth Evangelist's Concept of Correct (and Incorrect) Faith', *Salesianum* 40 (1978), pp. 817–43.

——— 'John 1:18 "in the Bosom of" or "Turned Towards" the Father', *Australian Biblical Review* 31 (1983), pp. 63–71.

——— *Belief in the Word: Reading John 1–4* (Minneapolis: Fortress, 1993).

——— 'The Faith of Mary and Martha: A Narrative Approach to John 11,17-40', *Biblica* 75 (1994), pp. 471–93.

——— *Signs and Shadows: Reading John 5–12* (Minneapolis: Fortress, 1996).

——— *Glory not Dishonor: Reading John 13–21* (Minneapolis: Fortress, 1998).

——— *The Gospel of John* (SP, 4; Collegeville, MN: Liturgical, 1998).

——— '"The Jews" in the Fourth Gospel: Another Perspective' *Pacifica* 15 (2002), pp. 16–36.

——— 'Can Everyone Be Wrong? A Reading of John 11.1–12.8', *New Testament Studies* 49 (2003), pp. 505–27.

——— *The Living Voice of the Gospels* (Peabody, MA: Hendrickson, 2007), pp. 309–42.

Moltmann-Wendel, E., *The Women Around Jesus: Reflections on Authentic Personhood* (trans. J. Bowden; London: SCM, 1982).

Moore, Stephen D., *Literary Criticism and the Gospels: The Theoretical Challenge* (New Haven: Yale University Press, 1989).

——— 'Are There Impurities in the Living Water that the Johannine Jesus Dispenses? Deconstruction, Feminism and the Samaritan Woman', *Biblical Interpretation* 1 (1993), pp. 207–27.

Mowley, Henry, 'John 1:14-18 in the Light of Exodus 33:7–34:35', *Expository Times* 95 (1984), pp. 135–7.

Muecke, Douglas Colin, *The Compass of Irony* (London: Methuen & Co., 1969).

Mussner, Franz, *Die Johanneische Sehweise Und Die Frage Nach Dem Historischen Jesus* (Quaestiones Disputatae, 28; Freiburg: Herder, 1965).

Neirynck, Frans, 'The "Other Disciple" in Jn 18:15-16', *Ephemerides Theologicae Lovaniensis* 51 (1975), pp. 113–41 (reprinted as 'The "Other Disciple" in Jn 18, 15-16', in idem, *Evangelica: Gospel Studies—Etudes d'Evangile* [BETL, 60; Leuven: University Press, 1982], pp. 335–64).

Neisser, Ulric, 'Memory: What are the Important Questions?', in idem (ed.), *Memory Observed: Remembering in Natural Contexts* (San Francisco: W.H. Freeman, 1982), pp. 3–19.

———— *Memory Observed: Remembering in Natural Contexts* (San Francisco: W.H. Freeman, 1982).

Nes, Solrunn, *The Mystical Language of Icons* (London: St Paul's, 2000).

Neyrey, Jerome H., 'Jacob Traditions and the Interpretation of John 4.10-26', *Catholic Biblical Quarterly* 41 (1979), pp. 419–37.

———— *The Gospel of John* (NCBC; Cambridge, UK: Cambridge University Press, 2007).

Neyrey, Jerome and Richard Rohrbaugh, 'He Must Increase, I Must Decrease (John 3:30): A Cultural and Social Interpretation', *Catholic Biblical Quarterly* 63 (2001), pp. 464–83.

Nolland, John, *Luke 9:21–18:34* (WBC, 35B; Dallas: Word Books, 1993).

O'Brien, Kelli S., 'Written That You May Believe: John 20 and Narrative Rhetoric', *Catholic Biblical Quarterly* 67 (2005), pp. 284–302.

O'Day, Gail R., *Revelation in the Fourth Gospel: Narrative Mode and Theological Claim* (Philadelphia: Fortress, 1986).

———— 'John', in Carol A. Newsom and Sharon H. Ringe (eds), *The Women's Bible Commentary* (London: SPCK, 1992), pp. 381–93.

———— 'The Citation of Scripture as a Key to Characterization in Acts', in Patrick Gray and Gail R. O'Day (eds), *Scripture and Traditions: Essays on Early Judaism and Christianity in Honor of Carl R. Holladay* (Leiden: Brill, 2008), pp. 207–21.

———— *The Gospel of John* (NIB; Vol. 9; Nashville: Abingdon, 1995).

Okure, Teresa, *The Johannine Approach to Mission: A Contextual Study of John 4.1-42* (WUNT, II/32; Tübingen: J.C.B. Mohr [Paul Siebeck], 1988).

Olsson, Birger, *Structure and Meaning in the Fourth Gospel: A Text-linguistic Analysis of John 2.1-11 and 4.1-42* (ConBib; New Testament Series, 6; Lund: Gleerup, 1974).

Osborn, Andrew, 'The Word Became Flesh: An Exposition of John 1:1-18', *Interpretation* 3 (1949), pp. 42–9.

Ouspensky, L., 'The Meaning and Language of Icons', in L. Ouspensky and V. Lossky (eds), *The Meaning of Icons* (New York: St Vladimir's Seminary Press, 1989).

Pamment, Margaret, 'The Fourth Gospel's Beloved Disciple', *Expository Times* 94 (1983), pp. 363–7.

———— 'Focus in the Fourth Gospel', *Expository Times* 97 (1985), pp. 71–5.

Pancaro, Severino, 'The Metamorphosis of a Legal Principle in the Fourth Gospel: A Closer Look at Jn 7,51', *Bib* 53 (1972), pp. 340–61.

Park, Sophia, 'The Galilean Jesus: Creating a Borderland at the Foot of the Cross (John 19:23-30)', *Theological Studies* 70 (2009), pp. 419–36.

Parunak, H. van Dyke, 'Some Axioms for Literary Architecture', *Semitics* 8 (1982), pp. 1–16.

———— 'Transitional Techniques in the Bible', *Journal of Biblical Literature* 102 (1983), pp. 525–48.

Paterson, Helen M. and Richard I. Kemp, 'Comparing Methods of Encountering Post-Event Information: The Power of Co-Witness Suggestion', *Applied Cognitive Psychology* 20 (2006), pp. 1083–99.

Pazdan, Margaret Mary, 'Nicodemus and the Samaritan Woman: Contrasting Models of Discipleship', *Biblical Theology Bulletin* 17 (1987), pp. 145–8.

Pelling, C. B. R., *Characterization and Individuality in Greek Literature* (Oxford: Clarendon, 1990).

Perkins, Pheme, *Peter: Apostle for the Whole Church* (Studies on Personalities of the New Testament; Columbia, SC: University of South Carolina Press, 1994).

Petersen, Norman R., 'The Reader in the Gospel', *Neotestamentica* 18 (1984), pp. 38–51.

Phelan, James, *Reading People, Reading Plots: Character, Progression, and the Interpretation of Narrative* (Chicago: University of Chicago Press, 1989).

———— 'Character and Judgment in Narrative and in Lyric: Toward an Understanding of the Audience's Engagement in *The Waves*', *Style* 24 (Fall 1990), pp. 408–21.

———— *Narrative as Rhetoric: Technique, Audiences, Ethics, Ideology* (Columbus, OH: Ohio State University Press, 1996).

———— *Living to Tell about It: A Rhetoric and Ethics of Character Narration* (Ithaca, NY: Cornell University Press, 2005).

Pillemer, David B., *Momentous Events, Vivid Memories* (Cambridge, MA: Harvard University Press, 1998).

Porter, Stanley E., 'The Ending of John's Gospel', in William H. Brackney and Craig A. Evans (eds), *From Biblical Criticism to Biblical Faith: Essays in Honor of Lee Martin McDonald* (Macon, GA: Mercer University Press, 2007), pp. 55–73.

Potin, Jacques, *La Fête juive de la Pentecôte* (LeDiv, 65; Paris: Cerf, 1971).

Powell, Mark Allan, *What Is Narrative Criticism?* (GBS; Minneapolis: Fortress, 1990).

———— 'Narrative Criticism: The Emergence of a Prominent Reading Strategy', in Kelly R. Iverson and Christopher W. Skinner (eds), *Mark as Story: Retrospect and Prospect* (SBLRBS, 65; Atlanta: Society of Biblical Literature, 2011), pp. 19–43.

Pryor, John, 'Covenant and Community in John's Gospel', *Reformed Theological Review* 47 (1988), pp. 44–51.

———— *John: Evangelist of the Covenant People: The Narrative & Themes of the Fourth Gospel* (Downers Grove, IL: InterVarsity, 1992).

———— 'John the Baptist and Jesus: Tradition and Text in John 3.25', *Journal for the Study of the New Testament* 66 (1997), pp. 15–26.

Quast, Kevin, *Peter and the Beloved Disciple: Figures for a Community in Crisis* (JSNTSup, 32; Sheffield: JSOT Press, 1989).

Rabinowitz, Peter J., 'Truth in Fiction: A Reexamination of Audiences', *Critical Inquiry* 4 (1977), pp. 121–41.

Rabinowitz, Peter J. and Michael W. Smith, *Authorizing Readers: Resistance and Respect in the Teaching of Literature* (Language and Literacy Series, New York: Teachers College Press, 1998).

Redman, Judith C. S., 'How Accurate are Eyewitnesses? Bauckham and the Eyewitnesses in the Light of Psychological Research', *Journal of Biblical Literature* 129 (2010), pp. 177–97.

Regev, Eyal, 'Were the Early Christians Sectarians?', *Journal of Biblical Literature* 130 (2011), pp. 771–93.

Reid, Barbara, *Choosing the Better Part? Women in the Gospel of Luke* [Collegeville, MN: Liturgical, 1996).

Reinhartz, Adele, 'The Gospel of John', in Elisabeth Schüssler Fiorenza (ed.), *Searching the Scriptures. Vol. 2: A Feminist Commentary* (New York: Crossroad, 1994), pp. 571–600.

———— 'The Johannine Community and its Jewish Neighbors: A Reappraisal', in Fernando F. Segovia (ed.), *What is John?* (Atlanta: Scholars, 1998), pp. 111–38.

———— 'The Gospel According to John', in Amy-Jill Levine and Marc Zvi Brettler (eds), *The Jewish Annotated New Testament: New Revised Standard Version Bible Translation* (2011), pp. 152–7.

Rengstorf, Karl H., 'ἑπτά', *Theological Dictionary of the New Testament*, Vol. 2, pp. 627–35.

Rensberger, David, *Overcoming the World: Politics and Community in the Gospel of John* (London: SPCK, 1988).

———— *Johannine Faith and Liberating Community* (Philadelphia: Westminster, 1989).

Renz, Gabi, 'Nicodemus: An Ambiguous Disciple? A Narrative Sensitive Investigation', in John Lierman (ed.), *Challenging Perspectives on the Gospel of John* (WUNT, II/219; Tübingen: Mohr Siebeck, 2006), pp. 255–83.

Resseguie, James L., *The Strange Gospel: Narrative Design and Point of View in John* (BIS, 56; Leiden: Brill, 2001).

———— *Narrative Criticism of the New Testament: An Introduction* (Grand Rapids: Baker Academic, 2005).

———— *The Revelation of John: A Narrative Commentary* (Grand Rapids: Baker Academic, 2009).

Rhoads, David, Joanna Dewey and Donald Michie, *Mark as Story: An Introduction to the Narrative of a Gospel* (Minneapolis: Fortress, 2nd edn, 1999).

Richards, I. A., *The Philosophy of Rhetoric* (New York: Oxford University Press, 1936).

Rimmon-Kenan, Shlomith, *Narrative Fiction: Contemporary Poetics* (New York: Methuen & Co., 1983).

Ringe, Sharon H., *Luke* (Louisville: Westminster John Knox, 1995).

Robertson, A. T., *A Grammar of the Greek New Testament in the Light of Historical Research* (New York: Hodder & Stoughton, 4th edn, 1923).

Robinson, John A. T., 'Elijah, John and Jesus, and Essay in Detection', *New Testament Studies* 4 (1957–58), pp. 263–81.

———— 'The Relation of the Prologue to the Gospel of St. John', *New Testament Studies* 9 (1963), pp. 120–9.

Roediger, Henry L., Michelle L. Meade and Erik T. Bergman, 'Social Contagion of Memory', *Psychonomic Bulletin and Review* 8 (2001), pp. 365–71.

Rohrbaugh, Richard, 'Models and Muddles: Discussions of the Social Facets Seminar', *Forum* 3 (1987), pp. 23–33.

———— 'What's the Matter with Nicodemus? A Social-Science Perspective on John 3:1-21', in Holly E. Hearon (ed.), *Distant Voices Drawing Near: Essays in Honor of Antoinette Clark Wire* (Collegeville, MN: Liturgical, 2004), pp. 145–58.

Ronning, John, *The Jewish Targums and John's Logos Theology* (Peabody, MA: Hendrickson, 2010).

Ruschmann, Susanne, *Maria von Magdala im Johannesevangelium: Jüngerin— Zeugin—Lebensbotin* (NTAbh, 40; Münster: Aschendorff, 2002).

Sanders, J. N., '"Those Whom Jesus Loved" (John xi.5)', *New Testament Studies* 1 (1954–55), pp. 29–41.

Satlow, Frank P., *Jewish Marriage in Antiquity* (Princeton, NJ: Princeton University Press, 2001).

Saxby, Harold, 'The Time-Scheme in the Gospel of John', *Expository Times* 104 (1992), pp. 9–13.

Schaberg, Jane, 'Luke', in Carol A. Newsom and Sharon H. Ringe (eds), *The Women's Bible Commentary* (London: SPCK, 1992).

Schacter, Daniel L., *The Seven Sins of Memory: How the Mind Forgets and Remembers* (Boston: Houghton Mifflin, 2001).

Schilling, Renee M., 'The Effects of Birth Order on Interpersonal Relationships', http://faculty.mckendree.edu/scholars/2001/schilling.htm.

Schnackenburg, Rudolf, 'Die situationsgelösten Redestücke in John 3', *Zeitschrift für die Neutestamentliche Wissenschaft* 49 (1958), pp. 88–99.

———— *The Gospel According to St John* (trans. K. Smyth, et al.; HTCNT, 3 vols; London: Burns & Oates, 1968–82).

Schneiders, Sandra M., *The Revelatory Text: Interpreting the New Testament as Sacred Scripture* (San Francisco: HarperCollins, 1991).

—— *Written That You May Believe: Encountering Jesus in the Fourth Gospel* (New York: Herder & Herder, 1999).

Scholtissek, Klaus, *In Ihm Sein und Bleiben: Die Sprache Der Immanenz Un Den Johanneischen Schriften* (Herder's Biblical Studies, 21; Freiburg: Herder, 2000).

—— '"Ich und der Vater, wir sind eins" (Joh 10,30) Zum Theologischen Potential und zur Hermeneutischen Kompetenz der Johanneischen Christologie', in G. van Belle, J. G. van der Watt and P. J. Maritz (eds), *Theology and Christology in the Fourth Gospel* (Leuven: University Press, 2005), pp. 315–45.

Scholes, Robert, *Elements of Fiction* (New York: Oxford University Press, 1968).

Scholes, Robert and Robert Kellogg, *The Nature of Narrative* (London: Oxford University Press, 1966).

Schremer, Adiel, *Brothers Estranged: Heresy, Christianity, and Jewish Identity in Late Antiquity* (Oxford: Oxford University Press, 2010).

Schüssler Fiorenza, Elisabeth, 'A Feminist Interpretation for Liberation: Martha and Mary: Lk. 10:38-42', *Religion and Intellectual Life* 3 (1986), pp. 21–36.

—— *But She Said: Feminist Practices of Biblical Interpretation* (Boston: Beacon, 1992).

—— 'The Practice of Biblical Interpretation: Luke 10.38-42', in N. K. Gottwald and R. A. Horsley (eds), *The Bible and Liberation: Political and Social Hermeneutics* (Maryknoll: Orbis, 1993), pp. 172–97.

Seim, Turid Karlsen, 'Roles of Women in the Gospel of John', in L. Hartman and B. Olsson (eds), *Aspects on the Johannine Literature* (ConBNT, 18; Uppsala: Almqvist & Wiksell, 1987), pp. 56–73.

—— *The Double Message: Patterns of Gender in Luke & Acts* (Nashville: Abingdon, 1994).

—— 'The Gospel of Luke', in Elisabeth Schüssler Fiorenza (ed.), *Searching the Scriptures. Vol. 2: A Feminist Commentary* (New York: Crossroad, 1994).

Servotte, Herman, *According to John: A Literary Reading of the Fourth Gospel* (London: Darton, Longman and Todd, 1994).

Shellard, Barbara, *New Light on Luke: Its Purpose, Sources and Literary Context* (JSNTSup, 215; Sheffield: Sheffield Academic Press, 2002).

Sheridan, Ruth, *Retelling Scripture: 'The Jews' and the Scriptural Citations in John 1:19–12:15* (BIS, 110; Leiden: Brill, 2012).

Skinner, Christopher W., 'Another Look at the "Lamb of God"', *Bibliotheca Sacra* 161 (2004), pp. 89–104.

—— *John and Thomas: Gospels in Conflict? Johannine Characterization and the Thomas Question* (PTMS, 115; Eugene, OR: Pickwick, 2009).

Smith, D. Moody, *The Fourth Gospel in Four Dimensions: Judaism and Jesus, the Gospels and Scripture* (Columbia, SC: University of South Carolina Press, 2008).

Sproston North, Wendy E., *The Lazarus Story within the Johannine Tradition* (Sheffield: Sheffield University Press, 2001).

Staley, Jeffrey, 'The Structure of John's Prologue: Its Implications for the Gospel's Narrative Structure', *Catholic Biblical Quarterly* 48 (1986), pp. 241–63.

——— *The Print's First Kiss: A Rhetorical Investigation of the Implied Reader in the Fourth Gospel* (SBLDS, 82; Atlanta: Scholars, 1988).

Stapfer, Edmond, *Palestine in the Time of Christ* (trans. A. H. Holmden; New York: Armstrong and Son, 1885).

Sternberg, Meir, *The Poetics of Biblical Narrative: Ideological Literature and the Drama of Reading* (Bloomington: Indiana University Press, 1985).

Stibbe, Mark W. G., *John as Storyteller: Narrative Criticism and the Fourth Gospel* (SNTSMS, 73; Cambridge, UK: Cambridge University Press, 1992).

——— *John* (Readings: A New Biblical Commentary; Sheffield: JSOT Press, 1993).

——— *John's Gospel* (New Testament Readings; London: Routledge, 1994).

——— 'Telling the Father's Story: The Gospel of John as Narrative Theology', in John Lierman (ed.), *Challenging Perpectives on the Gospel of John* (Tübingen: Mohr Siebeck, 2006), pp. 170–93.

Stramara Jr, Daniel F., 'The Chiastic Key to the Identity of the Beloved Disciple', *St. Vladimir's Theological Quarterly* 53 (2009), pp. 5–27.

Suggit, John, 'Nicodemus – The True Jew', *Neotestamentica* 14 (1981), pp. 90–110.

——— 'John XVII. 17, Ο ΛΟΓΟΣ Ο ΣΟΣ ΑΛΗΘΕΙΑ ΕΣΤΙΝ', *Journal of Theological Studies* 35 (1984), pp. 104–17.

Sulloway, F. J., *Born to Rebel: Birth Order, Family Dynamics, and Creative Lives* (New York: Random House, 1996).

Sutherland, Rachel and Harlene Hayne, 'The Effect of Postevent Information on Adults' Eyewitness Reports', *Applied Cognitive Psychology* 15 (2001), pp. 249–63.

Sylva, Dennis D., 'Nicodemus and His Spices (John 19.39)', *New Testament Studies* 34 (1988), pp. 148–51.

Syreeni, Kari, 'Peter as Character and Symbol', in David Rhoads and Kari Syreeni (eds), *Characterization in the Gospels: Reconceiving Narrative Criticism* (JSNTSup, 184; Sheffield: Sheffield Academic Press, 1999), pp. 106–52.

Talbert, Charles H., *Reading John* (Reading the New Testament; New York: Crossroad, 1992).

——— *Reading Luke: A Literary and Theological Commentary on the Third Gospel* (Macon, GA: Smyth & Helwys, 2002).

Talmon, Shemaryahu, 'The Presentation of Synchroneity and Simultaneity in Biblical Narrative', in Joseph Heinemann and Shnuel Werses (eds), *Scripta Hierosolymitana* (Jerusalem: Magnes, 1978), pp. 9–26.

Tannehill, Robert C., 'The Disciples in Mark: The Function of a Narrative Role', *Journal of Religion* 57 (1977), pp. 386–405.

—— *The Narrative Unity of Luke-Acts: A Literary Interpretation* (2 vols; Minneapolis: Fortress, 1986–89).

—— *Luke* (ANTC; Nashville: Abingdon, 1996).

Taylor, Joan E., 'Pontius Pilate and the Imperial Cult in Roman Judaea', *New Testament Studies* 52 (2006), pp. 555–82.

Teppler, Yaakov Y., *Birkat haMinim: Jews and Christians in Conflict in the Ancient World* (trans. Susan Weingarten; Tübingen: Mohr Siebeck, 2007).

Thatcher, Tom, 'Philo on Pilate: Rhetoric or Reality', *Restoration Quarterly* 37 (1995), pp. 215–18.

—— 'Jesus, Judas, and Peter: Character by Contrast in the Fourth Gospel', *Bibliotheca Sacra* 153 (1996), pp. 435–48.

—— 'Anatomies of the Fourth Gospel: Past, Present, and Future Probes', in Tom Thatcher and Stephen D. Moore (eds), *Anatomies of Narrative Criticism: The Past, Present, and Futures of the Fourth Gospel as Literature* (SBLRBS, 55; Atlanta: Society of Biblical Literature, 2008), pp. 1–35.

—— *Greater than Caesar: Christology and Empire in the Fourth Gospel* (Minneapolis: Fortress, 2009).

—— 'The Riddle of the Baptist and the Genesis of the Prologue: John 1:1-18 an Oral/Aural Media Culture', in Anthony LeDonne and Tom Thatcher (eds), *The Fourth Gospel in First-Century Media Culture* (LNTS, 426; London: T&T Clark, 2011), pp. 29–48.

Thatcher, Tom and Stephen D. Moore (eds), *Anatomies of Narrative Criticism: The Past, Present, and Futures of the Fourth Gospel as Literature* (SBLRBS, 55; Atlanta: Society of Biblical Literature, 2008).

Theissen, Gerd and Annette Merz, *The Historical Jesus: A Comprehensive Guide* (Minneapolis: Fortress, 1998).

Theobald, Michael, *Die Fleischwerdung des Logos: Studien zum Verhältnis des Johannesprologs zum Corpus des Evangeliums und zu Joh 1* (NTAbh, NF 20; Munster: Aschendorff, 1988).

Thiselton, Anthony C., *The Two Horizons* (Exeter: Paternoster, 1980).

—— *New Horizons in Hermeneutics* (San Francisco: HarperCollins, 1992).

Thompson, Marianne Meye, '"God's Voice You Have Never Heard, God's Form You Have Never Seen": The Characterization of God in the Gospel of John', *Semeia* 63 (1993), pp. 177–204.

—— 'The Raising of Lazarus in John 11: A Theological Reading', in Richard Bauckham and Carl Mosser (eds), *The Gospel of John and Christian Theology* (Grand Rapids: Eerdmans, 2008), pp. 233–44.

Thyen, Hartwig, 'Die Erzuahlung von den Bethanischen Geschwistern (Joh 11,1-12,19) als "Palimpsest" über Synoptishcen Texten', in F. Van Segbroeck, C. M. Tuckett, G. van Belle and J. Verheyden (eds), *The Four Gospels 1992: Festschrift F. Neirynck* (3 vols; Leuven: University Press, 1992), Vol. 3, pp. 2021–50.

——— *Das Johannesevengelium* (Handbuch zum Neuen Testament, 6; Tübingen: Mohr Siebeck, 2005).

Tilborg, Sjef van, *Imaginative Love in John* (BIS, 2; Leiden: Brill, 1993).

Tobin, Thomas, 'The Prologue of John and Hellenistic Jewish Speculation', *Catholic Biblical Quarterly* 52 (1990), pp. 252–69.

Tolmie, D. François, *Jesus' Farewell to the Disciples: John 13:1–17:26 in Narratological Perspective* (BIS, 12; Leiden: Brill, 1995).

——— 'The Characterization of God in the Fourth Gospel', *Journal for the Study of the New Testament* 68 (1997), pp. 57–75.

Tovey, Derek, *Narrative Art and Act in the Fourth Gospel* (JSNTSup, 151; Sheffield: Sheffield Academic Press, 1997).

——— 'Narrative Strategies in the Prologue and the Metaphor of ὁ λόγος in John's Gospel', *Pacifica* 15 (2002), pp. 138–53.

Trumbull, H. Clay, *Studies in Oriental Social Life* (Philadelphia: The Sunday School Times Co., 1894).

Tuckett, Christopher M., *Luke* (NTG; Sheffield: Sheffield Academic Press, 1996).

——— 'Pilate in John 18–19: A Narrative-Critical Approach', in G. J. Brooke and J.-D. Kaestli (eds), *Narrativity in Biblical and Related Texts* (BETL, 149; Leuven: Peeters, 2000), pp. 131–40.

Uspensky, Boris, *A Poetics of Composition: The Structure of the Artistic Text and Typology of a Compositional Form* (trans. V. Zavarin and S. Wittig; Berkeley: University of California Press, 1978).

Van Aarde, A. G., 'Narrative Criticism Applied to John 4:43-54', in P. Hartin and J. Petzer (eds), *Text & Interpretation: New Approaches in the Criticism of the NT* (NTTS, 15; Leiden: Brill, 1991), pp. 101–28.

van Belle, G., J. G. van der Watt and P. J. Maritz (eds), *Theology and Christology in the Fourth Gospel* (Leuven: Peeters, 2005).

van der Merwe, Dirk G., 'The Historical and Theological Significance of John the Baptist as He is Portrayed in John 1', *Neotestamentica* 33 (1999), pp. 267–92.

van der Watt, J. G., 'The Composition of the Prologue of John's Gospel: The Historical Jesus Introducing Divine Grace', *Westminster Theological Journal* 57 (1995), pp. 311–32.

van Selms, Adrian, 'The Best Man and Bride: From Sumer to St. John', *Journal of Near Eastern Studies* 9 (1950), pp. 65–70.

van Unnik, W. C., 'The Purpose of St John's Gospel', *Studia Evangelica* 1 (1959), pp. 382–411.

Vermes, Geza, *Jesus and the World of Judaism* (London: SCM, 1983).

von Wahlde, Urban C., 'The Witnesses to Jesus in John 5:31-40 and Belief in the Fourth Gospel', *Catholic Biblical Quarterly* 43 (1981), pp. 385–404.

——— *The Gospel and Letters of John* (Eerdmans Critical Commentary; Grand Rapids: Eerdmans, 2010).

Voorwinde, Stephen, *Jesus' Emotions in the Fourth Gospel: Human or Divine?* (LNTS, 284; London: T&T Clark, 2005).

Wallace, Daniel B., *Greek Grammar Beyond the Basics: An Exegetical Syntax of the New Testament* (Grand Rapids: Zondervan, 1997).

Waweru, Humphrey Mwangi, 'Jesus and Ordinary Women in the Gospel of John: An African Perspective', *Swedish Missiological Themes* 96 (2008), pp. 139–59.

Wead, David W., 'We Have a Law', *Novum Testamentum* 11 (1969), pp. 185–9.

Weldon, Mary Susan, 'Remembering as a Social Process', *The Psychology of Learning and Motivation: Advances in Research and Theory* (2000), pp. 67–120.

Weldon, Mary Susan and Krystal D. Bellinger, 'Collective Memory: Collaborative and Individual Processes in Remembering', *Journal of Experimental Psychology: Learning, Memory, and Cognition* 23 (1997), pp. 1160–75.

Whitters, Mark F., 'Discipleship in John: Four Profiles', *Word and World* 18 (1998), pp. 422–7.

Wight, Fred H., *Manners and Customs of Bible Lands* (Chicago: Moody, 1953).

Williams, Joel F., *Other Followers of Jesus: Minor Characters as Major Figures in Mark's Gospel* (JSNTSup, 102; Sheffield: Sheffield Academic Press, 1994).

Williams, P. J., 'Not the Prologue of John', *Journal for the Study of the New Testament* 33 (2011), pp. 375–86.

Wilson, Jeffrey, 'The Integrity of John 3:22-36', *Journal for the Study of the New Testament* 10 (1981), pp. 34–41.

Witherington, Ben, *What Have They Done to Jesus? Beyond Strange Theories and Bad History—Why We Can Trust the Bible* (San Francisco: Harper, 2006).

Wright, Daniel B., Gail Self and Chris Justice, 'Memory Conformity: Exploring Misinformation Effects When Presented by Another Person', *British Journal of Psychology* 91 (2000), pp. 189–202.

Wright IV, William M., 'Greco-Roman Character Typing and the Presentation of Judas in the Fourth Gospel', *Catholic Biblical Quarterly* 71 (2009), pp. 544–59.

Wuellner, Wilhelm, 'Putting Life Back into the Lazarus Story and Its Reading: The Narrative Rhetoric of John 11 as the Narration of Faith', *Semeia* 53 (1991), pp. 113–32.

Yak-hwee, Tan, *Re-Presenting the Johannine Community* (Studies in Biblical Literature, 107; New York: Peter Lang, 2008).

Yamaguchi, S., *Mary & Martha: Women in the World of Jesus* (Maryknoll: Orbis, 2002).

Yieh, John Y. H., 'Thomas', in Katharine Doob Sakenfeld (ed.), *New Interpreter's Dictionary of the Bible* (5 vols; Nashville: Abingdon, 2009), Vol. 5, p. 582.

Yoder, John Howard, *The Politics of Jesus* (Grand Rapids: Eerdmans, 2nd edn, 1994).

Zimmerman, Ruben, 'The Narrative Hermeneutics of John 11: Learning with Lazarus How to Understand Death, Life, and Resurrection', in Craig Koester and Reimund Bieringer (eds), *The Resurrection of Jesus in the Gospel of John* (WUNT, I/222; Tübingen: Mohr Siebeck, 2008), pp. 75–101.

Zumstein, Jean, 'Johannes 19, 25-27', *Zeitschrift für Theologie und Kirche* 94 (1997), pp. 131–54.

———*Kreative Erinnerung: Relecture und Auslegung im Johannesevangelium* (Zurich: Pano Verlag, 1999).

INDEX OF AUTHORS